Everyman, I will go with thee, and be thy guide,
In thy most need to go by thy side.

EVERYMAN'S LIBRARY

No. 508

FICTION

THE VIRGINIANS
BY WILLIAM MAKEPEACE THACKERAY
INTRODUCTION BY WALTER JERROLD
IN 2 VOLS.   VOL. 2

WILLIAM MAKEPEACE THACKERAY,
born at Calcutta in 1811. Came to England
in 1817; educated at Cambridge. Soon
abandoned law and entered journalism in
1832–3. Died on 24th December 1863.

THE VIRGINIANS
VOLUME TWO

WILLIAM MAKEPEACE THACKERAY

LONDON: J. M. DENT & SONS LTD.
NEW YORK: E. P. DUTTON & CO. INC.

CONTENTS

vii

v. 2 c. 1

THE VIRGINIANS

CHAPTER XLVIII

AN APPARITION

GOING off in his wrath from his morning's conversation with Harry, Mr. Draper thought he heard the young prisoner speak behind him; and, indeed, Harry had risen, and uttered a half exclamation to call the lawyer back. But he was proud, and the other offended: Harry checked his words, and Draper did not choose to stop. It wounded Harry's pride to be obliged to humble himself before the lawyer, and to have to yield from mere lack and desire of money. "An hour hence will do as well," thought Harry, and lapsed sulkily on to the bed again. No, he did not care for Maria Esmond. No: he was ashamed of the way in which he had been entrapped into that engagement. A wily and experienced woman, she had cheated his boyish ardour. She had taken unfair advantage of him, as her brother had at play. They were his own flesh and blood, and they ought to have spared him. Instead, one and the other had made a prey of him, and had used him for their selfish ends. He thought how they had betrayed the rights of hospitality: how they had made a victim of the young kinsman who came confiding within their gates. His heart was sore wounded: his head sank back on his pillow: bitter tears wetted it. "Had they come to Virginia," he thought, "I had given them a different welcome!"

He was roused from this mood of despondency by Gumbo's grinning face at his door, who said a lady was come to see Master Harry, and behind the lad came the lady in the capuchin, of whom we have just made mention. Harry sat up, pale and haggard, on his bed. The lady, with a sob, and almost ere the servant-man withdrew, ran towards the young prisoner, put her arms round his neck with real emotion and a maternal tenderness, sobbed over his pale cheek and kissed it in the midst of plentiful tears, and cried out—

" Oh, my Harry! Did I ever think to see thee here? "

He started back, scared as it seemed at her presence, but she sank down at the bedside, and seized his feverish hand, and embraced his knees. She had a real regard and tenderness for him. The wretched place in which she found him, his wretched look, filled her heart with a sincere love and pity.

" I—I thought none of you would come! " said poor Harry, with a groan.

More tears, more kisses of the hot young hand, more clasps and pressure with hers, were the lady's reply for a moment or two.

" Oh, my dear! my dear! I cannot bear to think of thee in misery," she sobbed out.

Hardened though it might be, that heart was not all marble —that dreary life not all desert. Harry's mother could not have been fonder, nor her tones more tender than those of his kinswoman now kneeling at his feet.

" Some of the debts, I fear, were owing to my extravagance! " she said (and this was true). " You bought trinkets and jewels in order to give me pleasure. Oh, how I hate them now! I little thought I ever could! I have brought them all with me, and more trinkets—here! and here! and all the money I have in the world! "

And she poured brooches, rings, a watch, and a score or so of guineas into Harry's lap. The sight of which strangely agitated and immensely touched the young man.

" Dearest, kindest cousin! " he sobbed out.

His lips found no more words to utter, but yet, no doubt, they served to express his gratitude, his affection, his emotion.

He became quite gay presently, and smiled as he put away some of the trinkets, his presents to Maria, and told her into what danger he had fallen by selling other goods which he had purchased on credit; and how a lawyer had insulted him just now upon this very point. He would not have his dear Maria's money—he had enough, quite enough for the present: but he valued her twenty guineas as much as if they had been twenty thousand. He would never forget her love and kindness; no, by all that was sacred he would not! His mother should know of all her goodness. It had cheered him when he was just on the point of breaking down under his disgrace and misery. Might Heaven bless her for it! There is no need to pursue beyond this the cousins' conversation. The dark day seemed brighter to Harry after Maria's visit: the imprisonment not so hard to bear. The world was not all selfish and cold. Here was a fond creature who really and truly loved him. Even Castlewood was not so bad as he had thought. He had expressed the deepest grief at not being able to assist his kinsman. He was hopelessly in debt. Every shilling he had won from Harry he had lost on the next day to others. Anything that lay in his power he would do. He would come soon and see Mr. Warrington: he was in waiting to-day, and as much a prisoner as Harry himself. So the pair talked on cheerfully and affectionately until the darkness began to close in, when Maria, with a sigh, bade Harry farewell.

The door scarcely closed upon her, when it opened to admit Draper.

"Your humble servant, sir," says the attorney. His voice jarred upon Harry's ear, and his presence offended the young man.

"I had expected you some hours ago, sir," he curtly said.

"A lawyer's time is not always his own, sir," said Mr. Draper, who had just been in consultation with a bottle of port at the "Grecian." "Never mind, I'm at your orders now. Presume it's all right, Mr. Warrington. Packed your trunk? Why now, there you are in your bed-gown still. Let me go down and settle whilst you call in your black man and titivate a bit. I've a coach at the door, and we'll be off and dine with the old lady."

"Are you going to dine with the Baroness de Bernstein, pray?"

"Not me—no such honour. Had my dinner already. It's you are a-going to dine with your aunt, I suppose?"

"Mr. Draper, you suppose a great deal more than you know," says Mr. Warrington, looking very fierce and tall, as he folds his brocade dressing-gown round him.

"Great goodness, sir, what do you mean?" asks Draper.

"I mean, sir, that I have considered, and that, having given my word to a faithful and honourable lady, it does not become me to withdraw it."

"Confound it, sir!" shrieks the lawyer. "I tell you she has lost the paper. There's nothing to bind you—nothing. Why, she's old enough to be——"

"Enough, sir," says Mr. Warrington, with a stamp of his foot. "You seem to think you are talking to some other pettifogger. I take it, Mr. Draper, you are not accustomed to have dealings with men of honour."

"Pettifogger, indeed," cries Draper in a fury. "Men of

honour, indeed! I'd have you to know, Mr. Warrington, that
I'm as good a man of honour as you. I don't know so many
gamblers and horse-jockeys, perhaps. I haven't gambled away
my patrimony, and lived as if I was a nobleman on two hundred
a year. I haven't bought watches on credit, and pawned—
touch me if you dare, sir," and the lawyer sprang to the door.

" That is the way out, sir. You can't go through the window,
because it is barred," says Mr. Warrington.

" And the answer I take to my client is No, then! " screamed
out Draper.

Harry stepped forward, with his two hands clenched. " If
you utter another word," he said, " I'll——" The door was
shut rapidly—the sentence was never finished, and Draper went
away furious to Madame de Bernstein, from whom, though he
gave her the best version of his story, he got still fiercer language
than he had received from Mr. Warrington himself.

" What? Shall she trust me, and I desert her? " says Harry,
stalking up and down his room in his flowing rustling brocade.
" Dear, faithful, generous woman! If I lie in prison for years,
I'll be true to her."

Her lawyer dismissed after a stormy interview, the desolate
old woman was fain to sit down to the meal which she had hoped
to share with her nephew. The chair was before her which he
was to have filled, the glasses shining by the silver. One dish
after another was laid before her by the silent major-domo, and
tasted and pushed away. The man pressed his mistress at last.
" It is eight o'clock," he said. " You have had nothing all day.
It is good for you to eat." She could not eat. She would have
her coffee. Let Case go get her coffee. The lacqueys bore the
dishes off the table, leaving their mistress sitting at it before
the vacant chair.

Presently the old servant re-entered the room without his
lady's coffee and with a strange scared face, and said, " MR.
WARRINGTON! "

The old woman uttered an exclamation, got up from her
arm-chair, but sank back in it trembling very much. " So you
are come, sir, are you? " she said with a fond shaking voice.
" Bring back the——Ah! " here she screamed. " Gracious
God, who is it? " Her eyes stared wildly: her white face looked
ghastly through her rouge. She clung to the arms of her chair
for support, as the visitor approached her.

A gentleman whose face and figure exactly resembled Harry
Warrington, and whose voice, when he spoke, had tones strangely

similar, had followed the servant into the room. He bowed low towards the Baroness.

" You expected my brother, madam? " he said. " I am but now arrived in London. I went to his house. I met his servant at your door, who was bearing this letter for you. I thought I would bring it to your Ladyship before going to him." And the stranger laid down a letter before Madam Bernstein.

" Are you "—gasped out the Baroness—" are you my nephew, that we supposed was——"

" Was killed—and is alive! I am George Warrington, madam, and I ask his kinsfolk, What have you done with my brother? "

" Look, George! " said the bewildered old lady. " I expected him here to-night—that chair was set for him—I have been waiting for him, sir, till now—till I am quite faint—— I don't like —I don't like being alone. Do stay and sup with me! "

" Pardon me, madam. Please God, my supper will be with Harry to-night! "

" Bring him back. Bring him back here on any conditions! It is but five hundred pounds! Here is the money, sir, if you need it! "

" I have no want, madam. I have money with me that can't be better employed than in my brother's service."

" And you will bring him to me, sir! Say you will bring him to me! "

Mr. Warrington made a very stately bow for answer, and quitted the room, passing by the amazed domestics, and calling with an air of authority to Gumbo to follow.

Had Mr. Harry received no letters from home? Master Harry had not opened all his letters the last day or two. Had he received no letter announcing his brother's escape from the French settlements and return to Virginia? Oh, no! No such letter had come, else Master Harry certainly tell Gumbo. Quick, horses! Quick by Strand to Temple Bar! Here is the house of Captivity, and the Deliverer come to the rescue!

CHAPTER XLIX

FRIENDS IN NEED

QUICK, hackney-coach steeds, and bear George Warrington through Strand and Fleet Street to his imprisoned brother's rescue! Any one who remembers Hogarth's picture of a London hackney-coach and a London street road at that period, may fancy how weary the quick time was, and how long seemed the journey—scarce any lights, save those carried by link-boys; badly hung coaches; bad pavements; great holes in the road, and vast quagmires of winter mud. That drive from Piccadilly to Fleet Street seemed almost as long to our young man as the journey from Marlborough to London which he had performed in the morning.

He had written to Harry announcing his arrival at Bristol. He had previously written to his brother, giving the great news of his existence and his return from captivity. There was war between England and France at that time; the French privateers were for ever on the look-out for British merchant-ships, and seized them often within sight of port. The letter bearing the intelligence of George's restoration must have been on board one of the many American ships of which the French took possession. The letter telling of George's arrival in England was never opened by poor Harry; it was lying at the latter's apartments, which it reached on the third morning after Harry's captivity, when the angry Mr. Ruff had refused to give up any single item more of his lodger's property.

To these apartments George first went on his arrival in London, and asked for his brother. Scared at the likeness between them, the maid-servant who opened the door screamed, and ran back to her mistress. The mistress not liking to tell the truth, or to own that poor Harry was actually a prisoner at her husband's suit, said Mr. Warrington had left his lodgings; she did not know where Mr. Warrington was. George knew that Clarges Street was close to Bond Street. Often and often had he looked over the London map. Aunt Bernstein would tell him where Harry was. He might be with her at that very moment. George had read in Harry's letters to Virginia about Aunt Bernstein's kindness to Harry. Even Madam Esmond was softened by it (and especially touched by a letter which the Baroness

wrote—the letter which caused George to pack off post haste for
Europe, indeed). She heartily hoped and trusted that Madam
Beatrix had found occasion to repent of her former bad ways.
It was time, indeed, at her age; and Heaven knows that she had
plenty to repent of! I have known a harmless good old soul of
eighty, still bepommelled and stoned by irreproachable ladies of
the straitest sect of the Pharisees, for a little slip which occurred
long before the present century was born, or she herself was
twenty years old. Rachel Esmond never mentioned her eldest
daughter: Madam Esmond Warrington never mentioned her
sister. No. In spite of the order for remission of the sentence
—in spite of the hand-writing on the floor of the Temple—there
is a crime which some folks never will pardon, and regarding
which female virtue especially is inexorable.

I suppose the Virginians' agent at Bristol had told George
fearful stories of his brother's doings. Gumbo, whom he met
at his aunt's door, as soon as the lad recovered from his terror
at the sudden re-appearance of the master whom he supposed
dead, had leisure to stammer out a word or two respecting his
young master's whereabouts, and present pitiable condition; and
hence Mr. George's sternness of demeanour when he presented
himself to the old lady. It seemed to him a matter of course that
his brother in difficulty should be rescued by his relations. Oh,
George, how little you know about London and London ways!
Whene'er you take your walks abroad, how many poor you
meet: if a philanthropist were for rescuing all of them, not all
the wealth of all the provinces of America would suffice him!

But the feeling and agitation displayed by the old lady touched
her nephew's heart, when, jolting through the dark streets
towards the house of his brother's captivity, George came to
think of his aunt's behaviour. "She *does* feel my poor Harry's
misfortune," he thought to himself. "I have been too hasty
in judging her." Again and again, in the course of his life, Mr.
George had to rebuke himself with the same crime of being too
hasty. How many of us have not? And, alas, the mischief
done, there's no repentance will mend it. Quick, coachman!
We are almost as slow as you are in getting from Clarges Street
to the Temple. Poor Gumbo knows the way to the bailiff's
house well enough. Again the bell is set ringing. The first door
is opened to George and his negro; then that first door is locked
warily upon them, and they find themselves in a little passage
with a little Jewish janitor; then a second door is unlocked, and
they enter into the house. The Jewish janitor stares, as by his

flaring tallow-torch he sees a second Mr. Warrington before him. Come to see that gentleman? Yes. But wait a moment. This is Mr. Warrington's brother from America. Gumbo must go and prepare his master first. Step into this room. There's a gentleman already there about Mr. W.'s business (the porter says), and another upstairs with him now. There's no end of people have been about him.

The room into which George was introduced was a small apartment which went by the name of Mr. Amos's office, and where, by a guttering candle, and talking to the bailiff, sat a stout gentleman in a cloak and a laced hat. The young porter carried his candle too, preceding Mr. George, so there was a sufficiency of light in the apartment.

"We are not angry any more, Harry!" says the stout gentleman, in a cheery voice, getting up and advancing with an outstretched hand to the newcomer. "Thank God, my boy! Mr. Amos here says there will be no difficulty about James and me being your bail, and we will do your business by breakfast-time in the morning. Why . . . Angels and ministers of grace! who are you?" And he started back as the other had hold of his hand.

But the stranger grasped it only the more strongly. "God bless you, sir!" he said. "I know who *you* are. You must be Colonel Lambert of whose kindness to him my poor Harry wrote. And I am the brother whom you have heard of, sir; and who was left for dead in Mr. Braddock's action; and came to life again after eighteen months amongst the French; and live to thank God and thank you for your kindness to my Harry," continued the lad, with a faltering voice.

"James! James! here is news!" cries Mr. Lambert to a gentleman in red, who now entered the room. "Here are the dead come alive! Here is Harry Scapegrace's brother come back, and with his scalp on his head, too!" (George had taken his hat off, and was standing by the light.) "This is my brother bail, Mr. Warrington! This is Lieutenant-Colonel James Wolfe, at your service. You must know there has been a little difference between Harry and me, Mr. George. He is pacified, is he, James?"

"He is full of gratitude," says Mr. Wolfe, after making his bow to Mr. Warrington.

"Harry wrote home about Mr. Wolfe, too, sir," said the young man, "and I hope my brother's friends will be so kind as to be mine."

" I wish he had none other but us, Mr. Warrington. Poor Harry's fine folks have been too fine for him, and have ended by landing him here."

" Nay, your honours, I have done my best to make the young gentleman comfortable; and, knowing your honour before, when you came to bail Captain Watkins, and that your security is perfectly good,—if your honour wishes, the young gentleman can go out this very night, and I will make it all right with the lawyer in the morning," says Harry's landlord, who knew the rank and respectability of the two gentlemen who had come to offer bail for his young prisoner.

" The debt is five hundred and odd pounds, I think? " said Mr. Warrington. " With a hundred thanks to these gentlemen, I can pay the amount at this moment into the officer's hands, taking the usual acknowledgment and caution. But I can never forget, gentlemen, that you helped my brother at his need, and, for doing so, I say thank you, and God bless you, in my mother's name and mine."

Gumbo had, meanwhile, gone upstairs to his master's apartment, where Harry would probably have scolded the negro for returning that night, but that the young gentleman was very much soothed and touched by the conversation he had had with the friend who had just left him. He was sitting over his pipe of Virginia in a sad mood (for, somehow, even Maria's goodness and affection, as she had just exhibited them, had not altogether consoled him; and he had thought, with a little dismay, of certain consequences to which that very kindness and fidelity bound him), when Mr. Wolfe's homely features and eager outstretched hand came to cheer the prisoner, and he heard how Mr. Lambert was below, and the errand upon which the two officers had come. In spite of himself, Lambert would be kind to him. In spite of Harry's ill-temper, and needless suspicion and anger, the good gentleman was determined to help him if he might—to help him even against Mr. Wolfe's own advice, as the latter frankly told Harry. " For you were wrong, Mr. Warrington," said the Colonel, " and you wouldn't be set right; and you, a young man, used hard words and unkind behaviour to your senior, and what is more, one of the best gentlemen who walk God's earth. You see, sir, what his answer hath been to your wayward temper. You will bear with a friend who speaks frankly with you? Martin Lambert hath acted in this as he always doth, as the best Christian, the best friend, the most kind and generous of men. Nay, if you want another proof of his goodness, here it is: he has converted me, who, as I don't care to disguise, was angry with you for your treatment of him, and has absolutely brought me down here to be your bail. Let us both cry Peccavimus! Harry, and shake our friend by the hand! He is sitting in the room below. He would not come here till he knew how you would receive him."

" I think he is a good man!" groaned out Harry. "I was very angry and wild at the time when he and I met last, Colonel Wolfe. Nay, perhaps he was right in sending back those trinkets, hurt as I was at his doing so. Go down to him, will you be so kind, sir? and tell him I am sorry, and ask his pardon, and—and, God bless him for his generous behaviour." And here the young gentleman turned his head away, and rubbed his hand across his eyes.

" Tell him all this thyself, Harry!" cries the Colonel, taking the young fellow's hand. "No deputy will ever say it half so well. Come with me now."

"You go first, and I'll—I'll follow,—on my word I will. See! I am in my morning-gown! I will but put on a coat and come to him. Give him my message first. Just—just prepare him for me!" says poor Harry, who knew he must do it, but yet did not much like that process of eating of humble-pie.

Wolfe went out smiling—understanding the lad's scruples well enough, perhaps. As he opened the door, Mr. Gumbo entered it; almost forgetting to bow to the gentleman, profusely courteous as he was on ordinary occasions,—his eyes glaring round, his great mouth grinning—himself in a state of such high excitement and delight that his master remarked his condition.

" What, Gum? What has happened to thee? Hast thou got a new sweetheart? "

No, Gum had not got no new sweetheart, Master.

" Give me my coat. What has brought thee back? "

Gum grinned prodigiously. " I have seen a ghost, Mas'r!" he said.

" A ghost! and whose, and where? "

" Whar? Saw him at Madam Bernstein's house. Come with him here in the coach! He downstairs now with Colonel Lambert!" Whilst Gumbo is speaking, as he is putting on his master's coat, his eyes are rolling, his head is wagging, his hands are trembling, his lips are grinning.

" Ghost—what ghost? " says Harry, in a strange agitation. " Is anybody—is—my mother come? "

"No, sir; no, Master Harry!" Gumbo's head rolls nearly off in its violent convolutions, and his master, looking oddly at him, flings the door open and goes rapidly down the stair.

He is at the foot of it, just as a voice within the little office, of which the door is open, is saying, "*and, for doing so, I say thank you, and God bless you, in my mother's name and mine.*"

"Whose voice is that?" calls out Harry Warrington, with a strange cry in his own voice.

"It's the *ghost's*, Mas'r!" says Gumbo, from behind; and Harry runs forward to the room,—where, if you please, we will pause a little minute before we enter. The two gentlemen who were there, turned their heads away. The lost was found again. The dead was alive. The prodigal was on his brother's heart,—his own full of love, gratitude, repentance.

"Come away, James! I think we are not wanted any more here," says the Colonel. "Good-night, boys. Some ladies in Hill Street won't be able to sleep for this strange news. Or will you go home and sup with 'em, and tell them the story!"

No, with many thanks, the boys would not go and sup to-night. They had stories of their own to tell. "Quick, Gumbo, with the trunks. Good-bye, Mr. Amos!" Harry felt almost unhappy when he went away.

CHAPTER L

CONTAINING A GREAT DEAL OF THE FINEST MORALITY

WHEN first we had the honour to be presented to Sir Miles Warrington at the King's drawing-room, in St. James's Palace, I confess that I, for one—looking at his jolly round face, his broad round waistcoat, his hearty country manner,—expected that I had lighted upon a most eligible and agreeable acquaint-ance at last, and was about to become intimate with that noblest specimen of the human race, the bepraised of songs and men, the good old English country gentleman. In fact, to be a good old country gentleman is to hold a position nearest the gods, and at the summit of earthly felicity. To have a large unencumbered rent-roll, and the rents regularly paid by adoring farmers, who bless their stars at having such a landlord as his honour; to have no tenant holding back with his money, excepting just one, perhaps, who does so in order to give occasion to Good Old Country Gentleman to show his sublime charity and universal benevolence of soul—to hunt three days a week, love the sport of all things, and have perfect good health and good appetite in consequence—to have not only good appetite, but a good dinner; to sit down at church in the midst of a chorus of blessings from the villagers, the first man in the parish, the benefactor of the parish, with a consciousness of consummate desert, saying, "Have mercy upon us miserable sinners," to be sure, but only for form's sake, because the words are written in the book, and to give other folks an example:—a G. O. C. G. a miserable sinner! So healthy, so wealthy, so jolly, so much respected by the vicar, so much honoured by the tenants, so much beloved and admired by his family, amongst whom his story of grouse in the gun-room causes laughter from generation to generation;—this perfect being a miserable sinner! *Allons donc!* Give any man good health and temper, five thousand a year, the adoration of his parish, and the love and worship of his family, and I'll defy you to make him so heartily dissatisfied with his spiritual condition as to set himself down a miserable anything. If you were a Royal Highness, and went to church in the most perfect health and comfort, the parson waiting to begin the service until Your R. H. came in, would you believe yourself to be a miserable etc.? You might when racked with gout, in solitude, the fear of death before your eyes, the doctor having cut off your bottle of claret, and ordered arrowroot and a little sherry,—you might *then* be humiliated, and acknowledge your own shortcomings, and the vanity of things in general; but, in high health, sunshine, spirits, that word miserable is only a form. You can't think in your heart that you are to be pitied much for the present. If you are to be miserable, what is Colin Ploughman, with the ague, seven children, two pounds a year rent to pay for his cottage, and eight shillings a week? No: a healthy, rich, jolly country gentleman, if miserable, has a very supportable misery: if a sinner, has very few people to tell him so.

It may be he becomes somewhat selfish; but at least he is satisfied with himself. Except my Lord at the Castle, there is nobody for miles and miles round so good or so great. His admirable wife ministers to him, and to the whole parish, indeed: his children bow before him: the vicar of the parish reverences him: he is respected at quarter-sessions: he causes poachers to tremble: off go all hats before him at market: and round about his great coach, in which his spotless daughters and sublime lady sit, all the country-town tradesmen cringe, bare-headed, and the farmers' women drop innumerable curtseys. From their cushions in the great coach the ladies look down beneficently, and smile on the poorer folk. They buy a yard of ribbon with affability; they condescend to purchase an ounce of salts, or a packet of flower-seeds: they deign to cheapen a goose: their drive is like a royal progress: a happy people is supposed to press round them and bless them. Tradesmen bow, farmers' wives bob, town-boys, waving their ragged hats, cheer the red-faced coachman as he drives the fat bays, and cry, " Sir Miles for ever! Throw us a halfpenny, my Lady!"

But suppose the market-woman should hide her fat goose when Sir Miles's coach comes, out of terror lest my Lady, spying the bird, should insist on purchasing it a bargain? Suppose no coppers ever were known to come out of the royal coach window? Suppose Sir Miles regaled his tenants with notoriously small beer, and his poor with especially thin broth? This may be our fine old English gentleman's way. There have been not a few fine English gentlemen and ladies of this sort; who patronised the poor without ever relieving them, who called out "Amen!" at church as loud as the clerk; who went through all the forms of piety, and discharged all the etiquette of old English gentleman-hood; who bought virtue a bargain, as it were, and had no doubt they were honouring her by the purchase. Poor Harry, in his distress, asked help from his relations: his aunt sent him a tract and her blessing; his uncle had business out of town, and could not, of course, answer the poor boy's petition. How much of this behaviour goes on daily in respectable life, think you? You can fancy Lord and Lady Macbeth concocting a murder, and coming together with some little awkwardness, perhaps, when the transaction was done and over; but my Lord and Lady Skinflint, when they consult in their bedroom about giving their luckless nephew a helping hand, and determine to refuse, and go down to family prayers, and meet their children and domestics, and discourse virtuously before them, and then remain together, and talk nose to nose,—what can they think of one another? and of the poor kinsman fallen among the thieves, and groaning for help unheeded? How can they go on with those virtuous airs? How can they dare look each other in the face?

Dare? Do you suppose they think they have done wrong? Do you suppose Skinflint is tortured with remorse at the idea of the distress which called to him in vain, and of the hunger which he sent empty away? Not he. He is indignant with

Prodigal for being a fool: he is not ashamed of himself for being a curmudgeon. What? a young man with such opportunities throw them away? A fortune spent amongst gamblers and spendthrifts? Horrible, horrible! Take warning, my child, by this unfortunate young man's behaviour, and see the consequences of extravagance. According to the great and always Established Church of the Pharisees, here is an admirable opportunity for a moral discourse, and an assertion of virtue. "And to think of his deceiving us so!" cries out Lady Warrington.

"Very sad, very sad, my dear!" says Sir Miles, wagging his head.

"To think of so much extravagance in one so young!" cries Lady Warrington. "Cards, bets, feasts at taverns of the most wicked profusion, carriage and riding horses, the company of the wealthy and profligate of his own sex, and, I fear, of the most iniquitous persons of ours."

"Hush, my Lady Warrington!" cries her husband, glancing towards the spotless Dora and Flora, who held down their blushing heads at the mention of the last naughty persons.

"No wonder my poor children hide their faces!" mamma continues. "My dears, I wish even the existence of such creatures could be kept from you!"

"They can't go to an opera, or the park, without seeing 'em, to be sure," says Sir Miles.

"To think we should have introduced such a young serpent into the bosom of our family! and have left him in the company of that guileless darling!" and she points to Master Miles.

"Who's a serpent, mamma?" inquires that youth. "First you said Cousin Harry was bad: then he was good: now he is bad again. Which is he, Sir Miles?"

"He has faults, like all of us, Miley, my dear. Your cousin has been wild, and you must take warning by him."

"Was not my elder brother, who died—my naughty brother —was not he wild too? He was not kind to me when I was quite a little boy. He never gave me money, nor toys, nor rode with me, nor—why do you cry, mamma? Sure I remember how Hugh and you were always fight——"

"Silence, sir!" cry out papa and the girls in a breath. "Don't you know you are never to mention that name?"

"I know I love Harry, and I didn't love Hugh," says the sturdy little rebel. "And if Cousin Harry is in prison, I'll give him my half-guinea that my god-papa gave me, and anything I have—yes, anything, except—except my little horse—and my silver waistcoat—and—and Snowball and Sweetlips at home—and—and, yes, my custard after dinner." This was in reply to a hint of sister Dora. "But I'd give him *some* of it," continues Miles, after a pause.

"Shut thy mouth with it, child, and then go about thy business," says papa, amused. Sir Miles Warrington had a considerable fund of easy humour.

"Who would have thought he should ever be so wild?" mamma goes on.

"Nay. Youth is the season for wild oats, my dear."

"That we should be so misled in him!" sighed the girls.

"That he should kiss us both!" cries papa.

"Sir Miles Warrington, I have no patience with that sort of vulgarity!" says the majestic matron.

"Which of you was the favourite yesterday, girls?" continues the father.

"Favourite, indeed! I told him over and over again of my engagement to dear Tom—I did, Dora,—why do you sneer, if you please?" says the handsome sister.

"Nay, to do her justice, so did Dora too," said papa.

"Because Flora seemed to wish to forget her engagement with dear Tom sometimes," remarks her sister.

"I never never never wished to break with Tom! It's wicked of you to say so, Dora! It is you who were for ever sneering at him: it is you who are always envious because I happen—at least, because gentlemen imagine that I am not ill-looking, and prefer me to some folks, in spite of all their learning and wit!" cries Flora, tossing her head over her shoulder, and looking at the glass.

"Why are you always looking there, sister?" says the artless Miles junior. "Sure, you must know your face well enough!"

"Some people look at it just as often, child, who haven't near such good reason," says papa gallantly.

"If you mean *me*, Sir Miles, I thank you," cries Dora. "My face is as Heaven made it, and my father and mother gave it me. 'Tis not my fault if I resemble my papa's family. If my head is homely, at least I have got some brains in it. I envious of Flora, indeed, because she has found favour in the sight of poor Tom Claypool! I should as soon be proud of captivating a ploughboy!"

"Pray, miss, was your Mr. Harry, of Virginia, much wiser

than Tom Claypool? You would have had him for the asking!"
exclaims Flora.

"And so would *you*, miss, and have dropped Tom Claypool
into the sea!" cries Dora.

"I wouldn't."

"You would."

"I wouldn't;"—and *da capo* goes the conversation—the
shuttlecock of wrath being briskly battled from one sister to
another.

"Oh, my children! Is this the way you dwell together in
unity?" exclaims their excellent female parent, laying down
her embroidery. "What an example you set to this Innocent!"

"Like to see 'em fight, my Lady!" cries the Innocent, rubbing
his hands.

"At her, Flora! Worry her, Dora! To it again, you little
rogues!" says facetious papa. "'Tis good sport, ain't it, Miley?"

"Oh, Sir Miles! Oh, my children! These disputes are
unseemly. They tear a fond mother's heart," says mamma,
with majestic action, though bearing the laceration of her bosom
with much seeming equanimity. "What cause for thankfulness
ought we to have, that watchful parents have prevented any
idle engagements between you and your misguided cousin! If
we have been mistaken in him, is it not a mercy that we have
found out our error in time? If either of you had any preference for him, your excellent good sense, my loves, will teach you
to overcome, to eradicate, the vain feeling. That we cherished
and were kind to him can *never* be a source of regret. 'Tis a
proof of our good nature. What *we* have to regret, I fear, is,
that your cousin should have proved unworthy of our kindness,
and, coming away from the society of gamblers, play-actors,
and the like, should have brought contamination—pollution, I
had almost said—into this pure family!"

"Oh, bother mamma's sermons!" says Flora, as my Lady
pursues an harangue of which we only give the commencement
here, but during which papa, whistling, gently quits the room
on tiptoe, while the artless Miles junior winds his top and pegs
it under the robes of his sisters. It has done humming, and
staggered and tumbled over, and expired in its usual tipsy
manner, long ere Lady Warrington has finished her sermon.

"Were you listening to me, my child?" she asks, laying her
hand on her darling's head.

"Yes, mother," says he, with the whipcord in his mouth, and
proceeding to wind up his sportive engine. "You was a-saying

that Harry was very poor now, and that we oughtn't to help him. That's what you were saying, wasn't it, madam?"

"My poor child, thou wilt understand me better when thou art older!" says mamma, turning towards that ceiling to which her eyes always have recourse.

"Get out, you little wretch!" cries one of the sisters. The artless one has pegged his top at Dora's toes, and laughs with the glee of merry boyhood at his sister's discomfiture.

But what is this? Who comes here? Why does Sir Miles return to the drawing-room, and why does Tom Claypool, who strides after the Baronet, wear a countenance so disturbed?

"Here's a pretty business, my Lady Warrington!" cries Sir Miles. "Here's a wonderful wonder of wonders, girls!"

"For goodness' sake, gentlemen, what is your intelligence?" asks the virtuous matron.

"The whole town's talking about it, my Lady!" says Tom Claypool, puffing for breath.

"Tom has seen him," continued Sir Miles.

"Seen both of them, my Lady Warrington. They were at Ranelagh last night, with a regular mob after 'em. And so like, that but for their different ribbons you would hardly have told one from the other. One was in blue, the other in brown; but I'm certain he has worn both the suits here."

"What suits?"

"What one,—what other?" call the girls.

"Why, your Fortunate Youth, to be sure."

"Our precious Virginian, and heir to the principality!" says Sir Miles.

"Is my nephew, then, released from his incarceration?" asks her Ladyship. "And he is again plunged in the vortex of dissip——"

"Confound him!" roars out the Baronet, with an expression which I fear was even stronger. "What should you think, my Lady Warrington, if this precious nephew of mine should turn out to be an impostor; by George! no better than an adventurer?"

"An inward monitor whispered me as much!" cried the lady; "but I dashed from me the unworthy suspicion. Speak, Sir Miles, we burn with impatience to listen to your intelligence."

"I'll speak, my love, when you've done," says Sir Miles. "Well, what do you think of my gentleman, who comes into my house, dines at my table, is treated as one of the family, kisses my——"

"What?" asks Tom Claypool, firing as red as his waistcoat.

"—Hem! Kisses my wife's hand, and is treated in the fondest manner, by George! What do you think of this fellow, who talks of his property and his principality, by Jupiter!— turning out to be a beggarly SECOND SON! A beggar, my Lady Warrington, by——"

"Sir Miles Warrington, no violence of language before these dear ones! I sink to the earth, confounded by this unutterable hypocrisy. And did I intrust thee to a pretender, my blessed boy? Did I leave thee with an impostor, my innocent one?" the matron cries, fondling her son.

"Who's an impostor, my Lady?" asks the child.

"That confounded young scamp of a Harry Warrington!" bawls out papa; on which the little Miles, after wearing a puzzled look for a moment, and yielding to I know not what hidden emotion, bursts out crying.

His admirable mother proposes to clutch him to her heart, but he rejects the pure caress, bawling only the louder, and kicking frantically about the maternal *gremium*. As the butler announces "Mr. George Warrington, Mr. Henry Warrington!" Miles is dropped from his mother's lap. Sir Miles's face emulates Mr. Claypool's waistcoat. The three ladies rise up, and make three most frigid curtseys, as our two young men enter the room.

Little Miles runs towards them. He holds out a little hand. "Oh, Harry! No! which is Harry? *You're* my Harry," and he chooses rightly this time. "Oh, you dear Harry! I'm so glad you are come! and they've been abusing you so!"

"I am come to pay my duty to my uncle," says the dark-haired Mr. Warrington; "and to thank him for his hospitalities to my brother Henry."

"What, Nephew George? My brother's face and eyes! Boys both, I am delighted to see you!" cries their uncle, grasping affectionately a hand of each, as his honest face radiates with pleasure.

"This indeed has been a most mysterious and most providential resuscitation," says Lady Warrington. "Only I wonder that my nephew Henry concealed the circumstance until now," she adds, with a sidelong glance at both young gentlemen.

"He knew it no more than your Ladyship," says Mr. Warrington. The young ladies looked at each other with downcast eyes.

"Indeed, sir! a most singular circumstance," says mamma, with another curtsey. "We had heard of it, sir; and Mr. Claypool, our county neighbour, had just brought us the intelligence, and it even now formed the subject of my conversation with my daughters."

" Yes," cries out a little voice, " and do you know, Harry, father and mother said you was a—a imp——"

" Silence, my child! Screwby, convey Master Warrington to his own apartment! These, Mr. Warrington—or, I suppose I should say Nephew George—are your cousins." Two curtseys —two cheeses are made—two hands are held out. Mr. Esmond Warrington makes a profound low bow, which embraces (and it is the only embrace which the gentleman offers) all three ladies. He lays his hat to his heart. He says, " It is my duty, madam, to pay my respects to my uncle and cousins, and to thank your Ladyship for such hospitality as you have been enabled to show to my brother."

" It was not much, nephew, but it was our best. Ods bobs! " cries the hearty Sir Miles, " it was our best! "

" And I appreciate it, sir," says Mr. Warrington, looking gravely round at the family.

" Give us thy hand. Not a word more," says Sir Miles. " What? do you think I'm a cannibal, and won't extend the hand of hospitality to my dear brother's son? What say you, lads? Will you eat our mutton at three? This is my neighbour, Tom Claypool, son to Sir Thomas Claypool, Baronet, and my very good friend. Hey, Tom! Thou wilt be of the party, Tom? Thou knowest our brew, hey, my boy? "

" Yes, I know it, Sir Miles," replies Tom, with no peculiar expression of rapture on his face.

" And thou shalt taste it, my boy, thou shalt taste it! What is there for dinner, my Lady Warrington? Our food is plain, but plenty, lads—plain, but plenty! "

" We cannot partake of it to-day, sir. We dine with a friend who occupies my Lord Wrotham's house, your neighbour. Colonel Lambert — Major-General Lambert he has just been made."

" With two daughters, I think—countrified-looking girls—are they not? " asks Flora.

" I think I have remarked two little rather dowdy things," says Dora.

" They are as good girls as any in England! " breaks out Harry, to whom no one had thought of saying a single word. His reign was over, you see. He was nobody. What wonder, then, that he should not be visible?

"Oh, indeed, cousin!" says Dora, with a glance at the young man, who sat with burning cheeks, chafing at the humiliation put upon him, but not knowing how or whether he should notice it. "Oh, indeed, cousin! You are very charitable—or very lucky, I'm sure! You see angels where we only see ordinary little persons. I'm sure I could not imagine who were those odd-looking people in Lord Wrotham's coach, with his handsome liveries. But if they were three *angels*, I have nothing to say."

"My brother is an enthusiast," interposes George. "He is often mistaken about women."

"Oh, really!" says Dora, looking a little uneasy.

"I fear my nephew Henry has indeed met with some unfavourable specimens of our sex," the matron remarks, with a groan.

"We are so easily taken in, madam—we are both very young yet—we shall grow older and learn better."

"Most sincerely, Nephew George, I trust you may. You have my best wishes, my prayers, for your brother's welfare and your own. No efforts of *ours* have been wanting. At a painful moment, to which I will not further allude——"

"And when my uncle Sir Miles was out of town," says George, looking towards the Baronet, who smiles at him with affectionate approval.

"—I sent your brother a work which I thought might comfort him, and I know might improve him. Nay, do not thank me; I claim no credit; I did but my duty—a humble woman's duty—for what are this world's goods, nephew, compared to the welfare of a soul? If I did good, I am thankful; if I was useful, I rejoice. If, through my means, you have been brought, Harry, to consider——"

"Oh! the sermon, is it?" breaks in downright Harry. "I hadn't time to read a single syllable of it, aunt—thank you. You see I don't care much about that kind of thing—but thank you all the same."

"The intention is everything," says Mr. Warrington, "and we are both grateful. Our dear friend, General Lambert, intended to give bail for Harry; but happily, I had funds of Harry's with me to meet any demands upon us. But the kindness is the same, and I am grateful to the friend who hastened to my brother's rescue when he had most need of aid, and when his own relations happened—so unfortunately—to be out of town."

"Anything I could do, my dear boy, I'm sure—my brother's

son—my own nephew—ods bobs! you know—that is, anything
—*anything*, you know!" cries Sir Miles, bringing his own hand
into George's with a generous smack. "You *can't* stay and dine
with us? Put off the Colonel—the General—do, now! Or
name a day. My Lady Warrington, make my nephew name a
day when he will sit under his grandfather's picture, and drink
some of his wine!"

"His intellectual faculties seem more developed than those
of his unlucky younger brother," remarked my Lady, when the
young gentlemen had taken their leave. "The younger must
be reckless and extravagant about money indeed, for did you
remark, Sir Miles, the loss of his reversion in Virginia—the
amount of which has, no doubt, been grossly exaggerated, but,
nevertheless, must be something considerable—did you, I say,
remark that the ruin of Harry's prospects scarcely seemed to
affect him?"

"I shouldn't be at all surprised that the elder turns out to
be as poor as the young one," says Dora, tossing her head.
"He! he! Did you see that Cousin George had one of Cousin
Harry's suits of clothes on—the brown and gold—that one he
wore when he went with you to the oratorio, Flora?"

"Did he take Flora to an oratorio?" asks Mr. Claypool
fiercely.

"I was ill and couldn't go, and my cousin went with her,"
says Dora.

"Far be it from *me* to object to any innocent amusement,
much less to the music of Mr. Handel, dear Mr. Claypool," says
mamma. "Music refines the soul, elevates the understanding,
is heard in our churches, and 'tis well known was practised by
King David. Your operas I shun as deleterious; your ballets
I would forbid to my children as most immoral; but music,
my dears! May we enjoy it, like everything else in reason—
may we——"

"There's the music of the dinner-bell," says papa, rubbing
his hands. "Come, girls. Screwby, go fetch Master Miley.
Tom, take down my Lady."

"Nay, dear Thomas, I walk but slowly. Go you with dearest
Flora downstairs," says Virtue.

But Dora took care to make the evening pleasant by talking
of Handel and oratorios constantly during dinner.

CHAPTER LI

CONTICUERE OMNES

ACROSS the way, if the gracious reader will please to step over with us, he will find our young gentlemen at Lord Wrotham's house, which his Lordship has lent to his friend the General and that little family party assembled, with which we made acquaintance at Oakhurst and Tunbridge Wells. James Wolfe has promised to come to dinner; but James is dancing attendance upon Miss Lowther, and would rather have a glance from her eyes than the finest kickshaws dressed by Lord Wrotham's cook, or the dessert which is promised for the entertainment at which you are just going to sit down. You will make the sixth. You may take Mr. Wolfe's place. You may be sure he won't come. As for me, I will stand at the sideboard and report the conversation.

Note first, how happy the women look! When Harry Warrington was taken by those bailiffs, I had intended to tell you how the good Mrs. Lambert, hearing of the boy's mishap, had flown to her husband, and had begged, implored, insisted, that her Martin should help him. "Never mind his rebeldom of the other day; never mind about his being angry that his presents were returned—of course anybody would be angry, much more such a high-spirited lad as Harry! Never mind about our being so poor, and wanting all our spare money for the boys at college; there *must* be some way of getting him out of the scrape. Did you not get Charles Watkins out of the scrape two years ago; and did he not pay you back every half-penny? Yes; and you made a whole family happy, blessed be God! and Mrs. Watkins prays for you and blesses you to this very day, and I think everything has prospered with us since. And I have no doubt it has made you a Major-General—no *earthly* doubt," says the fond wife.

Now, as Martin Lambert requires very little persuasion to do a kind action, he in this instance lets himself be persuaded easily enough, and having made up his mind to seek for friend James Wolfe, and give bail for Harry, he takes his leave and his hat, and squeezes Theo's hand, who seems to divine his errand (or perhaps that silly mamma has blabbed it), and kisses little Hetty's flushed cheek, and away he goes out of the apartment where the girls and their mother are sitting, though he is followed out of the room by the latter.

When she is alone with him, that enthusiastic matron cannot control her feelings any longer. She flings her arms round her husband's neck, kisses him a hundred and twenty-five times in an instant—calls God to bless him—cries plentifully on his shoulder; and in this sentimental attitude is discovered by old Mrs. Quiggett, my Lord's housekeeper, who is bustling about the house, and, I suppose, is quite astounded at the conjugal phenomenon.

"We have had a tiff, and we are making it up! Don't tell tales out of school, Mrs. Quiggett!" says the gentleman, walking off.

"Well, I never!" says Mrs. Quiggett, with a shrill strident laugh, like a venerable old cockatoo—which white, hook-nosed, long-lived bird Mrs. Quiggett strongly resembles. "Well, I never!" says Quiggett, laughing and shaking her old sides, all her keys, and, as one may fancy, her old ribs clatter and jingle.

"Oh, Quiggett!" sobs out Mrs. Lambert, "what a man that is!"

"You've been a-quarrelling, have you, mum, and making it up? That's right."

"Quarrel with *him*? He never told a greater story. My General is an angel, Quiggett. I should like to worship him. I should like to fall down at his boots and kiss 'em, I should! There never was a man so good as my General. What have I done to have such a man. How *dare* I have such a good husband?"

"My dear, I think there's a pair of you," says the old cockatoo; "and what would you like for your supper?"

When Lambert comes back very late to that meal, and tells what has happened, how Harry is free, and how his brother has come to life, and rescued him, you may fancy what a commotion the whole of those people are in! If Mrs. Lambert's General was an angel before, what is he now! If she wanted to embrace his boots in the morning, pray what further office of wallowing degradation would she prefer in the evening? Little Hetty comes and nestles up to her father quite silent, and drinks a little drop out of his glass. Theo's and mamma's faces beam with happiness, like two moons of brightness. . . . After supper, those four at a certain signal fall down on their knees

—glad homage paying in awful mirth—rejoicing, and with such pure joy as angels do, we read, for the sinner that repents. There comes a great knocking at the door whilst they are so gathered together. Who can be there? My Lord is in the country miles off. It is past midnight now; so late have they been, so long have they been talking! I think Mrs. Lambert guesses who is there.

"This is George," says a young gentleman, leading in another. "We have been to Aunt Bernstein. We couldn't go to bed, Aunt Lambert, without coming to thank you too. You dear dear good——" There is no more speech audible. Aunt Lambert is kissing Harry, Theo has snatched up Hetty, who is as pale as death, and is hugging her into life again. George Warrington stands with his hat off, and then (when Harry's transaction is concluded) goes up and kisses Mrs. Lambert's hand: the General passes his across his eyes. I protest they are all in a very tender and happy state. Generous hearts sometimes feel it, when Wrong is forgiven, when Peace is restored, when Love returns that had been thought lost.

"We came from Aunt Bernstein's; we saw lights here, you see; we couldn't go to sleep without saying good-night to you all," says Harry. "Could we, George?"

"'Tis certainly a famous nightcap you have brought us, boys," says the General. "When are you to come and dine with us? To-morrow?" No, they must go to Madam Bernstein's to-morrow. The next day, then? Yes, they would come the next day—and that is the very day we are writing about: and this is the very dinner at which, in the room of Lieutenant-Colonel James Wolfe, absent on private affairs, my gracious reader has just been invited to sit down.

To sit down, and why, if you please? Not to a mere Barmecide dinner—no, no—but to hear Mr. GEORGE ESMOND WARRINGTON'S STATEMENT, which of course he was going to make. Here they all sit—not in my Lord's grand dining-room, you know, but in the snug study or parlour in front. The cloth has been withdrawn, the General has given the King's health, the servants have left the room, the guests sit conticent, and so, after a little hemming and blushing, Mr. George proceeds:—

"I remember, at the table of our General, how the little Philadelphia agent, whose wit and shrewdness we had remarked at home, made the very objections to the conduct of the campaign of which its disastrous issue showed the justice. 'Of course,' says he, 'your Excellency's troops once before Fort

Duquesne, such a weak little place will never be able to resist such a general, such an army, such artillery, as will there be found attacking it. But do you calculate, sir, on the difficulty of reaching the place? Your Excellency's march will be through woods almost untrodden, over roads which you will have to make yourself, and your line will be some four miles long. This slender line having to make its way through the forest, will be subject to endless attacks in front, in rear, in flank, by enemies whom you will never see, and whose constant practice in war is the dexterous laying of ambuscades.' — 'Psha, sir!' says the General, 'the savages may frighten your raw American militia' (Thank your Excellency for the compliment, Mr. Washington seems to say, who is sitting at the table), ' but the Indians will never make any impression on His Majesty's regular troops.'—' I heartily hope not, sir,' says Mr. Franklin, with a sigh; and of course the gentlemen of the General's family sneered at the postmaster, as at a pert civilian who had no call to be giving his opinion on matters entirely beyond his comprehension.

" We despised the Indians on our own side, and our commander made light of them and their service. Our officers disgusted the chiefs who were with us by outrageous behaviour to their women. There were not above seven or eight who remained with our force. Had we had a couple of hundred in our front on that fatal 9th of July, the event of the day must have been very different. They would have flung off the attack of the French Indians; they would have prevented the surprise and panic which ensued. 'Tis known now that the French had even got ready to give up their fort, never dreaming of the possibility of a defence, and that the French Indians themselves remonstrated against the audacity of attacking such an overwhelming force as ours.

" I was with our General with the main body of the troops when the firing began in front of us, and one aide-de-camp after another was sent forwards. At first the enemy's attack was answered briskly by our own advanced people, and our men huzza'd and cheered with good heart. But very soon our fire grew slacker, whilst from behind every tree and bush round about us came single shots, which laid man after man low. We were marching in orderly line, the skirmishers in front, the colours and two of our small guns in the centre, the baggage well guarded bringing up the rear, and were moving over a ground which was open and clear for a mile or two, and for some half-mile in breadth, a thick tangled covert of brushwood and trees on either side of us. After the firing had continued for some brief time in front, it opened from both sides of the environing wood on our advancing column. The men dropped rapidly, the officers in greater number than the men. At first, as I said, these cheered and answered the enemy's fire, our guns even opening on the wood, and seeming to silence the French in ambuscade there. But the hidden rifle-firing began again. Our men halted, huddled up together, in spite of the shouts and orders of the General and officers to advance, and fired wildly into the brushwood—of course making no impression. Those in advance came running back on the main body frightened, and many of them wounded. They reported there were five thousand Frenchmen and a legion of yelling Indian devils in front, who were scalping our people as they fell. We could hear their cries from the wood around as our men dropped under their rifles. There was no inducing the people to go forward now. One aide-de-camp after another was sent forward, and never returned. At last it came to be my turn, and I was sent with a message to Captain Fraser of Halkett's in front, which he was never to receive nor I to deliver.

"I had not gone thirty yards in advance when a rifle-ball struck my leg, and I fell straightway to the ground. I recollect a rush forward of Indians and Frenchmen after that, the former crying their fiendish war-cries, the latter as fierce as their savage allies. I was amazed and mortified to see how few of the white-coats there were. Not above a score passed me; indeed there were not fifty in the accursed action in which two of the bravest regiments of the British army were put to rout.

"One of them, who was half Indian half Frenchman, with mocassins and a white uniform coat and cockade, seeing me prostrate on the ground, turned back and ran towards me, his musket clubbed over his head to dash my brains out and plunder me as I lay. I had my little fusil which my Harry gave me when I went on the campaign; it had fallen by me and within my reach, luckily: I seized it and down fell the Frenchman dead at six yards before me. I was saved for that time, but bleeding from my wound and very faint. I swooned almost in trying to load my piece, and it dropped from my hand, and the hand itself sank lifeless to the ground.

"I was scarcely in my senses, the yells and shots ringing dimly in my ears, when I saw an Indian before me, busied over the body of the Frenchman I had just shot, but glancing towards me as I lay on the ground bleeding. He first rifled the Frenchman, tearing open his coat, and feeling in his pockets: he then scalped him, and with his bleeding knife in his mouth advanced towards me. I saw him coming as through a film, as in a dream—I was powerless to move, or to resist him.

"He put his knee upon my chest: with one bloody hand he seized my long hair and lifted my head from the ground, and as he lifted it, he enabled me to see a French officer rapidly advancing behind him.

"Good God! It was young Florac, who was my second in the duel at Quebec. 'A moi, Florac!' I cried out. 'C'est Georges! aide-moi!'

"He started; ran up to me at the cry, laid his hand on the Indian's shoulder, and called him to hold. But the savage did not understand French, or choose to understand it. He clutched my hair firmer, and waving his dripping knife round it, motioned to the French lad to leave him to his prey. I could only cry out again and piteously, 'A moi!'

"'Ah, canaille, tu veux du sang? Prends!" said Florac, with a curse; and the next moment, and with an *ugh*, the Indian fell over my chest dead, with Florac's sword through his body.

"My friend looked round him. 'Eh!' says he, 'la belle affaire! Where art thou wounded, in the leg?' He bound my leg tight with his sash. 'The others will kill thee if they find thee here. Ah, tiens! Put me on this coat, and this hat with the white cockade. Call out in French if any of our people pass. They will take thee for one of us. Thou art Brunet of the Quebec Volunteers. God guard thee, Brunet! I must go forward. 'Tis a general débâcle, and the whole of your redcoats are on the run, my poor boy.' Ah, what a rout it was! What a day of disgrace for England!

"Florac's rough application stopped the bleeding of my leg, and the kind creature helped me to rest against a tree, and to load my fusil, which he placed within reach of me, to protect me in case any other marauder should have a mind to attack me. And he gave me the gourd of that unlucky French soldier, who had lost his own life in the deadly game which he had just played against me, and the drink the gourd contained served greatly to refresh and invigorate me. Taking a mark of the tree against which I lay, and noting the various bearings of the country, so as to be able again to find me, the young lad hastened on to the front. 'Thou seest how much I love thee, George,' he said, 'that I stay behind in a moment like this.' I forget

whether I told thee, Harry, that Florac was under some obliga-
tion to me. I had won money of him at cards, at Quebec—only
playing at his repeated entreaty—and there was a difficulty
about paying, and I remitted his debt to me, and lighted my
pipe with his note-of-hand. You see, sir, that you are not the
only gambler in the family.

" At evening, when the dismal pursuit was over, the faithful
fellow came back to me with a couple of Indians, who had each
reeking scalps at their belts, and whom he informed that I was
a Frenchman, his brother, who had been wounded early in the
day, and must be carried back to the fort. They laid me in
one of their blankets, and carried me, groaning, with the trusty
Florac by my side. Had he left me, they would assuredly have
laid me down, plundered me, and added my hair to that of the
wretches whose bleeding spoils hung at their girdles. He
promised them brandy at the fort, if they brought me safely
there. I have but a dim recollection of the journey; the
anguish of my wound was extreme: I fainted more than once.
We came to the end of our march at last. I was taken into the
fort, and carried to the officer's log-house, and laid upon Florac's
own bed.

" Happy for me was my insensibility. I had been brought
into the fort as a wounded French soldier of the garrison. I
heard afterwards, that, during my delirium, the few prisoners
who had been made on the day of our disaster, had been brought
under the walls of Duquesne by their savage captors, and there
horribly burned, tortured, and butchered by the Indians, under
the eyes of the garrison."

As George speaks, one may fancy a thrill of horror running
through his sympathising audience. Theo takes Hetty's hand,
and looks at George in a very alarmed manner. Harry strikes
his fist upon the table, and cries, " The bloody, murderous red-
skinned villains! There will never be peace for us until they
are all hunted down!"

" They were offering a hundred and thirty dollars apiece for
Indian scalps in Pennsylvania when I left home," says George
demurely, " and fifty for women."

" Fifty for women, my love! Do you hear that, Mrs.
Lambert?" cries the Colonel, lifting up his wife's hair.

" The murderous villains!" says Harry, again. " Hunt 'em
down, sir! Hunt 'em down!"

" I know not how long I lay in my fever," George resumed
" When I awoke to my senses, my dear Florac was gone. He

and his company had been despatched on an enterprise against
an English fort on the Pennsylvanian territory, which the
French claimed, too. In Duquesne, when I came to be able to
ask and understand what was said to me, there were not above
thirty Europeans left. The place might have been taken over
and over again, had any of our people had the courage to return
after their disaster.

" My old enemy the ague-fever set in again upon me as I lay
here by the river-side. 'Tis a wonder how I ever survived. But
for the goodness of a half-breed woman in the fort, who took
pity on me, and tended me, I never should have recovered, and
my poor Harry would be what he fancied himself yesterday,
our grandfather's heir, our mother's only son.

" I remembered how, when Florac laid me in his bed, he put
under my pillow my money, my watch, and a trinket or two
which I had. When I woke to myself these were all gone; and
a surly old sergeant, the only officer left in the quarter, told me,
with a curse, that I was lucky enough to be left with my life
at all; that it was only my white cockade and coat had saved
me from the fate which the other canaille of Rosbifs had
deservedly met with.

" At the time of my recovery the fort was almost emptied of
the garrison. The Indians had retired enriched with British
plunder, and the chief part of the French regulars were gone
upon expeditions northward. My good Florac had left me upon
his service, consigning me to the care of an invalided sergeant.
Monsieur de Contrecœur had accompanied one of these expeditions, leaving an old lieutenant, Museau by name, in
command at Duquesne.

" This man had long been out of France, and serving in the
colonies. His character, doubtless, had been indifferent at
home; and he knew that, according to the system pursued in
France, where almost all promotion is given to the noblesse, he
never would advance in rank. And he had made free with
my guineas, I suppose, as he had with my watch, for I saw it
one day on his chest when I was sitting with him in his
quarter.

" Monsieur Museau and I managed to be pretty good friends.
If I could be exchanged, or sent home, I told him that my mother
would pay liberally for my ransom; and I suppose this idea
excited the cupidity of the commandant, for a trapper coming
in the winter, whilst I still lay very ill with fever, Museau
consented that I should write home to my mother, but that the

letter should be in French, that he should see it, and that I should say I was in the hands of the Indians, and should not be ransomed under ten thousand livres.

"In vain I said I was a prisoner to the troops of His Most Christian Majesty, that I expected the treatment of a gentleman and an officer. Museau swore that letter should go, and no other; that if I hesitated, he would fling me out of the fort, or hand me over to the tender mercies of his ruffian Indian allies. He would not let the trapper communicate with me except in his presence. Life and liberty are sweet. I resisted for a while, but I was pulled down with weakness, and shuddering with fever; I wrote such a letter as the rascal consented to let pass, and the trapper went away with my missive, which he promised, in three weeks, to deliver to my mother in Virginia.

"Three weeks, six, twelve, passed. The messenger never returned. The winter came and went, and all our little plantations round the fort, where the French soldiers had cleared corn-ground and planted gardens and peach and apple trees down to the Monongahela, were in full blossom. Heaven knows how I crept through the weary time! When I was pretty well, I made drawings of the soldiers of the garrison, and of the half-breed and her child (Museau's child), and of Museau himself, whom, I am ashamed to say, I flattered outrageously; and there was an old guitar left in the fort, and I sang to it, and played on it some French airs which I knew, and ingratiated myself as best I could with my gaolers; and so the weary months passed, but the messenger never returned.

"At last news arrived that he had been shot by some British Indians in Maryland; so there was an end of my hope of ransom for some months more. This made Museau very savage and surly towards me; the more so as his sergeant inflamed his rage by telling him that the Indian woman was partial to me—as I believe, poor thing, she was. I was always gentle with her, and grateful to her. My small accomplishments seemed wonders in her eyes; I was ill and unhappy, too, and these are always claims to a woman's affection.

"A captive pulled down by malady, a ferocious gaoler, and a young woman touched by the prisoner's misfortunes—sure you expect that, with these three prime characters in a piece, some pathetic tragedy is going to be enacted? You, Miss Hetty, are about to guess that the woman saved me?"

"Why, of course she did!" cries mamma.

"What else is she good for?" says Hetty.

" You, Miss Theo, have painted her already as a dark beauty —is it not so? A swift huntress?——"

" Diana with a baby," says the Colonel.

" Who scours the plain with her nymphs, who brings down the game with her unerring bow, who is Queen of the forest— and I see by your looks that you think I am madly in love with her? "

" Well, I suppose she is an interesting creature, Mr. George? " says Theo, with a blush.

" What think you of a dark beauty, the colour of new mahogany? with long straight black hair, which was usually dressed with a hair-oil or pomade by no means pleasant to approach, with little eyes, with high cheek-bones, with a flat nose, sometimes ornamented with a ring, with rows of glass beads round her tawny throat, her cheeks and forehead grace- fully tattooed, a great love of finery, and inordinate passion for—oh! must I own it? "

" For coquetry. I know you are going to say that? " says Miss Hetty.

" For whisky, my dear Miss Hester—in which appetite my gaoler partook; so that I have often sat by, on the nights when I was in favour with Monsieur Museau, and seen him and his poor companion hob-and-nobbing together until they could scarce hold the noggin out of which they drank. In these evening entertainments they would sing, they would dance, they would fondle, they would quarrel, and knock the cans and furniture about; and, when I was in favour, I was admitted to share their society, for Museau, jealous of his dignity, or not willing that his men should witness his behaviour, would allow none of them to be familiar with him.

" Whilst the result of the trapper's mission to my home was yet uncertain, and Museau and I myself expected the payment of my ransom, I was treated kindly enough, allowed to crawl about the fort, and even to go into the adjoining fields and gardens, always keeping my parole, and duly returning before gun-fire. And I exercised a piece of hypocrisy, for which, I hope, you will hold me excused. When my leg was sound (the ball came out in the winter, after some pain and inflammation, and the wound healed up presently), I yet chose to walk as if I was dis- abled and a cripple: I hobbled on two sticks, and cried Ah! and Oh! at every minute, hoping that a day might come when I might treat my limbs to a run.

" Museau was very savage when he began to give up all hopes

of the first messenger. He fancied that the man might have got the ransom-money and fled with it himself. Of course he was prepared to disown any part in the transaction, should my letter be discovered. His treatment of me varied according to his hopes or fears, or even his mood for the time being. He would have me consigned to my quarters for several days at a time; then invite me to his tipsy supper-table, quarrel with me there and abuse my nation: or again break out into maudlin sentimentalities about his native country of Normandy, where he longed to spend his old age, to buy a field or two, and to die happy.

"'Eh, Monsieur Museau!' says I, 'ten thousand livres of your money would buy a pretty field or two in your native country! You can have it for a ransom of me, if you will but let me go. In a few months you must be superseded in your command here, and then adieu the crowns and the fields in Normandy! You had better trust a gentleman and a man of honour. Let me go home, and I give you my word the ten thousand livres shall be paid to any agent you may appoint in France or in Quebec.'

"'Ah, young traitor!' roars he, 'do you wish to tamper with my honour? Do you believe an officer of France will take a bribe? I have a mind to consign thee to my black-hole, and to have thee shot in the morning.'

"'My poor body will never fetch ten thousand livres,' says I; 'and a pretty field in Normandy with a cottage——'

"'And an orchard. Ah, sacré bleu!' says Museau, whimpering, 'and a dish of tripe à la mode du pays!'

"This talk happened between us again and again, and Museau would order me to my quarters, and then ask me to supper the next night, and return to the subject of Normandy, and cider, and tripes à la mode de Caen. My friend is dead now——"

"He was hung, I trust?" breaks in Colonel Lambert.

"And I need keep no secret about him. Ladies, I wish I had to offer you the account of a dreadful and tragical escape; how I slew all the sentinels of the fort; filed through the prison windows, destroyed a score or so of watchful dragons, overcame a million of dangers, and finally effected my freedom. But, in regard of that matter, I have no heroic deeds to tell of, and own that, by bribery and no other means, I am where I am."

"But you *would* have fought, Georgy, if need were," says Harry; "and you couldn't conquer a whole garrison, you know?" And herewith Mr. Harry blushed very much.

"See the women, how disappointed they are!" says Lambert. "Mrs. Lambert, you bloodthirsty woman, own that you are balked of a battle; and look at Hetty, quite angry because Mr. George did not shoot the commandant."

"You wished he was hung yourself, papa!" cries Miss Hetty, "and I am sure I wish anything my papa wishes."

"Nay, ladies," says George, turning a little red, "to wink at a prisoner's escape was not a very monstrous crime; and to take money? Sure other folks besides Frenchmen have condescended to a bribe before now. Although Monsieur Museau set me free, I am inclined, for my part, to forgive him. Will it please you to hear how that business was done? You see, Miss Hetty, I cannot help being alive to tell it."

"Oh, George!—that is, I mean, Mr. Warrington!—that is, I mean I beg your pardon!" cries Hester.

"No pardon, my dear! I never was angry yet or surprised that any one should like my Harry better than me. He deserves all the liking that any man or woman can give him. See, it is *his* turn to blush now," says George.

"Go on, Georgy, and tell them about the escape out of Duquesne!" cries Harry, and he said to Mrs. Lambert afterwards in confidence, "You know he is always going on saying that he ought never to have come to life again, and declaring that I am better than he is. The idea of my being better than George, Mrs. Lambert! a poor extravagant fellow like me! It's absurd!"

CHAPTER LII

INTENTIQUE ORA TENEBANT

"WE continued for months our weary life at the fort, and the commandant and I had our quarrels and reconciliations, our greasy games at cards, our dismal duets with his asthmatic flute and my cracked guitar. The poor Fawn took her beatings and her cans of liquor as her lord and master chose to administer them; and she nursed her papoose, or her master in the gout, or her prisoner in the ague; and so matters went on until the beginning of the fall of last year, when we were visited by a hunter who had important news to deliver to the commandant, and such as set the little garrison in no little excitement. The

Marquis de Montcalm had sent a considerable detachment to garrison the forts already in the French hands, and to take up farther positions in the enemy's—that is, in the British—possessions. The troops had left Quebec and Montreal, and were coming up the St. Lawrence and the lakes in bâteaux, with artillery and large provisions of warlike and other stores. Museau would be superseded in his command by an officer of superior rank, who might exchange me, or who might give me up to the Indians in reprisal for cruelties practised by our own people on many and many an officer and soldier of the enemy. The men of the fort were eager for the reinforcements; they would advance into Pennsylvania and New York; they would seize upon Albany and Philadelphia; they would drive the Rosbifs into the sea, and all America should be theirs from the Mississippi to Newfoundland.

"This was all very triumphant: but yet, somehow, the prospect of the French conquest did not add to Mr. Museau's satisfaction.

"'Eh, Commandant!' says I, ''tis fort bien, but meanwhile your farm in Normandy, the pot of cider, and the tripes à la mode de Caen, where are they?'

"'Yes; 'tis all very well, my garçon,' says he. 'But where will you be when poor old Museau is superseded? Other officers are not good companions like me. Very few men in the world have my humanity. When there is a great garrison here, will my successors give thee the indulgences which honest Museau has granted thee? Thou wilt be kept in a sty like a pig ready for killing. As sure as one of our officers falls into the hands of your brigands of frontier men, and evil comes to him, so surely wilt thou have to pay with thy skin for his. Thou wilt be given up to our red allies—to the brethren of La Biche yonder. Didst thou see, last year, what they did to thy countrymen whom we took in the action with Braddock? Roasting was the very smallest punishment, ma foi—was it not, La Biche?'

"And he entered into a variety of jocular descriptions of tortures inflicted, eyes burnt out of their sockets, teeth and nails wrenched out, limbs and bodies gashed—— You turn pale, dear Miss Theo! Well, I will have pity, and will spare you the tortures which honest Museau recounted in his pleasant way as likely to befall me.

"La Biche was by no means so affected as you seem to be, ladies, by the recital of these horrors. She had witnessed them in her time. She came from the Senecas, whose villages lie near the great cataract between Ontario and Erie; her people made war for the English, and against them: they had fought with other tribes; and, in the battles between us and them, it is difficult to say whether white-skin or red-skin is most savage.

" ' They may chop me into cutlets and broil me, 'tis true, Commandant,' say I coolly. ' But again, I say, you will never have the farm in Normandy.'

" ' Go get the whisky-bottle, La Biche,' says Museau.

" ' And it is not too late even now. I will give the guide who takes me home a large reward. And again I say I promise, as a man of honour, ten thousand livres to—whom shall I say? to any one who shall bring me any token—who shall bring me, say, my watch and seal with my grandfather's arms—which I have seen in a chest somewhere in this fort.'

" ' Ah, scélérat!' roars out the commandant, with a hoarse yell of laughter. ' Thou hast eyes, thou! All is good prize in war.'

" ' Think of a house in your village, of a fine field hard by with a half-dozen of cows—of a fine orchard all covered with fruit.'

" ' And Javotte at the door with her wheel, and a rascal of a child, or two, with cheeks as red as the apples! Oh, my country! Oh, my mother!' whimpers out the commandant. ' Quick, La Biche, the whisky!'

" All that night the commandant was deep in thought, and La Biche, too, silent, and melancholy. She sat away from us nursing her child, and whenever my eyes turned towards her I saw hers were fixed on me. The poor little infant began to cry, and was ordered away by Museau, with his usual foul language, to the building which the luckless Biche occupied with her child. When she was gone, we both of us spoke our minds freely; and I put such reasons before Monsieur as his cupidity could not resist.

" ' How do you know,' he asked, ' that this hunter will serve you?'

" ' That is my secret,' says I. But here, if you like, as we are not on honour, I may tell it. When they come into the settlements for their bargains, the hunters often stop a day or two for rest and drink and company, and our new friend loved all these. He played at cards with the men: he set his furs against their liquor: he enjoyed himself at the fort, singing, dancing, and gambling with them. I think I said they liked to listen to my songs, and for want of better things to do, I was often singing and guitar-scraping: and we would have many a concert, the men joining in chorus, or dancing to my homely music, until it was interrupted by the drums and the retraite.

"Our guest, the hunter, was present at one or two of these concerts, and I thought I would try if possibly he understood English. After we had had our little stock of French songs, I said, 'My lads, I will give you an English song,' and to the tune of ' Over the hills and far away,' which my good old grandfather used to hum as a favourite air in Marlborough's camp, I made some doggerel words:—' This long long year, a prisoner drear; Ah, me! I'm tired of lingering here: I'll give a hundred guineas gay, To be over the hills and far away.'

"' What is it? ' says the hunter. ' I don't understand.'

"' 'Tis a girl to her lover,' I answered; but I saw by the twinkle in the man's eye that he understood me.

"The next day, when there were no men within hearing, the trapper showed that I was right in my conjecture, for as he passed me he hummed in a low tone, but in perfectly good English, ' Over the hills and far away,' the burden of my yesterday's doggerel.

"' If you are ready,' says he, ' I am ready. I know who your people are, and the way to them. Talk to the Fawn, and she will tell you what to do. What! You will not play with me?' Here he pulled out some cards, and spoke in French, as two soldiers came up. ' Milor est trop grand-seigneur? Bonjour, my Lord!'

"And the man made me a mock bow, and walked away shrugging up his shoulders, to offer to play and drink elsewhere.

"I knew now that the Biche was to be the agent in the affair, and that my offer to Museau was accepted. The poor Fawn performed her part very faithfully and dexterously. I had not need of a word more with Museau; the matter was understood between us. The Fawn had long been allowed free communication with me. She had tended me during my wound and in my illnesses, helped to do the work of my little chamber, my cooking, and so forth. She was free to go out of the fort, as I have said, and to the river and the fields whence the corn and garden-stuff of the little garrison were brought in.

"Having gambled away most of the money which he received for his peltries, the trapper now got together his store of flints, powder, and blankets, and took his leave. And, three days after his departure, the Fawn gave me the signal that the time was come for me to make my little trial for freedom.

" When first wounded, I had been taken by my kind Florac and placed on his bed in the officers' room. When the fort was emptied of all officers except the old lieutenant left in command, I had been allowed to remain in my quarters, sometimes being left pretty free, sometimes being locked up and fed on prisoners' rations, sometimes invited to share his mess by my tipsy gaoler. This officers' house, or room, was of logs like the half-dozen others within the fort, which mounted only four guns of small calibre, of which one was on the bastion behind my cabin. Looking westward over this gun, you could see a small island at the confluence of the two rivers Ohio and Monongahela whereon Duquesne is situated. On the shore opposite this island were some trees.

" ' You see those trees?' my poor Biche said to me the day before in her French jargon. 'He wait for you behind those trees.'

" In the daytime the door of my quarters was open, and the Biche free to come and go. On the day before, she came in from the fields with a pick in her hand and a basketful of vegetables and potherbs for soup. She sat down on a bench at my door, the pick resting against it, and the basket at her side. I stood talking to her for a while: but I believe I was so idiotic that I never should have thought of putting the pick to any use had she not actually pushed it into my open door, so that it fell into my room. 'Hide it,' she said; 'want it soon.' And that afternoon it was she pointed out the trees to me.

" On the next day, she comes, pretending to be very angry, and calls out, 'My Lord! my Lord! why you not come to Commandant's dinner? He very bad! Entendez-vous?' And she peeps into the room as she speaks, and flings a coil of rope at me.

" ' I am coming, La Biche,' say I, and hobbled after her on my crutch. As I went into the commandant's quarters she says, ' Pour ce soir.' And then I knew the time was come.

" As for Museau, he knew nothing about the matter. Not he! He growled at me, and said the soup was cold. He looked me steadily in the face, and talked of this and that; not only whilst his servant was present, but afterwards when we smoked our pipes and played our game at picquet; whilst, according to her wont, the poor Biche sat cowering in a corner.

" My friend's whisky-bottle was empty; and he said, with rather a knowing look, he must have another glass—we must both have a glass that night. And, rising from the table, he stumped to the inner room, where he kept his fire-water under lock and key, and away from the poor Biche, who could not resist that temptation.

" As he turned his back the Biche raised herself; and he was no sooner gone but she was at my feet, kissing my hand, pressing it to her heart, and bursting into tears over my knees. I confess I was so troubled by this testimony of the poor creature's silent attachment and fondness, the extent of which I scarce had suspected before, that when Museau returned, I had not recovered my equanimity, though the poor Fawn was back in her corner again and shrouded in her blanket.

" He did not appear to remark anything strange in the be-haviour of either. We sat down to our game, though my thoughts were so preoccupied that I scarcely knew what cards were before me.

" ' I gain everything from you to-night, milor,' says he grimly. ' We play upon parole.'

" ' And you may count upon mine,' I replied.

" ' Eh! 'tis all that you have! ' says he.

" ' Monsieur,' says I, ' my word is good for ten thousand livres; ' and we continued our game.

" At last he said he had a headache, and would go to bed, and I understood the orders too, that I was to retire. ' I wish you a good night, mon petit milor,' says he,—' stay, you will fall without your crutch,' and his eyes twinkled at me, and his face wore a sarcastic grin. In the agitation of the moment I had quite forgotten that I was lame, and was walking away at a pace as good as a grenadier's.

" ' What a vilain night! ' says he, looking out. In fact there was a tempest abroad, and a great roaring, and wind. ' Bring a lanthorn, La Tulipe, and lock my Lord comfortably into his quarters! ' He stood a moment looking at me from his own door, and I saw a glimpse of the poor Biche behind him.

" The night was so rainy that the sentries preferred their boxes, and did not disturb me in my work. The log-house was built with upright posts, deeply fixed in the ground, and horizontal logs laid upon it. I had to dig under these, and work a hole sufficient to admit my body to pass. I began in the dark, soon after tattoo. It was some while after midnight before my work was done, when I lifted my hand up under the log and felt the rain from without falling upon it. I had to work very cautiously for two hours after that, and then crept through to the parapet and silently flung my rope over the gun; not without a little tremor of heart, lest the sentry should see me and send a charge of lead into my body.

"The wall was but twelve feet, and my fall into the ditch easy enough. I waited a while there, looking steadily under the gun, and trying to see the river and the island. I heard the sentry pacing up above and humming a tune. The darkness became more clear to me ere long and the moon rose, and I saw the river shining before me, and the dark rocks and trees of the island rising in the waters.

"I made for this mark as swiftly as I could, and for the clump of trees to which I had been directed. Oh, what a relief I had when I heard a low voice humming there, ' Over the hills and far away!'"

When Mr. George came to this part of his narrative, Miss Theo, who was seated by a harpsichord, turned round and dashed off the tune on the instrument, whilst all the little company broke out into the merry chorus.

"Our way," the speaker went on, "lay through a level tract of forest with which my guide was familiar upon the right bank of the Monongahela. By daylight we came to a clearer country, and my trapper asked me—Silverheels was the name by which he went—had I ever seen the spot before? It was the fatal field where Braddock had fallen and whence I had been wonderfully rescued in the summer of the previous year. Now, the leaves were beginning to be tinted with the magnificent hues of our autumn."

"Ah, brother!" cries Harry, seizing his brother's hand. "I was gambling and making a fool of myself at the Wells and in London, when my George was flying for his life in the wilderness! Oh, what a miserable spendthrift I have been!"

"But I think thou art not unworthy to be called thy mother's son," said Mrs. Lambert very softly, and with moistened eyes. Indeed if Harry had erred, to mark his repentance, his love, his unselfish joy and generosity, was to feel that there was hope for the humbled and kind young sinner.

"We presently crossed the river," George resumed, "taking our course along the base of the western slopes of the Alleghanies; and through a grand forest region of oaks and maple, and enormous poplars that grow a hundred feet high without a branch. It was the Indians whom we had to avoid, besides the outlying parties of French. Always of doubtful loyalty, the savages have been specially against us, since our ill-treatment of them, and the French triumph over us two years ago.

" I was but weak still, and our journey through the wilderness lasted a fortnight or more. As we advanced, the woods became redder and redder. The frost nipped sharply of nights. We lighted fires at our feet, and slept in our blankets as best we might. At this time of year, the hunters who live in the mountains get their sugar from the maples. We came upon more than one such family, camping near their trees by the mountain streams; and they welcomed us at their fires, and gave us of their venison. So we passed over the two ranges of the Laurel Hills and the Alleghanies. The last day's march of my trusty guide and myself took us down that wild magnificent pass of Will's Creek, a valley lying between cliffs near a thousand feet high—bald, white, and broken into towers like huge fortifications, with eagles wheeling round the summits of the rocks, and watching their nests among the crags.

" And hence we descended to Cumberland, whence we had marched in the year before, and where there was now a considerable garrison of our people. Oh, you may think it was a welcome day when I saw English colours again on the banks of our native Potomac! "

CHAPTER LIII

WHERE WE REMAIN AT THE COURT END OF THE TOWN

GEORGE WARRINGTON had related the same story, which we have just heard, to Madame de Bernstein on the previous evening—a portion, that is, of the history; for the old lady nodded off to sleep many times during the narration, only waking up when George paused, saying it was most interesting, and ordering him to continue. The young gentleman hem'd and ha'd, and stuttered, and blushed, and went on, much against his will, and did not speak half so well as he did to his friendly little auditory in Hill Street, where Hetty's eyes of wonder, and Theo's sympathising glances, and mamma's kind face, and papa's funny looks, were applause sufficient to cheer any modest youth who required encouragement for his eloquence. As for mamma's behaviour, the General said, 'twas as good as

Mr. Addison's trunkmaker, and she would make the fortune of any tragedy by simply being engaged to cry in the front boxes. That is why we chose my Lord Wrotham's house as the theatre where George's first piece should be performed, wishing that he should speak to advantage, and not as when he was heard by that sleepy cynical old lady, to whom he had to narrate his adventures.

"Very good and most interesting, I am sure, my dear sir," says Madam Bernstein, putting up three pretty little fingers covered with a lace mitten, to hide a convulsive movement of her mouth. "And your mother must have been delighted to see you."

George shrugged his shoulders ever so little, and made a low bow, as his aunt looked up at him for a moment with her keen old eyes.

"Have been delighted to see you," she continued drily, "and killed the fatted calf, and—and that kind of thing. Though why I say calf, I don't know, Nephew George, for you never were the prodigal. I may say calf to thee, my poor Harry! Thou hast been amongst the swine sure enough. And evil companions have robbed the money out of thy pocket and the coat off thy back."

"He came to his family in England, madam," says George, with some heat, "and his friends were your Ladyship's."

"He could not have come to worse advisers, Nephew Warrington, and so I should have told my sister earlier, had she condescended to write to me by him, as she has done by you," said the old lady, tossing up her head. "Hey! hey!" she said, at night, to her waiting-maid, as she arranged herself for the rout to which she was going: "this young gentleman's mother is half sorry that he has come to life again, I could see that in his face. She is half sorry, and I am perfectly furious! Why didn't he lie still when he dropped there under the tree, and why did that young Florac carry him to the fort? I knew those Floracs when I was at Paris, in the time of Monsieur le Régent. They were of the Floracs of Ivry. No great house before Henri IV. His ancestor was the King's favourite. His ancestor —he! he!—his ancestress! Brett! entendez-vous? Give me my card-purse. I don't like the grand airs of this Monsieur George; and yet he resembles, very much, his grandfather—the same look and sometimes the same tones. You have heard of Colonel Esmond when I was young? This boy has his eyes. I suppose I liked the Colonel's, because he loved me."

Being engaged, then, to a card-party,—an amusement which she never missed, week-day or Sabbath, as long as she had strength to hold trumps or sit in a chair,—very soon after George had ended his narration the old lady dismissed her two nephews, giving to the elder a couple of fingers and a very stately curtsey; but to Harry two hands and a kindly pat on the cheek.

" My poor child, now thou art disinherited, thou wilt see how differently the world will use thee! " she said. " There is only, in all London, a wicked heartless old woman who will treat thee as before. Here is a pocket-book for you, child! Do not lose it at Ranelagh to-night. That suit of yours does not become your brother half so well as it sat upon you; you will present your brother to everybody, and walk up and down the room for two hours at least, child. Were I you, I would then go to the Chocolate House, and play as if nothing had happened. Whilst you are there, your brother may come back to me and eat a bit of chicken with me. My Lady Flint gives wretched suppers, and I want to talk his mother's letter over with him. Au revoir, gentlemen! " and she went away to her toilette. Her chairmen and flambeaux were already waiting at the door.

The gentlemen went to Ranelagh, where but a few of Mr. Harry's acquaintances chanced to be present. They paced the round, and met Mr. Tom Claypool with some of his country friends; they heard the music; they drank tea in a box. Harry was master of ceremonies, and introduced his brother to the curiosities of the place; and George was even more excited than his brother had been on his first introduction to this palace of delight. George loved music much more than Harry ever did; he heard a full orchestra for the first time, and a piece of Mr. Handel's satisfactorily performed; and a not unpleasing instance of Harry's humility and regard for his elder brother was, that he could even hold George's love of music in respect at a time when fiddling was voted effeminate and unmanly in England, and Britons were, every day, called upon by the patriotic prints to sneer at the frivolous accomplishments of your Squallinis, Monsieurs, and the like. Nobody in Britain is proud of his ignorance now. There is no conceit left among us. There is no such thing as dulness. Arrogance is entirely unknown. . . . Well, at any rate, Art has obtained her letters of naturalisation, and lives here on terms of almost equality. If Mrs. Thrale chose to marry a music-master now, I don't think her friends would shudder at the mention of her name. If she had a good fortune and kept a good cook, people would even go and dine with her in spite of the *mésalliance*, and actually treat Mr. Piozzi with civility.

After Ranelagh, and pursuant to Madam Bernstein's advice, George returned to her Ladyship's house, whilst Harry showed himself at the club, where gentlemen were accustomed to assemble at night to sup, and then to gamble. No one, of course, alluded to Mr. Warrington's little temporary absence, and Mr. Ruff, his ex-landlord, waited upon him with the utmost gravity and civility, and as if there had never been any difference between them. Mr. Warrington had caused his trunks and habiliments to be conveyed away from Bond Street in the morning, and he and his brother were now established in apartments elsewhere.

But when the supper was done, and the gentlemen as usual were about to seek the macco-table upstairs, Harry said he was not going to play any more. He had burned his fingers already, and could afford no more extravagance.

"Why," says Mr. Morris, in a rather flippant manner, "you must have won more than you have lost, Mr. Warrington, after all said and done."

"And of course I don't know my own business as well as you do, Mr. Morris," says Harry sternly, who had not forgotten the other's behaviour on hearing of his arrest; "but I have another reason. A few months or days ago, I was heir to a great estate, and could afford to lose a little money. Now, thank God, I am heir to nothing." And he looked round, blushing not a little, to the knot of gentlemen, his gaming associates, who were lounging at the tables or gathered round the fire.

"How do you mean, Mr. Warrington?" cries my Lord March. "Have you lost Virginia, too? Who has won it? I always had a fancy to play you myself for that stake."

"And grow an improved breed of slaves in the colony," says another.

"The right owner has won it. You heard me tell of my twin elder brother!"

"Who was killed in that affair of Braddock's two years ago? Yes. Gracious goodness, my dear sir, I hope in Heaven he has not come to life again?"

"He arrived in London two days since. He has been a prisoner in a French fort for eighteen months; he only escaped a few months ago, and left our house in Virginia very soon after his release."

"You haven't had time to order mourning, I suppose, Mr.

Warrington?" asks Mr. Selwyn very good-naturedly, and simple
Harry hardly knew the meaning of his joke until his brother
interpreted it to him.

"Hang me, if I don't believe the fellow is absolutely glad of
the reappearance of his confounded brother!" cries my Lord
March, as they continued to talk of the matter when the young
Virginian had taken his leave.

"These savages practise the simple virtues of affection—they
are barely civilised in America yet," yawns Selwyn.

"They love their kindred, and they scalp their enemies,"
simpers Mr. Walpole. "It's not Christian, but natural.
Shouldn't you like to be present at a scalping match, George,
and see a fellow skinned alive?"

"A man's elder brother is his natural enemy," says Mr.
Selwyn, placidly ranging his money and counters before him.

"Torture is like broiled bones and pepper. You wouldn't
relish simple hanging afterwards, George!" continues Harry.

"I'm hanged if there's any man in England who would like
to see his elder brother alive," says my Lord.

"No, nor his father either, my Lord!" cries Jack Morris.

"First time I ever knew you had one, Jack. Give me
counters for five hundred."

"I say, 'tis all mighty fine about dead brothers coming to
life again," continues Jack. "Who is to know that it wasn't
a scheme arranged between these two fellows? Here comes a
young fellow who calls himself the Fortunate Youth, who says
he is a Virginian Prince and the deuce knows what, and who gets
into our society——"

A great laugh ensues at Jack's phrase of "our society."

"Who is to know that it wasn't a cross?" Jack continues.
"The young one is to come first. He is to marry an heiress,
and, when he has got her, up is to rise the elder brother! When
did this elder brother show? Why, when the younger's scheme
was blown and all was up with him! Who shall tell me that the
fellow hasn't been living in Seven Dials, or in a cellar dining off
tripe and cow-heel until my younger gentleman was disposed
of! Dammy, as gentlemen, I think we ought to take notice of
it: and that this Mr. Warrington has been taking a most outrageous liberty with the whole club."

"Who put him up? It was March, I think, put him up?"
asks a bystander.

"Yes. But my Lord thought he was putting up a very
different person. Didn't you, March?"

" Hold your confounded tongue, and mind your game ! "
says the nobleman addressed; but Jack Morris's opinion found
not a few supporters in the world. Many persons agreed that it
was most indecorous of Mr. Harry Warrington to have ever
believed in his brother's death; that there was something
suspicious about the young man's first appearance and subsequent actions, and, in fine, that regarding these foreigners,
adventurers, and the like, we ought to be especially cautious.

Though he was out of prison and difficulty; though he had
his aunt's liberal donation of money in his pocket; though his
dearest brother was restored to him, whose return to life Harry
never once thought of deploring, as his friends at White's supposed he would do; though Maria had shown herself in such a
favourable light by her behaviour during his misfortune: yet
Harry, when alone, felt himself not particularly cheerful, and
smoked his pipe of Virginia with a troubled mind. It was not
that he was deposed from his principality; the loss of it never
once vexed him; he knew that his brother would share with him
as he would have done with his brother; but after all those
struggles and doubts in his own mind, to find himself poor, and
yet irrevocably bound to his elderly cousin! Yes, she was
elderly, there was no doubt about it. When she came to that
horrible den in Cursitor Street and the tears washed her rouge
off, why, she looked as old as his mother! her face was all
wrinkled and yellow, and as he thought of her he felt just such
a qualm as he had when she was taken ill that day in the coach on
their road to Tunbridge. What would his mother say when he
brought her home, and, Lord, what battles there would be
between them! He would go and live on one of the plantations
—the farther from home the better—and have a few negroes,
and farm as best he might, and hunt a good deal; but at Castlewood or in her own home, such as he could make it for her, what
a life for poor Maria, who had been used to go to Court and to
cards and balls and assemblies every night! If he could be but
the overseer of the estates—oh, he would be an honest factor,
and try and make up for his useless life and extravagance in
these past days! Five thousand pounds, all his patrimony and
the accumulations of his long minority squandered in six months !
He a beggar, except for dear George's kindness, with nothing in
life left to him but an old wife: a pretty beggar, dressed out in
velvet and silver lace forsooth—the poor lad was arrayed in his
best clothes—a pretty figure he had made in Europe, and a nice
end he was come to! With all his fine friends at White's and

Newmarket, with all his extravagance, had he been happy a single day since he had been in Europe? Yes, three days, four days, yesterday evening, when he had been with dear dear Mrs. Lambert, and those affectionate kind girls, and that brave good Colonel. And the Colonel was right when he rebuked him for his spendthrift follies, and he had been a brute to be angry as he had been, and God bless them all for their generous exertions in his behalf! Such were the thoughts which Harry put into his pipe, and he smoked them whilst he waited his brother's return from Madam Bernstein.

CHAPTER LIV

DURING WHICH HARRY SITS SMOKING HIS PIPE AT HOME

THE maternal grandfather of our Virginians, the Colonel Esmond of whom frequent mention has been made, and who had quitted England to reside in the New World, had devoted some portion of his long American leisure to the composition of the Memoirs of his early life. In these volumes Madame de Bernstein (Mrs. Beatrix Esmond was her name as a spinster) played a very considerable part; and as George had read his grandfather's manuscript many times over, he had learned to know his kinswoman long before he saw her,—to know, at least, the lady, young, beautiful, and wilful, of half a century since, with whom he now became acquainted in the decline of her days. When cheeks are faded, and eyes are dim, is it sad or pleasant, I wonder, for the woman who is a beauty no more, to recall the period of her bloom? When the heart is withered, do the old love to remember how it once was fresh and beat with warm emotions? When the spirits are languid and weary, do we like to think how bright they were in other days, the hope how buoyant, the sympathies how ready, the enjoyment of life how keen and eager? So they fall,—the buds of prime, the roses of beauty, the florid harvests of summer,—fall and wither, and the naked branches shiver in the winter.

" And that was a beauty once! " thinks George Warrington, as his aunt, in her rouge and diamonds, comes in from her rout, " and that ruin was a splendid palace. Crowds of lovers have sighed before those decrepit feet, and been bewildered by the brightness of those eyes." He remembered a firework at home, at Williamsburg, on the King's birthday, and afterwards looking at the skeleton wheel, and the sockets of the exploded Roman candles. The dazzle and brilliancy of Aunt Beatrix's early career passed before him, as he thought over his grandsire's journals. Honest Harry had seen them, too, but Harry was no book man, and had not read the manuscript very carefully; nay, if he had, he would probably not have reasoned about it as his brother did, being by no means so much inclined to moralising as his melancholy senior.

Mr. Warrington thought that there was no cause why he should tell his aunt how intimate he was with her early history, and accordingly held his peace upon that point. When their meal was over, she pointed with her cane to her escritoire, and bade her attendant bring the letter which lay under the ink-stand there; and George, recognising the superscription, of course knew the letter to be that of which he had been the bearer from home.

" It would appear by this letter," said the old lady, looking hard at her nephew, " that ever since your return, there have been some differences between you and my sister."

" Indeed? I did not know that Madam Esmond had alluded to them," George said.

The Baroness puts a great pair of glasses upon eyes which shot fire and kindled who knows how many passions in old days, and, after glancing over the letter, hands it to George, who reads as follows:—

" RICHMOND, VIRGINIA: *December 26th*, 1756.

" HONOURED MADAM! AND SISTER!—I have received, and thank-fully acknowledge, your Ladyship's favour, per ' Rose ' packet, of October 23 ult.; and straightway answer you at a season which should be one of goodwill and peace to all men: but in which Heaven hath nevertheless decreed we should still bear our portion of earthly sorrow and trouble. My reply will be brought to you by my eldest son, Mr. Esmond Warrington, who returned to us so miraculously out of the Valley of the Shadow of Death (as our previous letters have informed my poor Henry), and who is desirous, not without my consent to his wish, to visit Europe, though he has been amongst us so short a while. I grieve to think that my dearest Harry should have appeared at home—I mean in England —*under false colours*, as it were; and should have been presented to His Majesty, to our family, and his own, as his father's heir, whilst my dear son George was still alive, though dead to us. Ah, madam! During the eighteen months of his captivity, what anguish have his mother's, his brother's, hearts undergone! My Harry's is the tenderest of any man's now alive. In the joy of seeing Mr. Esmond

Warrington returned to life, he will forget the worldly misfortune which befals him. He will return to (comparative) poverty without a pang. The most generous, *the most obedient* of human beings, of sons, he will gladly give up to his elder brother that inheritance which had been his own but for the accident of birth, and for the providential return of my son George.

" Your beneficent intentions towards dearest Harry will be more than ever welcome, now he is reduced to a younger brother's slender portion! Many years since, an advantageous opportunity occurred of providing for him in this province, and he would by this time have been master of a *noble estate* and negroes, and have been enabled to make a figure with most here, could his *mother's wishes* have been complied with, and his father's small portion, now lying in small interest in the British funds, have been invested in this most excellent purchase. But the forms of the law, and, I grieve to own, *my elder son's scruples*, prevailed, and this admirable opportunity was lost to me! Harry will find the savings of his income have been carefully accumulated—long, long may he live to enjoy them! May Heaven bless you, dear sister, for what your Ladyship may add to *his little store!* As I gather from your letter, that the sum which has been allowed to him has not been sufficient for his expenses *in the fine company* which he has kept (and the grandson of the Marquis of Esmond—one who had so *nearly* been his Lordship's *heir*—may sure claim equality with any other nobleman in Great Britain), and having a sum by me which I had always intended for the poor child's establishment, I intrust it to my eldest son, who, to do him justice, hath a most sincere regard for his brother, to lay it out for Harry's best advantage."

" It took him out of prison, yesterday, madam. I think that was the best use to which we could put it," interposed George, at this stage of his mother's letter.

" Nay, sir, I don't know any such thing! Why not have kept it to buy a pair of colours for him, or to help towards another estate and some negroes, if he has a fancy for home? " cried the old lady. " Besides, I had a fancy to pay that debt myself."

" I hope you will let his brother do that. I ask leave to be my brother's banker in this matter, and consider I have borrowed so much from my mother, to be paid back to my dear Harry."

" Do you say so, sir? Give me a glass of wine! You are an extravagant fellow! Read on, and you will see your mother thinks so. I drink to your health, Nephew George! 'Tis good Burgundy. Your grandfather never loved Burgundy. He loved claret, the little he drank."

And George proceeded with the letter:

" This remittance will, I trust, amply cover any expense which,

owing to the mistake respecting his position, dearest Harry may
have incurred. I wish I could trust his elder brother's prudence as
confidently as my Harry's! But I fear that, even in his captivity,
Mr. Esmond W. has learned little of that *humility* which becomes
all Christians, and which I have ever endeavoured to teach to my
children. Should you by chance show him these lines, when by
the blessing of Heaven on those who go down to the sea in ships,
the great Ocean divides us! he will know that a fond mother's
blessing and prayers follow both her children, and that there is no
act I have ever done, no desire I have ever expressed (however little
he may have been inclined to obey it!) but hath been dictated by
the fondest wishes for my dearest boys' welfare."

" There is a scratch with a penknife, and a great blot upon the
letter there, as if water had fallen on it. Your mother writes
well, George. I suppose you and she had a difference?" said
George's aunt, not unkindly.

" Yes, ma'am, many," answered the young man sadly.
" The last was about a question of money—of ransom which I
promised to the old lieutenant of the fort who aided me to make
my escape. I told you he had a mistress, a poor Indian woman,
who helped me, and was kind to me. Six weeks after my
arrival at home, the poor thing made her appearance at Richmond, having found her way through the woods by pretty
much the same track which I had followed, and bringing me the
token which Museau had promised to send me when he connived
at my flight. A commanding officer and a considerable reinforcement had arrived at Duquesne. Charges, I don't know of
what peculation (for his messenger could not express herself
very clearly), had been brought against this Museau. He had
been put under arrest, and had tried to escape; but, less fortunate than myself, he had been shot on the rampart, and he
sent the Indian woman to me, with my grandfather's watch,
and a line scrawled in his prison on his death-bed, begging me to
send *ce que je scavais* to a notary at Havre de Grâce in France to
be transmitted to his relatives at Caen in Normandy. My friend
Silverheels, the hunter, had helped my poor Indian on her way.
I don't know how she would have escaped scalping else. But
at home they received the poor thing sternly. They hardly
gave her a welcome. I won't say what suspicions they had
regarding her and me. The poor wretch fell to drinking whenever she could find means. I ordered that she should have food
and shelter, and she became the jest of our negroes, and formed
the subject of the scandal and tittle-tattle of the old fools in our
little town. Our Governor was, luckily, a man of sense, and I

made interest with him, and procured a pass to send her back to her people. Her grief at parting with me only served to confirm the suspicions against her. A fellow preached against me from the pulpit, I believe; I had to treat another with a cane. And I had a violent dispute with Madam Esmond—a difference which is not healed yet—because I insisted upon paying to the heirs Museau pointed out the money I had promised for my deliverance. You see that scandal flourishes at the borders of the wilderness, and in the New World as well as the Old."

"I have suffered from it myself, my dear," said Madam Bernstein, demurely. "Fill thy glass, child! A little tass of cherry-brandy! 'Twill do thee all the good in the world."

"As for my poor Harry's marriage," Madam Esmond's letter went on, "though I know *too well, from sad experience*, the dangers to which youth is subject, and would keep my boy, *at any price*, from them, though I should wish him to marry a person of rank, as becomes his birth, yet my Lady Maria Esmond is out of the question. Her age is almost the same as mine; and I know my brother Castlewood left his daughters with the very smallest portions. My Harry is so obedient that I know a desire from me will be sufficient to cause him to give up this imprudent match. Some foolish people once supposed that I myself once thought of a second union, and with a person of rank very different from ours. No! I knew what was due to my children. As succeeding to this estate after me, Mr. Esmond W. is amply provided for. Let my task now be to save for his less fortunate younger brother: and, as I do not love to live quite alone, let him return without delay to his fond and loving mother.

"The report which your Ladyship hath given of my Harry fills my heart with warmest gratitude. He is all indeed a mother may wish. A year in Europe will have given him a polish and refinement which he could not acquire in our homely Virginia. Mr. Stack, one of our invaluable ministers in Richmond, hath a letter from Mr. Ward—my darlings' tutor of early days—who knows my Lady Warrington and her excellent family, and saith that my Harry has lived much with his cousins of late. I am grateful to think that my boy has the privilege of being with his good aunt. May he follow her counsels, and listen to those around him who will guide him on the way of *his best welfare!* Adieu, dear madam and sister! For your kindness to my boy accept the grateful thanks of a mother's heart. Though we have been divided hitherto, may these kindly ties draw us nearer and nearer. I am thankful that you should speak of my dearest father so. He was, indeed, one of the best of men! He, too, thanks you, I know, for the love you have borne to one of his grandchildren; and his daughter subscribes herself, with sincere thanks, your Ladyship's most dutiful and grateful sister and servant. RACHEL ESMOND WN.

"*P.S.*—I have communicated with my Lady Maria; but there

will be no need to tell her and dear Harry that his mother or your
Ladyship hope to be able to increase his small fortune. The match
is altogether unsuitable."

"As far as regards myself, madam," George said, laying
down the paper, " my mother's letter conveys no news to me.
I always knew that Harry was the favourite son with Madam
Esmond, as he deserves indeed to be. He has a hundred good
qualities which I have not the good fortune to possess. He
has better looks——"

"Nay, that is not your fault," said the old lady, slily looking
at him; "and, but that he is fair and you are brown, one might
almost pass for the other."

Mr. George bowed, and a faint blush tinged his pale cheek.

"His disposition is bright, and mine is dark," he continued.
"Harry is cheerful, and I am otherwise, perhaps. He knows
how to make himself beloved by every one, and it has been my
lot to find but few friends."

"My sister and you have pretty little quarrels. There were
such in old days in our family," the Baroness said; "and if
Madam Esmond takes after our mother——"

"My mother has always described hers as an angel upon
earth," interposed George.

"Eh! That is a common character for people when they are
dead!" cried the Baroness; "and Rachel Castlewood was an
angel if you like—at least your grandfather thought so. But
let me tell you, sir, that angels are sometimes not very *commodes
à vivre*. It may be they are too good to live with us sinners, and
the air down below here don't agree with them. My poor
mother was so perfect that she never could forgive me for being
otherwise. Ah, mon Dieu! how she used to oppress me with
those angelical airs!"

George cast down his eyes, and thought of his own melancholy youth. He did not care to submit more of his family secrets
to the cynical inquisition of this old worldling, who seemed,
however, to understand him in spite of his reticence

"I quite comprehend you, sir, though you hold your tongue,"
the Baroness continued. "A sermon in the morning: a sermon
at night: and two or three of a Sunday. That is what people
call being good. Every pleasure cried fie upon; all us worldly
people excommunicated; a ball an abomination of desolation;
a play a forbidden pastime; and a game of cards perdition!
What a life! Mon Dieu, what a life!"

"We played at cards every night, if we were so inclined," said

George, smiling; "and my grandfather loved Shakspeare so much that my mother had not a word to say against her father's favourite author."

"I remember. He could say whole pages by heart; though, for my part, I like Mr. Congreve a great deal better. And then, there was that dreadful dreary Milton, whom he and Mr. Addison pretended to admire!" cried the old lady, tapping her fan.

"If your Ladyship does not like Shakspeare, you will not quarrel with my mother for being indifferent to him, too," said George. "And indeed I think, and I am sure, that you don't do her justice. Wherever there are any poor she relieves them; wherever there are any sick she——"

"She doses them with her horrible purges and boluses!" cried the Baroness. "Of course just as my mother did!"

"She does her best to cure them! She acts for the best, and performs her duty as far as she knows it."

"I don't blame you, sir, for doing yours, and keeping your own counsel about Madam Esmond," said the old lady. "But at least there is one point upon which we all three agree—that this absurd marriage must be prevented. Do you know how old the woman is? I can tell you, though she has torn the first leaf out of the family Bible at Castlewood."

"My mother has not forgotten her cousin's age, and is shocked at the disparity between her and my poor brother. Indeed, a city-bred lady of her time of life, accustomed to London gaiety and luxury, would find but a dismal home in our Virginian plantation. Besides, the house, such as it is, is not Harry's. He is welcome there, Heaven knows: more welcome, perhaps, than I, to whom the property comes in natural reversion; but, as I told him, I doubt how his wife would—would like our colony," George said, with a blush, and a hesitation in his sentence.

The old lady laughed shrilly. "He, he! Nephew Warrington!" she said, "you need not scruple to speak your mind out. I shall tell no tales to your mother: though 'tis no news to me that she has a high temper, and loves her own way. Harry has held his tongue, too; but it needed no conjuror to see who was the mistress at home, and what sort of a life my sister led you. I love my niece, my Lady Molly, so well, that I could wish her two or three years of Virginia, with your mother reigning over her. You may well look alarmed, sir! Harry has said quite enough to show me who governs the family."

"Madam," said George, smiling, "I may say as much as this,

that I don't envy any woman coming into our house, against my mother's will: and my poor brother knows this perfectly well."

"What? You two have talked the matter over? No doubt you have. And the foolish child considers himself bound in honour—of course he does, the gaby!"

"He says Lady Maria has behaved most nobly to him. When he was sent to prison, she brought him her trinkets and jewels, and every guinea she had in the world. This behaviour has touched him so, that he feels more deeply than ever bound to her Ladyship. But I own my brother seems bound by honour rather than love—such at least is his present feeling."

"My good creature," cried Madam Bernstein, "don't you see that Maria brings a few twopenny trinkets and a half-dozen guineas to Mr. Esmond, the heir of the great estate in Virginia, —not to the second son, who is a beggar, and has just squandered away every shilling of his fortune? I swear to you, on my credit as a gentlewoman, that, knowing Harry's obstinacy, and the misery he had in store for himself, I tried to bribe Maria to give up her engagement with him, and only failed because I could not bribe high enough! When he was in prison, I sent my lawyer to him, with orders to pay his debts immediately, if he would but part from her, but Maria had been beforehand with us, and Mr. Harry chose not to go back from his stupid word. Let me tell you what has passed in the last month!" And here the old lady narrated at length the history which we know already, but in that cynical language which was common in her times, when the finest folks and the most delicate ladies called things and people by names which we never utter in good company nowadays. And so much the better on the whole. We mayn't be more virtuous, but it is something to be more decent: perhaps we are not more pure, but of a surety we are more cleanly.

Madam Bernstein talked so much, so long, and so cleverly, that she was quite pleased with herself and her listener; and when she put herself into the hands of Mrs. Brett to retire for the night, informed the waiting-maid that she had changed her opinion about her eldest nephew, and that Mr. George was handsome, that he was certainly much wittier than poor Harry (whom Heaven, it must be confessed, had not furnished with a very great supply of brains), and that he had quite the *bel air*— a something melancholy—a noble and distinguished *je ne sçais quoy*—which reminded her of the Colonel. Had she ever told Brett about the Colonel? Scores of times, no doubt. And now she told Brett about the Colonel once more. Meanwhile, perhaps, her new favourite was not quite so well pleased with her as she was with him. What a strange picture of life and manners had the old lady unveiled to her nephew. How she railed at all the world round about her! How unconsciously did she paint her own family—her own self; how selfish, one and all; pursuing what mean ends; grasping and scrambling frantically for what petty prizes; ambitious for what shabby recompenses; tramping—from life's beginning to its close—through what scenes of stale dissipations and faded pleasures! "Are these the inheritors of noble blood?" thought George, as he went home quite late from his aunt's house, passing by doors whence the last guests of fashion were issuing, and where the chairmen were yawning over their expiring torches. "Are these the proud possessors of ancestral honours and ancient names, and were their forefathers, when in life, no better? We have our pedigree at home with noble coats-of-arms emblazoned all over the branches, and titles dating back before the Conquest and the Crusaders. When a knight of old found a friend in want, did he turn his back upon him, or an unprotected damsel, did he delude her and leave her? When a nobleman of the early time received a young kinsman, did he get the better of him at dice, and did the ancient chivalry cheat in horseflesh? Can it be that this wily woman of the world, as my aunt has represented, has inveigled my poor Harry into an engagement, that her tears are false, and that as soon as she finds him poor she will desert him? Had we not best pack the trunks and take a cabin in the next ship bound for home?" George reached his own door revolving these thoughts, and Gumbo came up yawning with a candle, and Harry was asleep before the extinguished fire, with the ashes of his emptied pipe on the table beside him.

He starts up; his eyes, for a moment dulled by sleep, lighten with pleasure as he sees his dear George. He puts his arm round his brother with a boyish laugh.

"There he is in flesh and blood, thank God!" he says; "I was dreaming of thee but now, George, and that Ward was hearing us our lesson! Dost thou remember the ruler, Georgy? Why, bless my soul, 'tis three o'clock! Where have you been a-gadding, Mr. George? Hast thou supped? I supped at White's, but I'm hungry again. I did not play, sir,—no, no; no more of that for younger brothers! And my Lord March paid me fifty he lost to me. I bet against his horse and on the Duke of Hamilton's! They both rode the match at Newmarket this morning, and he lost because he was under weight. And he paid me, and he was as sulky as a bear. Let us have one pipe, Georgy!—just one."

And after the smoke the young men went to bed, where I, for one, wish them a pleasant rest, for sure it is a good and pleasant thing to see brethren who love one another.

CHAPTER LV

BETWEEN BROTHERS

OF course our young men had had their private talk about home, and all the people and doings there, and each had imparted to the other full particulars of his history since their last meeting. How were Harry's dogs, and little Dempster, and good old Nathan, and the rest of the household? Was Mountain well, and Fanny grown to be a pretty girl? So Parson Broadbent's daughter was engaged to marry Tom Barker of Savannah, and they were to go and live in Georgia! Harry owns that at one period he was very sweet upon Parson Broadbent's daughter, and lost a great deal of pocket-money at cards, and drank a great quantity of strong waters with the father, in order to have a pretext for being near the girl. But, Heaven help us! Madam Esmond would never have consented to his throwing himself away upon Polly Broadbent. So Colonel G. Washington's wife was a pretty woman, very good-natured and pleasant, and with a good fortune? He had brought her into Richmond, and paid a visit of state to Madam Esmond. George described, with much humour, the awful ceremonials at the interview between these two personages, and the killing politeness of his mother to Mr. Washington's young wife. " Never mind, George my dear! " says Mrs. Mountain. " The Colonel has taken another wife, but I feel certain that at one time two young gentlemen I know of ran a very near chance of having a tall step-father six feet two in his boots." To be sure, Mountain was for ever match-making in her mind. Two people could not play a game at cards together, or sit down to a dish of tea, but she fancied their conjunction was for life. It was she, the foolish tattler, who had set the report abroad regarding the poor Indian woman. As for Madam Esmond, she had repelled the insinuation with scorn when Parson Stack brought it to her, and said, " I should as soon fancy Mr. Esmond stealing the spoons, or marrying a negro woman out of the kitchen." But though she disdained to find the poor Biche guilty, and even thanked her for attending her son in his illness, she treated her with such a chilling haughtiness of demeanour, that the Indian slunk away into the servants' quarters and there tried to drown her disappointments with drink. It was not a cheerful picture that which George gave of his two months at home. "The birthright is mine, Harry," he said, "but thou art the favourite, and God help me! I think my mother almost grudges it to me. Why should I have taken the *pas*, and preceded your worship into the world? Had you been the elder, you would have had the best cellar, and ridden the best nag, and been the most popular man in the country, whereas I have not a word to say for myself, and frighten people by my glum face: I should have been second son, and set up as lawyer, or come to England and got my degrees, and turned parson, and said grace at your honour's table. The time is out of joint, sir. O cursed spite, that ever I was born to set it right!"

"Why, Georgy, you are talking verses, I protest you are!" says Harry.

"I think, my dear, some one else talked those verses before me," says George, with a smile.

"It's out of one of your books. You know every book that ever was wrote, that I do believe!" cries Harry; and then told his brother how he had seen the two authors at Tunbridge, and how he had taken off his hat to them. "Not that *I* cared much about their books, not being clever enough. But I remembered how my dear old George used to speak of 'em," says Harry, with a choke in his voice, "and that's why I liked to see them. I say, dear, it's like a dream seeing you over again. Think of that bloody Indian with his knife at my George's head! I should like to give that Monsieur de Florac something for saving you—but I haven't got much now, only my little gold knee-buckles, and they ain't worth two guineas."

"You have got the half of what I have, child, and we'll divide as soon as I have paid the Frenchman," George said.

On which Harry broke out not merely into blessings but actual imprecations, indicating his intense love and satisfaction; and he swore that there never was such a brother in the world as his brother George. Indeed, for some days after his brother's arrival, his eyes followed George about: he would lay down his knife and fork, or his newspaper, when they were sitting together, and begin to laugh to himself. When he walked with George about the woman I had selected. Oh, the world is a nice charitable world! I was so enraged that I thought of going to Castlewood and living alone there,—for our mother finds the place dull, and the greatest consolation in precious Mr. Stack's ministry,—when the news arrived of *your* female perplexity, and I think we were all glad that I should have a pretext for coming to Europe."

"I should like to see any of the infernal scoundrels who said a word against you, and break their rascally bones," roars out Harry, striding up and down the room.

"I had to do something like it for Bob Clubber."

"What! that little sneaking, backbiting, toad-eating wretch, who is always hanging about my Lord at Greenway Court, and sponging on every gentleman in the country? If you whipped him, I hope you whipped him well, George!"

"We were bound over to keep the peace; and I offered to go into Maryland with him and settle our difference there, and of course the good folk said, that having made free with the seventh commandment I was inclined to break the sixth. So, by this and by that—and being as innocent of the crime imputed to me as you are—I left home, my dear Harry, with as awful a reputation as ever a young gentleman earned."

Ah, what an opportunity is there here to moralise! If the esteemed reader and his humble servant could but know—could but write down in a book—could but publish, with illustrations, a collection of the lies which have been told regarding each of us since we came to man's estate,—what a harrowing and thrilling work of fiction that romance would be! Not only is the world informed of everything about you, but of a great deal more. Not long since the kind postman brought a paper containing a valuable piece of criticism, which stated, "This author states he was born in such and such a year. It is a lie. He was born in the year so and so." The critic knew better: of course he did. Another (and both came from the country which gave MULLIGAN birth) warned some friend, saying, "Don't speak of New South Wales to him. He has a brother there, and the family *never mention his name*." But this subject is too vast and noble for a mere paragraph. I shall prepare a memoir, or let us rather have, *par une société de gens de lettres*, a series of Biographies,—of lives of gentlemen, as told by their dear friends whom they don't know.

George having related his exploits as champion and martyr, of course Harry had to unbosom himself to his brother, and lay before his elder an account of his private affairs. He gave up all the family of Castlewood—my Lord, not for getting the better of him at play; for Harry was a sporting man, and expected to pay when he lost, and receive when he won; but for refusing to aid the chaplain in his necessity, and dismissing him with such false and heartless pretexts. About Mr. Will he had made up his mind, after the horse-dealing matter, and freely marked his sense of the latter's conduct upon Mr. Will's eyes and nose. Respecting the Countess and Lady Fanny, Harry spoke in a manner more guarded, but not very favourable. He had heard all sorts of stories about them. The Countess was a card-playing old cat; Lady Fanny was a desperate flirt. Who told him? Well, he had heard the stories from a person who knew them both very well indeed. In fact, in their days of confidence, Maria had freely imparted to her cousin a number of anecdotes respecting her stepmother and her half-sister, which were by no means in favour of those ladies.

But in respect to Lady Maria herself, the young man was staunch and hearty. "It may be imprudent: I don't say no, George. I may be a fool: I think I am. I know there will be a dreadful piece of work at home, and that Madam and she will fight. Well! we must live apart. Our estate is big enough to live on without quarrelling, and I can go elsewhere than to Richmond or Castlewood. When you come to the property, you'll give me a bit—at any rate, Madam will let me off at an easy rent—or I'll make a famous farmer or factor. I can't and won't part from Maria. She has acted so nobly by me, that I should be a rascal to turn my back on her. Think of her bringing me every jewel she had in the world, dear brave creature! and flinging them into my lap with her last guineas, —and—and—God bless her!" Here Harry dashed his sleeve across his eyes, with a stamp of his foot; and said, "No, brother, I won't part with her, not to be made Governor of Virginia to-morrow; and my dearest old George would never advise me to do so, I know that."

"I am sent here to advise you," George replied. "I am sent to break the marriage off, if I can: and a more unhappy one I can't imagine. But I can't counsel you to break your word, my boy."

"I knew you couldn't! What's said is said, George. I have made my bed, and must lie on it," says Mr. Harry gloomily.

Such had been the settlement between our two young worthies, when they first talked over Mr. Harry's love-affair. But after as the man who feeds on his own flesh and blood. And now you have his all, you make merry over his misfortune!" And away she rustled from the room, flinging looks of defiance at all the party there assembled.

"Tell us what has happened, or what you have heard, Will, and my sister's grief will not interrupt us." And Will told, at greater length, and with immense exultation at Harry's discomfiture, the story now buzzed through all London of George Warrington's sudden apparition. Lord Castlewood was sorry for Harry: Harry was a good brave lad, and his kinsman liked him, as much as certain worldly folks like each other. To be sure, he played Harry at cards, and took the advantage of the market upon him; but why not? The peach which other men would certainly pluck, he might as well devour. "Eh! if that were all my conscience had to reproach me with, I need not be very uneasy!" my Lord thought. "Where does Mr. Warrington live?"

Will expressed himself ready to enter upon a state of reprobation if he knew or cared.

"He shall be invited here, and treated with every respect," says my Lord.

"Including picquet, I suppose?" growls Will.

"Or will you take him to the stables, and sell him one of your bargains of horseflesh, Will?" asks Lord Castlewood. "*You* would have won of Harry Warrington fast enough, if you could; but you cheat so clumsily at your game that you got paid with a cudgel. I desire, once more, that every attention may be paid to our cousin Warrington."

"And that you are not to be disturbed, when you sit down to play, of course, my Lord!" cries Lady Castlewood.

"Madam, I desire fair play, for Mr. Warrington, and for myself, and for every member of this amiable family," retorted Lord Castlewood fiercely.

"Heaven help the poor gentleman if your Lordship is going to be kind to him," said the step-mother, with a curtsey; and there is no knowing how far this family dispute might have been carried, had not, at this moment, a phaeton driven up to the house, in which were seated the two young Virginians.

It was the carriage which our young Prodigal had purchased in the days of his prosperity. He drove it still: George sat in it by his side; their negroes were behind them. Harry had been for meekly giving the whip and reins to his brother, and ceding the whole property to him. "What business has a poor devil like me with horses and carriages, Georgy?" Harry had humbly said. "Beyond the coat on my back, and the purse my aunt gave me, I have nothing in the world. You take the driving-seat, brother; it will ease my mind if you will take the driving-seat." George laughingly said he did not know the way, and Harry did; and that, as for the carriage, he would claim only a half of it, as he had already done with his brother's wardrobe. "But a bargain is a bargain; if I share thy coats, thou must divide my breeches' pocket, Harry; that is but fair dealing!" Again and again Harry swore there never was such a brother on earth. How he rattled his horses over the road! How pleased and proud he was to drive such a brother! They came to Kensington in famous high spirits; and Gumbo's thunder upon Lord Castlewood's door was worthy of the biggest footman in all St. James's.

Only my Lady Castlewood and her daughter Lady Fanny were in the room into which our young gentlemen were ushered. Will had no particular fancy to face Harry, my Lord was not dressed, Maria had her reasons for being away, at least till her eyes were dried. When we drive up to friends' houses nowadays in our coaches and six, when John carries up our noble names, when, finally, we enter the drawing-room with our best hat and best Sunday smile foremost, does it ever happen that we interrupt a family row? that we come simpering and smiling in, and stepping over the delusive ashes of a still burning domestic heat? that in the interval between the hall-door and the drawing-room, Mrs., Mr., and the Misses Jones have grouped themselves in a family tableau: this girl artlessly arranging flowers in a vase, let us say; that one reclining over an illuminated work of devotion; mamma on the sofa, with the butcher's and grocer's book pushed under the cushion, some elegant work in her hand, and a pretty little foot pushed out advantageously; while honest Jones, far from saying, "Curse that Brown, he is always calling here!" holds out a kindly hand, shows a pleased face, and exclaims, "What, Brown my boy, delighted to see you! Hope you've come to lunch!" I say, does it ever happen to *us* to be made the victims of domestic artifices, the spectators of domestic comedies got up for our special amusement? Oh, let us be thankful, not only for faces, but for masks! not only for honest welcome, but for hypocrisy, which hides unwelcome things from us! Whilst I am talking, for instance, in this easy chatty way, what right have you, my good sir, to know what is really passing in my mind! It may be that I am racked with gout, or that my eldest son has just sent me a thousand pounds' worth of college bills, or that I am writhing under an attack of the *Stoke Pogis Sentinel*, which has just been sent me under cover, or that there is a dreadfully scrappy dinner, the evident remains of a party to which I *didn't* invite you, and yet I conceal my agony, I wear a merry smile; I say, "What, come to take pot-luck with us, Brown my boy? Betsy! put a knife and fork for Mr. Brown. Eat! Welcome! Fall to! It's my best!" I say that humbug which I am performing is beautiful self-denial—that hypocrisy is true virtue. Oh, if every man spoke his mind, what an intolerable society ours would be to live in!

As the young gentlemen are announced, Lady Castlewood advances towards them with perfect ease and good-humour. "We have heard, Harry," she says, looking at the latter with a special friendliness, "of this most extraordinary circumstance. My Lord Castlewood said at breakfast that he should wait on you this very day, Mr. Warrington, and, Cousin Harry, we intend not to love you any the less because you are poor."

"We shall be able to show now that it is not for your acres that we like you, Harry!" says Lady Fanny, following her mamma's lead.

"And I to whom the acres have fallen?" says Mr. George, with a smile and a bow.

"Oh, cousin, we shall like you for being like Harry!" replied the arch Lady Fanny.

Ah! who that has seen the world, has not admired that astonishing ease with which fine ladies drop you and pick you up again? Both the ladies now addressed themselves almost exclusively to the younger brother. They were quite civil to Mr. George! but with Mr. Harry they were fond, they were softly familiar, they were gently kind, they were affectionately reproachful. Why had Harry not been for days and days to see them?

"Better to have had a dish of tea and a game at picquet with them than with some other folks," says Lady Castlewood. "If *we* had won enough to buy a paper of pins from you we should have been content; but young gentlemen don't know what is for their own good," says mamma.

"Now you have no more money to play with, you can come and play with us, cousin!" cries fond Lady Fanny, lifting up a finger, "and so your misfortune will be good fortune to us."

George was puzzled. This welcome of his brother was very different from that to which he had looked. All these compliments and attentions paid to the younger brother, though he was without a guinea! Perhaps the people were not so bad as they were painted? The Blackest of all Blacks is said not to be of *quite* so dark a complexion as some folks describe him.

This affectionate conversation continued for some twenty minutes, at the end of which period my Lord Castlewood made his appearance, wig on head, and sword by side. He greeted both the young men with much politeness: one not more than the other. "If you were to come to us—and I, for one, cordially rejoice to see you—what a pity it is you did not come a few months earlier! A certain evening at picquet would then most likely never have taken place. A younger son would have been more prudent."

"Yes, indeed," said Harry.

"Or a kinsman more compassionate. But I fear that love of play runs in the blood of all of us. I have it from my father, and it has made me the poorest peer in England. Those fair ladies whom you see before you are not exempt. My poor brother Will is a martyr to it; and what I, for my part, win on one day, I lose on the next. 'Tis shocking, positively, the rage for play in England. All my poor cousin's bank-notes parted company from me within twenty-four hours after I got them."

"I have played like other gentlemen, but never to hurt myself, and never indeed caring much for the sport," remarked Mr. Warrington.

"When we heard that my Lord had played with Harry, we did *so* scold him," cried the ladies.

"But if it had not been I, thou knowest, Cousin Warrington, some other person would have had thy money. 'Tis a poor consolation, but as such Harry must please to take it, and be glad that friends won his money, who wish him well, not strangers, who cared nothing for him, and fleeced him."

"Eh! a tooth out is a tooth out, though it be your brother that pulls it, my Lord!" said Mr. George, laughing. "Harry must bear the penalty of his faults, and pay his debts, like other men."

"I am sure I have never said or thought otherwise. 'Tis not like an Englishman to be sulky because he is beaten," says Harry.

"Your hand, cousin! You speak like a man!" cries my Lord, with delight. The ladies smile to each other.

"My sister, in Virginia, has known how to bring up her sons as gentlemen!" exclaims Lady Castlewood enthusiastically.

"I protest you must not be growing so amiable now you are

poor, Cousin Harry!" cries Cousin Fanny. "Why, mamma, we did not know half his good qualities when he was only Fortunate Youth and Prince of Virginia! You are exactly like him, Cousin George, but I vow you can't be as amiable as your brother!"

"I am the Prince of Virginia, but I fear I am not the Fortunate Youth," said George gravely.

Harry was beginning, "By Jove, he is the best——" when the noise of a harpsichord was heard from the upper room. The lad blushed: the ladies smiled.

"'Tis Maria above," said Lady Castlewood. "Let some of us go up to her."

The ladies rose, and made way towards the door: and Harry followed them, blushing very much. George was about to join the party, but Lord Castlewood checked him. "Nay, if all the ladies follow your brother," his Lordship said, "let me at least have the benefit of your company and conversation. I long to hear the account of your captivity and rescue, Cousin George!"

"Oh, we must hear that too!" cried one of the ladies, lingering.

"I am greedy, and should like it all by myself," said Lord Castlewood, looking at her very sternly; and followed the women to the door, and closed it upon them, with a low bow.

"Your brother has no doubt acquainted you with the history of all that has happened to him in this house, Cousin George?" asked George's kinsman.

"Yes, including the quarrel with Mr. Will, and the engagement to my Lady Maria," replies George, with a bow. "I may be pardoned for saying that he hath met with but ill fortune here, my Lord."

"Which no one can deplore more cordially than myself. My brother lives with horse-jockeys and trainers, and the wildest bloods of the town, and between us there is very little sympathy. We should not all live together, were we not so poor. This is the house which our grandmother occupied before she went to America and married Colonel Esmond. Much of the old furniture belonged to her." George looked round the wainscoted parlour with some interest. "Our house has not flourished in the last twenty years: though we had a promotion of rank a score of years since, owing to some interest we had at Court, then. But the malady of play has been the ruin of us all. I am a miserable victim to it; only too proud to sell myself and title to a *roturière*, as many noblemen, less scrupulous, have done. Pride is my fault, my dear cousin. I remember how I was born!" And his Lordship laid his hand on his shirt-frill, turned out his toe, and looked his cousin nobly in the face.

Young George Warrington's natural disposition was to believe everything which everybody said to him. When once deceived, however, or undeceived about the character of a person, he became utterly incredulous, and he saluted this fine speech of my Lord's with a sardonical inward laughter, preserving his gravity, however, and scarce allowing any of his scorn to appear in his words.

"We have all our faults, my Lord. That of play hath been condoned over and over again in gentlemen of our rank. Having heartily forgiven my brother, surely I cannot presume to be your Lordship's judge in the matter; and instead of playing and losing, I wish sincerely that you had both played and won!"

"So do I, with all my heart!" says my Lord, with a sigh. "I augur well for your goodness when you can speak in this way, and for your experience and knowledge of the world, too, cousin, of which you seem to possess a greater share than most young men of your age. Your poor Harry hath the best heart in the world; but I doubt whether his head be very strong."

"Not very strong, indeed. But he hath the art to make friends wherever he goes, and in spite of all his imprudences most people love him."

"I do—we all do, I'm sure! as if he were our brother!" cries my Lord.

"He has often described in his letters his welcome at your Lordship's house. My mother keeps them all, you may be sure. Harry's style is not very learned, but his heart is so good, that to read him is better than wit."

"I may be mistaken, but I fancy his brother possesses a good heart and a good wit, too!" says my Lord, obstinately gracious.

"I am as Heaven made me, cousin; and perhaps have had some more experience and sorrow than has fallen to the lot of most young men."

"This misfortune of your poor brother—I mean this piece of good fortune, your sudden re-appearance—has not quite left Harry without resources?" continued Lord Castlewood, very gently.

"With nothing but what his mother can leave him, or I, at her death, can spare him. What is the usual portion here of a younger brother, my Lord?"

"Eh! a younger brother here is—you know—in fine, everybody knows what a younger brother is," said my Lord, and shrugged his shoulders and looked his guest in the face.

The other went on: " We are the best of friends, but we are flesh and blood: and I don't pretend to do more for him than is usually done for younger brothers. Why give him money? That he should squander it at cards or horse-racing? My Lord, we have cards and jockeys in Virginia, too; and my poor Harry hath distinguished himself in his own country already, before he came to yours. He inherits the family failing for dissipation."

" Poor fellow, poor fellow, I pity him! "

" Our estate, you see, is great, but our income is small. We have little more money than that which we get from England for our tobacco—and very little of that too—for our tobacco comes back to us in the shape of goods, clothes, leather, groceries, ironmongery, nay, wine and beer for our people and ourselves. Harry may come back and share all these; there is a nag in the stable for him, a piece of venison on the table, a little ready money to keep his pocket warm, and a coat or two every year. This will go on whilst my mother lives, unless, which is far from improbable, he gets into some quarrel with Madam Esmond. Then, whilst I live, he will have the run of the house and all it contains: then, if I die leaving children, he will be less and less welcome. His future, my Lord, is a dismal one, unless some strange piece of luck turn up on which we were fools to speculate. Henceforth he is doomed to dependence, and I know no worse lot than to be dependent on a self-willed woman like our mother. The means he had to make himself respected at home he hath squandered away here. He has flung his patrimony to the dogs, and poverty and subserviency are now his only portion." Mr. Warrington delivered this speech with considerable spirit and volubility, and his cousin heard him respectfully.

" You speak well, Mr. Warrington. Have you ever thought of public life? " said my Lord.

" Of course I have thought of public life like every man of my station—every man, that is, who cares for something beyond a dice-box or a stable," replies George. " I hope, my Lord, to be able to take my own place, and my unlucky brother must content himself with his. This I say advisedly, having heard from him of certain engagements which he has formed, and which it would be misery to all parties were he to attempt to execute now."

" Your logic is very strong," said my Lord. " Shall we go up and see the ladies? There is a picture above-stairs which your grandfather is said to have executed. Before you go, my dear cousin, you will please to fix a day when our family may have the honour of receiving you. Castlewood, you know, is always your home when we are there. It is something like your Virginian Castlewood, cousin, from your account. We have beef, and mutton, and ale, and wood, in plenty; but money is woefully scarce amongst us."

They ascended to the drawing-room, where, however, they found only one of the ladies of the family. This was my Lady Maria, who came out of the embrasure of a window, where she and Harry Warrington had been engaged in talk.

George made his best bow, Maria her lowest curtsey. "You are indeed wonderfully like your brother," she said, giving him her hand. "And from what he says, Cousin George, I think you are as good as he is."

At the sight of her swollen eyes and tearful face George felt a pang of remorse. "Poor thing," he thought. "Harry has been vaunting my generosity and virtue to her, and I have been playing the selfish elder brother downstairs! How old she looks! How could he ever have a passion for such a woman as that?" How? Because he did not see with your eyes, Mr. George. He saw rightly too now with his own, perhaps. I never know whether to pity or congratulate a man on coming to his senses.

After the introduction a little talk took place, which for a while Lady Maria managed to carry on in an easy manner: but though ladies in this matter of social hypocrisy are, I think, far more consummate performers than men, after a sentence or two the poor lady broke out into a sob, and, motioning Harry away with her hand, fairly fled from the room.

Harry was rushing forward, but stopped—checked by that sign. My Lord said his poor sister was subject to these fits of nerves, and had already been ill that morning. After this event our young gentlemen thought it was needless to prolong their visit. Lord Castlewood followed them downstairs, accompanied them to the door, admired their nags in the phaeton, and waved them a friendly farewell.

"And so we have been coaxing and cuddling in the window, and we part good friends, Harry? Is it not so?" says George to his charioteer.

"Oh, she *is* a good woman!" cries Harry, lashing the horses. "I know you'll think so when you come to know her."

"When you take her home to Virginia? A pretty welcome

our mother will give her. She will never forgive me for not breaking the match off, nor you for making it."

" I can't help it, George! Don't you be popping your ugly head so close to my ears, Gumbo! After what has passed between us, I am bound in honour to stand by her. If she sees no objection, I must find none. I told her all. I told her that Madam would be very rusty at first; but that she was very fond of me, and must end by relenting. And when *you* come to the property, I told her that I knew my dearest George so well, that I might count upon sharing with him."

" The deuce you did! Let me tell you, my dear, that I have been telling my Lord Castlewood quite a different story. That as an elder brother I intend to have all my rights—there, don't flog that near horse so—and that you can but look forward to poverty and dependence."

" What? You won't help me?" cries Harry, turning quite pale. " George, I don't believe it, though I hear it out of your own mouth!"

There was a minute's pause after this outbreak, during which Harry did not even look at his brother, but sat, gazing blindly before him, the picture of grief and gloom. He was driving so near to a road-post that the carriage might have been upset but for George's pulling the rein.

" You had better take the reins, sir," said Harry. " I told you you had better take them."

" Did you ever know me fail you, Harry?" George asked.

" No," said the other, " not till now "—the tears were rolling down his cheeks as he spoke.

" My dear, I think one day you will say I have done my duty."

" What have you done?" asked Harry.

" I have said you were a younger brother—that you have spent all your patrimony, and that your portion at home must be very slender. Is it not true?"

" Yes, but I would not have believed it if ten thousand men had told me," said Harry. " Whatever happened to me, I thought I could trust *you*, George Warrington." And in this frame of mind Harry remained during the rest of the drive.

Their dinner was served soon after their return to their lodgings, of which Harry scarce ate any, though he drank freely of the wine before him.

" That wine is a bad consoler in trouble, Harry," his brother remarked.

"I have no other, sir," said Harry grimly; and having drunk glass after glass in silence, he presently seized his hat, and left the room.

He did not return for three hours. George, in much anxiety about his brother, had not left home meanwhile, but read his book, and smoked the pipe of patience. "It *was* shabby to say I would not aid him, and God help me, it was not true. I won't leave him, though he marries a blackamoor," thought George: "have I not done him harm enough already, by coming to life again? Where has he gone? has he gone to play?"

"Good God! what has happened to thee?" cried George Warrington, presently, when his brother came in, looking ghastly pale.

He came up and took his brother's hand. "I can take it now, Georgy," he said. "Perhaps what you did was right, though I for one will never believe that you would throw your brother off in distress. I'll tell you what. At dinner, I thought suddenly, I'll go back to her and speak to her. I'll say to her, 'Maria, poor as I am, your conduct to me has been so noble, that, by Heaven! I am yours to take or to leave. If you will have me, here I am: I will enlist: I will work: I will try and make a livelihood for myself, somehow, and my bro—my relations will relent, and give us enough to live on.' That's what I determined to tell her; and I did, George. I ran all the way to Kensington in the rain—look, I am splashed from head to foot,—and found them all at dinner, all except Will, that is. I spoke out that very moment to them all, sitting round the table, over their wine. 'Maria,' says I, 'a poor fellow wants to redeem his promise which he made when he fancied he was rich. Will you take him?' I found I had plenty of words, and didn't hem and stutter as I am doing now. I spoke ever so long, and I ended by saying I would do my best and my duty by her, so help me God!

"When I had done, she came up to me quite kind. She took my hand, and kissed it before the rest. 'My dearest, best Harry!' she said (those were her words, I don't want otherwise to be praising myself), 'you are a noble heart, and I thank you with all mine. But, my dear, I have long seen it was only duty, and a foolish promise made by a young man to an old woman, that has held you to your engagement. To keep it would make you miserable, my dear. I absolve you from it, thanking you with all my heart for your fidelity, and blessing and loving my dear cousin always.' And she came up and kissed me before

them all, and went out of the room quite stately, and without
a single tear. They were all crying, especially my Lord, who
was sobbing quite loud. I didn't think he had so much feeling.
And she, George? Oh, isn't she a noble creature?"

"Here's her health!" cries George, filling one of the glasses
that still stood before him.

"Hip, hip, huzzay!" says Harry. He was wild with delight
at being free.

CHAPTER LVII

IN WHICH MR. HARRY'S NOSE CONTINUES TO BE PUT OUT OF JOINT

MADAME DE BERNSTEIN was scarcely less pleased than her
Virginian nephews at the result of Harry's final interview with
Lady Maria. George informed the Baroness of what had
passed, in a billet which he sent to her the same evening; and
shortly afterwards her nephew Castlewood, whose visits to his
aunt were very rare, came to pay his respects to her, and frankly
spoke about the circumstances which had taken place; for no
man knew better than my Lord Castlewood how to be frank
upon occasion, and now that the business between Maria and
Harry was ended, what need was there of reticence or hypocrisy?
The game had been played, and was over: he had no objection
now to speak of its various moves, stratagems, finesses. "She
is my own sister," said my Lord affectionately: "she won't
have many more chances—many more *such* chances of marrying
and establishing herself. I might not approve of the match
in all respects, and I might pity your Ladyship's young
Virginian favourite: but of course such a piece of good fortune
was not to be thrown away, and I was bound to stand by my
own flesh and blood."

"Your candour does your Lordship honour," says Madame
de Bernstein, "and your love for your sister is quite edifying!"

"Nay, we have lost the game, and I am speaking *sans rancune*.
It is not for you, who have won, to bear malice," says my
Lord, with a bow.

Madame Bernstein protested she was never in her life in
better humour. "Confess now, Eugene, that visit of Maria to
Harry at the sponging-house—that touching giving up of all his
presents to her, was a stroke of thy invention?"

"Pity for the young man, and a sense of what was due from Maria to her friend—her affianced lover—in misfortune, sure these were motives sufficient to make her act as she did?" replies Lord Castlewood demurely.

"But 'twas you advised her, my good nephew?"

Castlewood, with a shrug of his shoulders, owned that he *did* advise his sister to see Mr. Henry Warrington. "But we should have won in spite of your Ladyship," he continued, "had not the elder brother made his appearance. And I have been trying to console my poor Maria by showing her what a piece of good fortune it is, after all, that we lost."

"Suppose she had married Harry, and then Cousin George had made his appearance?" remarks the Baroness.

"*Effectivement*," cries Eugene, taking snuff. "As the grave was to give up its dead, let us be thankful to the grave for disgorging in time! I am bound to say, that Mr. George Warrington seems to be a man of sense, and not more selfish than other elder sons and men of the world. My poor Molly fancied that he might be a—what shall I say?—a greenhorn perhaps is the term—like his younger brother. She fondly hoped that he might be inclined to go share and share alike with Twin junior; in which case, so infatuated was she about the young fellow, that I believe she would have taken him. 'Harry Warrington, with half a loaf, might do very well,' says I, 'but Harry Warrington with no bread, my dear!'"

"How no bread?" asks the Baroness.

"Well, no bread except at his brother's side-table. The elder said as much."

"What a hard-hearted wretch!" cries Madame de Bernstein.

"Ah, bah! I play with you, aunt, *cartes sur table!* Mr. George only did what everybody else would do: and we have no right to be angry with him—really we haven't. Molly herself acknowledged as much, after her first burst of grief was over and I brought her to listen to reason. The silly old creature! to be so wild about a young lad at her time of life."

"'Twas a real passion, I almost do believe," said Madame de Bernstein.

"You should have heard her take leave of him! C'était touchant, ma parole d'honneur! I cried. Before George, I could not help myself. The young fellow with muddy stockings, and his hair about his eyes, flings himself amongst us when we were at dinner; makes his offer to Molly in a very frank and noble manner, and in good language too; and she replies.

Begad, it put me in mind of Mrs. Woffington in the new Scotch play, that Lord Bute's man has wrote—Douglas—what d'ye call it? She clings round the lad; she bids him adieu in heartrending accents. She steps out of the room in a stately despair —no more chocolate, thank you. If she had made a *mauvais pas*, no one could retire from it with more dignity. 'Twas a masterly retreat after a defeat. We were starved out of our position, but we retired with all the honours of war."

" Molly won't die of the disappointment!" said my Lord's aunt, sipping her cup.

My Lord snarled a grin, and showed his yellow teeth. " He, he!" he said, " she hath once or twice before had the malady very severely, and recovered perfectly. It don't kill, as your Ladyship knows, at Molly's age."

How should her Ladyship know? She did not marry Dr. Tusher until she was advanced in life. She did not become Madame de Bernstein until still later. Old Dido, a poet remarks, was not ignorant of misfortune, and hence learned to have compassion on the wretched.

People in the little world, as I have been told, quarrel and fight, and go on abusing each other, and are not reconciled for ever so long. But people in the great world are surely wiser in their generation. They have differences; they cease seeing each other. They make it up and come together again, and no questions are asked. A stray prodigal, or a stray puppy-dog, is thus brought in under the benefit of an amnesty, though you know he has been away in ugly company. For six months past, ever since the Castlewoods and Madame de Bernstein had been battling for possession of poor Harry Warrington, these two branches of the Esmond family had remained apart. Now, the question being settled, they were free to meet again, as though no difference ever had separated them: and Madame de Bernstein drove in her great coach to Lady Castlewood's rout, and the Esmond ladies appeared smiling at Madame de Bernstein's drums, and loved each other just as much as they previously had done.

" So, sir, I hear you have acted like a hard-hearted monster about your poor brother Harry!" says the Baroness, delighted, and menacing George with her stick.

" I acted but upon your Ladyship's hint, and desired to see whether it was for himself or his reputed money that his kinsfolk wanted to have him," replies George, turning rather red.

" Nay, Maria could not marry a poor fellow who was utterly

penniless, and whose elder brother said he would give him nothing!"

"I did it for the best, madam," says George, still blushing.

"And so thou didst, O thou hypocrite!" cries the old lady.

"Hypocrite, madam! and why?" asks Mr. Warrington, drawing himself up in much state.

"I know all, my infant!" says the Baroness in French. "Thou art very like thy grandfather. Come, that I embrace thee! Harry has told me all, and that thou hast divided thy little patrimony with him!"

"It was but natural, madam. We have had common hearts and purses since we were born. I but feigned hard-heartedness in order to try those people yonder," says George, with filling eyes.

"And thou wilt divide Virginia with him too?" asks the Bernstein.

"I don't say so. It were not just," replied Mr. Warrington. "The land must go to the eldest born, and Harry would not have it otherwise: and it may be I shall die, or my mother outlive the pair of us. But half of what is mine is his: and he, it must be remembered, only was extravagant because he was mistaken as to his position."

"But it is a knight of old, it is a Bayard, it is the grandfather come to life!" cried Madame de Bernstein to her attendant, as she was retiring for the night. And that evening, when the lads left her, it was to poor Harry she gave the two fingers, and to George the rouged cheek, who blushed for his part, almost as deep as that often-dyed rose, at such a mark of his old kinswoman's favour.

Although Harry Warrington was the least envious of men, and did honour to his brother as in all respects his chief, guide, and superior, yet no wonder a certain feeling of humiliation and disappointment oppressed the young man after his deposition from his eminence as Fortunate Youth and heir to boundless Virginian territories. Our friends at Kensington might promise and vow that they would love him all the better after his fall; Harry made a low bow and professed himself very thankful; but he could not help perceiving, when he went with his brother to the state entertainment with which my Lord Castlewood regaled his new-found kinsman, that George was all in all to his cousins; had all the talk, compliments, and *petits soins* for himself, whilst of Harry no one took any notice save poor Maria, who followed him with wistful looks, pursued him with eyes conveying dismal reproaches, and, as it were, blamed him because she had left him. "Ah!" the eyes seemed to say, "'tis mighty well of you, Harry, to have accepted the freedom which I gave you; but I had no intention, sir, that you should be so pleased at being let off." She gave him up, but yet she did not quite forgive him for taking her at her word. She would not have him, and yet she would. Oh, my young friends, how delightful is the beginning of a love-business, and how undignified, sometimes, the end!

This is what Harry Warrington, no doubt, felt when he went to Kensington and encountered the melancholy reproachful eyes of his cousin. Yes! it is a foolish position to be in; but it is also melancholy to look into a house you have once lived in, and see black casements and emptiness where once shone the fires of welcome. Melancholy? Yes; but, ah! how bitter, how melancholy, how absurd to look up as you pass sentimentally by No. 13, and see somebody else grinning out of window, and evidently on the best terms with the landlady. I always feel hurt, even at an inn which I frequent, if I see other folks' trunks and boots at the doors of the rooms which were once mine. Have those boots lolled on the sofa which once I reclined on? I kick you from before me, you muddy, vulgar highlows!

So considering that his period of occupation was over, and Maria's rooms, if not given up to a new tenant, were, at any rate, to let, Harry did not feel very easy in his cousin's company, nor she possibly in his. He found either that he had nothing to say to her, or that what she had to say to him was rather dull and commonplace, and that the red lip of a white-necked pipe of Virginia was decidedly more agreeable to him now than Maria's softest accents and most melancholy *moue*. When George went to Kensington, then, Harry did not care much about going, and pleaded other engagements.

At his uncle's house in Hill Street the poor lad was no better amused, and, indeed, was treated by the virtuous people there with scarce any attention at all. The ladies did not scruple to deny themselves when he came; he could scarce have believed in such insincerity after their caresses, their welcome, their repeated vows of affection; but happening to sit with the Lamberts for an hour after he had called upon his aunt, he saw her Ladyship's chairman arrive with an empty chair, and his aunt step out and enter the vehicle, and not even blush when he made her a bow from the opposite window. To be denied by his own relations—to have that door which had opened to

him so kindly, slammed in his face! He would not have believed
such a thing possible, poor simple Harry said. Perhaps he
thought the door-knocker had a tender heart, and was not made
of brass: not more changed than the head of that knocker was
my Lady Warrington's virtuous face when she passed her
nephew.

"My father's own brother's wife! What have I done to
offend her? Oh, Aunt Lambert, Aunt Lambert, did you ever
see such cold-heartedness?" cries out Harry, with his usual
impetuosity.

"Do we make any difference to you, my dear Harry?" says
Aunt Lambert, with a side look at her youngest daughter. "The
world may look coldly at you, but we don't belong to it: so you
may come to us in safety."

"In this house you are different from other people," replies
Harry. "I don't know how, but I always feel quiet and happy
somehow when I come to you."

> "Quis me uno vivit felicior? aut magis hâc quid
> Optandum vitâ dicere quis poterit?"

calls out General Lambert. "Do you know where I got these
verses, Mr. Gownsman?" and he addresses his son from college,
who is come to pass an Easter holiday with his parents.

"You got them out of Catullus, sir," says the scholar.

"I got them out of no such thing, sir. I got them out of
my favourite Democritus Junior—out of old Burton, who has
provided many different scholars with learning;" and who and
Montaigne were favourite authors with the good General.

CHAPTER LVIII

WHERE WE DO WHAT CATS MAY DO

WE have said how our Virginians, with a wisdom not uncommon
in youth, had chosen to adopt strong Jacobite opinions, and to
profess a prodigious affection for the exiled Royal family. The
banished prince had recognised Madam Esmond's father as
Marquis of Esmond, and she did not choose to be very angry
with an unfortunate race, that, after all, was so willing to
acknowledge the merits of her family. As for any little scandal
about her sister, Madam de Bernstein, and the Old Chevalier,
she tossed away from her with scorn the recollection of that

odious circumstance, asserting, with perfect truth, that the two first monarchs of the House of Hanover were quite as bad as any Stuarts in regard to their domestic morality. But the King *de facto* was the King, as well as His Majesty *de jure*. De Facto had been solemnly crowned and anointed at church, and had likewise utterly discomfited De Jure, when they came to battle for the kingdom together. Madam's clear opinion was, then, that her sons owed it to themselves as well as the Sovereign to appear at his Royal Court. And if His Majesty should have been minded to confer a lucrative post, or a blue or red ribbon upon either of them, she, for her part, would not have been in the least surprised. She made no doubt but that the King knew the Virginian Esmonds as well as any other members of his nobility. The lads were specially commanded, then, to present themselves at Court, and, I dare say, their mother would have been very angry had she known that George took Harry's laced coat on the day when he went to make his bow at Kensington.

A hundred years ago the King's drawing-room was open almost every day to his nobility and gentry; and loyalty— especially since the war had begun—could gratify itself a score of times in a month with the august sight of the sovereign. A wise avoidance of the enemy's ships-of-war, a gracious acknowledgment of the inestimable loss the British Isles would suffer by the seizure of the Royal person at sea, caused the monarch to forego those visits to his native Hanover which were so dear to his Royal heart, and compelled him to remain, it must be owned unwillingly, amongst his loving Britons. A Hanoverian lady, however, whose virtues had endeared her to the Prince, strove to console him for his enforced absence from Herrenhausen. And from the lips of the Countess of Walmoden (on whom the imperial beneficence had gracefully conferred a high title of British honour) the revered Defender of the Faith could hear the accents of his native home.

To this beloved Sovereign, Mr. Warrington requested his uncle, an assiduous courtier, to present him: and as Mr. Lambert had to go to Court likewise, and thank His Majesty for his promotion, the two gentlemen made the journey to Kensington together, engaging a hackney-coach for the purpose, as my Lord Wrotham's carriage was now wanted by its rightful owner, who had returned to his house in town. They alighted at Kensington Palace Gate, where the sentries on duty knew and saluted the good General, and hence modestly made their way on foot to the summer residence of the Sovereign. Walking under the portico of the Palace, they entered the gallery which leads to the great black marble staircase (which hath been so richly decorated and painted by Mr. Kent), and then passed through several rooms richly hung with tapestry and adorned with pictures and bustos, until they came to the King's great drawing-room, where that famous " Venus " by Titian is, and, amongst other masterpieces, the picture of " St. Francis adoring the infant Saviour," performed by Sir Peter Paul Rubens; and here, with the rest of the visitors to the Court, the gentlemen waited until His Majesty issued from his private apartments, where he was in conference with certain personages who were called in the newspaper language of that day His M-j—ty's M-n-st-rs.

George Warrington, who had never been in a palace before, had leisure to admire the place, and regard the people round him. He saw fine pictures for the first time too, and I dare say delighted in that charming piece of Sir Anthony Vandyke representing King Charles the First, his Queen and Family, and the noble picture of " Esther before Ahasuerus," painted by Tintoret, and in which all the figures are dressed in the magnificent Venetian habit. With the contemplation of these works he was so enraptured, that he scarce heard all the remarks of his good friend the General, who was whispering into his young companion's almost heedless ear the names of some of the personages round about them.

" Yonder," says Mr. Lambert, " are two of my Lords of the Admiralty, Mr. Gilbert Elliot and Admiral Boscawen: *your* Boscawen, whose fleet fired the first gun in your waters two years ago. That stout gentleman all belaced with gold is Mr. Fox, that was Minister, and is now content to be Paymaster with a great salary."

" He carries the *auri fames* on his person. Why, his waistcoat is a perfect Potosi! " says George.

" *Alieni appetens*—how goes the text? He loves to get money and to spend it," continues General Lambert. " Yon is my Lord Chief Justice Willes, talking to my Lord of Salisbury, Dr. Hoadley, who, if he serve his God as he serves his King, will be translated to some very high promotion in heaven. He belongs to your grandfather's time, and was loved by Dick Steele and hated by the Dean. With them is my Lord of London, the learned Doctor Sherlock. My Lords of the lawn sleeves have lost half their honours now. I remember when I was a boy in my mother's hand, she made me go down on my

knees to the Bishop of Rochester; him who went over the
water, and became Minister to somebody who shall be nameless
—Perkin's Bishop. That handsome fair man is Admiral Smith.
He was president of poor Byng's court-martial, and strove in
vain to get him off his penalty; Tom of Ten Thousand they call
him in the fleet. The French Ambassador had him broke, when
he was a lieutenant, for making a French man-of-war lower
topsails to him, and the King made Tom a captain the next day.
That tall haughty-looking man is my Lord George Sackville,
who, now I am a Major-General myself, will treat me somewhat
better than a footman. I wish my stout old Blakeney were
here; he is the soldier's darling, and as kind and brave as
yonder poker of a nobleman is brave and—— I am your
Lordship's very humble servant. This is a young gentleman
who is just from America, and was in Braddock's sad business
two years ago."

"Oh, indeed!" says the poker of a nobleman. "I have the
honour of speaking to Mr.——"

"To Major-General Lambert, at your Lordship's service, and
who was in His Majesty's some time before you entered it.
That, Mr. Warrington, is the first commoner in England, Mr.
Speaker Onslow. Where is your uncle? I shall have to present
you myself to His Majesty if Sir Miles delays much longer."
As he spoke the worthy General addressed himself entirely to
his young friend, making no sort of account of his colleague,
who stalked away with a scared look as if amazed at the other's
audacity. A hundred years ago, a nobleman was a nobleman,
and expected to be admired as such.

Sir Miles's red waistcoat appeared in sight presently, and
many cordial greetings passed between him, his nephew, and
General Lambert: for we have described how Sir Miles was the
most affectionate of men. So the General had quitted my
Lord Wrotham's house? It was time, as his Lordship himself
wished to occupy it? Very good; but consider what a loss for
the neighbours!

"We miss you, we positively miss you, my dear General,"
cries Sir Miles. "My daughters were in love with those lovely
young ladies—upon my word they were; and my Lady Warrington and my girls were debating over and over again how
they should find an opportunity of making the acquaintance of
your charming family. We feel as if we were old friends already;
indeed we do, General, if you will permit me the liberty of
saying so; and we love you, if I may be allowed to speak

frankly, on account of your friendship and kindness to our dear
nephews: though we were a little jealous, I own a little jealous
of them, because they went so often to see you. Often and
often have I said to my Lady Warrington, 'My dear, why don't
we make acquaintance with the General? Why don't we ask
him and his ladies to come over in a family way and dine with
some other plain country gentlefolks?' Carry my most sincere
respects to Mrs. Lambert, I pray, sir; and thank her for her
goodness to these young gentlemen. My own flesh and blood,
sir; my dear dear brother's boys!" He passed his hand across
his manly eyes: he was choking almost with generous and
affectionate emotion.

Whilst they were discoursing—George Warrington the while
restraining his laughter with admirable gravity—the door of
the King's apartments opened, and the pages entered, preceding
His Majesty. He was followed by his burly son, His Royal
Highness the Duke, a very corpulent prince, with a coat and
face of blazing scarlet: behind them came various gentlemen
and officers of state, among whom George at once recognised
the famous Mr. Secretary Pitt, by his tall stature, his eagle eye
and beak, his grave and majestic presence. As I see that
solemn figure passing, even a hundred years off, I protest I feel
a present awe, and a desire to take my hat off. I am not
frightened at George the Second; nor are my eyes dazzled by
the portentous appearance of His Royal Highness the Duke
of Culloden and Fontenoy; but the Great Commoner, the
terrible Cornet of Horse! His figure bestrides our narrow isle
of a century back like a Colossus; and I hush as he passes in his
gouty shoes, his thunderbolt hand wrapped in flannel. Perhaps
as we see him now, issuing with dark looks from the Royal
closet, angry scenes have been passing between him and his
august master. He has been boring that old monarch for
hours with prodigious long speeches, full of eloquence, voluble
with the noblest phrases upon the commonest topics; but, it
must be confessed, utterly repulsive to the little shrewd old
gentleman, "at whose feet he lays himself," as the phrase is,
and who has the most thorough dislike for fine *boedry* and for
fine *brose* too! The sublime Minister passes solemnly through
the crowd; the company ranges itself respectfully round the
wall; and His Majesty walks round the circle, his Royal son
lagging a little behind, and engaging select individuals in
conversation for his own part.

The monarch is a little keen fresh-coloured old man, with

very protruding eyes, attired in plain old-fashioned snuff-coloured clothes and brown stockings, his only ornament the blue ribbon of his Order of the Garter. He speaks in a German accent, but with ease, shrewdness, and simplicity, addressing those individuals whom he has a mind to notice, or passing on with a bow. He knew Mr. Lambert well, who had served under His Majesty at Dettingen, and with his Royal son in Scotland, and he congratulated him good-humouredly on his promotion.

"It is not always," His Majesty was pleased to say, "that we can do as we like; but I was glad when, for once, I could give myself that pleasure in your case, General; for my army contains no better officer as you."

The veteran blushed and bowed, deeply gratified at this speech. Meanwhile, the Best of Monarchs was looking at Sir Miles Warrington (whom His Majesty knew perfectly, as the eager recipient of all favours from all Ministers), and at the young gentleman by his side.

"Who is this?" the Defender of the Faith condescended to ask, pointing towards George Warrington, who stood before his sovereign in a respectful attitude, clad in poor Harry's best embroidered suit.

With the deepest reverence Sir Miles informed his King, that the young gentleman was his nephew, Mr. George Warrington, of Virginia, who asked leave to pay his humble duty.

"This, then, is the other brother?" the venerated Prince deigned to observe. "He came in time, else the other brother would have spent all the money. My Lord Bishop of Salisbury, why do you come out in this bitter weather? You had much better stay at home!" and with this, the revered wielder of Britannia's sceptre passed on to other lords and gentlemen of his Court. Sir Miles Warrington was deeply affected at the Royal condescension. He clapped his nephew's hands. "God bless you, my boy," he cried; "I told you that you would see the greatest monarch and the finest gentleman in the world. Is he not so, my Lord Bishop?"

"That, that he is!" cried his Lordship, clasping his ruffled hands, and turning his fine eyes up to the sky, "the best of princes and of men."

"That is Master Louis, my Lady Yarmouth's favourite nephew," says Lambert, pointing to a young gentleman who stood with a crowd round him; and presently the stout Duke of Cumberland came up to our little group.

His Royal Highness held out his hand to his old companion

in arms. "Congratulate you on your promotion, Lambert," he said good-naturedly. Sir Miles Warrington's eyes were ready to burst out of his head with rapture.

"I owe it, sir, to your Royal Highness's good offices," said the grateful General.

"Not at all; not at all: ought to have had it a long time before. Always been a good officer; perhaps there'll be some employment for you soon. This is the gentleman whom James Wolfe introduced to me?"

"His brother, sir."

"Oh, the real Fortunate Youth! You were with poor Ned Braddock in America—a prisoner, and lucky enough to escape. Come and see me, sir, in Pall Mall. Bring him to my levée, Lambert." And the broad back of the Royal Prince was turned to our friends.

"It is raining! You came on foot, General Lambert? You and George must come home in my coach. You must and *shall* come home with me, I say. By George, you must! I'll have no denial," cried the enthusiastic Baronet; and he drove George and the General back to Hill Street, and presented the latter to my Lady Warrington and his darlings, Flora and Dora, and insisted upon their partaking of a collation, as they must be hungry after their ride. "What, there is only cold mutton? Well, an old soldier can eat cold mutton. And a good glass of my Lady Warrington's own cordial, prepared with her own hands, will keep the cold wind out. Delicious cordial! Capital mutton! Our own, my dear General," says the hospitable Baronet, "our own from the country, six years old if a day. We keep a plain table; but all the Warringtons since the Conqueror have been remarkable for their love of mutton; and our meal may look a little scanty, and is, for we are plain people, and I am obliged to keep my rascals of servants on board wages. Can't give them seven-year-old mutton, you know."

Sir Miles, in his nephew's presence and hearing, described to his wife and daughters George's reception at Court in such flattering terms that George hardly knew himself, or the scene at which he had been present, or how to look his uncle in the face, or how to contradict him before his family in the midst of the astonishing narrative he was relating. Lambert sat by for a while with open eyes. He, too, had been at Kensington. He had seen none of the wonders which Sir Miles described.

"We are proud of you, dear George. We love you, my dear nephew—we all love you, we are all proud of you——"

" Yes; but I like Harry best," says a little voice.

"—not because you are wealthy! Screwby, take Master Miles to his governor. Go, dear child. Not because you are blest with great estates and an ancient name; but because, George, you have put to good use the talents with which Heaven has adorned you: because you have fought and bled in your country's cause, in your monarch's cause, and as such are indeed worthy of the favour of the best of sovereigns. General Lambert, you have kindly condescended to look in on a country family, and partake of our unpretending meal. I hope we may see you some day when our hospitality is a little less homely. Yes, by George, General, you must and shall name a day when you and Mrs. Lambert, and your dear girls, will dine with us. I'll take no refusal now, by George I won't," bawls the knight.

" You will accompany us, I trust, to my drawing-room? " says my Lady, rising.

Mr. Lambert pleaded to be excused; but the ladies on no account would let dear George go away. No, positively, he should *not* go. They wanted to make acquaintance with their cousin. They must hear about that dreadful battle and escape from the Indians. Tom Claypool came in and heard some of the story. Flora was listening to it with her handkerchief to her eyes, and little Miles had just said—

" Why do you take your handkerchief, Flora? You're not crying a bit."

Being a man of great humour, Martin Lambert, when he went home, could not help entertaining his wife with an account of the new family with which he had made acquaintance. A certain cant word called humbug had lately come into vogue. Will it be believed that the General used it to designate the family of this virtuous country gentleman? He described the eager hospitalities of the father, the pompous flatteries of the mother, and the daughters' looks of admiration; the toughness and scarcity of the mutton, and the abominable taste and odour of the cordial; and we may be sure Mrs. Lambert contrasted Lady Warrington's recent behaviour to poor Harry with her present conduct to George.

" Is this Miss Warrington really handsome? " asks Mrs. Lambert.

" Yes; she is very handsome indeed, and the most astounding flirt I have ever set eyes on," replies the General.

" The hypocrite! I have no patience with such people! " cries the lady.

To which the General, strange to say, only replied by the monosyllable " Bo ! "

" Why do you say ' Bo !' Martin? " asks the lady.

" I say ' Bo !' to a goose, my dear," answers the General.

And his wife vows she does not know what he means, or of what he is thinking, and the General says—

" Of course not."

CHAPTER LIX

IN WHICH WE ARE TREATED TO A PLAY

THE real business of life, I fancy, can form but little portion of the novelist's budget. When he is speaking of the profession of arms, in which men can show courage or the reverse, and in treating of which the writer naturally has to deal with interesting circumstances, actions, and characters, introducing recitals of danger, devotedness, heroic deaths, and the like, the novelist may perhaps venture to deal with actual affairs of life: but otherwise, they scarcely can enter into our stories. The main part of Ficulnus's life, for instance, is spent in selling sugar, spices, and cheese; of Causidicus's in poring over musty volumes of black-letter law; of Sartorius's in sitting, cross-legged on a board, after measuring gentlemen for coats and breeches. What can a story-teller say about the professional existence of these men? Would a real rustical history of hobnails and eighteenpence a day be endurable? In the days whereof we are writing, the poets of the time chose to represent a shepherd in pink breeches and a chintz waistcoat, dancing before his flocks, and playing a flageolet tied up with a blue satin ribbon. I say, in reply to some objections which have been urged by potent and friendly critics, that of the actual affairs of life the novelist cannot be expected to treat—with the almost single exception of war before named. But law, stockbroking, polemical theology, linen-drapery, apothecary-business, and the like, how can writers manage fully to develop these in their stories? All authors can do, is to depict men *out* of their business—in their passions, loves, laughters, amusements, hatreds, and what not—and describe these as well as they can, taking the business part for granted, and leaving it as it were for subaudition.

Thus, in talking of the present or the past world, I know I am only dangling about the theatre-lobbies, coffee-houses, ridottos, pleasure-haunts, fair-booths, and feasting and fiddling rooms of life; that, meanwhile, the great serious past or present world is plodding in its chambers, toiling at its humdrum looms, or jogging on its accustomed labours, and we are only seeing our characters away from their work. Corydon has to cart the litter and thresh the barley, as well as to make love to Phyllis; Ancillula has to dress and wash the nursery, to wait at breakfast and on her misses, to take the children out, etc., before she can have her brief sweet interview through the area-railings with Boopis, the policeman. All day long have his heels to beat the stale pavement before he has the opportunity to snatch the hasty kiss or the furtive cold pie. It is only at moments, and away from these labours, that we can light upon one character or the other; and hence, though most of the persons of whom we are writing have doubtless their grave employments and avocations, it is only when they are disengaged and away from their work, that we can bring them and the equally disengaged reader together.

The macaronis and fine gentlemen at White's and Arthur's continued to show poor Harry Warrington such a very cold shoulder, that he sought their society less and less, and the Ring and the Mall and the gambling-table knew him no more. Madame de Bernstein was for her nephew's braving the indifference of the world, and vowed that it would be conquered, if he would but have courage to face it; but the young man was too honest to wear a smiling face when he was discontented; to disguise mortification or anger; to parry slights by adroit flatteries or cunning impudence; as many gentlemen and gentlewomen must and do who wish to succeed in society.

"You pull a long face, Harry, and complain of the world's treatment of you," the old lady said. "Fiddle-de-dee, sir! Everybody has to put up with impertinences; and if you get a box on the ear now you are poor and cast down, you must say nothing about it, bear it with a smile, and, if you can, revenge it ten years after. Moi qui vous parle, sir!—do you suppose I have had no humble pie to eat? All of us in our turn are called upon to swallow it; and now you are no longer the Fortunate Youth, be the Clever Youth, and win back the place you have lost by your ill-luck. Go about more than ever. Go to all the routs and parties to which you are asked, and to more still. Be civil to everybody—to all women especially. Only of course take care to show your spirit, of which you have plenty. With economy, and by your brother's, I must say, admirable generosity, you can still make a genteel figure. With your handsome person, sir, you can't fail to get a rich heiress! Tenez! You should go amongst the merchants in the City, and look out there. They won't know that you are out of fashion at the Court end of the town. With a little management, there is not the least reason, sir, why you should not make a good position for yourself still. When did you go to see my Lady Yarmouth, pray? Why did you not improve that connection? She took a great fancy to you. I desire you will be constant at her Ladyship's evenings, and lose no opportunity of paying court to her."

Thus the old woman who had loved Harry *so* on his first appearance in England, who had been so eager for his company, and pleased with his artless conversation, was taking the side of the world, and turning against him. Instead of the smiles and kisses with which the fickle old creature used once to greet him, she received him with coldness; she became peevish and patronising; she cast jibes and scorn at him before her guests, making his honest face flush with humiliation, and awaking the keenest pangs of grief and amazement in his gentle manly heart. Madame de Bernstein's servants, who used to treat him with such eager respect, scarcely paid him now any attention. My Lady was often indisposed or engaged when he called on her; her people did not press him to wait; did not volunteer to ask whether he would stay and dine, as they used in the days when he was the Fortunate Youth and companion of the wealthy and great. Harry carried his woes to Mrs. Lambert. In a passion of sorrow he told her of his aunt's cruel behaviour to him. He was stricken down and dismayed by the fickleness and heartlessness of the world in its treatment of him. While the good lady and her daughters would move to and fro, and busy themselves with the cares of the house, our poor lad would sit glum in a window-seat, heart-sick and silent.

" I know you are the best people alive," he would say to the ladies, " and the kindest, and that I must be the dullest company in the world—yes, that I am."

" Well, you are not very lively, Harry," says Miss Hetty, who began to command him, and perhaps to ask herself, " What? Is this the gentleman whom I took to be such a hero? "

" If he is unhappy, why should he be lively? " asks Theo gently. " He has a good heart, and is pained at his friends' desertion of him. Sure, there is no harm in that? "

"I would have too much spirit to show I was hurt, though," cries Hetty, clenching her little fists. "And I would smile, though that horrible old painted woman boxed my ears. She *is* horrible, mamma. You think so yourself, Theo! Own, now, you think so yourself! You said so last night, and acted her coming in on her crutch, and grinning round to the company."

"I mayn't like her," said Theo, turning very red. "But there is no reason why I should call Harry's aunt names before Harry's face."

"You provoking thing; you are always right!" cries Hetty, "and that's what makes me so angry. Indeed, Harry, it was very wrong of me to make rude remarks about any of your relations."

"I don't care about the others, Hetty; but it seems hard that this one should turn upon me. I had got to be very fond of her; and you see, it makes me mad, somehow, when people I'm very fond of turn away from me, or act unkind to me."

"Suppose George were to do so?" asks Hetty. You see, it was George and Hetty, and Theo and Harry, amongst them now.

"You are very clever and very lively, and you may suppose a number of things; but not that, Hetty, if you please," cried Harry, standing up, and looking very resolute and angry. "You don't know my brother as I know him—or you wouldn't take—such a—liberty as to suppose—my brother, George, could do anything unkind or unworthy!" Mr. Harry was quite in a flush as he spoke.

Hetty turned very white. Then she looked up at Harry, and then she did not say a single word.

Then Harry said, in his simple way, before taking leave, "I'm very sorry, and I beg your pardon, Hetty, if I said anything rough, or that seemed unkind; but I always fight up if anybody says anything against George."

Hetty did not answer a word out of her pale lips, but gave him her hand, and dropped a prim little curtsey.

When she and Theo were together at night, making curl-paper confidences, "Oh!" said Hetty, "I thought it would be so happy to see him every day, and was so glad when papa said we were to stay in London! And now I do see him, you see, I go on offending him. I can't help offending him; and I know he is not clever, Theo. But oh! isn't he good, and kind, and brave? Didn't he look handsome when he was angry?"

"You silly little thing, you are always trying to make him look handsome," Theo replied.

It was Theo and Hetty, and Harry and George, among these young people, then; and I dare say the reason why General Lambert chose to apply the monosyllable " Bo " to the mother of his daughters, was as a rebuke to that good woman for the inveterate love of sentiment and propensity to match-making which belonged to her (and every other woman in the world whose heart is worth a fig); and as a hint that Madam Lambert was a goose if she fancied the two Virginian lads were going to fall in love with the young women of the Lambert house. Little Het might have her fancy: little girls will: but they get it over: " and you know, Molly " (which dear soft-hearted Mrs. Lambert could not deny), " you fancied somebody else before you fancied me," says the General, " but Harry had evidently not been smitten by Hetty; and now he was superseded, as it were, by having an elder brother over him, and could not even call the coat upon his back his own, Master Harry was no great catch."

" Oh, yes: now he is poor we will show him the door, as all the rest of the world does, I suppose," says Mrs. Lambert.

" That is what I always do, isn't it, Molly? turn my back on my friends in distress? " asks the General.

" No, my dear! I *am* a goose, now, and that I own, Martin," says the wife, having recourse to the usual pocket-handkerchief.

" Let the poor boy come to us and welcome: ours is almost the only house in this selfish place where so much can be said for him. He is unhappy, and to be with us puts him at ease; in God's name let him be with us! " says the kind-hearted officer. Accordingly, whenever poor crestfallen Hal wanted a dinner, or an evening's entertainment, Mr. Lambert's table had a corner for him. So was George welcome, too. He went among the Lamberts, not at first with the cordiality which Harry felt for these people, and inspired among them: for George was colder in his manner, and more mistrustful of himself and others than his twin-brother; but there was a goodness and friendliness about the family which touched almost all people who came into frequent contact with them; and George soon learned to love them for their own sake, as well as for their constant regard and kindness to his brother. He could not but see and own how sad Harry was, and pity his brother's depression. In his sarcastic way, George would often take himself to task before his brother for coming to life again, and say, " Dear Harry, I am George the Unlucky, though you have ceased to be Harry the Fortunate. Florac would have done much better not to pass his sword through that Indian's body, and to have left my scalp as an ornament for the fellow's belt. I say he would, sir! At White's the people would have respected you. Our mother would have wept over me, as a defunct angel, instead of being angry with me for again supplanting her favourite—you *are* her favourite, you deserve to be her favourite; everybody's favourite: only, if I had not come back, *your* favourite, Maria, would have insisted on marrying you; and that is how the gods would have revenged themselves upon you for your prosperity."

" I never know whether you are laughing at me or yourself, George," says the brother. " I never know whether you are serious or jesting."

" Precisely my own case, Harry my dear! " says George.

" But this I know, that there never was a better brother in all the world; and never better people than the Lamberts."

" Never was truer word said! " cries George, taking his brother's hand.

" And if I'm unhappy, 'tis not your fault—nor their fault—nor perhaps mine, George," continues the younger. " 'Tis fate, you see; 'tis the having nothing to do. I *must* work; and how, George, that is the question! "

" We will see what our mother says. We must wait till we hear from her," says George.

" I say, George! Do you know, I don't think I should much like going back to Virginia? " says Harry, in a low alarmed voice.

" What! in love with one of the lasses here? "

" Love 'em like sisters—with all my heart, of course, dearest, best girls! but, having come out of that business, thanks to you, I don't want to go back, you know. No! no! It is not for that I fancy staying in Europe better than going home. But, you see, I don't fancy hunting, duck-shooting, tobacco-planting, whist-playing, and going to sermon, over and over and over again for all my life, George. And what else is there to do at home? What on earth is there for me to do at all, I say? That's what makes me miserable. It would not matter for you to be a younger son; you are so clever you would make your way anywhere; but, for a poor fellow like me, what chance is there? Until I do something, George, I shall be miserable, that's what I shall! "

" Have I not always said so? Art thou not coming round to my opinion? "

" What opinion, George? You know pretty much whatever
you think, I think, George!" says the dutiful junior.

"That Florac had best have left the Indian to take my
scalp, my dear!"

At which Harry bursts away with an angry exclamation;
and they continue to puff their pipes in friendly union.

They lived together, each going his own gait; and not much
intercourse, save that of affection, was carried on between them.
Harry never would venture to meddle with George's books, and
would sit as dumb as a mouse at the lodgings whilst his brother
was studying. They removed presently from the Court end
of the town, Madame de Bernstein pishing and pshaing at their
change of residence. But George took a great fancy to frequenting Sir Hans Sloane's new reading-room and museum, just set
up in Montagu House, and he took cheerful lodgings in Southampton Row, Bloomsbury, looking over the delightful fields
towards Hampstead, at the back of the Duke of Bedford's
gardens. And Lord Wrotham's family coming to Mayfair, and
Mr. Lambert having business which detained him in London,
had to change his house, too, and engaged furnished apartments
in Soho, not very far off from the dwelling of our young men;
and it was, as we have said, with the Lamberts that Harry,
night after night, took refuge.

George was with them often, too; and, as the acquaintance
ripened, he frequented their house with increasing assiduity,
finding their company more to his taste than that of Aunt
Bernstein's polite circle of gamblers, than Sir Miles Warrington's
port and mutton, or the daily noise and clatter of the coffee-
houses. And as he and the Lambert ladies were alike strangers
in London, they partook of its pleasures together, and, no doubt,
went to " Vauxhall " and " Ranelagh," to " Marybone Gardens,"
and the play, and the Tower, and wherever else there was
honest amusement to be had in those days. Martin Lambert
loved that his children should have all the innocent pleasure
which he could procure for them, and Mr. George, who was of a
most generous, open-handed disposition, liked to treat his friends
likewise, especially those who had been so admirably kind to
his brother.

With all the passion of his heart Mr. Warrington loved a
play. He had never enjoyed this amusement in Virginia, and
only once or twice at Quebec, when he visited Canada; and
when he came to London, where the two houses were in their
full glory, I believe he thought he never could have enough

of the delightful entertainment. Anything he liked himself, he naturally wished to share amongst his companions. No wonder that he was eager to take his friends to the theatre, and we may be sure our young country folks were not unwilling. Shall it be " Drury Lane " or " Covent Garden," ladies? There was Garrick and Shakspeare at " Drury Lane." Well, will it be believed, the ladies wanted to hear the famous new author whose piece was being played at " Covent Garden " ?

At this time a star of genius had arisen, and was blazing with quite a dazzling brilliancy. The great Mr. John Home, of Scotland, had produced a tragedy, than which, since the days of the ancients, there had been nothing more classic and elegant. What had Mr. Garrick meant by refusing such a masterpiece for his theatre? Say what you will about Shakspeare; in the works of that undoubted great poet (who had begun to grow vastly more popular in England since Monsieur Voltaire attacked him) there were many barbarisms that could not but shock a polite auditory; whereas Mr. Home, the modern author, knew how to be refined in the very midst of grief and passion; to represent death, not merely as awful, but graceful and pathetic; and never condescended to degrade the majesty of the Tragic Muse by the ludicrous apposition of buffoonery and familiar punning, such as the elder playwright certainly had resort to. Besides, Mr. Home's performance had been admired in quarters so high, and by personages whose taste was known to be as elevated as their rank, that all Britons could not but join in the plaudits for which august hands had given the signal. Such, it was said, was the opinion of the very best company, in the coffee-houses, and amongst the wits about town. Why, the famous Mr. Gray, of Cambridge, said there had not been for a hundred years any dramatic dialogue of such a true style; and as for the poet's native capital of Edinburgh, where the piece was first brought out, it was even said that the triumphant Scots called out from the pit (in their dialect), " Where's Wully Shakspeare noo? "

" I should like to see the man who could beat Willy Shakspeare? " says the General, laughing.

" Mere national prejudice," says Mr. Warrington.

" Beat Shakspeare indeed! " cries Mrs. Lambert.

" Pooh, pooh! you have cried more over Mr. Sam Richardson than ever you did over Mr. Shakspeare, Molly! " remarks the General. " I think few women love to read ' Shakspeare ' ! they say they love it, but they don't."

" Oh, papa! " cry three ladies, throwing up three pair of hands.

" Well, then, why do you all three prefer ' Douglas '? And you, boys, who are such Tories, will you go see a play which is wrote by a Whig Scotchman, who was actually made prisoner at Falkirk? "

" Relictâ non bene parmulâ," says Mr. Jack the scholar.

" Nay—it was relictâ bene parmulâ," cried the General. " It was the Highlanders who flung their targes down, and made fierce work among us redcoats. If they had fought all their fields as well as that, and young Perkin had not turned back from Derby——"

" I know which side would be rebels, and who would be called the Young Pretender," interposed George.

" Hush! you must please to remember my cloth, Mr. War-rington," said the General, with some gravity; " and that the cockade I wear is a black, not a white one! Well, if you will not love Mr. Home for his politics, there is, I think, another reason, George, why you should like him."

" I may have Tory fancies, Mr. Lambert; but I think I know how to love and honour a good Whig," said George, with a bow to the General: " and why should I like this Mr. Home, sir? "

" Because, being a Presbyterian clergyman, he has committed the heinous crime of writing a play, and his brother parsons have barked out an excommunication at him. They took the poor fellow's means of livelihood away from him for his performance; and he would have starved, but that the young Pretender on *our* side of the water has given him a pension."

" If he has been persecuted by the parsons, there is hope for him," says George, smiling. " And henceforth I declare myself ready to hear his sermons."

" Mrs. Woffington is divine in it, though not generally famous in tragedy. Barry is drawing tears from all eyes; and Garrick is wild at having refused the piece. Girls, you must bring each half-a-dozen handkerchiefs! As for mamma, I cannot trust her; and she positively must be left at home."

But mamma persisted she would go; and, if need were to weep, she would sit and cry her eyes out in a corner. They all went to " Covent Garden," then; the most of the party duly prepared to see one of the masterpieces of the age and drama. Could they not all speak long pages of Congreve; had they not wept and kindled over Otway and Rowe? O ye past literary glories, that were to be eternal, how long have you been dead?

Who knows much more now than where your graves are? Poor neglected Muse of the bygone theatre! She pipes for us, and we will not dance! she tears her hair, and we will not weep. And the immortals of our time, how soon shall they be dead and buried, think you? How many will survive? How long shall it be ere Nox et Domus Plutonia shall overtake them?

So away went the pleased party to "Covent Garden" to see the tragedy of the immortal John Home. The ladies and the General were conveyed in a glass coach, and found the young men in waiting to receive them at the theatre door. Hence they elbowed their way through a crowd of torch-boys, and a whole regiment of footmen. Little Hetty fell to Harry's arm in this expedition, and the blushing Miss Theo was handed to the box by Mr. George. Gumbo had kept the places until his masters arrived, when he retired, with many bows, to take his own seat in the footman's gallery. They had good places in a front box, and there was luckily a pillar behind which mamma could weep in comfort. And opposite them they had the honour to see the august hope of the empire, His Royal Highness George Prince of Wales, with the Princess Dowager his mother, whom the people greeted with loyal, but not very enthusiastic, plaudits.

That handsome man standing behind His Royal Highness was my Lord Bute, the Prince's Groom of the Stole, the patron of the poet whose performance they had come to see, and over whose work the Royal party had already wept more than once.

How can we help it, if during the course of the performance Mr. Lambert would make his jokes and mar the solemnity of the scene? At first, as the reader of the tragedy well knows, the characters are occupied in making a number of explanations. Lady Randolph explains how it is that she is so melancholy. Married to Lord Randolph somewhat late in life, she owns, and his Lordship perceives, that a dead lover yet occupies all her heart, and her husband is fain to put up with this dismal second-hand regard, which is all that my Lady can bestow. Hence, an invasion of Scotland by the Danes is rather a cause of excitement than disgust to my Lord, who rushes to meet the foe, and forget the dreariness of his domestic circumstances. Welcome Vikings and Norsemen! Blow, northern blasts, the invaders' keels to Scotland's shore! Randolph and other heroes will be on the beach to give the foeman a welcome! His Lordship has no sooner disappeared behind the trees of the forest, but Lady Randolph begins to explain to her confidante the circumstances of her early life. The fact was she had made a private marriage,

and what would the confidante say, if, in early youth, she,
Lady Randolph, had lost a husband? In the cold bosom of the
earth was lodged the husband of her youth, and in some cavern
of the ocean lies her child and his!

Up to this the General behaved with as great gravity as any
of his young companions to the play; but when Lady Randolph
proceeded to say, "Alas! Hereditary evil was the cause of my
misfortunes," he nudged George Warrington, and looked so droll,
that the young man burst out laughing.

The magic of the scene was destroyed after that. These two
gentlemen went on cracking jokes during the whole of the
subsequent performance, to their own amusement, but the
indignation of their company, and perhaps of the people in the
adjacent boxes. Young Douglas, in those days, used to wear
a white satin " shape " slashed at the legs and body, and when
Mr. Barry appeared in his droll costume, the General vowed it
was the exact dress of the Highlanders in the late war. The
Chevalier's Guard, he declared, had all white satin slashed
breeches, and red boots—" only they left them at home, my
dear," adds this wag. Not one pennyworth of sublimity would
he or George allow henceforth to Mr. Home's performance. As
for Harry, he sat in very deep meditation over the scene; and
when Mrs. Lambert offered him a penny for his thoughts, he
said, " That he thought Young Norval, Douglas, What-d'ye-
call-'im, the fellow in white satin—who looked as old as his
mother—was very lucky to be able to distinguish himself so soon.
I wish I could get a chance, Aunt Lambert," says he, drumming
on his hat; on which mamma sighed, and Theo, smiling, said,
" We must wait, and perhaps the Danes will land."

" How do you mean? " asks simple Harry.

" Oh, the Danes always land, pour qui sçait attendre! " says
kind Theo, who had hold of her sister's little hand and, I dare
say, felt its pressure.

She did not behave unkindly—that was not in Miss Theo's
nature—but somewhat coldly to Mr. George, on whom she
turned her back, addressing remarks, from time to time, to
Harry. In spite of the gentlemen's scorn, the women choose
to be affected. A mother and son, meeting in love and parting
in tears, will always awaken emotion in female hearts.

" Look, papa! there is an answer to all your jokes! " says
Theo, pointing towards the stage.

At a part of the dialogue between Lady Randolph and her
son, one of the grenadiers on guard on each side of the stage, as

the custom of those days was, could not restrain his tears, and was visibly weeping before the side-box.

" You are right, my dear," says papa.

" Didn't I tell you she always is? " interposes Hetty.

" Yonder sentry is a better critic than we are, and a touch of nature masters us all."

" Tamen usque recurrit! " cries the young student from college.

George felt abashed somehow, and interested, too. He had been sneering, and Theo sympathising. Her kindness was better—nay, wiser—than his scepticism, perhaps. Nevertheless, when, at the beginning of the fifth act of the play, young Douglas, drawing his sword and looking up at the gallery, bawled out—

> " Ye glorious stars! high heaven's resplendent host!
> To whom I oft have of my lot complained,
> Hear and record my soul's unaltered wish:
> Living or dead, let me but be renowned!
> May Heaven inspire some fierce gigantic Dane
> To give a bold defiance to our host!
> Before he speaks it out, I will accept,—
> Like Douglas conquer, or like Douglas die! "

—the gods, to whom Mr. Barry appealed, saluted this heroic wish with immense applause, and the General clapped his hands prodigiously. His daughter was rather disconcerted.

" This Douglas is not only brave, but he is modest! " says papa.

" I own I think he need not have asked for a gigantic Dane," says Theo, smiling, as Lady Randolph entered in the midst of the gallery thunder.

When the applause had subsided, Lady Randolph is made to say—

> " My son, I heard a voice! "

" I think she *did* hear a voice! " cries papa. " Why, the fellow was bellowing like a bull of Bashan." And the General would scarcely behave himself from thenceforth to the end of the performance. He said he was heartily glad that the young gentleman was put to death behind the scenes. When Lady Randolph's friend described how her mistress had " flown like lightning up the hill, and plunged herself into the empty air," Mr. Lambert said he was delighted to be rid of her. " And as for that story of her early marriage," says he, " I have my very strongest doubts about it."

"Nonsense, Martin! Look, children, their Royal Highnesses are moving."

The tragedy over, the Princess Dowager and the Prince were, in fact, retiring; though, I dare say, the latter, who was always fond of a farce, would have been far better pleased with that which followed, than he had been with Mr. Home's dreary tragic masterpiece.

CHAPTER LX

WHICH TREATS OF MACBETH, A SUPPER, AND A PRETTY KETTLE OF FISH

WHEN the performances were concluded, our friends took coach for Mr. Warrington's lodging, where the Virginians had provided an elegant supper. Mr. Warrington was eager to treat them in the handsomest manner, and the General and his wife accepted the invitation of the two bachelors, pleased to think that they could give their young friends pleasure. General and Mrs. Lambert, their son from college, their two blooming daughters, and Mr. Spencer of the Temple, a new friend, whom George had met at the coffee-house, formed the party, and partook with cheerfulness of the landlady's fare. The order of their sitting I have not been able exactly to ascertain; but, somehow, Miss Theo had a place next to the chickens and Mr. George Warrington, whilst Miss Hetty and a ham divided the attentions of Mr. Harry. Mrs. Lambert *must* have been on George's right hand, so that we have but to settle the three places of the General, his son, and the Templar.

Mr. Spencer had been at the other theatre, where, on a former day, he had actually introduced George to the green-room. The conversation about the play was resumed, and some of the party persisted in being delighted with it.

"As for what our gentlemen say, sir," cries Mrs. Lambert to Mr. Spencer, "you must not believe a word of it. 'Tis a delightful piece, and my husband and Mr. George behaved as ill as possible."

"We laughed in the wrong place, and when we ought to have cried," the General owned, "that's the truth."

"You caused all the people in the boxes about us to look round and cry, 'Hush!' You made the pit-folks say, 'Silence in the boxes, yonder!' Such behaviour I never knew, and quite blushed for you, Mr. Lambert!"

"Mamma thought it was a tragedy, and we thought it was a piece of fun," says the General. "George and I behaved perfectly well, didn't we, Theo?"

"Not when I was looking your way, papa!" Theo replies. At which the General asks, "Was there ever such a saucy baggage seen?"

"You know, sir, I didn't speak till I was bid," Theo continues modestly. "I own I was very much moved by the play, and the beauty and acting of Mrs. Woffington. I was sorry that the poor mother should find her child and lose him. I am sorry too, papa, if I oughtn't to have been sorry!" adds the young lady, with a smile.

"Women are not so clever as men, you know, Theo," cries Hetty from her end of the table, with a sly look at Harry. "The next time we go to the play, please, brother Jack, pinch us when we ought to cry, or give us a nudge when it is right to laugh."

"I wish we could have had the fight," said General Lambert —"the fight between little Norval and the gigantic Norwegian —that would have been rare sport: and you should write, Jack, and suggest it to Mr. Rich, the manager."

"I have not seen that: but I saw Slack and Broughton at Marybone Gardens!" says Harry gravely; and wondered if he had said something witty, as all the company laughed so. "It would require no giant," he added, "to knock over yonder little fellow in the red boots. I, for one, could throw him over my shoulder."

"Mr. Garrick is a little man. But there are times when he looks a giant," says Mr. Spencer. "How grand he was in Macbeth, Mr. Warrington! How awful that dagger-scene was! You should have seen our host, ladies! I presented Mr. Warrington, in the green-room, to Mr. Garrick and Mrs. Pritchard, and Lady Macbeth did him the honour to take a pinch out of his box."

"Did the wife of the Thane of Cawdor sneeze?" asked the General, in an awful voice.

"She thanked Mr. Warrington in tones so hollow and tragic, that he started back, and must have upset some of his rappee, for Macbeth sneezed thrice."

"Macbeth, Macbeth, Macbeth!" cries the General.

"And the great philosopher who was standing by,—Mr.

Johnson, says, 'You must mind, Davy, lest thy sneeze should awaken Duncan!' who, by the way, was talking with the three witches, as they sat against the wall."

"What! Have you been behind the scenes at the play? Oh, I would give worlds to go behind the scenes!" cries Theo.

"And see the ropes pulled, and smell the tallow-candles, and look at the pasteboard gold, and the tinsel jewels, and the painted old women, Theo? No, do not look too close," says the sceptical young host, demurely drinking a glass of hock. "You were angry with your papa and me."

"Nay, George!" cries the girl.

"Nay? I say, yes! You were angry with us because we laughed when you were disposed to be crying. If I may speak for you, sir, as well as myself," says George (with a bow to his guest, General Lambert), "I think we were not inclined to weep, like the ladies, because we stood behind the author's scenes of the play, as it were. Looking close up to the young hero, we saw how much of him was rant and tinsel; and as for the pale tragical mother, that her pallor was white chalk, and her grief her pocket-handkerchief. Own now, Theo, you thought me very unfeeling?"

"If you find it out, sir, without my owning it,—what is the good of my confessing?" says Theo.

"Suppose I were to die?" goes on George, "and you saw Harry in grief, you would be seeing a genuine affliction, a real tragedy: you would grieve too. But you wouldn't be affected if you saw the undertaker in weepers and a black cloak!"

"Indeed, but I should, sir!" says Mrs. Lambert; "and so, I promise you, would any daughter of mine."

"Perhaps we might find weepers of our own, Mr. Warrington," says Theo, "in such a case."

"Would you?" cries George, and his cheeks and Theo's simultaneously flushed up with red; I suppose because they both saw Hetty's bright young eyes watching them.

"The elder writers understood but little of the pathetic," remarked Mr. Spencer, the Temple wit.

"What do you think of Sophocles and Antigone?" calls out Mr. John Lambert.

"Faith, our wits trouble themselves little about *him*, unless an Oxford gentleman comes to remind us of him! I did not mean to go back further than Mr. Shakspeare, who, as you will all agree, does not understand the elegant and pathetic as well as the moderns. Has he ever approached Belvidera, or

Monimia, or Jane Shore; or can you find in his comic female characters the elegance of Congreve?" and the Templar offered snuff to the right and left.

"I think Mr. Spencer himself must have tried his hand?" asks some one.

"Many gentlemen of leisure have. Mr. Garrick, I own, has had a piece of mine, and returned it."

"And I confess that I have four acts of a play in one of my boxes," says George.

"I'll be bound to say it's as good as any of 'em," whispers Harry to his neighbour.

"Is it a tragedy or a comedy?" asks Mrs. Lambert.

"Oh, a tragedy, and two or three dreadful murders at least!" George replies.

"Let us play it, and let the audience look to their eyes! Yet my chief humour is for a tyrant," says the General.

"The tragedy, the tragedy! Go and fetch the tragedy this moment, Gumbo!" calls Mrs. Lambert to the black. Gumbo makes a low bow and says, "Tragedy? yes, madam."

"In the great cowskin trunk, Gumbo," George says gravely. Gumbo bows and says, "Yes, sir," with still superior gravity.

"But my tragedy is at the bottom of I don't know how much linen, packages, books, and boots, Hetty."

"Never mind, let us have it, and fling the linen out of window!" cries Miss Hetty.

"And the great cowskin trunk is at our agent's at Bristol: so Gumbo must get post-horses, and we can keep it up till he returns the day after to-morrow," says George.

The ladies groaned a comical "Oh!" and papa, perhaps, more seriously said: "Let us be thankful for the escape. Let us be thinking of going home too. Our young gentlemen have treated us nobly, and we will all drink a parting bumper to Madam Esmond Warrington of Castlewood, in Virginia. Suppose, boys, you were to find a tall handsome step-father when you got home? Ladies as old as she have been known to marry before now."

"To Madam Esmond Warrington, my old schoolfellow!" cries Mrs. Lambert. "I shall write and tell her what a pretty supper her sons have given us: and, Mr. George, I won't say how ill you behaved at the play!" And, with this last toast, the company took leave; the General's coach and servant, with a flambeau, being in waiting to carry his family home.

After such an entertainment as that which Mr. Warrington had given, what could be more natural or proper than a visit from him to his guests, to inquire how they had reached home and rested? Why, their coach might have taken the open country behind Montagu House, in the direction of Oxford Road, and been waylaid by footpads in the fields. The ladies might have caught cold or slept ill after the excitement of the tragedy. In a word, there was no reason why he should make any excuse at all to himself or them for visiting his kind friends; and he shut his books early at the Sloane Museum, and perhaps thought, as he walked away thence, that he remembered very little about what he had been reading.

Pray what is the meaning of this eagerness, this hesitation, this pshaing and shilly-shallying, these doubts, this tremor as he knocks at the door of Mr. Lambert's lodgings in Dean Street, and surveys the footman who comes to his summons? Does any young man read? does any old one remember? does any wearied, worn, disappointed pulseless heart recall the time of its full beat and early throbbing? It is ever so many hundred years since some of us were young; and we forget, but do not all forget. No, madam, we remember with advantages, as Shakspeare's Harry promised his soldiers they should do if they survived Agincourt and that day of St. Crispin. Worn old chargers turned out to grass, if the trumpet sounds over the hedge, may we not kick up our old heels, and gallop a minute or so about the paddock, till we are brought up roaring? I do not care for clown and pantaloon now, and think the fairy ugly, and her verses insufferable: but I like to see children at a pantomime. I do not dance, or eat supper any more; but I like to watch Eugenio and Flirtilla twirling round in a pretty waltz, or Lucinda and Ardentio pulling a cracker. Burn your little fingers, children! Blaze out little kindly flames from each other's eyes! And then draw close together and read the motto (that old namby-pamby motto, so stale and so new!)—I say, let her lips read it and his construe it; and so divide the sweetmeat, young people, and crunch it between you. I have no teeth. Bitter almonds and sugar disagree with me, I tell you; but, for all that, shall not bon-bons melt in the mouth?

We follow John upstairs to the General's apartments, and enter with Mr. George Esmond Warrington, who makes a prodigious fine bow. There is only one lady in the room, seated near a window: there is not often much sunshine in Dean Street: the young lady in the window is no special beauty: but it is spring-time, and she is blooming vernally. A bunch of fresh roses is flushing in her cheek. I suppose her eyes are violets. If we lived a hundred years ago, and wrote in the "Gentleman's" or the "London Magazine," we should tell Mr. Sylvanus Urban that her neck was the lily, and her shape the nymph's; we should write an acrostic about her, and celebrate our Lambertella in an elegant poem, still to be read between a neat new engraved plan of the city of Prague and the King of Prussia's camp, and a map of Maryland and the Delaware counties.

Here is Miss Theo blushing like a rose. What could mamma have meant an hour since by insisting that she was very pale and tired, and had best not come out to-day with the rest of the party? They were gone to pay their compliments to my Lord Wrotham's ladies, and thank them for the house in their absence; and papa was at the Horse Guards. He is in great spirits. I believe he expects some command, though mamma is in a sad tremor lest he should again be ordered abroad.

"Your brother and mine are going to see our little brother at his school at the Chartreux. My brothers are both to be clergymen, I think," Miss Theo continues. She is assiduously hemming at some article of boyish wearing-apparel as she talks. A hundred years ago, young ladies were not afraid either to make shirts, or to name them. Mind, I don't say they were the worse or the better for that plain stitching or plain speaking: and have not the least desire, my dear young lady, that you should make puddings, or I should black boots.

So Harry has been with them? "He often comes, almost every day," Theo says, looking up in George's face. "Poor fellow! He likes us better than the fine folks, who don't care for him now—now he is no longer a fine folk himself," adds the girl, smiling. "Why have you not set up for the fashion, and frequented the chocolate-houses and the race-courses, Mr. Warrington?"

"Has my brother got so much good out of his gay haunts or his grand friends, that I should imitate him?"

"You might at least go to Sir Miles Warrington; sure his arms are open to receive you. Her Ladyship was here this morning in her chair, and to hear her praises of you! She declares you are in a certain way to preferment. She says His Royal Highness the Duke made much of you at Court. When you are a great man, will you forget us, Mr. Warrington?"

"Yes, when I am a great man I will, Miss Lambert."

"Well! Mr. George, then——"

" *Mr.* George! "

" When papa and mamma are here, I suppose there need be no mistering," says Theo, looking out of the window, ever so little frightened. " And what have you been doing, sir? Reading books, or writing more of your tragedy? Is it going to be a tragedy to make us cry, as we like them, or only to frighten us, as *you* like them? "

" There is plenty of killing, but, I fear, not much crying. I have not met many women. I have not been very intimate with those. I daresay what I have written is only taken out of books or parodied from poems which I have read and imitated like other young men. Women do not speak to me, generally; I am said to have a sarcastic way which displeases them."

" Perhaps you never cared to please them? " inquires Miss Theo, with a blush.

" I displeased you last night; you know I did? "

" Yes; only it can't be called displeasure, and afterwards I thought I was wrong."

" Did you think about me at all when I was away, Theo? "

" Yes, George—that is, Mr.—well, George! I thought you and papa were right about the play; and, as you said, that it was not real sorrow, only affectation, which was moving us. I wonder whether it is good or ill fortune to see so clearly? Hetty and I agreed that we would be very careful, for the future, how we allowed ourselves to enjoy a tragedy. So, be careful when yours comes! What is the name of it? "

" He is not christened. Will you be the godmother? The name of the chief character is——" But at this very moment mamma and Miss Hetty arrived from their walk; and mamma straightway began protesting that she never expected to see Mr. Warrington at all that day—that is, she thought he might come—that is, it was very good of him to come, and the play and the supper of yesterday were all charming, except that Theo had a little headache this morning.

" I dare say it is better now, mamma," says Miss Hetty.

" Indeed, my dear, it never was of any consequence; and I told mamma so," says Miss Theo, with a toss of her head.

Then they fell to talking about Harry. He was very low. He must have something to do. He was always going to the Military Coffee-house, and perpetually poring over the King of Prussia's campaigns. It was not fair upon him, to bid him remain in London, after his deposition, as it were. He said nothing, but you could see how he regretted his previous useless life, and felt his present dependence, by the manner in which he avoided his former haunts and associates. Passing by the guard at St. James's, with John Lambert, he had said to brother Jack, " Why mayn't I be a soldier too? I am as tall as yonder fellow, and can kill with a fowling-piece as well as any man I know. But I can't earn so much as sixpence a day. I have squandered my own bread, and now I am eating half my brother's. He is the best of brothers, but so much the more shame that I should live upon him. Don't tell my brother, Jack Lambert." " And my boy promised he *wouldn't* tell," says Mrs. Lambert. No doubt. The girls were both out of the room when their mother made this speech to George Warrington. He, for his part, said he had written home to his mother—that half his little patrimony, the other half likewise, if wanted, were at Harry's disposal, for purchasing a commission, or for any other project which might bring him occupation or advancement.

" He *has* got a good brother, that is sure. Let us hope for good times for him," sighs the lady.

" The Danes always come pour qui sçait attendre," George said, in a low voice.

" What, you heard that? Ah, George! my Theo is an—— Ah! never mind *what* she is, George Warrington," cried the pleased mother, with brimful eyes. " Bah! I am going to make a gaby of myself, as I did at the tragedy."

Now Mr. George had been revolving a fine private scheme, which he thought might turn to his brother's advantage. After George's presentation to His Royal Highness at Kensington, more persons than one, his friend General Lambert included, had told him that the Duke had inquired regarding him, and had asked why the young man did not come to his levée. Importunity so august could not but be satisfied. A day was appointed between Mr. Lambert and his young friend, and they went to pay their duty to His Royal Highness at his house in Pall Mall.

When it came to George's turn to make a bow, the Prince was especially gracious; he spoke to Mr. Warrington at some length about Braddock and the war, and was apparently pleased with the modesty and intelligence of the young gentleman's answers. George ascribed the failure of the expedition to the panic and surprise certainly, but more especially to the delays occasioned by the rapacity, selfishness, and unfair dealing of the people of the colonies towards the King's troops who were come to defend them. "Could we have moved, sir, a month sooner, the fort was certainly ours, and the little army had never been defeated," Mr. Warrington said; in which observation His Royal Highness entirely concurred.

"I am told you saved yourself, sir, mainly by your knowledge of the French language," the Royal Duke then affably observed. Mr. Warrington modestly mentioned how he had been in the French colonies in his youth, and had opportunities of acquiring that tongue.

The Prince (who had a great urbanity when well pleased, and the finest sense of humour) condescended to ask who had taught Mr. Warrington the language; and to express his opinion, that, for the pronunciation, the French ladies were by far the best teachers.

The young Virginian gentleman made a low bow, and said it was not for him to gainsay His Royal Highness; upon which the Duke was good enough to say (in a jocose manner) that Mr. Warrington was a sly dog.

Mr. W. remaining respectfully silent, the Prince continued most kindly: "I take the field immediately against the French, who, as you know, are threatening His Majesty's Electoral dominions. If you have a mind to make the campaign with me, your skill in the language may be useful, and I hope we shall be more fortunate than poor Braddock!" Every eye was fixed on a young man to whom so great a Prince offered so signal a favour.

And now it was that Mr. George thought he would make his very cleverest speech. "Sir," he said, "your Royal Highness's most kind proposal does me infinite honour, but——"

"But what, sir?" says the Prince, staring at him.

"But I have entered myself of the Temple, to study our laws, and to fit myself for my duties at home. If my having been wounded in the service of my country be any claim on your kindness, I would humbly ask that my brother, who knows the French language as well as myself, and has far more strength, courage, and military genius, might be allowed to serve your Royal Highness in the place of——"

"Enough, enough, sir!" cried out the justly irritated son of the monarch. "What? I offer you a favour, and you hand it over to your brother? Wait, sir, till I offer you another!" And with this the Prince turned his back upon Mr. Warrington, just as abruptly as he turned it on the French a few months afterwards.

"Oh, George! oh, George! Here's a pretty kettle of fish!" groaned General Lambert, as he and his young friend walked home together.

CHAPTER LXI

IN WHICH THE PRINCE MARCHES UP THE HILL AND DOWN AGAIN

WE understand the respectful indignation of all loyal Britons when they come to read of Mr. George Warrington's conduct towards a gallant and gracious Prince, the beloved son of the best of monarchs, and the Captain-General of the British army. What an inestimable favour has not the young man slighted! What a chance of promotion had he not thrown away! Will Esmond, whose language was always rich in blasphemies, employed his very strongest curses in speaking of his cousin's behaviour, and expressed his delight that the confounded young Mohock was cutting his own throat. Cousin Castlewood said that a savage gentleman had a right to scalp himself if he liked: or perhaps, he added charitably, our cousin Mr. Warrington heard enough of the war-whoop in Braddock's affair, and has no more stomach for fighting. Mr. Will rejoiced that the younger brother had gone to the deuce, and he rejoiced to think that the elder was following him. The first time he met the fellow, Will said, he should take care to let Mr. George know what he thought of him.

"If you intend to insult George, at least you had best take care that his brother Harry is out of hearing!" cried Lady Maria —on which we may fancy more curses uttered by Mr. Will, with regard to his twin kinsfolk.

"Ta, ta, ta!" says my Lord. "No more of this squabbling! We can't be all warriors in the family!"

"I never heard your Lordship laid claim to be one!" says Maria.

"Never, my dear; quite the contrary! Will is our champion, and one is quite enough in the house. So I dare say with the two Mohocks:—George is the student, and Harry is the fighting man. When you intended to quarrel, Will, what a pity it was you had not George, instead of t'other, to your hand!"

"Your Lordship's hand is famous—at picquet," says Will's mother.

"It *is* a pretty one!" says my Lord, surveying his fingers, with a simper. "My Lord Hervey's glove and mine were of a size. Yes, my hand, as you say, is more fitted for cards than for war. Yours, my Lady Castlewood, is pretty dexterous, too. How I bless the day when you bestowed it on my lamented father!" In this play of sarcasm, as in some other games of skill, his Lordship was not sorry to engage, having a cool head, and being able to beat his family all round.

Madame de Bernstein, when she heard of Mr. Warrington's *bévue*, was exceedingly angry, stormed, and scolded her immediate household; and would have scolded George, but she was growing old, and had not the courage of her early days. Moreover, she was a little afraid of her nephew, and respectful in her behaviour to him. "You will never make your fortune at Court, nephew!" she groaned, when, soon after his discomfiture, the young gentleman went to wait upon her.

"It was never my wish, madam!" said Mr. George, in a very stately manner.

"Your wish was to help Harry? You might hereafter have been of service to your brother, had you accepted the Duke's offer. Princes do not love to have their favours refused, and I don't wonder that His Royal Highness was offended."

"General Lambert said the same thing," George confessed, turning rather red; "and I see now that I was wrong. But you must please remember that I had never seen a Court before, and I suppose I am scarce likely to shine in one."

"I think possibly not, my good nephew," says the aunt, taking snuff.

"And what then?" asked George. "I never had ambition for that kind of glory, and can make myself quite easy without it. When his Royal Highness spoke to me—most kindly, as I own—my thought was, I shall make a very bad soldier, and my brother would be a very good one. He has a hundred good qualities for the profession, in which I am deficient; and would have served a Commanding Officer far better than I ever could. Say the Duke is in battle, and his horse is shot, as my poor chief's was at home, would he not be better for a beast that had courage and strength to bear him anywhere, than with one that could not carry his weight?"

"*Au fait.* His Royal Highness's charger must be a strong one, my dear!" says the old lady.

"Expende Hannibalem," mutters George, with a shrug. "*Our* Hannibal weighs no trifle."

"I don't quite follow you, sir, and your Hannibal," the Baroness remarks.

"When Mr. Wolfe and Mr. Lambert remonstrated with me as you have done, madam," George rejoins, with a laugh, "I made this same defence which I am making to you. I said I offered to the Prince the best soldier in the family, and the two gentlemen allowed that my blunder at least had some excuse. Who knows but that they may set me right with His Royal Highness? The taste I have had of battles has shown me how little my genius inclines that way. We saw the Scotch play which everybody is talking about t'other night. And when the hero, young Norval, said how he longed to follow to the field some warlike lord, I thought to myself, 'How like my Harry is to him, except that he doth not brag!' Harry is pining now for a red coat, and if we don't mind, will take the shilling. He has the map of Germany for ever under his eyes, and follows the King of Prussia everywhere. He is not afraid of men or gods. As for me, I love my books and quiet best, and to read about battles in Homer or Lucan."

"Then what made a soldier of you at all, my dear? And why did you not send Harry with Mr. Braddock, instead of going yourself?" asked Madame de Bernstein.

"My mother loved her younger son the best," said George darkly. "Besides, with the enemy invading our country, it was my duty, as the head of our family, to go on the campaign. Had I been a Scotchman twelve years ago, I should have been a——"

"Hush, sir! or I shall be more angry than ever!" said the old lady, with a perfectly pleased face.

George's explanation might thus appease Madame de Bernstein, an old woman whose principles, we fear, were but loose: but to the loyal heart of Sir Miles Warrington and his lady, the young man's conduct gave a severe blow indeed! "I should have thought," her Ladyship said, "from my sister Esmond Warrington's letter, that my brother's widow was a woman of good sense and judgment, and that she had educated her sons in a becoming manner. But what, Sir Miles, what, my dear Thomas Claypool, can we think of an education which has resulted so lamentably for both these young men?"

"The elder seems to know a power of Latin, though, and speaks the French and the German, too. I heard him with the Hanover Envoy, at the Baroness's rout," says Mr. Claypool. "The French he jabbered quite easy: and when he was at a loss for the High Dutch, he and the Envoy began in Latin, and talked away till all the room stared."

"It is not language, but principles, Thomas Claypool!" exclaims the virtuous matron. "What must Mr. Warrington's principles be, when he could reject an offer made him by his Prince? Can he speak the High Dutch? So much the more ought he to have accepted His Royal Highness's condescension, and made himself useful in the campaign! Look at our son, look at Miles!"

"Hold up thy head, Miley my boy!" says papa.

"I trust, Sir Miles, that, as a member of the House of Commons, as an English gentleman, you will attend His Royal Highness's levée to-morrow, and say, if such an offer had been made to us for that child, we would have taken it, though our boy is but ten years of age."

"Faith, Miley, thou wouldst make a good little drummer or fifer!" says papa. "Shouldst like to be a little soldier, Miley?"

"Anything, sir, anything! a Warrington ought to be ready at any moment to have himself cut in pieces for his sovereign!" cries the matron, pointing to the boy; who, as soon as he comprehended his mother's proposal, protested against it by a loud roar, in the midst of which he was removed by Screwby. In obedience to the conjugal orders, Sir Miles went to His Royal Highness's levée the next day, and made a protest of his love and duty, which the Prince deigned to accept, saying—

"Nobody ever supposed that Sir Miles Warrington would ever refuse any place offered to him."

A compliment gracious indeed, and repeated everywhere by Lady Warrington, as showing how implicitly the august family on the throne could rely on the loyalty of the Warringtons.

Accordingly, when this worthy couple saw George, they received him with a ghastly commiseration, such as our dear relatives or friends will sometimes extend to us when we have done something fatal or clumsy in life: when we have come badly out of our lawsuit; when we enter the room just as the company has been abusing us; when our banker has broke; or we for our sad part have had to figure in the commercial columns of the *London Gazette*; when, in a word, we are guilty of some notorious fault, or blunder, or misfortune. Who does not know that face of pity? Whose dear relations have not so deplored him, not dead, but living? Not yours? Then, sir, if you have never been in scrapes; if you have never sowed a handful of wild oats or two; if you have always been fortunate, and good, and careful, and butter has never melted in your mouth, and an imprudent word has never come out of it; if you have never sinned and repented, and been a fool and been sorry—then, sir, you are a wiseacre who won't waste your time over an idle novel, and it is not *de te* that the fable is narrated.

Not that it was just on Sir Miles's part to turn upon George, and be angry with his nephew for refusing the offer of promotion made by His Royal Highness, for Sir Miles himself had agreed in George's view of pursuing quite other than a military career, and it was in respect to this plan of her son's that Madam Esmond had written from Virginia to Sir Miles Warrington. George had announced to her his intention of entering at the Temple, and qualifying himself for the magisterial and civil duties which, in the course of nature, he would be called to fulfil; nor could any one applaud his resolution more cordially than his uncle Sir Miles, who introduced George to a lawyer of reputation, under whose guidance we may fancy the young gentleman reading leisurely. Madam Esmond from home signified her approval of her son's course, fully agreeing with Sir Miles (to whom and his lady she begged to send her grateful remembrances) that the British Constitution was the envy of the world, and the proper object of every English gentleman's admiring study. The chief point to which George's mother objected was the notion that Mr. Warrington should have to sit down in the Temple dinner-hall, and cut at a shoulder of mutton, and drink small-beer out of tin pannikins, by the side of rough students who wore gowns like the parish-clerk. George's loyal younger brother shared, too, this repugnance. Anything was good enough for *him*, Harry said; he was a younger son, and prepared to rough it; but George in a gown, and dining in a mess with three nobody's sons off dirty pewter platters! Harry never could relish this condescension on his brother's part, or fancy George in his proper place at any except the high table; and was sorry that a plan Madam Esmond hinted at in her letters was not feasible—viz., that an application should be made to the Master of the Temple, who should be informed that Mr. George Warrington was a gentleman of most noble birth, and of great property in America, and ought only to sit *with the very best company* in the Hall. Rather to Harry's discomfiture, when he communicated his own and his mother's ideas to the gentlemen's new coffee-house friend Mr. Spencer, Mr. Spencer received the proposal with roars of laughter; and I cannot learn, from the Warrington papers, that any application was made to the Master of the Temple on this subject. Besides his literary and historical pursuits, which were those he most especially loved, Mr. Warrington studied the laws of his country, attended the courts at Westminster, where he heard a Henley, a Pratt, a Murray, and those other great famous schools of eloquence and patriotism, the two houses of Parliament.

Gradually Mr. Warrington made acquaintance with some of the members of the House and the Bar; who, when they came to know him, spoke of him as a young gentleman of good parts and good breeding, and in terms so generally complimentary that his good uncle's heart relented towards him, and Dora and Flora began once more to smile upon him. This reconciliation dated from the time when His Royal Highness the Duke, after having been defeated by the French, in the affair of Hastenbeck, concluded the famous capitulation with the French, which His Majesty George the Second refused to ratify. His Royal Highness, as 'tis well known, flung up his commissions after this disgrace, laid down his commander's baton — which, it must be confessed, he had not wielded with much luck or dexterity—and never again appeared at the head of armies or in public life. The stout warrior would not allow a word of complaint against his father and sovereign to escape his lips; but, as he retired with his wounded honour, and as he would have no interest or authority more, nor any places to give, it may be supposed that Sir Miles Warrington's anger against his nephew diminished as his respect for His Royal Highness diminished.

As our two gentlemen were walking in St. James's Park, one day, with their friend Mr. Lambert, they met His Royal Highness in plain clothes and without a star, and made profound bows to the Prince, who was pleased to stop and speak to them.

He asked Mr. Lambert how he liked my Lord Ligonier, his new chief at the Horse Guards, and the new duties there in which he was engaged? And, recognising the young men, with that fidelity of memory for which his Royal race hath ever been remarkable, he said to Mr. Warrington—

" You did well, sir, not to come with me when I asked you in the spring."

" I was sorry, then, sir," Mr. Warrington said, making a very low reverence, " but I am more sorry now."

On which the Prince said, " Thank you, sir," and touching

his hat, walked away. And the circumstances of this interview, and the discourse which passed at it, being related to Mrs. Esmond Warrington in a letter from her younger son, created so deep an impression in that lady's mind, that she narrated the anecdote many hundreds of times until all her friends and acquaintances knew, and, perhaps, were tired of it.

Our gentlemen went through the Park, and so towards the Strand, where they had business. And Mr. Lambert, pointing to the lion on the top of the Earl of Northumberland's house at Charing Cross, says—

" Harry Warrington! your brother is like yonder lion."

" Because he is as brave as one," says Harry.

" Because I respect virgins! " says George, laughing.

" Because you are a stupid lion. Because you turn your back on the East, and absolutely salute the setting sun. Why, child, what earthly good can you get by being civil to a man in hopeless dudgeon and disgrace? Your uncle will be more angry with you than ever—and so am I, sir." But Mr. Lambert was always laughing in his waggish way, and, indeed, he did not look the least angry.

CHAPTER LXII

ARMA VIRUMQUE

INDEED, if Harry Warrington had a passion for military pursuits and studies, there was enough of war stirring in Europe, and enough talk in all societies which he frequented in London, to excite and inflame him. Though our own gracious Prince of the house of Hanover had been beaten, the Protestant Hero, the King of Prussia, was filling the world with his glory, and winning those astonishing victories, in which I deem it fortunate on my own account that my poor Harry took no part; for then his veracious biographer would have had to narrate battles the description whereof has been undertaken by another pen. I am glad, I say, that Harry Warrington was not at Rossbach on that famous Gunpowder Fête-day, on the 5th of November, in the year 1757; nor at that tremendous slaughtering-match at Leuthen, which the Prussian King played a month afterwards; for these prodigious actions will presently be narrated in other volumes, which I and all the world are eager to behold. Would

you have this history compete with yonder book? Could my
jaunty yellow park-phaeton run counter to that grim chariot of
thundering war? Could my meek little jog-trot Pegasus meet
the shock of yon steed of foaming bit and flaming nostril?
Dear kind reader (with whom I love to talk from time to time,
stepping down from the stage where our figures are performing,
attired in the habits and using the parlance of past ages),—my
kind patient reader! it is a mercy for both of us that Harry
Warrington did not follow the King of the Borussians, as he
was minded to do, for then I should have had to describe battles
which Carlyle is going to paint: and I don't wish you should
make odious comparisons between me and that master.

Harry Warrington not only did not join the King of the
Borussians, but he pined and chafed at not going. He led a
sulky useless life, that is the fact. He dangled about the
military coffee-houses. He did not care for reading anything
save a newspaper. His turn was not literary. He even thought
novels were stupid; and, as for the ladies crying their eyes out
over Mr. Richardson, he could not imagine how they could be
moved by any such nonsense. He used to laugh in a very
hearty jolly way, but a little late, and some time after the joke
was over. Pray, why should all gentlemen have a literary
taste? and do we like some of our friends the worse because
they never turned a couplet in their lives? Ruined, perforce
idle, dependent on his brother for supplies, if he read a book
falling asleep over it, with no fitting work for his great strong
hands to do—how lucky it is that he did not get into more
trouble. Why, in the case of Achilles himself, when he was
sent by his mamma to the court of King What-d'ye-call-'im
in order to be put out of harm's reach, what happened to him
amongst a parcel of women with whom he was made to idle his
life away? And how did Pyrrhus come into the world? A
powerful mettlesome young Achilles ought not to be leading-
stringed by women too much; is out of his place dawdling by
distaffs or handing coffee-cups; and when he is not fighting,
depend on it, is likely to fall into much worse mischief.

Those soft-hearted women, the two elder ladies of the
Lambert family, with whom he mainly consorted, had an untiring pity and kindness for Harry, such as women only—and
only a few of those—can give. If a man is in grief, who cheers
him? in trouble, who consoles him? in wrath, who soothes
him? in joy, who makes him doubly happy? in prosperity, who
rejoices? in disgrace, who backs him against the world, and

dresses with gentle unguents and warm poultices the rankling wounds made by the slings and arrows of outrageous Fortune? Who, but woman, if you please? You who are ill and sore from the buffets of Fate, have you one or two of these sweet physicians? Return thanks to the gods that they have left you so much of consolation. What gentleman is not more or less a Prometheus! Who has not his rock (ai, ai), his chain (ea, ea), and his liver in a deuce of a condition? But the sea-nymphs come—the gentle, the sympathising; they kiss our writhing feet; they moisten our parched lips with their tears; they do their blessed best to console us Titans; *they* don't turn their backs upon us after our overthrow.

Now Theo and her mother were full of pity for Harry; but Hetty's heart was rather hard and seemingly savage towards him. She chafed that his position was not more glorious; she was angry that he was still dependent and idle. The whole world was in arms, and could he not carry a musket? It was harvest time, and hundreds of thousands of reapers were out with their flashing sickles: could he not use his, and cut down his sheaf or two of glory?

"Why, how savage the little thing is with him!" says papa, after a scene in which, according to her wont, Miss Hetty had been firing little shots into that quivering target which came and set itself up in Mrs. Lambert's drawing-room every day.

"Her conduct is perfectly abominable!" cries mamma; "she deserves to be whipped, and sent to bed."

"Perhaps, mother, it is because she likes him better than any of us do," says Theo, "and it is for his sake that Hetty is angry. If I were fond of—of some one, I should like to be able to admire and respect him always—to think everything he did right—and my gentleman better than all the gentlemen in the world!"

"The truth is, my dear," answers Mrs. Lambert, "that your father is so much better than all the world, he has spoiled us. Did you ever see any one to compare with him?"

"Very few indeed," owns Theo, with a blush.

"Very few. Who is so good-tempered?"

"I think nobody, mamma," Theo acknowledges.

"Or so brave?"

"Why, I dare say, Mr. Wolfe, or Harry, or Mr. George are very brave."

"Or so learned and witty?"

"I am sure Mr. George seems very learned, and witty too, in

his way," says Theo; "and his manners are very fine—you own they are. Madame de Bernstein says they are, and she hath seen the world. Indeed, Mr. George has a lofty way with him, which I don't see in other people; and in reading books, I find he chooses the fine noble things always, and loves them in spite of all his satire. He certainly is of a satirical turn, but then he is only bitter against mean things and people. No gentleman hath a more tender heart, I am sure; and but yesterday, after he had been talking so bitterly as you said, I happened to look out of window, and saw him stop and treat a whole crowd of little children to apples at the stall at the corner. And the day before yesterday, when he was coming and brought me the Molière, he stopped and gave money to a beggar, and how charmingly, sure, he reads the French! I agree with him though about Tartuffe, though 'tis so wonderfully clever and lively, that a mere villain and hypocrite is a figure too mean to be made the chief of a great piece. Iago, Mr. George said, is near as great a villain; but then he is not the first character of the tragedy, which is Othello, with his noble weakness. But what fine ladies and gentlemen Molière represents,—so Mr. George thinks—and—but oh, I don't dare to repeat the verses after *him*."

"But you know them by heart, my dear?" asks Mrs. Lambert.

And Theo replies, "O yes, mamma! I know them by—— Nonsense!"

I here fancy osculations, palpitations, and exit Miss Theo, blushing like a rose. Why had she stopped in her sentence? Because mamma was looking at her so oddly. And why was mamma looking at her so oddly? And why had she looked after Mr. George, when he was going away, and looked for him when he was coming! Ah, and why do cheeks blush, and why do roses bloom? Old Time is still a-flying. Old spring and bud time; old summer and bloom time: old autumn and seed time; old winter time when the cracking shivering old tree-tops are bald or covered with snow.

A few minutes after George arrived, Theo would come downstairs with a fluttering heart, may be, and a sweet nosegay in her cheeks, just culled, as it were, fresh in his honour; and I suppose she must have been constantly at that window which commanded the street, and whence she could espy his generosity to the sweep, or his purchases from the apple-woman. But if it was Harry who knocked, she remained in her own apartment

with her work or her books, sending her sister to receive the
young gentleman, or her brothers when the elder was at home
from college, or Doctor Crusius from the Chartreux gave the
younger leave to go home. And what good eyes Theo must
have had—and often in the evening, too—to note the difference
between Harry's yellow hair and George's dark locks, and
between their figures, though they were so like that people
continually were mistaking one for the other brother. Now
it is certain that Theo never mistook one or t'other; and that
Hetty, for her part, was not in the least excited, or rude, or
pert, when she found the black-haired gentleman in her mother's
drawing-room.

Our friends could come when they liked to Mr. Lambert's
house, and stay as long as they chose; and, one day, he of the
golden locks was sitting on a couch there, in an attitude of
more than ordinary idleness and despondency, when who should
come down to him but Miss Hetty? I say it was a most curious
thing (though the girls would have gone to the rack rather
than own any collusion), that when Harry called, Hetty appeared; when George arrived, Theo somehow came; and so,
according to the usual dispensation, it was Miss Lambert,
junior, who now arrived to entertain the younger Virginian.

After usual ceremonies and compliments, we may imagine
that the lady says to the gentleman—

"And pray, sir, what makes your honour look so glum this
morning?"

"Ah, Hetty!" says he. "I have nothing else to do but to
look glum. I remember when we were boys—and I a rare idle
one, you may be sure—I would always be asking my tutor for
a holiday, which I would pass very likely swinging on a gate,
or making ducks and drakes over the pond, and those do-nothing
days were always the most melancholy. What have I got to
do now from morning till night?"

"Breakfast, walk—dinner, walk—tea, supper, I suppose;
and a pipe of your Virginia," says Miss Hetty, tossing her
head.

"I tell you what, when I went back with Charley to the
Chartreux t'other night, I had a mind to say to the master,
'Teach me, sir. Here's a boy knows a deal more Latin and
Greek, at thirteen, than I do, who am ten years older. I have
nothing to do from morning till night, and I might as well go
to my books again, and see if I can repair my idleness as a
boy.' Why do you laugh, Hetty?"

" I laugh to fancy you at the head of a class, and called up by the master! " cries Hetty.

" I shouldn't be at the head of the class," Harry says humbly. " George might be at the head of any class, but I am not a book-man, you see; and when I was young, neglected myself, and was very idle. We would not let our tutors cane us much at home, but, if we had, it might have done me good."

Hetty drubbed with her little foot, and looked at the young man sitting before her—strong, idle, melancholy.

" Upon my word, it might do you good now! " she was minded to say. " What does Charley say about the caning at school? Does his account of it set you longing for it, pray? " she asked.

" His account of his school," Harry answered simply, " makes me see that I have been idle when I ought to have worked, and that I have not a genius for books, and for what am I good? Only to spend my patrimony when I come abroad, or to lounge at coffee-houses or race-courses, or to gallop behind dogs when I am at home. I am good for nothing, I am."

" What, such a great, brave, strong fellow as you good for nothing? " cries Het. " I would not confess as much to any woman, if I were *twice* as good for nothing! "

" What am I to do? I ask for leave to go into the army, and Madam Esmond does not answer me. 'Tis the only thing I am fit for. I have no money to buy. Having spent all my own, and so much of my brother's, I cannot and won't ask for more. If my mother would but send me to the army, you know I would jump to go."

" Eh! A gentleman of spirit does not want a woman to buckle his sword on for him, or to clean his firelock! What was that our papa told us of the young gentleman at Court yesterday? Sir John Armytage——"

" Sir John Armytage? I used to know him when I frequented White's and the club-houses—a fine noble young gentleman, of a great estate in the North."

" And engaged to be married to a famous beauty, too—Miss Howe, my Lord Howe's sister—but *that*, I suppose, is not an obstacle to gentlemen? "

" An obstacle to what? " asks the gentleman.

" An obstacle to glory! " says Miss Hetty. " I think no woman of spirit would stay 'Stay!' though she adored her lover ever so much, when his country said 'Go!' Sir John had volunteered for the expedition which is preparing, and being at Court yesterday His Majesty asked him when he would be ready to go? 'To-morrow, please your Majesty,' replies Sir John, and the King said that was a soldier's answer. My father himself is longing to go, though he has mamma and all us brats at home. O dear, O dear! Why wasn't I a man myself. Both my brothers are for the Church; but, as for me, I know I should have made a famous little soldier!" And so speaking, this young person strode about the room, wearing a most courageous military aspect, and looking as bold as Joan of Arc.

Harry beheld her with a tender admiration. "I think," says he, "I would hardly like to see a musket on that little shoulder, nor a wound on that pretty face, Hetty."

"Wounds! who fears wounds?" cries the little maid. "Muskets? If I could carry one, I would use it. You men fancy that we women are good for nothing but to make puddings or stitch samplers. Why wasn't I a man, I say. George was reading to us yesterday out of Tasso—look, here it is, and I thought the verses applied to me. See! Here is the book, with the mark in it where we left off."

"With the mark in it?" says Harry dutifully.

"Yes! it is about a woman who is disappointed because—because her brother does not go to war, and she says of herself—

> "'Alas! why did not Heaven these members frail
> With lively force and vigour strengthen, so
> That I this silken gown . . .'"

"Silken gown?" says downright Harry, with a look of inquiry.

"Well, sir, I know 'tis but calimanco;—but so it is in the book—

> "'. . . this silken gown and slender veil
> Might for a breastplate and a helm forego;
> Then should not heat, nor cold, nor rain, nor hail,
> Nor storms that fall, nor blust'ring winds that blow,
> Withhold me; but I would, both day and night,
> In pitched field or private combat fight'——

Fight? Yes, that I would! Why are both my brothers to be parsons, I say? One of my papa's children ought to be a soldier!"

Harry laughed, a very gentle kind of laugh, as he looked at her. He felt that he would not like much to hit such a tender little warrior as that.

"Why," says he, holding a finger out, "I think here is a finger nigh as big as your arm. How would you stand up before a great strong man? I should like to see a man try and injure you, though; I should just like to see him! You little, delicate, tender creature! Do you suppose any scoundrel would dare to do anything unkind to *you*?" And, excited by this flight of his imagination, Harry fell to walking up and down the room, too, chafing at the idea of any rogue of a Frenchman daring to be rude to Miss Hester Lambert.

It was a belief in this silent courage of his which subjugated Hetty, and this quality which she supposed him to possess, which caused her specially to admire him. Miss Hetty was no more bold, in reality, than Madam Erminia, whose speech she had been reading out of the book, and about whom Mr. Harry Warrington never heard one single word. He may have been in the room when brother George was reading his poetry out to the ladies, but his thoughts were busy with his own affairs, and he was entirely bewildered with your Clotildas and Erminias, and giants, and enchanters, and nonsense. No, Miss Hetty, I say and believe, had nothing of the virago in her composition; else, no doubt, she would have taken a fancy to a soft young fellow with a literary turn, or a genius for playing the flute, according to the laws of contrast and nature provided in those cases; and who has not heard how great strong men have an affinity for frail tender little women; how tender little women are attracted by great honest strong men; and how your burly heroes and champions of war are constantly henpecked? *If* Mr. Harry Warrington falls in love with a woman who is like Miss Lambert in disposition, and if he marries her—without being conjurors, I think we may all see what the end will be.

So, whilst Hetty was firing her little sarcasms into Harry, he for a while scarcely felt that they were stinging him, and let her shoot on without so much as taking the trouble to shake the little arrows out of his hide. Did she mean by her sneers and innuendoes to rouse him into action? He was too magnanimous to understand such small hints. Did she mean to shame him by saying that she, a weak woman, would don the casque and breastplate? The simple fellow either melted at the idea of her being in danger, or at the notion of her fighting fell a-laughing.

" Pray what is the use of having a strong hand if you only use it to hold a skein of silk for my mother? " cries Miss Hester; " and what is the good of being ever so strong in a drawing-room? Nobody wants you to throw anybody out of window, Harry! A strong man, indeed! I suppose there's a stronger at Bartholomew Fair. James Wolfe is not a strong man. He seems quite weakly and ill. When he was here last, he was coughing the whole time, and as pale as if he had seen a ghost."

"I never could understand why a man should be frightened at a ghost," says Harry.

"Pray have you seen one, sir?" asks the pert young lady.

"No. I thought I did once at home—when we were boys; but it was only Nathan in his night-shirt; but I wasn't frightened when I thought he *was* a ghost. I believe there's no such things. Our nurses tell a pack of lies about 'em," says Harry gravely. "George was a little frightened; but then he's——" Here he paused.

"Then George is what?" asked Hetty.

"George is different from me, that's all. Our mother's a bold woman as ever you saw, but she screams at seeing a mouse —always does—can't help it. It's her nature. So, you see, perhaps my brother can't bear ghosts. I don't mind 'em."

"George always says you would have made a better soldier than he."

"So I think I should, if I had been allowed to try. But he can do a thousand things better than me, or anybody else in the world. Why didn't he let me volunteer on Braddock's expedition? I might have got knocked on the head, and then I should have been pretty much as useful as I am now, and then I shouldn't have ruined myself, and brought people to point at me and say that I had disgraced the name of Warrington. Why mayn't I go on this expedition, and volunteer, like Sir John Armytage? Oh, Hetty! I'm a miserable fellow—that's what I am." And the miserable fellow paced the room at double quick time. "I wish I had never come to Europe," he groaned out.

"What a compliment to us! Thank you, Harry!" But presently, on an appealing look from the gentleman, she added, "Are you—are you thinking of going home?"

"And have all Virginia jeering at me! There's not a gentleman there that wouldn't, except one, and him my mother doesn't like. I should be ashamed to go home now, I think. You don't know my mother, Hetty. I ain't afraid of most things; but, somehow, I am of her. What shall I say to her, when she says, 'Harry, where's your patrimony?' 'Spent, mother,' I shall have to say. 'What have you done with it?' 'Wasted it, mother, and went to prison after.' 'Who took you out of prison?' 'Brother George, ma'am, he took me out of prison; and now I'm come back, having done no good for myself, with no profession, no prospects, no nothing,—only to look after negroes, and be scolded at home: or to go to sleep at sermons; or to play at cards, and drink, and fight cocks at the taverns about.' How can I look the gentlemen of the country in the face? I'm ashamed to go home in this way, I say. I must and will do something! What shall I do, Hetty? Ah! what shall I do?"

"Do? What did Mr. Wolfe do at Louisbourg! Ill as he was, and in love as we knew him to be, he didn't stop to be nursed by his mother, Harry, or to dawdle with his sweetheart. He went on the King's service, and hath come back covered with honour. If there is to be another great campaign in America, papa says he is sure of a great command."

"I wish he would take me with him, and that a ball would knock me on the head and finish me," groaned Harry. "You speak to me, Hetty, as though I know were my fault that I am not in the army, when you know I would give—give, forsooth, what have I to give?—yes! my life to go on service!"

"Life indeed!" says Miss Hetty, with a shrug of her shoulders.

"You don't seem to think that of much value, Hetty," remarked Harry sadly. "No more it is—to anybody. I'm a poor useless fellow. I'm not even free to throw it away as I would like, being under orders here and at home."

"Orders, indeed! Why under orders?" cries Miss Hetty. "Aren't you tall enough, and old enough, to act for yourself, and must you have George for a master here, and your mother for a schoolmistress at home? If I were a man, I would do something famous before I was two and twenty years old, that I would! I would have the world speak of me. I wouldn't dawdle at apron-strings. I wouldn't curse my fortune—I'd make it. I vow and declare I would!"

Now, for the first time, Harry began to wince at the words of his young lecturer.

"No negro on our estate is more a slave than I am, Hetty," he said, turning very red as he addressed her; "but then, Miss Lambert, we don't reproach the poor fellow for not being free. That isn't generous. At least that isn't the way I understand honour. Perhaps with women it's different, or I may be wrong, and have no right to be hurt at a young girl telling me what my faults are. Perhaps my faults are not my faults—only my cursed luck. You have been talking ever so long about this gentleman volunteering, and that man winning glory, and cracking up their courage as if I had none of my own. I suppose, for the matter of that, I'm as well provided as other gentlemen. I don't brag: but I'm not afraid of Mr. Wolfe, nor of Sir John Armytage, nor of anybody else that ever I saw. How can I buy a commission when I've spent my last shilling, or ask my brother for more who has already halved with me? A gentleman of my rank can't go a common soldier—else, by Jupiter, I would! And if a ball finished me, I suppose Miss Hetty Lambert wouldn't be very sorry. It isn't kind, Hetty—I didn't think it of you."

"What is it I have said?" asks the young lady. "I have only said Sir John Armytage has volunteered, and Mr. Wolfe has covered himself with honour, and you begin to scold me! How can I help it if Mr. Wolfe is brave and famous? Is that any reason you should be angry, pray?"

"I didn't say angry," said Harry gravely. "I said I was hurt."

"Oh, indeed! I thought such a little creature as I am couldn't hurt anybody! I'm sure 'tis mighty complimentary to me to say that a young lady whose arm is no bigger than your little finger can hurt such a great strong man as you!"

"I scarce thought you would try, Hetty," the young man said. "You see, I'm not used to this kind of welcome in this house."

"What is it, my poor boy?" asks kind Mrs. Lambert, looking in at the door at this juncture, and finding the youth with a very woe-worn countenance.

"Oh, we have heard the story before, mamma!" says Hetty hurriedly. "Harry is making his old complaint of having nothing to do. And he is quite unhappy; and he is telling us so over and over again, that's all."

"So are you hungry over and over again, my dear! Is that a reason why your papa and I should leave off giving you dinner?" cries mamma, with some emotion. "Will you stay and have ours, Harry? 'Tis just three o'clock!" Harry agreed to stay, after a few faint negations. "My husband dines abroad. We are but three women, so you will have a dull dinner," remarks Mrs. Lambert.

"We shall have a gentleman to enliven us, mamma, I dare say!" says Madam Pert, and then looked in mamma's face with that admirable gaze of blank innocence which Madam Pert knows how to assume when she has been specially and successfully wicked.

When the dinner appeared Miss Hetty came downstairs, and

was exceedingly chatty, lively, and entertaining. Theo did not know that any little difference had occurred (such, alas, my Christian friends, will happen in the most charming families), did not know, I say, that anything had happened until Hetty's uncommon sprightliness and gaiety aroused her suspicions. Hetty would start a dozen subjects of conversation—the King of Prussia, and the news from America; the last masquerade, and the highwayman shot near Barnet; and when her sister, admiring this volubility, inquired the reason of it, with her eyes,—

"Oh, my dear, you need not nod and wink at me!" cries Hetty. "Mamma asked Harry on purpose to enliven us, and I am talking until he begins,—just like the fiddles at the playhouse, you know, Theo! First the fiddles. Then the play. Pray begin, Harry!"

"Hester!" cries mamma.

"I merely asked Harry to entertain us. You said yourself, mother, that we were only three women, and the dinner would be dull for a gentleman; unless, indeed, he chose to be very lively."

"I'm not that on most days—and, Heaven knows, on this day less than most," says poor Harry.

"Why on this day less than another? Tuesday is as good a day to be lively as Wednesday. The only day when we mustn't be lively is Sunday. Well, you know it is, ma'am! We mustn't sing, nor dance, nor do anything on Sunday."

And in this naughty way the young woman went on for the rest of the evening, and was complimented by her mother and sister when poor Harry took his leave. He was not ready of wit, and could not fling back the taunts which Hetty cast against him. Nay, had he been able to retort, he would have been silent. He was too generous to engage in that small war, and chose to take all Hester's sarcasms without an attempt to parry or evade them. Very likely the young lady watched and admired that magnanimity, while she tried it so cruelly. And after one of her fits of ill-behaviour, her parents and friends had not the least need to scold her, as she candidly told them, because she suffered a great deal more than they would ever have had her, and her conscience punished her a great deal more severely than her kind elders would have thought of doing. I suppose she lies awake all that night, and tosses and tumbles in her bed. I suppose she wets her pillow with tears, and should not mind about her sobbing: unless it kept her sister awake; unless she was unwell the next day, and the doctor had to be fetched: unless the whole family is to be put to discomfort; mother to choke over her dinner in flurry and indignation; father to eat his roast-beef in silence and with bitter sauce: everybody to look at the door each time it opens, with a vague hope that Harry is coming in. If Harry does not come, why at least does not George come? thinks Miss Theo.

Some time in the course of the evening comes a billet from George Warrington, with a large nosegay of lilacs, per Mr. Gumbo. "I send my best duty and regards to Mrs. Lambert and the ladies," George says, "and humbly beg to present to Miss Theo this nosegay of lilacs, which she says she loves in the early spring. You must not thank me for them, please, but the gardener of Bedford House, with whom I have made great friends by presenting him with some dried specimens of a Virginian plant which some ladies don't think as fragrant as lilacs.

"I have been in the garden almost all the day. It is alive with sunshine and spring: and I have been composing two scenes of you know what, and polishing the verses which the Page sings in the fourth act, under Sybilla's window, which she cannot hear, poor thing, because she has just had her head off."

"Provoking! I wish he would not always sneer and laugh! The verses are beautiful," says Theo.

"You really think so, my dear? How very odd!" remarks papa.

Little Het looks up from her dismal corner with a faint smile of humour. Theo's secret is a secret for nobody in the house, it seems. Can any young people guess what it is? The lady continues to read:—

"Spencer has asked the famous Mr. Johnson to breakfast to-morrow, who condescends to hear the play, and who won't, I hope, be too angry because my heroine undergoes the fate of his in 'Irene.' I have heard he came up to London himself as a young man with only his tragedy in his wallet. Shall I ever be able to get mine played? Can you fancy the cat-call music beginning, and the pit hissing at the perilous part of the fourth act, where my executioner comes out from the closet with his great sword, at the awful moment when he is called upon to *amputate*? They say Mr. Fielding, when the pit hissed at a part of one of his pieces about which Mr. Garrick had warned him, said, 'Hang them, they *have* found it out, have they?' and finished his punch in tranquillity. I suppose his wife was not in the boxes. There are some women to whom I would be very unwilling to give pain, and there are some to whom I would give the best I have."

"Whom can he mean? The letter is to you, my dear. I protest he is making love to your mother before my face!" cries papa to Hetty, who only gives a little sigh, puts her hand in her father's hand, and then withdraws it.

"To whom I would give the best I have. To-day it is only a bunch of lilacs. To-morrow it may be what?—a branch of rue—a sprig of bays, perhaps—anything, so it be my best and my all.

"I have had a fine long day, and all to myself. What do you think of Harry playing truant?" (Here we may imagine what they call in France, or what they used to call, when men dared to speak or citizens to hear, *sensation dans l'auditoire.*)

"I suppose Carpezan wearied the poor fellow's existence out. Certain it is he has been miserable for weeks past; and a change of air and scene may do him good. This morning, quite early, he came to my room; and told me he had taken a seat in the Portsmouth machine, and proposed to go to the Isle of Wight, to the army there."

The army! Hetty looks very pale at this announcement, and her mother continues:—

"And a little portion of it, namely, the Thirty-second Regiment, is commanded by Lieutenant-Colonel Richmond Webb—the nephew of the famous old General under whom my grandfather Esmond served in the great wars of Marlborough. Mr. Webb met us at our uncle's, accosting us very politely, and giving us an invitation to visit him at his regiment. Let my poor brother go and listen to his darling music of fife and drum! He bade me tell the ladies that they should hear from him. I kiss their hands, and go to dress for dinner, at the 'Star and Garter,' in Pall Mall. We are to have Mr. Soame Jenyns, Mr. Cambridge, Mr. Walpole, possibly, if he is not too fine to dine in a tavern; a young Irishman, a Mr. Bourke, who, they say, is a wonder of eloquence and learning—in fine, all the wits of Mr. Dodsley's shop. Quick, Gumbo, a coach, and my French grey suit! And if gentlemen ask me, 'Who gave you that sprig of lilac you wear on your heart-side?' I shall call a bumper, and give Lilac for a toast."

I fear there is no more rest for Hetty on this night than on the previous one, when she had behaved so mutinously to poor Harry Warrington. Some secret resolution must have inspired that gentleman, for, after leaving Mr. Lambert's table, he paced the streets for a while, and appeared at a late hour in the even-

ing at Madame de Bernstein's house in Clarges Street. Her
Ladyship's health had been somewhat ailing of late, so that even
her favourite routs were denied her, and she was sitting over a
quiet game of écarté, with a divine of whom our last news was
from a lock-up house hard by that in which Harry Warrington
had been himself confined. George, at Harry's request, had paid
the little debt under which Mr. Sampson had suffered tem-
porarily. He had been at his living for a year. He may have
paid and contracted ever so many debts, have been in and out
of jail many times since we saw him. For some time past he
had been back in London, stout and hearty as usual, and ready
for any invitation to cards or claret. Madame de Bernstein did
not care to have her game interrupted by her nephew, whose
conversation had little interest now for the fickle old woman.
Next to the very young, I suppose the very old are the most
selfish. Alas! the heart hardens as the blood ceases to run.
The cold snow strikes down from the head, and checks the glow
of feeling. Who wants to survive into old age after abdicating
all his faculties one by one, and be sans teeth, sans eyes, sans
memory, sans hope, sans sympathy? How fared it with those
patriarchs of old who lived for their nine centuries, and when
were life's conditions so changed that, after threescore years and
ten, it became but a vexation and a burden?

Getting no reply but Yes and No to his brief speeches, poor
Harry sat a while on a couch, opposite his aunt, who shrugged
her shoulders, had her back to her nephew, and continued her
game with the chaplain. Sampson sat opposite Mr. Warrington, and could see that something disturbed him. His face
was very pale, and his countenance disturbed and full of gloom.
"Something has happened to him, ma'am," he whispered to the
Baroness.

"Bah!" She shrugged her shoulders again, and continued
to deal her cards. "What is the matter with you, sir," she at
last said, at a pause in the game, "that you have such a dismal
countenance? Chaplain, that last game makes us even, I think!"

Harry got up from his place. "I am going on a journey:
I am come to bid you good-bye, aunt," he said, in a very tragical
voice.

"On a journey! Are you going home to America? I mark
the king, Chaplain, and play him."

No, Harry said: he was not going to America yet: he was
going to the Isle of Wight for the present.

"Indeed!—a lovely spot!" says the Baroness. "Bon jour,

mon ami, et bon voyage!" And she kissed a hand to her nephew.

"I mayn't come back for some time, aunt," he groaned out.

"Indeed? We shall be inconsolable without you! Unless you have a spade, Mr. Sampson, the game is mine. Good-bye, my child! No more about your journey at present: tell us about it when you come back!" And she gaily bade him farewell. He looked for a moment piteously at her, and was gone.

"Something grave has happened, madam," says the chaplain.

"Oh! the boy is always getting into scrapes! I suppose he has been falling in love with one of those country girls—what are their names, Lamberts?—with whom he is ever dawdling about. He has been doing no good here for some time. I am disappointed in him, really quite grieved about him—I will take two cards, if you please—again?—quite grieved. What do you think they say of his cousin—the Miss Warrington who made eyes at him when she thought he was a prize—they say the King has remarked her, and the Yarmouth is crêving with rage. He, he!—those methodistical Warringtons! They are not a bit less worldly than their neighbours; and, old as he is, if the Grand Signior throws his pocket-handkerchief, they will jump to catch it!"

"Ah, madam; how your Ladyship knows the world!" sighs the chaplain. "I propose, if you please!"

"I have lived long enough in it, Mr. Sampson, to know something of it. 'Tis sadly selfish, my dear sir, sadly selfish; and everybody is struggling to pass his neighbour! No, I can't give you any more cards. You haven't the king? I play queen, knave, and a ten,—a sadly selfish world, indeed. And here comes my chocolate!"

The more immediate interest of the cards entirely absorbs the old woman. The door shuts out her nephew and his cares. Under his hat, he bears them into the street, and paces the dark town for a while.

"Good God!" he thinks, "what a miserable fellow I am, and what a spendthrift of my life I have been! I sit silent with George and his friends. I am not clever and witty as he is. I am only a burthen to him: and if I would help him ever so much, don't know how. My dear Aunt Lambert's kindness never tires, but I begin to be ashamed of trying it. Why, even Hetty can't help turning on me; and when she tells me I am idle and should be doing something, ought I to be angry? The rest have left me. There's my cousins and uncle and my Lady my aunt, they have showed me the cold shoulder this long time. They didn't even ask me to Norfolk when they went down to the country, and offer me so much as a day's partridge-shooting. I can't go to Castlewood—after what has happened: I should break that scoundrel William's bones; and, faith, am well out of the place altogether."

He laughs a fierce laugh as he recalls his adventures since he has been in Europe. Money, friends, pleasure, all have passed away, and he feels the past like a dream. He strolls into White's Chocolate House, where the waiters have scarce seen him for a year. The Parliament is up. Gentlemen are away; there is not even any play going on—not that he would join it, if there were. He has but a few pieces in his pocket; George's drawer is open, and he may take what money he likes thence; but very very sparingly will he avail himself of his brother's repeated invitation. He sits and drinks his glass in moody silence. Two or three officers of the Guards enter from St. James's. He knew them in former days, and the young men, who have been already dining and drinking on guard, insist on more drink at the club. The other battalion of their regiment is at Winchester: it is going on this great expedition, no one knows whither, which everybody is talking about. Cursed fate that they do not belong to the other battalion; and must stay and do duty in London and at Kensington! There is Webb, who was of their regiment: he did well to exchange his company in the Coldstreams for the lieutenant-colonelcy of the Thirty-second. He will be of the expedition. Why, everybody is going; and the young gentlemen mention a score of names of men of the first birth and fashion, who have volunteered. "It ain't Hanoverians this time, commanded by the big Prince," says one young gentleman (whose relatives may have been Tories forty years ago)—"it's Englishmen, with the Guards at the head of 'em, and a Marlborough for a leader! Will the Frenchmen ever stand against *them*? No, by George, they are irresistible." And a fresh bowl is called, and loud toasts are drunk to the success of the expedition.

Mr. Warrington, who is a cup too low, the young Guardsmen say, walks away when they are not steady enough to be able to follow him, thinks over the matter on his way to his lodgings, and lies thinking of it all through the night.

"What is it, my boy?" asks George Warrington of his brother, when the latter enters his chamber very early on a blushing May morning.

"I want a little money out of the drawer," says Harry, looking at his brother. "I am sick and tired of London."

"Good heavens! Can anybody be tired of London?" George asks, who has reasons for thinking it the most delightful place in the world.

"I am for one. I am sick and ill," says Harry.

"You and Hetty have been quarrelling?"

"She don't care a penny-piece about me, nor I for her neither," says Harry, nodding his head. "But I am ill, and a little country air will do me good." And he mentions how he thinks of going to visit Mr. Webb in the Isle of Wight, and how a Portsmouth coach starts from Holborn.

"There's the till, Harry," says George, pointing from his bed. "Put your hand in, and take what you will. What a lovely morning, and how fresh the Bedford House Garden looks!"

"God bless you, brother!" Harry says.

"Have a good time, Harry!" and down goes George's head on the pillow again, and he takes his pencil and note-book from under his bolster, and falls to polishing his verses, as Harry, with his cloak over his shoulder and a little valise in his hand, walks to the inn in Holborn whence the Portsmouth machine starts.

CHAPTER LXIII

MELPOMENE

GEORGE WARRINGTON by no means allowed his legal studies to obstruct his comfort and pleasures, or interfere with his precious health. Madam Esmond had pointed out to him in her letters that, though he wore a student's gown, and sat down with a crowd of nameless people to hall commons, he had himself a name, and a very ancient one, to support, and could take rank with the first persons at home or in his own country; and desired that he would study as a gentleman, not a mere professional drudge. With this injunction the young man complied obediently enough: so that he may be said not to have belonged to the rank and file of the law, but may be considered to have been a volunteer in her service, like some young gentlemen of whom we have just heard. Though not so exacting as she since has become—though she allowed her disciples much more leisure, much more pleasure, much more punch, much more frequenting of coffee-houses and holiday-making, than she admits now-a-days, when she scarce gives her votaries time for amusement, recreation, instruction, sleep, or dinner—the law a hundred years ago was still a jealous mistress, and demanded a pretty exclusive attention. Murray, we are told, might have been an Ovid, but he preferred to be Lord Chief Justice, and to wear ermine instead of bays. Perhaps Mr. Warrington might have risen to a peerage and the woolsack, had he studied very long and assiduously,—had he been a dexterous courtier, and a favourite of attorneys: had he been other than he was, in a word. He behaved to Themis with a very decent respect and attention; but he loved letters more than law always; and the black letter of Chaucer was infinitely more agreeable to him than the Gothic pages of Hale and Coke.

Letters were loved indeed in those quaint times, and authors were actually authorities. Gentlemen appealed to Virgil or Lucan in the courts or the House of Commons. What said Statius, Juvenal—let alone Tully or Tacitus—on such and such a point? Their reign is over now, the good old Heathens: the worship of Jupiter and Juno is not more out of mode than the cultivation of Pagan poetry or ethics. The age of economists and calculators has succeeded, and Tooke's Pantheon is deserted and ridiculous. Now and then, perhaps, a Stanley kills a kid, a Gladstone hangs up a wreath, a Lytton burns incense, in honour of the Olympians. But what do they care at Lambeth, Birmingham, the Tower Hamlets, for the ancient rites, divinities, worship? Who the plague are the Muses, and what is the use of all that Greek and Latin rubbish? What is Helicon, and who cares? Who was Thalia, pray, and what is the length of her i? Is Melpomene's name in three syllables or four?

Now, it has been said how Mr. George in his youth, and in the long leisure which he enjoyed at home, and during his imprisonment in the French fort on the banks of Monongahela, had whiled away his idleness by paying court to Melpomene; and the result of their union was a tragedy, which has been omitted in Bell's " Theatre," though I dare say it is no worse than some of the pieces printed there. Most young men pay their respects to the Tragic Muse first, as they fall in love with women who are a great deal older than themselves. Let the candid reader own, if ever he had a literary turn, that his ambition was of the very highest, and that however in his riper age

he might come down in his pretensions, and think that to translate an ode of Horace, or to turn a song of Waller or Prior into
decent alcaics or sapphics, was about the utmost of his capa-
bility, tragedy and epic only did his green unknowing youth
engage, and no prize but the highest was fit for him.

George Warrington, then, on coming to London, attended the
theatrical performances at both houses, frequented the theatrical
coffee-houses, and heard the opinions of the critics, and might
be seen at the " Bedford " between the plays, or supping at the
" Cecil " along with the wits and actors when the performances
were over. Here he gradually became acquainted with the
players and such of the writers and poets as were known to the
public. The tough old Macklin, the frolicsome Foote, the
vivacious Hippisley, the sprightly Mr. Garrick himself, might
occasionally be seen at these houses of entertainment; and our
gentleman, by his wit and modesty, as well, perhaps, as for the
high character for wealth which he possessed, came to be very
much liked in the coffee-house circles, and found that the actors
would drink a bowl of punch with him, and the critics sup at his
expense with great affability. To be on terms of intimacy with
an author or an actor has been an object of delight to many a
young man; actually to hob and nob with Bodadil or Henry
the Fifth or Alexander the Great, to accept a pinch out of
Aristarchus's own box, to put Juliet into her coach, or hand
Monimia to her chair, are privileges which would delight most
young men of a poetic turn; and no wonder George Warrington
loved the theatre. Then he had the satisfaction of thinking
that his mother only half approved of plays and play-houses,
and of feasting on fruit forbidden at home. He gave more
than one elegant entertainment to the players, and it was even
said that one or two distinguished geniuses had condescended
to borrow money of him.

And as he polished and added new beauties to his masterpiece, we may be sure that he took advice of certain friends
of his, and that they gave him applause and counsel. Mr.
Spencer, his new acquaintance of the Temple, gave a breakfast
at his chambers in Fig Tree Court, when Mr. Warrington read
part of his play, and the gentlemen present pronounced that it
had uncommon merit. Even the learned Mr. Johnson, who was
invited, was good enough to say that the piece showed talent.
It warred against the unities, to be sure; but these had been
violated by other authors, and Mr. Warrington might sacrifice
them as well as another. There was in Mr. W.'s tragedy a

something which reminded him both of "Coriolanus" and "Othello." "And two very good things too, sir!" the author pleaded. "Well, well, there was no doubt on that point; and 'tis certain your catastrophe is terrible, just, and being in part true, is not the less awful," remarks Mr. Spencer.

Now the plot of Mr. Warrington's tragedy was quite full indeed of battle and murder. A favourite book of his grandfather had been the life of old George Frundsberg of Mindelheim, a colonel of footfolk in the Imperial service at Pavia fight, and during the wars of the Constable Bourbon: and one of Frundsberg's military companions was a certain Carpzow, or Carpezan, whom our friend selected as his tragedy hero.

His first act, as it at present stands in Sir George Warrington's manuscript, is supposed to take place before a convent on the Rhine, which the Lutherans, under Carpezan, are besieging. A godless gang these Lutherans are. They have pulled the beards of Roman friars, and torn the veils of hundreds of religious women. A score of these are trembling within the walls of the convent yonder, of which the garrison, unless the expected succours arrive before mid-day, has promised to surrender. Meanwhile there is armistice, and the sentries within look on with hungry eyes, as the soldiers and camp people gamble on the grass before the gate. Twelve o'clock, ding, ding, dong! it sounds upon the convent bell. No succours have arrived. Open gates, warder! and give admission to the famous Protestant hero, the terror of Turks on the Danube, and Papists in the Lombard plains—Colonel *Carpezan !* See, here he comes, clad in complete steel, his hammer of battle over his shoulder, with which he has battered so many infidel sconces, his flags displayed, his trumpets blowing. "No rudeness, my men," says Carpezan, "the wine is yours, and the convent larder and cellar are good; the church plate shall be melted: any of the garrison who choose to take service with Gaspar Carpezan are welcome, and shall have good pay. No insult to the religious ladies! I have promised them a safe-conduct, and he who lays a finger on them, hangs! Mind that, Provost Marshal!" The Provost Marshal, a huge fellow in a red doublet, nods his head.

"We shall see more of that Provost Marshal, or executioner," Mr. Spencer explains to his guests.

"A very agreeable acquaintance, I am sure,—shall be delighted to meet the gentleman again!" says Mr. Johnson, wagging his head over his tea. "This scene of the mercenaries, the camp-followers, and their wild sports, is novel and stirring, Mr. Warrington, and I make you my compliments on it. The Colonel has gone into the convent, I think? Now let us hear what he is going to do there."

The Abbess, and one or two of her oldest ladies, make their appearance before the conqueror. Conqueror as he is, they beard him in the sacred halls. They have heard of his violent behaviour in conventual establishments before. That hammer, which he always carries in action, has smashed many sacred images in religious houses. Pounds and pounds of convent plate is he known to have melted, the sacrilegious plunderer! No wonder the Abbess-Princess of Saint Mary's, a lady of violent prejudices, free language, and noble birth, has a dislike to the low-born heretic who lords it in her convent, and tells Carpezan a bit of her mind, as the phrase is. This scene, in which the lady gets somewhat better of the Colonel, was liked not a little by Mr. Warrington's audience at the Temple. Terrible as he might be in war, Carpezan was shaken at first by the Abbess's brisk opening charge of words; and, conqueror as he was, seemed at first to be conquered by his actual prisoner. But such an old soldier was not to be beaten ultimately by any woman. "Pray, madam," says he, "how many ladies are there in your convent, for whom my people shall provide conveyance?" The Abbess, with a look of much trouble and anger, says that, "besides herself, the noble Sisters of Saint Mary's House are twenty—twenty-three." She was going to say twenty-four, and now says twenty-three! "Ha! why this hesitation?" asks Captain Ulric, one of Carpezan's gayest officers.

The dark chief pulls a letter from his pocket. "I require from you, madam," he says sternly to the Lady Abbess, "the body of the noble Lady Sybilla of Hoya. Her brother was my favourite captain, slain by my side, in the Milanese. By his death, she becomes heiress of his lands. 'Tis said a greedy uncle brought her hither; and fast immured the lady against her will. The damsel shall herself pronounce her fate—to stay a cloistered sister of Saint Mary's, or to return to home and liberty, as Lady Sybil, Baroness of——" Ha! The Abbess was greatly disturbed by this question. She says haughtily: "There is no Lady Sybil in this house: of which every inmate is under your protection, and sworn to go free. The Sister Agnes was a nun professed, and what was her land and wealth revert to this Order."

" Give me straightway the body of the Lady Sybil of Hoya ! "
roars Carpezan in great wrath. " If not, I make a signal to my
reiters, and give you and your convent up to war."

" Faith, if I lead the storm and have my right, 'tis not my
Lady Abbess that I'll choose," says Captain Ulric, " but rather
some plump, smiling, red-lipped maid like—like——" Here,
as he, the sly fellow, is looking under the veils of the two attendant nuns, the stern Abbess cries, " Silence, fellow, with thy
ribald talk ! The lady, warrior, whom you ask of me is passed
away from sin, temptation, vanity, and three days since our
Sister Agnes—*died*."

At this announcement Carpezan is immensely agitated. The
Abbess calls upon the Chaplain to confirm her statement.
Ghastly and pale, the old man has to own that three days since
the wretched Sister Agnes was buried.

This is too much ! In the pocket of his coat of mail Carpezan
has a letter from Sister Agnes herself, in which she announces
that she is going to be buried indeed, but in an *oubliette* of the
convent, where she may either be kept on water and bread, or
die starved outright. He seizes the unflinching Abbess by the
arm, whilst Captain Ulric lays hold of the Chaplain by the throat.
The Colonel blows a blast upon his horn; in rush his furious
lanzknechts from without. Crash, bang ! They knock the
convent walls about. And in the midst of flames, screams and
slaughter, who is presently brought in by Carpezan himself, and
fainting on his shoulder, but Sybilla herself ? A little sister nun
(that gay one with the red lips) had pointed out to the Colonel
and Ulric the way to Sister Agnes's dungeon, and, indeed, had
been the means of making her situation known to the Lutheran
chief.

" The convent is suppressed with a vengeance," says Mr.
Warrington. " We end our first act with the burning of the
place, the roars of triumph of the soldiery, and the outcries of
the nuns. They had best go change their dresses immediately,
for they will have to be Court ladies in the next act—as you
will see." Here the gentlemen talked the matter over. If the
piece were to be done at " Drury Lane," Mrs. Pritchard would
hardly like to be Lady Abbess, as she doth but appear in the
first act. Miss Pritchard might make a pretty Sybilla, and
Miss Gates the attendant nun. Mr. Garrick was scarce tall
enough for Carpezan—though, when he is excited, nobody ever
thinks of him but as big as a grenadier. Mr. Johnson owns
Woodward will be a good Ulric, as he plays the Mercutio parts

very gaily; and so, by one and t'other, the audience fancies the play already on the boards, and casts the characters.

In act the second, Carpezan has married Sybilla. He has enriched himself in the wars, has been ennobled by the Emperor, and lives at his castle on the Danube in state and splendour.

But, truth to say, though married, rich, and ennobled, the Lord Carpezan was not happy. It may be that in his wild life, as condottiere on both sides, he had committed crimes which agitated his mind with remorse. It may be that his rough soldier-manners consorted ill with his imperious high-born bride. She led him such a life—I am narrating as it were the Warrington manuscript, which is too long to print in entire—taunting him with his low birth, his vulgar companions, whom the old soldier loved to see about him, and so forth—that there were times when he rather wished that he had never rescued this lovely, quarrelsome, wayward vixen from the *oubliette* out of which he fished her. After the bustle of the first act this is a quiet one, and passed chiefly in quarrelling between the Baron and Baroness Carpezan, until horns blow, and it is announced that the young King of Bohemia and Hungary is coming hunting that way.

Act III. is passed at Prague, whither His Majesty has invited Lord Carpezan and his wife, with noble offers of preferment to the Baron. From Baron he shall be promoted to be Count; from Colonel he shall be General-in-Chief. His wife is the most brilliant and fascinating of all the ladies of the Court—and as for Carpzoff—

"Oh, stay—I have it—I know your story, sir, now," says Mr. Johnson. "'Tis in 'Meteranus,' in the 'Theatrum Universum.' I read it in Oxford as a boy—Carpezanus or Carpzoff——"

"That is the fourth act," says Mr. Warrington. In the fourth act the young King's attentions towards Sybilla grow more and more marked; but her husband, battling against his jealousy, long refuses to yield to it, until his wife's criminality is put beyond a doubt—and here he read the act, which closes with the terrible tragedy which actually happened. Being convinced of his wife's guilt, Carpezan caused the executioner who followed his regiment to slay her in her own palace. And the curtain of the act falls just after the dreadful deed is done, in a side-chamber illuminated by the moon shining through a great oriel window, under which the King comes with his lute, and plays the song which was to be the signal between him and his guilty victim.

This song (writ in the ancient style, and repeated in the piece, being sung in the third act previously at a great festival given by the King and Queen) was pronounced by Mr. Johnson to be a happy imitation of Mr. Waller's manner, and its gay repetition at the moment of guilt, murder, and horror, very much deepened the tragic gloom of the scene.

" But whatever came afterwards? " he asked. " I remember in the 'Theatrum,' Carpezan is said to have been taken into favour again by Count Mansfield, and doubtless to have murdered other folks on the reformed side."

Here our poet has departed from historic truth. In the fifth act of " Carpezan " King Louis of Hungary and Bohemia (sufficiently terror-stricken, no doubt, by the sanguinary termination of his intrigue) has received word that the Emperor Solyman is invading his Hungarian dominions. Enter two noblemen who relate how, in the council which the King held upon the news, the injured Carpezan rushed infuriated into the Royal presence, broke his sword, and flung it at the King's feet—along with a glove which he dared him to wear, and which he swore he would one day claim. After that wild challenge the rebel fled from Prague, and had not since been heard of; but it was reported that he had joined the Turkish invader, assumed the turban, and was now in the camp of the Sultan, whose white tents glance across the river yonder, and against whom the King was now on his march. Then the King comes to his tent with his generals, prepares his order of battle, and dismisses them to their posts, keeping by his side an aged and faithful knight, his master of the horse, to whom he expresses his repentance for his past crimes, his esteem for his good and injured Queen, and his determination to meet the day's battle like a man.

" What is this field called? "

" Mohacz, my liege! " says the old warrior, adding the remark that " Ere set of sun, Mohacz will see a battle bravely won."

Trumpets and alarms now sound; they are the cymbals and barbaric music of the janissaries; we are in the Turkish camp, and yonder, surrounded by turbaned chiefs, walks the Sultan Solyman's friend, the conquerer of Rhodes, the redoubted Grand Vizier.

Who is that warrior in an Eastern habit, but with a glove in his cap? 'Tis Carpezan. Even Solyman knew his courage and ferocity as a soldier. He knows the ordnance of the Hungarian host; in what arms King Louis is weakest: how his cavalry, of which the shock is tremendous, should be received, and inveigled into yonder morass, where certain death may await them—he prays for a command in the front, and as near as possible to the place where the traitor King Louis will engage. "'Tis well," says the grim Vizier, "our invincible Emperor surveys the battle from yonder tower. At the end of the day, he will know how to reward your valour." The signal-guns fire—the trumpets blow—the Turkish captains retire, vowing death to the infidel, and eternal fidelity to the Sultan.

And now the battle begins in earnest, and with those various incidents which the lover of the theatre knoweth. Christian knights and Turkish warriors clash and skirmish over the stage. Continued alarms are sounded. Troops on both sides advance and retreat. Carpezan, with his glove in his cap, and his dreadful hammer smashing all before him, rages about the field, calling for King Louis. The renegade is about to slay a warrior who faces him, but recognising young Ulric, his ex-captain, he drops the uplifted hammer, and bids him fly and think of Carpezan. He is softened at seeing his young friend, and thinking of former times when they fought and conquered together in the cause of Protestantism. Ulric bids him to return, but of course that is now out of the question. They fight, Ulric *will* have it, and down he goes under the hammer. The renegade melts in sight of his wounded comrade, when who appears but King Louis, his plumes torn, his sword hacked, his shield dented with a thousand blows which he has received and delivered during the day's battle. Ha! who is this? The guilty monarch would turn away (perhaps Macbeth may have done so before), but Carpezan is on him. All his softness is gone. He rages like a fury. "An equal fight!" he roars. "A traitor against a traitor! Stand, King Louis! False King, false knight, false friend—by this glove in my helmet, I challenge you!" And he tears the guilty token out of his cap, and flings it at the King.

Of course they set to, and the monarch falls under the terrible arm of the man whom he has injured. He dies uttering a few incoherent words of repentance, and Carpezan, leaning upon his murderous mace, utters a heartbroken soliloquy over the royal corpse. The Turkish warriors have gathered meanwhile: the dreadful day is their own. Yonder stands the dark Vizier, surrounded by his janissaries, whose bows and swords are tired of drinking death. He surveys the renegade standing over the corpse of the King.

"Christian renegade!" he says, "Allah has given us a great victory. The arms of the Sublime Emperor are everywhere triumphant. The Christian King is slain by you."

"Peace to his soul! He died like a good knight," gasps Ulric, himself dying on the field.

"In this day's battle," the grim Vizier continues, "no man hath comported himself more bravely than you. You are made Bassa of Transylvania! Advance, bowmen—Fire!"

An arrow quivers in the breast of Carpezan.

"Bassa of Transylvania, you were a traitor to your King, who lies murdered by your hand!" continues grim Vizier. "You contributed more than any soldier to this day's great victory. 'Tis thus my sublime Emperor meetly rewards you. Sound trumpets! We march for Vienna to-night!"

And the curtain drops as Carpezan, crawling towards his dying comrade, kisses his hand, and gasps—

"Forgive me, Ulric!"

When Mr. Warrington has finished reading his tragedy, he turns round to Mr. Johnson, modestly, and asks—

"What say you, sir? Is there any chance for me?"

But the opinion of this most eminent critic is scarce to be given, for Mr. Johnson had been asleep for some time, and frankly owned that he had lost the latter part of the play.

The little auditory begins to hum and stir as the noise of the speaker ceased. George may have been very nervous when he first commenced to read; but everybody allows that he read the last two acts uncommonly well, and makes him a compliment upon his matter and manner. Perhaps everybody is in good humour because the piece has come to an end. Mr. Spencer's servant hands about refreshing drinks. The Templars speak out their various opinions whilst they sip the negus. They are a choice band of critics, familiar with the pit of the theatre, and they treat Mr. Warrington's play with the gravity which such a subject demands.

Mr. Fountain suggests that the Vizier should not say " Fire!" when he bids the archers kill Carpezan,—as you certainly don't *fire* with a bow and arrows. A note is taken of the objection.

Mr. Figtree, who is of a sentimental turn, regrets that Ulric could not be saved, and married to the comic heroine.

"Nay, sir, there was an utter annihilation of the Hungarian

army at Mohacz," says Mr. Johnson, "and Ulric must take
his knock on the head with the rest. He could only be saved
by flight, and you wouldn't have a hero run away! Pronounce sentence of death against Captain Ulric, but kill him
with honours of war."

Messrs. Essex and Tanfield wonder to one another who is this
queer-looking *put* whom Spencer has invited, and who con-
tradicts everybody; and they suggest a boat up the river and
a little fresh air after the fatigues of the tragedy.

The general opinion is decidedly favourable to Mr. Warrington's performance; and Mr. Johnson's opinion, on which he
sets a special value, is the most favourable of all. Perhaps
Mr. Johnson is not sorry to compliment a young gentleman
of fashion and figure like Mr. W. "Up to the death of the
heroine," he says, "I am frankly with you, sir. And I may
speak, as a playwright who have killed my own heroine, and
had my share of the *plausus in theatro*. To hear your own lines
nobly delivered to an applauding house, is indeed a noble excitement. I like to see a young man of good name and lineage
who condescends to think that the Tragic Muse is not below
his advances. It was to a sordid roof that I invited her, and I
asked her to rescue me from poverty and squalor. Happy you,
sir, who can meet her upon equal terms, and can afford to
marry her without a portion."

"I doubt whether the greatest genius is not debased who has
to make a bargain with Poetry," remarks Mr. Spencer.

"Nay, sir," Mr. Johnson answered, "I doubt if many a great
genius would work at all without bribes and necessities; and
so a man had better marry a poor Muse for good and all, for
better or worse, than dally with a rich one. I make you my
compliment of your play, Mr. Warrington, and if you want an
introduction to the stage, shall be very happy, if I can induce
my friend Mr. Garrick to present you."

"Mr. Garrick shall be his sponsor," cried the florid Mr.
Figtree. "Melpomene shall be his godmother, and he shall
have the witches' cauldron in 'Macbeth' for a christening
font."

"Sir, I neither said font nor godmother," remarks the man
of letters. "I would have no play contrary to morals or
religion: nor, as I conceive, is Mr. Warrington's piece otherwise
than friendly to them. Vice is chastised, as it should be, even
in kings, though perhaps we judge of their temptations too
lightly. Revenge is punished—as not to be lightly exercised

by our limited notion of justice. It may have been Carpezan's wife who perverted the King, and not the King who led the woman astray. At any rate, Louis is rightly humiliated for his crime, and the Renegade most justly executed for his. I wish you a good afternoon, gentlemen." And with these remarks, the great author took his leave of the company.

Towards the close of the reading, General Lambert had made his appearance at Mr. Spencer's chambers, and had listened to the latter part of the tragedy. The performance over, he and George took their way to the latter's lodgings in the first place, and subsequently to the General's own house, where the young author was expected, in order to recount the reception which his play had met from his Temple critics.

At Mr. Warrington's apartments in Southampton Row, they found a letter awaiting George, which the latter placed in his pocket unread, so that he might proceed immediately with his companion to Soho. We may be sure the ladies there were eager to know about the Carpezan's fate in the morning's small rehearsal. Hetty said George was so shy, that perhaps it would be better for all parties if some other person had read the play. Theo, on the contrary, cried out—

"Read it, indeed! Who can read a poem better than the author who feels it in his heart? And George had his whole heart in the piece!"

Mr. Lambert very likely thought that somebody else's whole heart was in the piece too, but did not utter this opinion to Miss Theo.

"I think Harry would look very well in your figure of a Prince," says the General. "That scene where he takes leave of his wife before departing for the wars reminds me of your brother's manner not a little."

"Oh, papa! surely Mr. Warrington himself would act the Prince's part best!" cries Miss Theo.

"And be deservedly slain in battle at the end?" asks the father of the house.

"I did not say that; only that Mr. George would make a very good Prince, papa!" cries Miss Theo.

"In which case he would find a suitable Princess, I have no doubt. What news of your brother Harry?"

George, who has been thinking about theatrical triumphs; about *monumentum ære perennius;* about lilacs; about love whispered and tenderly accepted, remembers that he has a letter from Harry in his pocket, and gaily produces it.

"Let us hear what Mr. Truant says for himself, Aunt Lambert!" cries George, breaking the seal.

Why is he so disturbed, as he reads the contents of his letter? Why do the women look at him with alarmed eyes? And why, above all, is Hetty so pale?

"Here is the letter," says George, and begins to read it:—

"RYDE: *June* 1, 1758.

"I DID not tell my dearest George what I hoped and intended, when I left home on Wednesday. 'Twas to see Mr. Webb at Portsmouth or the Isle of Wight, wherever his Regt. was, and if need was to *go down on my knees* to him to take me as volunteer with him on the Expedition. I took boat from Portsmouth, where I learned that he was with *our regiment* incampt at the village of Ryde. Was received by him most kindly, and my petition granted out of hand. That is why I say our regiment. We are eight gentlemen volunteers with Mr. Webb, all men of birth, and *good fortunes* except poor me, who don't deserve one. We are to mess with the officers; we take the right of the collumn, *and have always the right to be in front*, and in an hour we embark on board His Majesty's Ship the 'Rochester' of 60 guns, while our Commodore's, Mr. Howe's, is the 'Essex,' 70. His squadron is about 20 ships, and I should think 100 transports at least. Though 'tis a secret expedition, we make no doubt France is our destination—where I hope to see my friend the Monsieurs once more, and win my colours *à la poinct de mon épée*, as we used to say in Canada. Perhaps my service as interpreter may be useful; I speaking the language not so well *as someone I know*, but better than most here.

"I scarce venture to write to our mother to tell her of this step. Will you, who have a *coxing tongue will wheadle any one*, write to her as soon as you have finisht the famous *tradgedy?* Will you give my affectionate respects to dear General Lambert and ladies; and if any accident should happen, I know you will take care of poor Gumbo as belonging to my dearest best George's most affectionate brother,   HENRY E. WARRINGTON.

"P.S.—Love to all at home when you write, including Dempster, Mountain, and Fanny M. and all the people, and duty to my honored mother, wishing I had pleased her better. And if I said anything unkind to dear Miss Hester Lambert, I know she will forgive me, and pray God bless all.   H. E. W.

"To G. ESMOND WARRINGTON, Esq.,
  "At Mr. Scrace's house in Southampton Row,
      opposite Bedford House Gardens, London."

He has not read the last words with a very steady voice. Mr. Lambert sits silent, though not a little moved. Theo and her mother look at one another; but Hetty remains with a cold face and a stricken heart. She thinks, "He is gone to danger, perhaps to death, and it was I sent him!"

CHAPTER LXIV

IN WHICH HARRY LIVES TO FIGHT ANOTHER DAY

THE trusty Gumbo could not console himself for the departure of his beloved master: at least, to judge from his tears and howls on first hearing the news of Mr. Harry's enlistment, you would have thought the negro's heart must break at the separation. No wonder he went for sympathy to the maid-servants at Mr. Lambert's lodgings. Wherever that dusky youth was, he sought comfort in the society of females. Their fair and tender bosoms knew how to feel pity for the poor African, and the darkness of Gumbo's complexion was no more repulsive to them than Othello's to Desdemona. I believe Europe has never been so squeamish in regard to Africa, as a certain other respected quarter. Nay, some Africans—witness the Chevalier de St. Georges, for instance—have been notorious favourites with the fair sex.

So, in his humbler walk, was Mr. Gumbo. The Lambert servants wept freely in his company: the maids kindly considered him not only Mr. Harry's man, but their brother. Hetty could not help laughing when she found Gumbo roaring because his master had gone a volunteer, as he called it, and had not taken him. He was ready to save Master Harry's life any day, and would have done it, and had himself cut in twenty tousand hundred pieces for Master Harry, that he would! Meanwhile, Nature must be supported, and he condescended to fortify her by large supplies of beer and cold meat in the kitchen. That he was greedy, idle, and told lies, is certain; but yet Hetty gave him half-a-crown, and was especially kind to him. Her tongue, that was wont to wag so pertly, was so gentle now, that you might fancy it had never made a joke. She moved about the house mum and meek. She was humble to mamma; thankful to John and Betty when they waited at dinner; patient to Polly when the latter pulled her hair in combing it; long-suffering when Charley from school trod on her toes, or deranged her workbox; silent in papa's company,—oh, such a transmogrified little Hetty! If papa had ordered her to roast the leg of mutton, or walk to church arm-in-arm with Gumbo, she would have made a curtsey, and said, " Yes, if you please, dear papa! " Leg of mutton! What sort of meal were some poor volunteers having, with the cannon-balls flying about their heads? Church?

When it comes to the prayer in time of war, oh how her knees smite together as she kneels, and hides her head in the pew! She holds down her head when the parson reads out, "Thou shalt do no murder," from the communion-rail, and fancies he must be looking at her. How she thinks of all travellers by land or by water! How she sickens as she runs to the paper to read if there is news of the Expedition! How she watches papa when he comes home from his Ordnance Office, and looks in his face to see if there is good news or bad! Is he well? Is he made a General yet? Is he wounded and made a prisoner? ah me! or, perhaps, are both his legs taken off by one shot, like that pensioner they saw in Chelsea Garden t'other day? She would go on wooden legs all her life, if his can but bring him safe home; at least, she ought never to get up off her knees until he is returned. "Haven't you heard of people, Theo," says she, "whose hair has grown grey in a single night? I shouldn't wonder if mine did—shouldn't wonder in the least." And she looks in the glass to ascertain that phenomenon.

"Hetty dear, you used not to be so nervous when papa was away in Minorca," remarks Theo.

"Ah, Theo! one may very well see that George is not with the army, but safe at home," rejoins Hetty; whereat the elder sister blushes and looks very pensive. *Au fait*, if Mr. George had been in the army, that, you see, would have been another pair of boots. Meanwhile, we don't intend to harrow anybody's kind feelings any longer, but may as well state that Harry is, for the present, as safe as any officer of the Life Guards at Regent's Park Barracks.

The first expedition in which our gallant volunteer was engaged may be called successful, but certainly was not glorious. The British Lion, or any other lion, cannot always have a worthy enemy to combat, or a battle royal to deliver. Suppose he goes forth in quest of a tiger, who won't come, and lays his paws on a goose and gobbles him up? Lions, we know, must live like any other animals. But suppose, advancing into the forest in search of the tiger aforesaid, and bellowing his challenge of war, he espies not one but six tigers coming towards him? This manifestly is not his game at all. He puts his tail between his Royal legs, and retreats into his own snug den as quickly as he may. Were he to attempt to go and fight six tigers, you might write that Lion down an Ass.

Now Harry Warrington's first feat of war was in this wise. He and about 13,000 other fighting men embarked in various ships and transports on the 1st of June, from the Isle of Wight, and at daybreak on the 5th the fleet stood in to the Bay of Cancale in Brittany. For a while he and the gentlemen volunteers had the pleasure of examining the French coast from their ships, whilst the Commander-in-Chief and the Commodore reconnoitred the bay in a cutter. Cattle were seen and some dragoons, who trotted off into the distance; and a little fort with a couple of guns had the audacity to fire at his Grace of Marlborough and the Commodore in the cutter. By two o'clock the whole British fleet was at anchor, and signal was made for all the grenadier companies of eleven regiments, to embark on board flat-bottomed boats and assemble round the Commodore's ship, the "Essex." Meanwhile, Mr. Howe, hoisting his broad pennant on board the "Success" frigate, went in as near as possible to shore, followed by the other frigates to protect the landing of the troops; and, now, with Lord George Sackville and General Drury in command, the gentlemen volunteers, the grenadier companies, and three battalions of Guards pulled to shore.

The gentlemen volunteers could not do any heroic deed upon this occasion, because the French, who should have stayed to fight them, ran away, and the frigates having silenced the fire of the little fort which had disturbed the reconnaissance of the Commander-in-Chief, the army presently assaulted it, taking the whole garrison prisoner, and shooting him in the leg. Indeed he was but one old gentleman, who gallantly had fired his two guns, and who told his conquerors, "If every Frenchman had acted like me, you would not have landed at Cancale at all."

The advanced detachment of invaders took possession of the village of Cancale, where they lay upon their arms all night: and our volunteer was joked by his comrades about his eagerness to go out upon the war-path, and bring in two or three scalps of Frenchmen. None such, however, fell under his tomahawk; the only person slain on the whole day being a French gentleman, who was riding with his servant, and was surprised by volunteer Lord Downe, marching in the front with a company of Kingsley's. My Lord Downe offered the gentleman quarter, which he foolishly refused, whereupon he, his servant, and the two horses, were straightway shot.

Next day the whole force was landed, and advanced from Cancale to St. Malo. All the villages were emptied through which the troops passed, and the roads were so narrow in many places that the men had to march single file, and might have been shot down from behind the tall leafy hedges had there been any enemy to disturb them.

At nightfall the army arrived before St. Malo, and were saluted by a fire of artillery from that town, which did little damage in the darkness. Under cover of this, the British set fire to the ships, wooden buildings, pitch and tar magazines in the harbour, and made a prodigious conflagration that lasted the whole night.

This feat was achieved without any attempt on the part of the French to molest the British force; but, as it was confidently asserted that there was a considerable French force in the town of St. Malo, though they wouldn't come out, his Grace the Duke of Marlborough and my Lord George Sackville determined not to disturb the garrison, marched back to Cancale again, and —and so got on board their ships.

If this were not a veracious history, don't you see that it would have been easy to send our Virginian on a more glorious campaign? Exactly four weeks after his departure from England, Mr. Warrington found himself at Portsmouth again, and addressed a letter to his brother George, with which the latter ran off to Dean Street so soon as ever he received it.

"Glorious news, ladies!" cries he, finding the Lambert family all at breakfast. "Our champion has come back. He has undergone all sorts of dangers, but has survived them all. He has seen dragons—upon my word, he says so."

"Dragons! What do you mean, Mr. Warrington?"

"But not killed any—he says so, as you shall hear. He writes:—

"DEAREST BROTHER,—I think you will be glad to hear that I am returned, without any commission as yet; without any wounds or glory; but at any rate, *alive and harty*. On board our ship, we were almost as crowded as poor Mr. Holwell and his friends in their Black Hole at Calicutta. We had rough weather, and some of the gentlemen volunteers, who prefer smooth water, grumbled not a little. My gentlemen's stomachs are dainty; and after Braund's cookery and White's kickshaws, they don't like plain sailor's *rum and bisket*. But I, who have been at sea before, took my rations and can of flip very contentedly: being determined to put a good face on everything before our fine English *macaronis*, and show that a Virginia gentleman is as good as the best of 'em. I wish, for the honour of old Virginia, that I had more to brag about. But all I can say in truth is, that we have been to France and come back again. Why, I don't think even *your tragick pen* could make anything of such a campaign as ours has been. We landed on the 6 at Cancalle Bay, we saw a few dragons on a hill——"

"There! Did I not tell you there were dragons?" asks George, laughing.

"Mercy! What can he mean by dragons?" cries Hetty.

"Immense, long-tailed monsters, with steel scales on their backs, who vomit fire, and gobble up a virgin a-day. Haven't you read about them in 'The Seven Champions'?" says papa. "Seeing St. George's flag, I suppose, they slunk off."

"I have read of 'em," says the little boy from Chartreux, solemnly. "They like to eat women. One was going to eat Andromeda, you know, papa: and Jason killed another, who was guarding the apple-tree."

"—A few dragons on a hill," George resumes, "who rode away from us without engaging. We slept under canvass. We marched to St. Malo, and burned ever so many privateers there. And we went on board shipp again, without ever crossing swords with an enemy or meeting any except a few poor devils whom the troops plundered. Better luck next time! This hasn't been very much nor *particular glorious;* but I have liked it for my part. I have *smelt powder,* besides a deal of rosn and pitch we burned. I've seen the enemy; have sleppt under canvass, and been dreadful crowdid and sick at sea. I like it. My best compliments to dear Aunt Lambert, and tell Miss Hetty I wasn't *very much fritened* when I saw the French horse.—Your most affectionate brother,

"H. E. WARRINGTON."

We hope Miss Hetty's qualms of conscience were allayed by Harry's announcement that his expedition was over, and that he had so far taken no hurt. Far otherwise. Mr. Lambert, in the course of his official duties, had occasion to visit the troops at Portsmouth and the Isle of Wight, and George Warrington bore him company. They found Harry vastly improved in spirits and health from the excitement produced by the little campaign, quite eager and pleased to learn his new military duties, active, cheerful, and healthy, and altogether a different person from the listless moping lad who had dawdled in London coffee-houses and Mrs. Lambert's drawing-room. The troops were under canvas; the weather was glorious, and George found his brother a ready pupil in a fine brisk open-air school of war. Not a little amused, the elder brother, arm-in-arm with the young volunteer, paced the streets of the warlike city, recalled his own brief military experiences of two years back, and saw here a much greater army than that ill-fated one of which he had shared the disasters. The expedition, such as we have seen it, was certainly not glorious, and yet the troops and the nation were in high spirits with it. We were *said* to have

humiliated the proud Gaul. We should have vanquished as
well as humbled him had he dared to appear. What valour,
after all, is like British valour? I dare say some such expressions have been heard in later times. Not that I would
hint that our people brag much more than any other, or more
now than formerly. Have not these eyes beheld the battle-
grounds of Leipzig, Jena, Dresden, Waterloo, Blenheim, Bunker's
Hill, New Orleans? What heroic nation has not fought, has
not conquered, has not run away, has not bragged in its turn?
Well, the British nation was much excited by the glorious
victory of St. Malo. Captured treasures were sent home and
exhibited in London. The people were so excited, that more
laurels and more victories were demanded, and the enthusiastic
army went forth to seek some.

With this new expedition went a volunteer so distinguished,
that we must give him precedence of all other amateur soldiers
or sailors. This was our sailor prince, H.R.H. Prince Edward,
who was conveyed on board the " Essex " in the ship's twelve-
oared barge, the standard of England flying in the bow of the
boat, the Admiral with his flag and boat following the Prince's,
and all the captains following in seniority.

Away sails the fleet, Harry, in high health and spirits, waving
his hat to his friends as they cheer from the shore. He must
and will have his commission before long. There can be no
difficulty about that, George thinks. There is plenty of money
in his little store to buy his brother's ensigncy; but if he can
win it without purchase by gallantry and good conduct, that
were best. The colonel of the regiment reports highly of his
recruit; men and officers like him. It is easy to see that he is
a young fellow of good promise and spirit.

Hip, hip, huzzay! What famous news is this which arrives
ten days after the expedition has sailed? On the 7th and 8th
of August His Majesty's troops have effected a landing in the
Bay des Marais, two leagues westward of Cherbourg, in the face
of a large body of the enemy. Awed by the appearance of
British valour, that large body of the enemy has disappeared.
Cherbourg has surrendered at discretion; and the English
colours are hoisted on the three outlying forts. Seven-and-
twenty ships have been burned in the harbours, and a prodigious
number of fine brass cannon taken. As for your common iron
guns, we have destroyed 'em, likewise the basin (about which
the Mounseers bragged so), and the two piers at the entrance
to the harbour.

There is no end of jubilation in London; just as Mr. Howe's guns arrive from Cherbourg, come Mr. Wolfe's colours captured at Louisbourg. The colours are taken from Kensington to St. Paul's, escorted by fourscore Life Guards and fourscore Horse Grenadiers with officers in proportion, their standards, kettle-drums, and trumpets. At St. Paul's they are received by the Dean and Chapter at the West Gate, and at that minute —bang, bong, bung—the Tower and Park guns salute them! Next day is the turn of the Cherbourg cannon and mortars. These are the guns *we* took. Look at them with their carving and flaunting emblems—their lilies, and crowns, and mottoes! Here they are, the Téméraire, the Malfaisant, the Vainqueur (the Vainqueur, indeed! a pretty *vainqueer* of Britons!), and ever so many more. How the people shout as the pieces are trailed through the streets in procession! As for Hetty and Mrs. Lambert, I believe they are of opinion that Harry took every one of the guns himself, dragging them out of the batteries, and destroying the artillery-men. He has immensely risen in the general estimation in the last few days. Madame de Bernstein has asked about him. Lady Maria has begged her dear Cousin George to see her, and, if possible, give her news of his brother. George, who was quite the head of the family a couple of months since, finds himself deposed, and of scarce any account, in Miss Hetty's eyes at least. Your wit, and your learning, and your tragedies, may be all very well; but what are these in comparison to victories and brass cannon? George takes his deposition very meekly. They are fifteen thousand Britons. Why should they not march and take Paris itself? Nothing more probable, think some of the ladies. They embrace, they congratulate each other; they are in a high state of excitement. For once, they long that Sir Miles and Lady Warrington were in town, so that they might pay her Ladyship a visit, and ask, " What do you say to your nephew, now, pray? Has he not taken twenty-one finest brass cannon; flung a hundred and twenty iron guns into the water, seized twenty-seven ships in the harbour, and destroyed the basin and the two piers at the entrance? " As the whole town rejoices and illuminates, so these worthy folks display brilliant red hangings in their cheeks, and light up candles of joy in their eyes, in honour of their champion and conqueror.

But now, I grieve to say, comes a cloudy day after the fair weather. The appetite of our commanders, growing by what it fed on, led them to think they had not feasted enough on the plunder of St. Malo; and thither, after staying a brief time at Portsmouth, and the Wight, the conquerors of Cherbourg returned. They were landed in the bay of St. Lunar, at the distance of a few miles from the place, and marched towards it intending to destroy it this time. Meanwhile the harbour of St. Lunar was found insecure, and the fleet moved up to St. Cas, keeping up its communication with the invading army.

Now the British Lion found that the town of St. Malo—which he had proposed to swallow at a single mouthful—was guarded by an army of French, which the Governor of Brittany had brought to the succour of his good town, and the meditated *coup de main* being thus impossible, our leaders marched for their ships again, which lay duly awaiting our warriors in the Bay of St. Cas.

Hide, blushing glory, hide St. Cas's day! As our troops were marching down to their ships they became aware of an army following them, which the French governor of the province had sent from Brest. Two-thirds of the troops, and all the artillery, were already embarked, when the Frenchmen came down upon the remainder. Four companies of the First Regiment of Guards and the Grenadier companies of the army, faced about on the beach to await the enemy, whilst the remaining troops were carried off in the boats. As the French descended from the heights round the bay, these Guards and Grenadiers marched out to attack them, leaving an excellent position which they had occupied—a great dyke raised on the shore, and behind which they might have resisted to advantage. And now, eleven hundred men were engaged with six—nay, ten times their number; and, after a while, broke and made for the boats with a *sauve qui peut !* Seven hundred out of the eleven were killed, drowned, or taken prisoners—the General himself was killed—and ah! where were the volunteers?

A man of peace myself, and little intelligent of the practice or the details of war, I own I think less of the engaged troops than of the people they leave behind. Jack the Guardsman and La Tulipe of the Royal Bretagne are face to face, and striving to knock each other's brains out. Bon! It is their nature to —like the bears and lions—and we will not say Heaven, but some power or other has made them so to do. But the girl of Tower Hill, who hung on Jack's neck before he departed; and the lass at Quimper, who gave the Frenchman his *brûle-gueule* and tobacco-box before he departed on the *noir trajet ?* What have you done, poor little tender hearts, that you should grieve so? My business is not with the army, but with the people left behind. What a fine state Miss Hetty Lambert must be in, when she hears of the disaster to the troops and the slaughter of the Grenadier companies! What grief and doubt are in George Warrington's breast; what commiseration in Martin Lambert's, as he looks into his little girl's face and reads her piteous story there? Howe, the brave Commodore, rowing in his barge under the enemy's fire, has rescued with his boats scores and scores of our flying people. More are drowned; hundreds are prisoners, or shot on the beach. Among these where is our Virginian?

CHAPTER LXV

SOLDIER'S RETURN

GREAT Powers! will the vainglory of men, especially of Frenchmen, never cease? Will it be believed, that after the action of St. Cas—a mere affair of cutting off a rearguard, as you are aware—they were so unfeeling as to fire away I don't know how much powder at the Invalides at Paris, and brag and bluster over our misfortune? Is there any magnanimity in hallooing and huzzaying because five or six hundred brave fellows have been caught by ten thousand on a sea-shore, and that fate has overtaken them which is said to befall the hindmost? I had a mind to design an authentic picture of the rejoicings at London upon our glorious success at St. Malo. I fancied the polished guns dragged in procession by our gallant tars; the stout Horse Grenadiers prancing by; the mob waving hats, roaring cheers, picking pockets, and our friends in a balcony in Fleet Street looking on and blessing this scene of British triumph. But now that the French Invalides have been so vulgar as to imitate the Tower, and set up their St. Cas against our St. Malo, I scorn to allude to the stale subject. I say Nolo, not Malo: content, for my part, if Harry has returned from one expedition and t'other with a whole skin. And have I ever said he was so much as bruised? Have I not, for fear of exciting my fair young reader, said that he was as well as ever he had been in his life? The sea air had browned his cheek, and the ball whistling by his side-curl had spared it. The ocean had wet his gaiters and other garments, without swallowing up his body. He had, it is true, shown the lapels of his coat to the enemy; but for as short a time as possible, withdrawing out of their sight as quick as might be. And what, pray, are lapels but reverses? Coats have them, as well as men; and our duty is to wear them with courage and good-humour.

"I can tell you," said Harry, "we all had to run for it; and when our line broke, it was he who could get to the boats who was most lucky. The French horse and foot pursued us down to the sea, and were mingled among us, cutting our men down, and bayoneting them on the ground. Poor Armytage was shot in advance of me, and fell: and I took him up and staggered through the surf to a boat. It was lucky that the sailors in our boat weren't afraid; for the shot were whistling about their ears, breaking the blades of their oars, and riddling their flag with shot; but the officer in command was as cool as if he had been drinking a bowl of punch at Portsmouth, which we had one on landing, I can promise you. Poor Sir John was less lucky than me. He never lived to reach the ship, and the service has lost a fine soldier, and Miss Howe a true gentleman to her husband. There must be these casualties, you see; and his brother gets the promotion—the baronetcy."

"It is of the poor lady I am thinking," says Miss Hetty (to whom haply our volunteer is telling his story); "and the King. Why did the King encourage Sir John Armytage to go? A gentleman could not refuse a command from such a quarter. And now the poor gentleman is dead! Oh, what a state His Majesty must be in!"

"I have no doubt His Majesty will be in a deep state of grief," says papa, wagging his head.

"Now you are laughing! Do you mean, sir, that when a gentleman dies in his service, almost at his feet, the King of England won't feel for him?" Hetty asks. "If I thought that, I vow I would be for the Pretender!"

"The sauce-box would make a pretty little head for Temple Bar," says the General, who could see Miss Hetty's meaning behind her words, and was aware in what a tumult of remorse, of consternation, of gratitude that the danger was over, the little heart was beating. "No," says he, "my dear. Were kings to weep for every soldier, what a life you would make for them! I think better of His Majesty than to suppose him so weak; and, if Miss Hester Lambert got her Pretender, I doubt whether she would be any the happier. That family was never famous for too much feeling."

"But if the King sent Harry—I mean Sir John Armytage—actually to the war in which he lost his life, oughtn't His Majesty to repent very much?" asks the young lady.

"If Harry had fallen, no doubt the Court would have gone into mourning: as it is, gentlemen and ladies were in coloured clothes, yesterday," remarks the General.

"Why should we not make bonfires for a defeat, and put on sackcloth and ashes after a victory?" asks George. "I protest I don't want to thank Heaven for helping us to burn the ships at Cherbourg."

"Yes, you do, George! Not that I have a right to speak, and you ain't ever so much cleverer. But when your country wins you're glad—I know *I* am. When I run away before Frenchmen I'm ashamed—I can't help it, though I *done* it," says Harry. "It don't seem to me right somehow that Englishmen should have to do it," he added gravely. And George smiled; but did not choose to ask his brother what, on the other hand, was the Frenchman's opinion.

"'Tis a bad business," continued Harry gravely: "but 'tis lucky 'twas no worse. The story about the French is, that their Governor, the Duke of Aiguillon, was rather what you call a *moistened chicken*. Our whole retreat might have been cut off, only, to be sure, we ourselves were in a mighty hurry to move. The French local militia behaved famous, I am happy to say; and there was ever so many gentlemen volunteers with 'em, who showed, as they ought to do, in the front. They say the Chevalier of Tour d'Auvergne engaged in spite of the Duke of Aiguillon's orders. Officers told us, who came off with a list of our prisoners and wounded to General Bligh and Lord Howe. He is a Lord now, since the news came of his brother's death to home, George. He is a brave fellow, whether lord or commoner."

"And his sister, who was to have married poor Sir John Armytage, think what *her* state must be!" sighs Miss Hetty, who has grown of late so sentimental.

"And his mother," cries Mrs. Lambert. "Have you seen her Ladyship's address in the papers to the electors of Nottingham? 'Lord Howe being now absent upon the publick service and Lieutenant-Colonel Howe with his regiment at Louisbourg, it rests upon me to beg the favour of your votes and interests that Lieutenant-Colonel Howe may supply the place of his late brother as your representative in Parliament.' Isn't this a gallant woman?"

"A laconic woman," says George.

"How can sons help being brave who have been nursed by such a mother as that?" asks the General.

Our two young men looked at each other.

"If one of us were to fall in defence of his country, we have a mother in Sparta who would think and write so too," says George.

"If Sparta is anywhere Virginia way, I reckon we have," remarks Mr. Harry. "And to think that we should both of us have met the enemy, and both of us been whipped by him, brother!" he adds pensively.

Hetty looks at him, and thinks of him only as he was the other day, tottering through the water towards the boats, his comrade bleeding on his shoulder, the enemy in pursuit, the shot flying round. And it was she who drove him into the danger! Her words provoked him. He never rebukes her now he is returned. Except when asked he scarcely speaks about his adventures at all. He is very grave and courteous with Hetty; with the rest of the family especially frank and tender. But those taunts of hers wounded him. "Little hand!" his looks and demeanour seem to say, "*thou* shouldst not have been lifted against me! It is ill to scorn any one, much more one who has been so devoted to you and all yours. I may not be over quick of wit, but in as far as the heart goes, I am the equal of the best, and the best of my heart your family has had."

Harry's wrong, and his magnanimous endurance of it served him to regain in Miss Hetty's esteem that place which he had lost during the previous month's inglorious idleness. The respect which the fair pay to the brave she gave him. She was no longer pert in her answers, or sarcastic in her observations regarding his conduct. In a word, she was a humiliated, an altered, an improved Miss Hetty.

And all the world seemed to change towards Harry, as he towards the world. He was no longer sulky and indolent; he no more desponded about himself, or defied his neighbours. The colonel of his regiment reported his behaviour as exemplary, and recommended him for one of the commissions vacated by the casualties during the expedition. Unlucky as its termination was, it at least was fortunate to him. His brother volunteers, when they came back to St. James's Street, reported highly of his behaviour. These volunteers and their actions were the theme of everybody's praise. Had he been a general commanding, and slain in the moment of victory, Sir John Armytage could scarce have had more sympathy than that which the nation showed him. The papers teemed with letters about him, and men of wit and sensibility vied with each other in composing epitaphs in his honour. The fate of his affianced bride was bewailed. She was, as we have said, the sister of the brave Commodore who had just returned from this unfortunate expedition, and succeeded to the title of his elder brother, an officer as gallant as himself, who had just fallen in America.

My Lord Howe was heard to speak in special praise of Mr. Warrington, and so he had a handsome share of the fashion and favour which the town now bestowed on the volunteers. Doubtless there were thousands of men employed who were as good as they: but the English ever love their gentlemen, and love that they should distinguish themselves; and these volunteers were voted Paladins and heroes by common accord. As our young noblemen will, they accepted their popularity very affably. White's and Almack's illuminated when they returned, and St. James's embraced its young knights. Harry was restored to full favour amongst them. Their hands were held out eagerly to him again. Even his relations congratulated him; and there came a letter from Castlewood, whither Aunt Bernstein had by this time betaken herself, containing praises of his valour, and a pretty little bank-bill, as a token of his affectionate aunt's approbation. This was under my Lord Castlewood's frank, who sent his regards to both his kinsmen, and an offer of the hospitality of his country house, if they were minded to come to him. And besides this there came to him a private letter through the post—not very well spelt, but in a handwriting which Harry smiled to see again, in which his affectionate cousin, Maria Esmond, told him she always loved to hear his praises (which were in everybody's mouth now), and sympathised in his good or evil fortune; and that, whatever occurred to him, she begged to keep a little place in his heart. Parson Sampson, she wrote, had preached a beautiful sermon about the horrors of war, and the noble actions of men who volunteered to face battle and danger in the service of their country. Indeed, the chaplain wrote himself, presently, a letter full of enthusiasm, in which he saluted Mr. Harry as his friend, his benefactor, his glorious hero. Even Sir Miles Warrington despatched a basket of game from Norfolk: and one bird (shot sitting), with love to my cousin, had a string and paper round the leg, and was sent as the first victim of young Miles's fowling-piece.

And presently, with joy beaming in his countenance, Mr.

Lambert came to visit his young friends at their lodgings in Southampton Row, and announced to them that Mr. Henry Warrington was forthwith to be gazetted as Ensign in the Second Battalion of Kingsley's, the 20th Regiment, which had been engaged in the campaign, and which now at this time was formed into a separate regiment, the 67th. Its colonel was not with his regiment during its expedition to Brittany. He was away at Cape Breton, and was engaged in capturing those guns at Louisbourg, of which the arrival in England had caused such exultation.

CHAPTER LXVI

IN WHICH WE GO A-COURTING

SOME of my amiable readers no doubt are in the custom of visiting that famous garden in the Regent's Park, in which so many of our finned, feathered, four-footed fellow-creatures are accommodated with board and lodging, in return for which they exhibit themselves for our instruction and amusement: and there, as a man's business and private thoughts follow him everywhere and mix themselves with all life and nature round about him, I found myself, whilst looking at some fish in the aquarium, still actually thinking of our friends the Virginians. One of the most beautiful motion-masters I ever beheld, sweeping through his green bath in harmonious curves, now turning his black glistening back to me, now exhibiting his fair white chest, in every movement active and graceful, turned out to be our old homely friend the flounder, whom we have all gobbled up out of his bath of water souchy at Greenwich, without having the slightest idea that he was a beauty.

As is the race of man, so is the race of flounders. If you can but see the latter in his right element, you may view him agile, healthy, and comely: put him out of his place, and behold his beauty is gone, his motions are disgraceful; he flaps the unfeeling ground ridiculously with his tail, and will presently gasp his feeble life out. Take him up tenderly, ere it be too late, and cast him into his native Thames again—— But stop: I believe there is a certain proverb about fish out of water, and that other profound naturalists have remarked on them before me. Now Harry Warrington had been floundering for ever so long a time past and out of his proper element. As soon as he found it, health, strength, spirits, energy, returned to him, and with the tap of the epaulet on his shoulder he sprang up an altered being. He delighted in his new profession; he engaged in all its details, and mastered them with eager quickness. Had I the skill of my friend Lorrequer, I would follow the other Harry into camp, and see him on the march, at the mess, on the parade-ground; I would have many a carouse with him and his companions; I would cheerfully live with him under the tents; I would knowingly explain all the manœuvres of war, and all the details of the life military. As it is the reader must please, out of his experience and imagination, to fill in the colours of the picture of which I can give but meagre hints and outlines, and, above all, fancy Mr. Harry Warrington in his new red coat and yellow facings, very happy to bear the King's colours, and pleased to learn and perform all the duties of his new profession.

As each young man delighted in the excellence of the other, and cordially recognised his brother's superior qualities, George, we may be sure, was proud of Harry's success, and rejoiced in his returning good fortune. He wrote an affectionate letter to his mother in Virginia, recounting all the praises which he had heard of Harry, and which his brother's modesty, George knew, would never allow him to repeat. He described how Harry had won his own first step in the army, and how he, George, would ask his mother leave to share with her the expense of purchasing a higher rank for him.

Nothing, said George, would give him a greater delight than to be able to help his brother, and the more so, as, by his sudden return into life as it were, he had deprived Harry of an inheritance which he had legitimately considered as his own. Labouring under that misconception, Harry had indulged in greater expenses than he ever would have thought of incurring as a younger brother: and George thought it was but fair, and, as it were, as a thank-offering for his own deliverance, that he should contribute liberally to any scheme for his brother's advantage.

And now, having concluded his statement respecting Harry's affairs, George took occasion to speak of his own, and addressed his honoured mother on a point which very deeply concerned himself. She was aware that the best friends he and his brother had found in England were the good Mr. and Mrs. Lambert, the latter Madam Esmond's schoolfellow of earlier years. Where their own blood relations had been worldly and unfeeling, these true friends had ever been generous and kind. The General was respected by the whole army, and beloved by all who knew him. No mother's affection could have been more touching than Mrs. Lambert's for both Madam Esmond's children; and now, wrote Mr. George, he himself had formed an attachment for the elder Miss Lambert, on which he thought the happiness of his life depended, and which he besought his honoured mother to approve. He had made no precise offers to the young lady or her parents; but he was bound to say that he had made little disguise of his sentiments, and that the young lady, as well as her parents, seemed favourable to him. She had been so admirable and exemplary a daughter to her own mother, that he felt sure she would do her duty by his. In a word, Mr. Warrington described the young lady as a model of perfection, and expressed his firm belief that the happiness or misery of his own future life depended upon possessing or losing her. Why do you not produce this letter? haply asks some sentimental reader, of the present Editor, who has said how he has the whole Warrington correspondence in his hands. Why not? Because 'tis cruel to babble the secrets of a young man's love: to overhear his incoherent vows and wild raptures, and to note, in cold blood, the secrets—it may be, the follies—of his passion. Shall we play eavesdropper at twilight embrasures, count sighs and hand-shakes, bottle hot tears: lay our stethoscope on delicate young breasts, and feel their heart throbs? I protest for one, love is sacred. Wherever I see it (as one sometimes may in this world) shooting suddenly out of two pair of eyes; or glancing sadly even from one pair; or looking down from the mother to the baby in her lap; or from papa at his girl's happiness as she is whirling round the room with the captain; or from John Anderson, as his old wife comes into the room—the *bonne vieille*, the ever peerless among women: wherever we see that signal, I say, let us salute it. It is not only wrong to kiss and tell, but to tell about kisses. Everybody who has been admitted to the mystery,—hush about it. Down with him *qui Deæ sacrum vulgarit arcanæ*. Beware how you dine with him: he will print your private talk; as sure as you sail with him, he will throw you over.

Whilst Harry's love of battle has led him to smell powder—to rush upon *reluctantes dracones*, and to carry wounded comrades out of fire, George has been pursuing an amusement much more peaceful and delightful to him: penning sonnets to his mistress's eyebrow, mayhap; pacing in the darkness under her window, and watching the little lamp which shone upon her in her chamber; finding all sorts of pretexts for sending little notes which don't seem to require little answers, but get them; culling bits out of his favourite poets, and flowers out of Covent Garden for somebody's special adornment and pleasure; walking to St. James's Church, singing very likely out of the same Prayer-book, and never hearing one word of the sermon, so much do other thoughts engross him; being prodigiously affectionate to all Miss Theo's relations—to her little brother and sister at school; to the elder at college; to Miss Hetty with whom he engages in gay passages of wit; and to mamma, who is half in love with him herself, Martin Lambert says; for if fathers are sometimes sulky at the appearance of the destined son-in-law, is it not a fact that mothers become sentimental, and, as it were, love their own loves over again?

Gumbo and Sady are for ever on the trot between South-ampton Row and Dean Street. In the summer months, all sorts of junketings and pleasure-parties are devised; and there are countless proposals to go to Ranelagh, to Hampstead, to Vauxhall, to Marylebone Gardens, and what not? George wants the famous tragedy copied out fair for the stage, and who can write such a beautiful Italian hand as Miss Theo? As the sheets pass to and fro they are accompanied by little notes of thanks, of interrogation, of admiration, always. See, here is the packet, marked in Warrington's neat hand, "T's letters, 1758-9." Shall we open them and reveal their tender secrets to the public gaze? Those virgin words were whispered for one ear alone. Years after they were written, the husband read, no doubt, with sweet pangs of remembrance, the fond lines addressed to the lover. It were a sacrilege to show the pair to public eyes: only let kind readers be pleased to take our word that the young lady's letters are modest and pure, the gentle-man's most respectful and tender. In fine, you see, we have said very little about it; but, in these few last months, Mr. George Warrington has made up his mind that he has found the woman of women. She mayn't be the most beautiful. Why, there is Cousin Flora, there is Cœlia, and Ardelia, and a hundred more, who are ever so much more handsome: but her sweet face pleases *him* better than any other in the world. She mayn't be the most clever, but her voice is the dearest and pleasantest to hear; and in her company he is so clever himself; he has such fine thoughts; he uses such eloquent words; he is so generous, noble, witty, that no wonder he delights in it. And, in regard to the young lady,—as thank Heaven I never thought so ill of women as to suppose them to be just,—we may be sure that there is no amount of wit, of wisdom, of beauty, of valour, of virtue with which she does not endow her young hero.

When George's letter reached home, we may fancy that it created no small excitement in the little circle round Madam Esmond's fireside. So he was in love, and wished to marry! It was but natural, and would keep him out of harm's way. If he proposed to unite himself with a well-bred Christian young woman, Madam saw no harm.

" I knew they would be setting their caps at him," says Mountain. " They fancy that his wealth is as great as his estate. He does not say whether the young lady has money. I fear otherwise."

" People would set their caps at him here, I dare say," says Madam Esmond, grimly looking at her dependant, " and try and catch Mr. Esmond Warrington for their own daughters, who are no richer than Miss Lambert may be."

" I suppose your ladyship means me ! " says Mountain. " My Fanny is poor, as you say; and 'tis kind of you to remind me of her poverty ! "

" I said people would set their caps at him. If the cap fits you, *tant pis !* as my papa used to say."

" You think, madam, I am scheming to keep George for my daughter? I thank you, on my word ! A good opinion you seem to have of us after the years we have lived together ! "

" My dear Mountain, I know you much better than to suppose you could ever fancy your daughter would be a suitable match for a gentleman of Mr. Esmond's rank and station," says Madam, with much dignity.

" Fanny Parker was as good as Molly Benson at school, and Mr. Mountain's daughter is as good as Mr. Lambert's ! " Mrs. Mountain cries out.

" Then you *did* think of marrying her to my son? I shall write to Mr. Esmond Warrington, and say how sorry I am that you should be disappointed ! " says the mistress of Castlewood. And we, for our parts, may suppose that Mrs. Mountain was disappointed, and had some ambitious views respecting her daughter—else, why should she have been so angry at the notion of Mr. Warrington's marriage?

In reply to her son, Madam Esmond wrote back that she was pleased with the fraternal love George exhibited; that it was indeed but right in some measure to compensate Harry, whose expectations had led him to adopt a more costly mode of life than he would have entered on had he known he was only a younger son. And with respect to purchasing his promotion, she would gladly halve the expense with Harry's elder brother, being thankful to think his own gallantry had won him his first step. This bestowal of George's money, Madam Esmond added, was at least much more satisfactory than some other extravagances to which she would not advert.

The other extravagance to which Madam alluded was the payment of the ransom to the French captain's family, to which tax George's mother never would choose to submit. She had a determined spirit of her own, which her son inherited. *His* persistence she called pride and obstinacy. What she thought of her own pertinacity, her biographer who lives so far from her time does not pretend to say. Only I dare say people a hundred years ago pretty much resembled their grandchildren of the present date, and loved to have their own way, and to make others follow it.

Now, after paying his own ransom, his brother's debts, and half the price for his promotion, George calculated that no inconsiderable portion of his private patrimony would be swallowed up: nevertheless he made the sacrifice with a perfect good heart. His good mother always enjoined him in her letters to remember who his grandfather was, and to support the dignity of his family accordingly. She gave him various commissions to purchase goods in England, and though she as yet had sent him very trifling remittances, she alluded so constantly to the exalted rank of the Esmonds, to her desire that he should do nothing unworthy of that illustrious family; she advised him so peremptorily and frequently to appear in the first society of the country, to frequent the Court where his ancestors had been accustomed to move, and to appear always in the world in a manner worthy of his name, that George made no doubt his mother's money would be forthcoming when his own ran short, and generously obeyed her injunctions as to his style of life. I find in the Esmond papers of this period, bills for genteel entertainments, tailors' bills for Court suits supplied, and liveries for his honour's negro servants and chairmen, horse-dealers' receipts, and so forth; and am thus led to believe that the elder of our Virginians was also after a while living at a considerable expense.

He was not wild or extravagant like his brother. There was no talk of gambling or race-horses against Mr. George; his table was liberal, his equipages handsome, his purse always full, the estate to which he was heir was known to be immense. I mention these circumstances because they may probably have influenced the conduct both of George and his friends in that very matter concerning which, as I have said, he and his mother had been just corresponding. The young heir of Virginia was travelling for his pleasure and improvement in foreign kingdoms. The queen his mother was in daily correspondence with his Highness, and constantly enjoined him to act as became his lofty station. There could be no doubt from her letters that she desired he should live liberally and magnificently. He was perpetually making purchases at his parent's order. She had not settled as yet; on the contrary, she had wrote out by the last mail for twelve new sets of waggon-harness, and an organ that should play fourteen specified psalm-tunes; which articles George dutifully ordered. She had not paid as yet, and might not to-day or to-morrow, but eventually, of course, she would: and Mr. Warrington never thought of troubling his friends about these calculations, or discussing with them his mother's domestic affairs. They, on their side, took for granted that he was in a state of competence and ease, and, without being mercenary folks, Mr. and Mrs. Lambert were no doubt pleased to see an attachment growing up between their daughter and a young gentleman of such good principles, talents, family, and expectations. There was honesty in all Mr. Esmond Warrington's words and actions, and in his behaviour to the world a certain grandeur and simplicity, which showed him to be a true gentleman. Somewhat cold and haughty in his demeanour to strangers, especially towards the great, he was not in the least supercilious: he was perfectly courteous towards women, and with those people whom he loved, especially kind, amiable, lively, and tender.

No wonder that one young woman we know of got to think him the best man in all the world—alas! not even excepting papa. A great love felt by a man towards a woman makes him better, as regards her, than all other men. We have said that George used to wonder himself when he found how witty, how eloquent, how wise he was, when he talked with the fair young creature whose heart had become all his. . . . I say we will not again listen to their love whispers. Those soft words do not bear being written down. If you please—good sir, or madam, who are sentimentally inclined—lay down the book and think over certain things for yourself. You may be ever so old now; but you remember. It may be all dead and buried; but in a moment, up it springs out of its grave, and looks, and smiles, and whispers as of yore when it clung to your arm, and dropped fresh tears on your heart. It is here, and alive, did I say? O far far away! O lonely hearth and cold ashes! Here is the vase, but the roses are gone; here is the shore, and yonder the ship was moored; but the anchors are up, and it has sailed away for ever.

Et cetera, et cetera, et cetera. This, however, is mere sentimentality; and as regards George and Theo, is neither here nor there. What I mean to say is, that the young lady's family were perfectly satisfied with the state of affairs between her and Mr. Warrington; and though he had not as yet asked the decisive question, everybody else knew what the answer would be when it came.

Mamma perhaps thought the question was a long time coming.

"Psha! my dear!" says the General. "There is time enough in all conscience. Theo is not much more than seventeen; George, if I mistake not, is under forty; and, besides, he must have time to write to Virginia, and ask mamma."

"But suppose she refuses?"

"That will be a bad day for old and young," says the General. "Let us rather say, suppose she consents, my love? —I can't fancy anybody in the world refusing Theo anything she has set her heart on," adds the father: "and I am sure 'tis bent upon this match."

So they all waited with the utmost anxiety until an answer from Madam Esmond should arrive; and trembled lest the French privateers should take the packet-ship by which the precious letter was conveyed.

CHAPTER LXVII

IN WHICH A TRAGEDY IS ACTED, AND TWO MORE ARE BEGUN

JAMES WOLFE, Harry's new Colonel, came back from America a few weeks after our Virginian had joined his regiment. Wolfe had previously been Lieutenant-Colonel of Kingsley's, and a second battalion of the regiment had been formed and given to him in reward for his distinguished gallantry and services at Cape Breton. Harry went with quite unfeigned respect and cordiality to pay his duty to his new commander, on whom the eyes of the world began to be turned now,—the common opinion being that he was likely to become a great General. In the late affairs in France, several officers of great previous repute had been tried and found lamentably wanting. The Duke of Marlborough had shown himself no worthy descendant of his great ancestor. About my Lord George Sackville's military genius there were doubts, even before his unhappy behaviour at Minden prevented a great victory. The nation was longing for military glory, and the Minister was anxious to find a General who might gratify the eager desire of the people. Mr. Wolfe's and Mr. Lambert's business keeping them both in London, the friendly intercourse between those officers was renewed, no one being more delighted than Lambert at his younger friend's good fortune.

Harry, when he was away from his duty, was never tired of hearing Mr. Wolfe's details of the military operations of the last year, about which Wolfe talked very freely and openly. Whatever thought was in his mind, he appears to have spoken it out generously. He had that heroic simplicity which distinguished Nelson afterwards: he talked frankly of his actions. Some of the fine gentlemen at St. James's might wonder and sneer at him; but amongst our little circle of friends we may be sure he found admiring listeners. The young General had the romance of a boy on many matters. He delighted in music and poetry. On the last day of his life he said he would rather have written Gray's " Elegy " than have won a battle. We may be sure that with a gentleman of such literary tastes our friend George would become familiar; and as they were both in love, and both accepted lovers, and both eager for happiness, no doubt they must have had many sentimental conversations together, which would be very interesting to report could we only have accurate accounts of them. In one of his later letters, Warrington writes:—

" I had the honour of knowing the famous General Wolfe, and seeing much of him during his last stay in London. We had a subject of conversation then which was of unfailing interest to both of us, and I could not but admire Mr. Wolfe's simplicity, his frankness, and a sort of glorious bravery which characterised him. He was much in love, and he wanted heaps and heaps of laurels to take to his mistress. ' If it be a sin to covet honour,' he used to say with Harry the Fifth (he was passionately fond of plays and poetry), ' I am the most offending soul alive.' Surely on his last day he had a feast which was enough to satisfy the greediest appetite for glory. He hungered after it. He seemed to me not merely like a soldier going resolutely to do his duty, but rather like a knight in quest of dragons and giants. My own country has furnished of late a chief of a very different order, and quite an opposite genius. I scarce know which to admire most, the Briton's chivalrous ardour, or the more than Roman constancy of our great Virginian."

As Mr. Lambert's official duties detained him in London, his family remained contentedly with him, and I suppose Mr. Warrington was so satisfied with the rural quiet of Southampton Row and the beautiful flowers and trees of Bedford Gardens, that he did not care to quit London for any long period. He made his pilgrimage to Castlewood, and passed a few days there, occupying the chamber of which he had often heard his grandfather talk, and which Colonel Esmond had occupied as a boy: and he was received kindly enough by such members of the family as happened to be at home. But no doubt he loved better to be in London by the side of a young person in whose society he found greater pleasure than any which my Lord Castlewood's circle could afford him, though all the ladies were civil, and Lady Maria especially gracious, and enchanted with the tragedy which George and Parson Sampson read out to the ladies. The chaplain was enthusiastic in its praises, and indeed it was through his interest, and not through Mr. Johnson's after all, that Mr. Warrington's piece ever came on the stage. Mr. Johnson, it is true, pressed the play on his friend Mr. Garrick for " Drury Lane," but Garrick had just made an arrangement with the famous Mr. Home for a tragedy from the pen of the author of " Douglas." Accordingly, " Carpezan " was carried to Mr. Rich at " Covent Garden," and accepted by that manager.

On the night of the production of the piece, Mr. Warrington gave an elegant entertainment to his friends at the " Bedford Head " in Covent Garden, whence they adjourned in a body to the theatre; leaving only one or two with our young author, who remained at the Coffee-house, where friends from time to time came to him with an account of the performance. The part of Carpezan was filled by Barry, Shuter was the old nobleman, Reddish, I need scarcely say, made an excellent Ulric, and the King of Bohemia was by a young actor from Dublin,

Mr. Geoghegan, or Hagan, as he was called on the stage, and who looked and performed the part to admiration. Mrs. Woffington looked too old in the first act as the heroine, but her murder in the fourth act, about which great doubts were expressed, went off to the terror and delight of the audience. Miss Wayn sang the ballad which is supposed to be sung by the King's page, just at the moment of the unhappy wife's execution, and all agreed that Barry was very terrible and pathetic as Carpezan, especially in the execution scene. The grace and elegance of the young actor, Hagan, won general applause. The piece was put very elegantly on the stage by Mr. Rich, though there was some doubt whether, in the march of janissaries in the last, the manager was correct in introducing a favourite elephant, which had figured in various pantomimes, and by which one of Mr. Warrington's black servants marched in a Turkish habit. The other sat in the footman's gallery, and uproariously wept and applauded at the proper intervals.

The execution of Sybilla was the turning-point of the piece. Her head off, George's friends breathed freely, and one messenger after another came to him at the Coffee-house, to announce the complete success of the tragedy. Mr. Barry, amidst general applause, announced the play for repetition, and that it was the work of a young gentleman of Virginia, his first attempt in the dramatic style.

We should like to have been in the box where all our friends were seated during the performance, to have watched Theo's flutter and anxiety whilst the success of the play seemed dubious, and have beheld the blushes and the sparkles in her eyes, when the victory was assured. Harry, during the little trouble in the fourth act, was deadly pale—whiter, Mrs. Lambert said, than Barry, with all his chalk. But if Briareus could have clapped hands, he could scarcely have made more noise than Harry at the end of the piece. Mr. Wolfe and General Lambert huzzayed enthusiastically. Mrs. Lambert, of course, cried; and though Hetty said, " Why do you cry, mamma? you don't want any of them alive again; you know it serves them all right: "—the girl was really as much delighted as any person present, including little Charley from the Chartreux, who had leave from Dr. Crusius for that evening, and Miss Lucy, who had been brought from boarding-school on purpose to be present on the great occasion. My Lord Castlewood and his sister, Lady Maria, were present; and his Lordship went from his box and complimented Mr. Barry and the other actors on the stage; and Parson

Sampson was invaluable in the pit, where he led the applause, having, I believe, given previous instructions to Gumbo to keep an eye upon him from the gallery, and do as he did.

Be sure there was a very jolly supper of Mr. Warrington's friends that night—much more jolly than Mr. Garrick's, for example, who made but a very poor success with his " Agis " and its dreary choruses, and who must have again felt that he had missed a good chance, in preferring Mr. Home's tragedy to our young author's. A jolly supper, did we say?—many jolly suppers. Mr. Gumbo gave an entertainment to several gentlemen of the shoulder-knot, who had concurred in supporting his master's masterpiece: Mr. Henry Warrington gave a supper at the " Star and Garter," in Pall Mall, to ten officers of his new regiment, who had come up for the express purpose of backing " Carpezan; " and finally, Mr. Warrington received the three principal actors of the tragedy, our family-party from the side-box, Mr. Johnson and his ingenious friend, Mr. Reynolds the painter, my Lord Castlewood and his sister, and one or two more. My Lady Maria happened to sit next to the young actor who had performed the part of the King. Mr. Warrington somehow had Miss Theo for a neighbour, and no doubt passed a pleasant evening beside her. The greatest animation and cordiality prevailed, and when toasts were called, Lady Maria gaily gave " The King of Hungary " for hers. That gentleman, who had plenty of eloquence and fire, and excellent manners, on as well as off the stage, protested that he had already suffered death in the course of the evening, hoped that he should die a hundred times more on the same field; but, dead or living, vowed he knew whose humble servant he ever should be. Ah, if he had but a real crown in place of his diadem of pasteboard and tinsel, with what joy would he lay it at her Ladyship's feet! Neither my Lord nor Mr. Esmond were over well pleased with the gentleman's exceeding gallantry—a part of which they attributed, no doubt justly, to the wine and punch, of which he had been partaking very freely. Theo and her sister, who were quite new to the world, were a little frightened by the exceeding energy of Mr. Hagan's manner—but Lady Maria, much more experienced, took it in perfectly good part. At a late hour coaches were called, to which the gentlemen attended the ladies, after whose departure some of them returned to the supper-room, and the end was that Carpezan had to be carried away in a chair, and that the King of Hungary had a severe headache; and that the Poet, though he remembered making a great number of speeches, was quite astounded when half-a-dozen of his guests appeared at his house the next day, whom he had invited overnight to come and sup with him once more.

As he put Mrs. Lambert and her daughters into their coach on the night previous, all the ladies were flurried, delighted, excited; and you may be sure our gentleman was with them the next day, to talk of the play and the audience, and the actors, and the beauties of the piece, over and over again. Mrs. Lambert had heard that the ladies of the theatre were dangerous company for young men. She hoped George would have a care, and not frequent the green-room too much.

George smiled, and said he had a preventive against all green-room temptations, of which he was not in the least afraid; and as he spoke he looked in Theo's face, as if in those eyes lay the amulet which was to preserve him from all danger.

"Why should he be afraid, mamma?" asks the maiden simply. She had no idea of danger or of guile.

"No, my darling, I don't think he need be afraid," says the mother, kissing her.

"You don't suppose Mr. George would fall in love with that painted old creature who performed the chief part?" asks Miss Hetty, with a toss of her head. "She must be old enough to be his mother."

"Pray, do you suppose that at our age nobody can care for us, or that we have no hearts left?" asks mamma, very tartly. "I believe, or I may say, I hope and trust, your father thinks otherwise. *He* is, I imagine, perfectly satisfied, miss. *He* does not sneer at age, whatever little girls out of the school-room may do. And they had much better be back there, and they had much better remember what the fifth commandment is—that they had, Hetty!"

"I didn't think I was breaking it by saying that an actress was as old as George's mother," pleaded Hetty.

"George's mother is as old as I am, miss!—at least she was when we were *at school*. And Fanny Parker—Mrs. Mountain who now is—was seven months older, and we were in the French class together; and I have no idea that our age is to be made the subject of remarks and ridicule by our children, and I will thank you to spare it, if you please! Do you consider your mother too old, George?"

"I am glad my mother is of your age, Aunt Lambert," says George, in the most sentimental manner.

Strange infatuation of passion—singular perversity of reason!

At some period before his marriage, it not unfrequently happens that a man actually is fond of his mother-in-law! At this time our good General vowed, and with some reason, that he was jealous. Mrs. Lambert made much more of George than of any other person in the family. She dressed up Theo to the utmost advantage in order to meet him; she was for ever caressing her, and appealing to her when he spoke. It was " Don't you think he looks well? "—" Don't you think he looks pale, Theo, to-day? "—' Don't you think he has been sitting up over his books too much at night? " and so forth. If he had a cold, she would have liked to make gruel for him and see his feet in hot water. She sent him recipes of her own for his health. When he was away, she never ceased talking about him to her daughter. I dare say Miss Theo liked the subject well enough. When he came she was sure to be wanted in some part of the house, and would bid Theo take care of him till she returned. Why, before she returned to the room, could you hear her talking outside the door to her youngest innocent children, to her servants in the upper regions, and so forth? When she re-appeared, was not Mr. George always standing or sitting at a considerable distance from Miss Theo—except, to be sure, on that one day when she had just happened to drop her scissors, and he had naturally stooped down to pick them up? Why was she blushing? Were not youthful cheeks made to blush, and roses to bloom in the spring? Not that mamma ever noted the blushes, but began quite an artless conversation about this or that, as she sat down brimful of happiness to her work-table.

And at last there came a letter from Virginia in Madam Esmond's neat well-known hand, and over which George trembled and blushed before he broke the seal. It was in answer to the letter which he had sent home, respecting his brother's commission and his own attachment to Miss Lambert. Of his intentions respecting Harry, Madam Esmond fully approved. As for his marriage, she was not against early marriages. She would take his picture of Miss Lambert with the allowance that was to be made for lover's portraits, and hope, for his sake, that the young lady was all he described her to be. With money, as Madam Esmond gathered from her son's letter, she did not appear to be provided at all, which was a pity, as, though wealthy in land, their family had but little ready-money. However, by Heaven's blessing, there was plenty at home for children and children's children, and the wives of her sons should share all she had. When she heard

more at length from Mr. and Mrs. Lambert, she would reply
for her part more fully. She did not pretend to say that she
had not greater hopes for her son, as a gentleman of his name
and prospects might pretend to the hand of the first lady of
the land; but as Heaven had willed that her son's choice should
fall upon her old friend's daughter, she acquiesced, and would
welcome George's wife as her own child. This letter was
brought by Mr. Van den Bosch of Albany, who had lately
bought a very large estate in Virginia, and who was bound for
England to put his granddaughter to a boarding-school. She,
Madam Esmond, was not mercenary, nor was it because this
young lady was heiress of a very great fortune that she desired
her sons to pay Mr. Van d. B. every attention. Their properties
lay close together, and could Harry find in the young lady
those qualities of person and mind *suitable for a companion for
life*, at least she would have the satisfaction of seeing both her
children near her in her declining years. Madam Esmond
concluded by sending her affectionate compliments to Mrs.
Lambert, from whom she begged to hear further, and her
blessing to the young lady who was to be her daughter-in-law.

The letter was not cordial, and the writer evidently but half-
satisfied; but, such as it was, her consent was here formally
announced. How eagerly George ran away to Soho with the
long-desired news in his pocket! I suppose our worthy friends
there must have read his news in his countenance—else why
should Mrs. Lambert take her daughter's hand and kiss her
with such uncommon warmth, when George announced that he
had received letters from home? Then, with a break in his
voice, a pallid face, and a considerable tremor, turning to Mr.
Lambert, he said: "Madam Esmond's letter, sir, is in reply
to one of mine, in which I acquainted her that I had formed an
attachment in England, for which I asked my mother's approval.
She gives her consent, I am grateful to say, and I have to pray
my dear friends to be equally kind to me."

"God bless thee, my dear boy!" says the good General,
laying a hand on the young man's head. "I am glad to have
thee for a son, George. There, there, don't go down on your
knees, young folks! George may, to be sure, and thank God
for giving him the best little wife in all England. Yes, my dear,
except when you were ill, you never caused me a heartache—
and happy is the man, I say, who wins thee!"

I have no doubt the young people knelt before their parents,
as was the fashion in those days; and am perfectly certain that

Mrs. Lambert kissed both of them, and likewise bedewed her pocket-handkerchief in the most plentiful manner. Hetty was not present at this sentimental scene, and when she heard of it, spoke with considerable asperity, and a laugh that was by no means pleasant, saying, " Is this all the news you have to give me? Why, I have known it these months past. Do you think I have no eyes to see, and no ears to hear, indeed? " But in private she was much more gentle. She flung herself on her sister's neck, embracing her passionately, and vowing that never never would Theo find any one to love her like her sister. With Theo she became entirely mild and humble. She could not abstain from her jokes and satire with George, but he was too happy to heed her much, and too generous not to see the cause of her jealousy.

When all parties concerned came to read Madam Esmond's letter, that document, it is true, appeared rather vague. It contained only a promise that she would receive the young people at her house, and no sort of proposal for a settlement. The General shook his head over the letter—he did not think of examining it until some days after the engagement had been made between George and his daughter: but now he read Madam Esmond's words, they gave him but small encouragement.

" Bah! " says George. " I shall have three hundred pounds for my tragedy. I can easily write a play a year; and if the worst comes to the worst, we can live on that."

" On that and your patrimony," says Theo's father.

George now had to explain, with some hesitation, that what with paying bills for his mother, and Harry's commission and debts, and his own ransom—George's patrimony proper was well nigh spent.

Mr. Lambert's countenance looked graver still at this announcement, but he saw his girl's eyes turned towards him with an alarm so tender, that he took her in his arms and vowed that, let the worst come to the worst, his darling should not be balked of her wish.

About the going back to Virginia, George frankly owned that he little liked the notion of returning to be entirely dependent on his mother. He gave General Lambert an idea of his life at home, and explained how little to his taste that slavery was. No. Why should he not stay in England, write more tragedies, study for the bar, get a place, perhaps? Why, indeed? He straightway began to form a plan for another tragedy. He brought portions of his work, from time to time, to Miss Theo and her sister; Hetty yawned over the work, but Theo pronounced it to be still more beautiful and admirable than the last, which was perfect.

The engagement of our young friends was made known to the members of their respective families, and announced to Sir Miles Warrington, in a ceremonious letter from his nephew. For a while Sir Miles saw no particular objection to the marriage; though, to be sure, considering his name and prospects, Mr. Warrington might have looked higher. The truth was, that Sir Miles imagined that Madam Esmond had made some considerable settlement on her son, and that his circumstances were more than easy. But when he heard that George was entirely dependent on his mother, and that his own small patrimony was dissipated, as Harry's had been before, Sir Miles's indignation at his nephew's imprudence knew no bounds; he could not find words to express his horror and anger at the want of principle exhibited by both these unhappy young men: he thought it his duty to speak his mind about them, and wrote his opinion to his sister Esmond in Virginia. As for General and Mrs. Lambert, who passed for respectable persons, was it to be borne that such people should inveigle a penniless young man into a marriage with their penniless daughter? Regarding them, and George's behaviour, Sir Miles fully explained his views to Madam Esmond, gave half a finger to George whenever his nephew called on him in town, and did not even invite him to partake of the famous family small-beer. Towards Harry his uncle somewhat unbent; Harry had done his duty in the campaign, and was mentioned with praise in high quarters. He had sowed his wild oats,—he at least was endeavouring to amend; but George was a young prodigal, fast careering to ruin, and his name was only mentioned in the family with a groan. Are there any poor fellows nowadays, I wonder, whose polite families fall on them and persecute them; groan over them and stone them, and hand stones to their neighbours that they may do likewise? All the patrimony spent? Gracious heavens! Sir Miles turned pale when he saw his nephew coming. Lady Warrington prayed for him as a dangerous reprobate; and, in the meantime, George was walking the town, quite unconscious that he was occasioning so much wrath and so much devotion. He took little Miley to the play and brought him back again. He sent tickets to his aunts and cousins which they could not refuse, you know; it would look too marked

were they to break altogether. So they not only took the
tickets, but whenever country constituents came to town they
asked for more, taking care to give the very worst motives to
George's intimacy with the theatre, and to suppose that he and
the actresses were on terms of the most disgraceful intimacy.
An august personage having been to the theatre, and expressed
his approbation of Mr. Warrington's drama to Sir Miles, when
he attended his R-y-l H-g-n-ss's levée at Saville House, Sir
Miles, to be sure, modified his opinion regarding the piece, and
spoke henceforth more respectfully of it. Meanwhile, as we
have said, George was passing his life entirely careless of the
opinion of all the uncles, aunts, and cousins in the world.

Most of the Esmond cousins were at least more polite and
cordial than George's kinsfolk of the Warrington side. In spite
of his behaviour over the cards, Lord Castlewood, George always
maintained, had a liking for our Virginians, and George was
pleased enough to be in his company. He was a far abler man
than many who succeeded in life. He had a good name, and
somehow only stained it; a considerable wit, and nobody
trusted it; and a very shrewd experience and knowledge of
mankind, which made him mistrust them, and himself most of
all, and which perhaps was the bar to his own advancement.
My Lady Castlewood, a woman of the world, wore always a
bland mask, and received Mr. George with perfect civility, and
welcomed him to lose as many guineas as he liked at her Ladyship's card-tables. Between Mr. William and the Virginian
brothers there never was any love lost; but, as for Lady Maria,
though her love-affair was over, she had no rancour; she professed for her cousins a very great regard and affection, a part
of which the young gentlemen very gratefully returned. She
was charmed to hear of Harry's valour in the campaign; she
was delighted with George's success at the theatre; she was
for ever going to the play, and had all the favourite passages of
" Carpezan " by heart. One day, as Mr. George and Miss Theo
were taking a sentimental walk in Kensington Gardens, whom
should they light upon but their cousin Maria in company with
a gentleman in a smart suit and handsome laced hat, and who
should the gentleman be but His Majesty King Louis of Hungary,
Mr. Hagan? He saluted the party, and left them presently.
Lady Maria had only just happened to meet him. Mr. Hagan
came sometimes, he said, for quiet, to study his parts in
Kensington Gardens, and George and the two ladies walked
together to Lord Castlewood's door in Kensington Square, Lady

Maria uttering a thousand compliments to Theo upon her good looks, upon her virtue, upon her future happiness, upon her papa and mamma, upon her destined husband, upon her paduasoy cloak and dear little feet and shoe-buckles.

Harry happened to come to London that evening, and slept at his accustomed quarters. When George appeared at breakfast, the Captain was already in the room (the custom of that day was to call all army gentlemen Captains), and looking at the letters on the breakfast-table.

" Why, George," he cries, " there is a letter from Maria ! "

" Little boy bring it from Common Garden last night— Master George asleep," says Gumbo.

" What can it be about ? " asks Harry, as George peruses his letter with a queer expression of face.

" About my play, to be sure," George answers, tearing up the paper, and still wearing his queer look.

" What, she is not writing love-letters to *you*, is she, Georgy ? "

" No, certainly not to me," replies the other. But he spoke no word more about the letter; and when at dinner in Dean Street, Mrs. Lambert said, " So you met somebody walking with the King of Hungary yesterday in Kensington Gardens ? "

" What little tell-tale told you ? A mere casual rencontre— the King goes there to study his parts, and Lady Maria happened to be crossing the garden to visit some of the *other* King's servants at Kensington Palace." And so there was an end to that matter for the time being.

Other events were at hand fraught with interest to our Virginians. One evening after Christmas, the two gentlemen, with a few more friends, were met round General Lambert's supper-table, and among the company was Harry's new Colonel of the 67th, Major-General Wolfe. The young General was more than ordinarily grave. The conversation all related to the war. Events of great importance were pending. The great Minister now in power was determined to carry on the war on a much more extended scale than had been attempted hitherto: an army was ordered to Germany to help Prince Ferdinand; another great expedition was preparing for America, and here says Mr. Lambert, " I will give you the health of the Commander—a glorious campaign, and a happy return to him ! "

" Why do you not drink the toast, General James ? " asked the hostess of her guest.

" He must not drink his own toast," says General Lambert; " it is we must do that ! "

What, was James appointed?—All the ladies must drink such a toast as that, and they mingled their kind voices with the applause of the rest of the company.

Why did he look so melancholy? the ladies asked of one another when they withdrew. In after days they remembered his pale face.

"Perhaps he has been parting from his sweetheart," suggests tender-hearted Mrs. Lambert. And at this sentimental notion, no doubt all the ladies looked sad.

The gentlemen, meanwhile, continued their talk about the war and its chances. Mr. Wolfe did not contradict the speakers when they said that the expedition was to be directed against Canada.

"Ah, sir," says Harry, "I wish your regiment was going with you, and that I might pay another visit to my old friends at Quebec."

What, had Harry been there? Yes. He described his visit to the place five years before, and knew the city, and the neighbourhood, well. He lays a number of bits of biscuit on the table before him, and makes a couple of rivulets of punch on each side. "This fork is the Isle d'Orleans," says he, "with the north and south branches of St. Lawrence on each side. Here's the Low Town, with a battery—how many guns was mounted there in our time, brother?—but at long shots from the St. Joseph shore you might play the same game. Here's what they call the little river, the St. Charles, and bridge of boats with a *tête de pont* over to the place of arms. Here's the citadel, and here's convents—ever so many convents—and the cathedral; and here, outside the lines to the west and south, is what they call the Plains of Abraham—where a certain little affair took place, do you remember, brother? He and a young officer of the Roussillon regiment *ça-ça*'d at each other for twenty minutes, and George pinked him, and then they *juré*'d each other an *amitié éternelle*. Well it was for George: for his second saved his life on that awful day of Braddock's defeat. He was a fine little fellow, and I give his toast: Je bois à la santé du Chevalier de Florac!"

"What, can you speak French, too, Harry?" asks Mr. Wolfe. The young man looked at the General with eager eyes.

"Yes," says he, "I can speak, but not so well as George."

"But he remembers the city, and can place the batteries, you see, and knows the ground a thousand times better than I do!" cries the elder brother.

The two elder officers exchanged looks with one another; Mr. Lambert smiled and nodded, as if in reply to the mute queries of his comrade: on which the other spoke. "Mr. Harry," he said, "if you have had enough of fine folks, and White's and horse-racing——"

"Oh, sir!" says the young man, turning very red.

"And if you have a mind to a sea-voyage at a short notice, come and see me at my lodgings to-morrow."

What was that sudden uproar of cheers which the ladies heard in their drawing-room? It was the hurrah which Harry Warrington gave when he leaped up at hearing the General's invitation.

The women saw no more of the gentlemen that night. General Lambert had to be away upon his business early next morning, before seeing any of his family; nor had he mentioned a word of Harry's outbreak on the previous evening. But when he rejoined his folks at dinner, a look at Miss Hetty's face informed the worthy gentleman that she knew what had passed on the night previous, and what was about to happen to the young Virginian. After dinner Mrs. Lambert sat demurely at her work, Miss Theo took her book of Italian poetry. Neither of the General's customary guests happened to be present that evening.

He took little Hetty's hand in his, and began to talk with her. He did not allude to the subject which he knew was uppermost in her mind, except that by a more than ordinary gentleness and kindness he perhaps caused her to understand that her thoughts were known to him.

"I have breakfasted," says he, "with James Wolfe this morning, and our friend Harry was of the party. When he and the other guests were gone, I remained and talked with James about the great expedition on which he is going to sail. Would that his brave father had lived a few months longer to see him come back covered with honours from Louisbourg, and knowing that all England was looking to him to achieve still greater glory! James is dreadfully ill in body—so ill that I am frightened for him—and not a little depressed in mind at having to part from the young lady whom he has loved so long. A little rest, he thinks, might have set his shattered frame up, and to call her his has been the object of his life. But, great as his love is (and he is as romantic as one of you young folks of seventeen), honour and duty are greater, and he leaves home, and wife, and ease, and health, at their bidding. Every man of honour would do the like; every woman who loves him truly would buckle on his armour for him. James goes to take leave of his mother to-night; and though she loves him devotedly, and is one of the tenderest women in the world, I am sure she will show no sign of weakness at his going away."

" When does he sail, papa? " the girl asked.

" He will be on board in five days." And Hetty knew quite well who sailed with him.

CHAPTER LXVIII

IN WHICH HARRY GOES WESTWARD

OUR tender hearts are averse to all ideas and descriptions of parting; and I shall therefore say nothing of Harry Warrington's feelings at taking leave of his brother and friends. Were not thousands of men in the same plight? Had not Mr. Wolfe his mother to kiss (his brave father had quitted life during his son's absence on the glorious Louisbourg campaign), and his sweetheart to clasp in a farewell embrace? Had not stout Admiral Holmes, before sailing westward, with his squadron, the " Somerset," the " Terrible," the " Northumberland," the " Royal William," the " Trident," the " Diana," the " Seahorse "—his own flag being hoisted on board the " Dublin "—to take leave of Mrs. and the Misses Holmes? Was Admiral Saunders, who sailed the day after him, exempt from human feeling? Away go William and his crew of jovial sailors, ploughing through the tumbling waves, and poor Black-eyed Susan on shore watches the ship as it dwindles in the sunset!

It dwindles in the west. The night falls darkling over the ocean. They are gone: but their hearts are at home yet awhile. In silence, with a heart inexpressibly soft and tender, how each man thinks of those he has left! What a chorus of pitiful prayer rises up to the Father, at sea and on shore, on that parting night: at home by the vacant bedside, where the wife kneels in tears; round the fire, where the mother and children together pour out their supplications; or on deck, where the seafarer looks up to the stars of heaven, as the ship cleaves through the roaring midnight waters! To-morrow the sun rises upon our common life again, and we commence our daily task of toil and duty.

George accompanies his brother, and stays a while with him at Portsmouth whilst they are waiting for a wind. He shakes Mr. Wolfe's hand, looks at his pale face for the last time, and sees the vessels depart amid the clangour of bells, and the thunder of cannon from the shore. Next day he is back at his home, and at that business which is sure one of the most selfish and absorbing of the world's occupations, to which almost every man who is thirty years old has served, ere this, his apprenticeship. He has a pang of sadness as he looks in at the lodgings to the little room which Harry used to occupy, and sees his half-burned papers still in the grate. In a few minutes he is on his way to Dean Street again, and whispering by the fitful firelight in the ear of the clinging sweetheart. She is very happy—oh, so happy! at his return. She is ashamed of being so. Is it not heartless to be so, when poor Hetty is so melancholy? Poor little Hetty! Indeed, it *is* selfish to be glad when she is in such a sad way. It makes one quite wretched to see her. "Don't, sir! Well I *ought* to be wretched, and it's very very wicked of me if I'm not," says Theo; and one can understand her soft-hearted repentance. What she means by "Don't" who can tell? I have said the room was dark, and the fire burned fitfully —and "Don't" is no doubt uttered in one of the dark fits. Enter servants with supper and lights. The family arrives; the conversation becomes general. The destination of the fleet is known everywhere now. The force on board is sufficient to beat all the French in Canada; and, under such an officer as Wolfe, to repair the blunders and disasters of previous campaigns. He looked dreadfully ill, indeed. But he has a great soul in a feeble body. The Ministers, the country hope the utmost from him. After supper, according to custom, Mr. Lambert assembles his modest household, of whom George Warrington may be said quite to form a part; and as he prays for all travellers by land and water, Theo and her sister are kneeling together. And so, as the ship speeds farther and farther into the West, the fond thoughts pursue it; and the night passes, and the sun rises.

A day or two more, and everybody is at his books or his usual work. As for George Warrington, that celebrated dramatist is busy about another composition. When the tragedy of "Carpezan" had run some thirty or twoscore nights, other persons of genius took possession of the theatre.

There may have been persons who wondered how the town could be so fickle as ever to tire of such a masterpiece as the tragedy—who could not bear to see the actors dressed in other habits, reciting other men's verses; but George, of a sceptical turn of mind, took the fate of his tragedy very philosophically, and pocketed the proceeds with much quiet satisfaction. From Mr. Dodsley, the bookseller, he had the usual compliment of a hundred pounds; from the manager of the theatre two hundred or more; and such praises from the critics and his friends that he set to work to prepare another piece, with which he hoped to achieve even greater successes than by his first performance.

Over these studies, and the other charming business which occupies him, months pass away. Happy business! Happiest time of youth and life, when love is first spoken and returned; when the dearest eyes are daily shining welcome, and the fondest lips never tire of whispering their sweet secrets: when the parting look that accompanies " Good night! " gives delightful warning of to-morrow; when the heart is so overflowing with love and happiness, that it has to spare for all the world; when the day closes with glad prayers, and opens with joyful hopes; when doubt seems cowardice, misfortune impossible, poverty only a sweet trial of constancy! Theo's elders, thankfully remembering their own prime, sit softly by and witness this pretty comedy performed by their young people. And in one of his later letters, dutifully written to his wife during a temporary absence from home, George Warrington records how he had been to look up at the windows of the dear old house in Dean Street, and wondered who was sitting in the chamber where he and Theo had been so happy.

Meanwhile we can learn how the time passes, and our friends are engaged, by some extracts from George's letters to his brother.

" *From the old Window opposite Bedford Gardens,*
this 20th August, 1759.

" WHY are you gone back to rugged rocks, bleak shores, burning summers, nipping winters, at home, when you might have been cropping ever so many laurels in Germany? Kingsley's are coming back as covered with 'em as Jack-a-Green on May-day. Our six regiments did wonders; and our horse would have done if my Lord George Sackville only had let them. But when Prince Ferdinand said ' Charge! ' his Lordship could not hear, or could not translate the German word for ' Forward; ' and so we only beat the French, without utterly annihilating them, as we might, had Lord Granby or Mr. Warrington had the command. My Lord is come back to town, and is shouting for a Court-martial. He held his head high enough in prosperity: in misfortune he shows such a constancy of arrogance that one almost admires him. He looks as if he rather envied poor Mr. Byng, and the not shooting him were a *manque d'égards* towards him.

" The Duke has had notice to get himself in readiness for departing from this world of grandeurs and victories, and downfalls and disappointments. An attack of palsy has visited His Royal Highness; and *pallida mors* has just peeped in at his door, as it were, and said, ' I will call again.' Tyrant as he was, this Prince has been noble in disgrace; and no king has ever had a truer servant than ours has found in his son. Why do I like the losing side always, and am I disposed to revolt against the winners? Your famous Mr. P——, your chief's patron and discoverer, I have been to hear in the House of Commons twice or thrice. I revolt against his magniloquence. I wish some little David would topple over that swelling giant. His thoughts and his language are always attitudinising. I like Barry's manner best, though the other is the more awful actor.

" Pocahontas gets on apace. Barry likes his part of Captain Smith; and, though he will have him wear a red coat and blue facings and an epaulet, I have a fancy to dress him exactly like one of the pictures of Queen Elizabeth's gentlemen at Hampton Court; with a ruff and a square beard and square shoes. ' And Pocahontas —would you like her to be tattooed? ' asks Uncle Lambert. Hagan's part as the warrior who is in love with her, and, seeing her partiality for the Captain, nobly rescues him from death, I trust will prove a hit. A strange fish is this Hagan: his mouth full of stage-plays and rant, but good, honest, and brave, if I don't err. He is angry at having been cast lately for Sir O'Brallaghan, in Mr. Macklin's new farce of ' Love A-la-mode.' He says that he does not keer to disgreece his tongue with imiteetions of that rascal brogue. As if there was any call for imiteetions, when he has such an admirable twang of his own!

" Shall I tell you? Shall I hide the circumstance? Shall I hurt your feelings? Shall I set you in a rage of jealousy, and cause you to ask for leave to return to Europe? Know, then, that though Carpezan is long since dead, Cousin Maria is for ever coming to the playhouse. Tom Spencer has spied her out night after night in the gallery, and she comes on the nights when Hagan performs. Quick, Borroughs, Mr. Warrington's boots and portmanteau! Order a chaise and four for Portsmouth immediately! The letter which I burned one morning when we were at breakfast (I may let the cat out of the bag, now puss has such a prodigious way to run) was from Cousin M., hinting that she wished me to tell no tales about her: but I can't help just whispering to you that Maria at this moment is busy consoling herself as fast as possible. Shall I spoil sport? Shall I tell her brother? Is the affair any business of mine? What have the Esmonds done for you and me but win our money at cards? Yet I like our noble cousin. It seems to me that he would be good if he could—or rather, he would have been once. He has been set on a wrong way of life, from which 'tis now probably too late to rescue him. *O beati agricolæ!* Our Virginia was dull, but let us thank Heaven we were bred there. We were made little slaves, but not slaves to wickedness, gambling, bad male and female company. It was not until my poor Harry left home that he fell among thieves. I mean thieves *en grand* such as waylaid him and stripped him on English highroads. I consider you none the worse because you were the unlucky one, and had to deliver your purse up. And now you are going to retrieve, and make a good name for yourself; and kill more ' French dragons,' and become a great commander. And our mother will talk of her son the Captain, the Colonel, the General, and have his picture painted with all his stars and epaulets, while poor I shall be but a dawdling poetaster, or, if we may hope for the best, a snug-place man, with a little box at Richmond or Kew, and a half-score of little picaninnies, that will come and bob curtseys at the garden-gate when their uncle the General rides up on his great charger, with his aide-de-camp's pockets filled with gingerbread for the nephews and nieces. 'Tis for you to brandish the sword of Mars. As for me I look forward to a quiet life: a quiet little home, a quiet little library full of books, and a little Some-one *dulce ridentem, dulce loquentem*, on t'other side of the fire, as I scribble away at my papers. I am so pleased with this prospect, so utterly contented and happy, that I feel afraid as I think of it, lest it should escape me: and even to my dearest Hal, am shy of speaking of my happiness. What is ambition to me, with this certainty? What do I care for wars, with this beatific peace smiling near?

" Our mother's friend, Mynheer Van den Bosch, has been away on a tour to discover his family in Holland, and, strange to say, has found one. Miss (who was intended by maternal solicitude to be a wife for your worship) has had six months at Kensington School, and is coming out with a hundred pretty accomplishments, which are to complete her a perfect fine lady. Her grandpapa brought her to make a curtsey in Dean Street, and a mighty elegant curtsey she made. Though she is scarce seventeen, no dowager of sixty can be more at her ease. She conversed with Aunt Lambert on an equal footing; she treated the girls as chits—to Hetty's wrath and Theo's amusement. She talked politics with the General, and the last routs, dresses, operas, fashions, scandal, with such perfect ease that, but for a blunder or two, you might have fancied Miss Lydia was born in Mayfair. At the Court end of the town she will live, she says; and has no patience with her grandfather, who has a lodging in Monument Yard. For those who love a brown beauty, a prettier little *mignonne* creature cannot be seen. But my taste, you know, dearest brother, and . . ."

Here follows a page of raptures and quotations of verse, which, out of a regard for the reader, and the writer's memory, the Editor of the present pages declines to reprint. Gentlemen and ladies of a certain age may remember the time when they indulged in these rapturous follies on their own accounts; when the praises of the charmer were for ever warbling from their lips or trickling from their pens; when the flowers of life were in full bloom, and all the birds of spring were singing. The twigs are now bare, perhaps, and the leaves have fallen; but, for all that, shall we not remember the vernal time? As for you, young people, whose May (or April, is it?) has not

commenced yet, you need not be detained over other folks'
love-rhapsodies; depend on it, when your spring season arrives,
kindly Nature will warm all your flowers into bloom, and rouse
your glad bosoms to pour out their full song.

CHAPTER LXIX

A LITTLE INNOCENT

GEORGE WARRINGTON has mentioned in the letter just quoted,
that in spite of my Lord Castlewood's previous play transactions
with Harry, my Lord and George remained friends, and met on
terms of good kinsmanship. Did George want franks, or an
introduction at Court, or a place in the House of Lords to hear
a debate, his cousin was always ready to serve him, was a
pleasant and witty companion, and would do anything which
might promote his relative's interests, provided his own were
not prejudiced.

Now he even went so far as to promise that he would do his
best with the people in power to provide a place for Mr. George
Warrington, who daily showed a greater disinclination to return
to his native country, and place himself once more under the
maternal servitude. George had not merely a sentimental
motive for remaining in England: the pursuits and society of
London pleased him infinitely better than any which he could
have at home. A planter's life of idleness might have suited
him could he have enjoyed independence with it. But in
Virginia he was only the first, and, as he thought, the worst
treated, of his mother's subjects. He dreaded to think of
returning with his young bride to his home, and of the life which
she would be destined to lead there. Better freedom and
poverty in England, with congenial society, and a hope per-
chance of future distinction, than the wearisome routine of
home life, the tedious subordination, the frequent bickerings,
the certain jealousies and differences of opinion, to which he must
subject his wife so soon as they turned their faces homeward.

So Lord Castlewood's promise to provide for George was very
eagerly accepted by the Virginian. My Lord had not provided
very well for his own brother to be sure, and his own position,
peer as he was, was anything but enviable: but we believe what
we wish to believe, and George Warrington chose to put great

stress upon his kinsman's offer of patronage. Unlike the
Warrington family, Lord Castlewood was quite gracious when
he was made acquainted with George's engagement to Miss
Lambert; came to wait upon her parents; praised George to
them and the young lady to George, and made himself so prodigiously agreeable in their company that these charitable folk
forgot his bad reputation, and thought it must be a very wicked
and scandalous world which maligned him. He said, indeed,
that he was improved in their society, as every man must be
who came into it. Among them he was witty, lively, good for
the time being. He left his wickedness and worldliness with his
cloak in the hall, and only put them on again when he stepped
into his chair. What worldling on life's voyage does not know
of some such harbour of rest and calm, some haven where he
puts in out of the storm? Very likely Lord Castlewood was
actually better whilst he stayed with those good people, and for
the time being at least, no hypocrite.

And, I daresay, the Lambert elders thought no worse of his
Lordship for openly proclaiming his admiration for Miss Theo.
It was quite genuine, and he did not profess it was very deep.

"It don't affect my sleep, and I am not going to break my
heart because Miss Lambert prefers somebody else," he remarked. "Only I wish when I was a young man, madam, I
had had the good fortune to meet with somebody so innocent
and good as your daughter. I might have been kept out of a
deal of harm's way: but innocent and good young women
did not fall into mine, or they would have made me better than
I am."

"Sure, my Lord, it is not too late!" says Mrs. Lambert,
very softly.

Castlewood started back, misunderstanding her.

"Not too late, madam?" he inquired.

She blushed. "It is too late to court my dear daughter, my
Lord, but not too late to repent. We read, 'tis never too late
to do that. If others have been received at the eleventh hour,
is there any reason why you should give up hope?"

"Perhaps I know my own heart better than you," he says,
in a plaintive tone. "I can speak French and German very
well, and why? because I was taught both in the nursery. A
man who learns them late can never get the practice of them
on his tongue. And so 'tis the case with goodness, I can't learn
it at my age. I can only see others practise it, and admire
them. When I am on—on the side opposite to Lazarus, will

Miss Theo give me a drop of water? Don't frown! I know I shall be there, Mrs. Lambert. Some folks are doomed so; and I think some of our family are amongst these. Some people are vacillating, and one hardly knows which way the scale will turn. Whereas some are predestined angels, and fly heavenwards naturally, and do what they will."

" Oh, my Lord, and why should you not be of the predestined? Whilst there is a day left—whilst there is an hour—there is hope!" says the fond matron.

" I know what is passing in your mind, my dear madam— nay, I read your prayers in your looks; but how can they avail? " Lord Castlewood asked sadly. " You don't know all, my good lady. You don't know what a life ours is of the world: how early it began; how selfish nature, and then necessity and education have made us. It is Fate holds the reins of the chariot, and we can't escape our doom. I know better: I see better people: I go my own way. My own? No, not mine— Fate's: and it is not altogether without pity for us, since it allows us, from time to time, to see such people as you." And he took her hand, and looked her full in the face, and bowed with a melancholy grace. Every word he said was true. No greater error than to suppose that weak and bad men are strangers to good feelings, or deficient of sensibility. Only the good feeling does not last—nay, the tears are a kind of debauch of sentiment, as old libertines are said to find that the tears and grief of their victims add a zest to their pleasure. But Mrs. Lambert knew little of what was passing in this man's mind (how should she?), and so prayed for him with the fond persistence of woman. He was much better—yes, much better than he was supposed to be. He was a most interesting man. There were hopes, why should there not be the most precious hopes for him still?

It remains to be seen which of the two speakers formed the correct estimate of my Lord's character. Meanwhile, if the gentleman was right, the lady was mollified, and her kind wishes and prayers for this experienced sinner's repentance, if they were of no avail for his amendment, at least could do him no harm. Kind-souled doctors (and what good woman is not of the faculty?) look after a reprobate as physicians after a perilous case. When the patient is converted to health their interest ceases in him, and they drive to feel pulses and prescribe medicines elsewhere.

But, while the malady was under treatment, our kind lady

could not see too much of her sick man. Quite an intimacy sprang up between my Lord Castlewood and the Lamberts. I am not sure that some worldly views might not suit even with good Mrs. Lambert's spiritual plans (for who knows into what pure Eden, though guarded by flaming-sworded angels, worldliness will not creep?). Her son was about to take orders. My Lord Castlewood feared very much that his present chaplain's, Mr. Sampson's, careless life and heterodox conversation might lead him to give up his chaplaincy: in which case, my Lord hinted, the little modest cure would be vacant, and at the service of some young divine of good principles and good manners, who would be content with a small stipend, and a small but friendly congregation.

Thus an acquaintance was established between the two families, and the ladies of Castlewood, always on their good behaviour, came more than once to make their curtseys in Mrs. Lambert's drawing-room. They were civil to the parents and the young ladies. My Lady Castlewood's card-assemblies were open to Mrs. Lambert and her family. There was play, certainly—all the world played—His Majesty, the Bishops, every Peer and Peeress in the land. But nobody need play who did not like; and surely nobody need have scruples regarding the practice when such august and venerable personages were daily found to abet it. More than once Mrs. Lambert made her appearance at her Ladyship's routs, and was grateful for the welcome she received, and pleased with the admiration which her daughters excited.

Mention has been made, in a foregoing page and letter, of an American family of Dutch extraction, who had come to England very strongly recommended by Madam Esmond, their Virginian neighbour, to her sons in Europe. The views expressed in Madam Esmond's letter were so clear, that that arch matchmaker, Mrs. Lambert, could not but understand them. As for George, he was engaged already; as for poor Hetty's flame, Harry, he was gone on service, for which circumstance Hetty's mother was not very sorry perhaps. She laughingly told George that he ought to obey his mamma's injunctions, break off his engagement with Theo, and make up to Miss Lydia, who was ten times—ten times! a hundred times as rich as her poor girl, and certainly much handsomer. "Yes, indeed," says George, "that I own: she is handsomer, and she is richer, and perhaps even cleverer." (All which praises Mrs. Lambert but half liked.) "But say she is all these! So is Mr. Johnson much cleverer than I am: so is whom shall we say?—so is Mr. Hagan the actor much taller and handsomer: so is Sir James Lowther much richer: yet pray, ma'am, do you suppose I am going to be jealous of any one of these three, or think my Theo would jilt me for their sakes? Why should I not allow that Miss Lydia is handsomer, then? and richer, and clever too, and lively, and well-bred, if you insist on it, and an angel if you will have it so? Theo is not afraid: art thou, child?"

"No, George," says Theo, with such an honest look of the eyes, as would convince any scepticism, or shame any jealousy. And if after this pair of speeches, mamma takes occasion to leave the room for a minute to fetch her scissors, or her thimble, or a boot-jack and slippers, or the cross and ball on the top of St. Paul's, or her pocket-handkerchief which she has forgotten in the parlour,—if, I say, Mrs. Lambert quits the room on any errand or pretext, natural or preposterous, I shall not be in the least surprised if, at her return in a couple of minutes, she finds George in near proximity to Theo, who has a heightened colour, and whose hand George is just dropping—I shall not have the least idea of what they have been doing. Have you, madam? Have you any remembrance of what used to happen when Mr. Grundy came a-courting? Are you, who, after all, were not in the room with our young people, going to cry out fie and for shame? Then fie and for shame upon you, Mrs. Grundy!

Well, Harry being away, and Theo and George irrevocably engaged, so that there was no possibility of bringing Madam Esmond's little plans to bear, why should not Mrs. Lambert have plans of her own; and if a rich, handsome, beautiful little wife should fall in his way, why should not Jack Lambert from Oxford have her? So thinks mamma, who was always thinking of marrying and giving in marriage, and so she prattles to General Lambert, who, as usual, calls her a goose for her pains. At any rate, Mrs. Lambert says beauty and riches are no objection; at any rate, Madam Esmond desired that this family should be hospitably entertained, and it was not her fault that Harry was gone away to Canada. Would the General wish him to come back; leave the army and his reputation, perhaps; yes, and come to England and marry this American, and break poor Hetty's heart—would her father wish that? Let us spare further arguments, and not be so rude as to hint that Mr. Lambert was in the right in calling a fond wife by the name of that absurd splay-footed bird annually sacrificed at the feast of St. Michael.

In those early days, there were vast distinctions of rank drawn between the Court and City people: and Mr. Van den Bosch, when he first came to London, scarcely associated with any but the latter sort. He had a lodging near his agent's in the City. When his pretty girl came from school for a holiday, he took her an airing to Islington or Highgate, or an occasional promenade in the Artillery Ground in Bunhill Fields. They went to that Baptist meeting-house in Finsbury Fields, and on the sly to see Mr. Garrick once or twice, or that funny rogue Mr. Foote, at the Little Theatre. To go to a Lord Mayor's feast was a treat to the gentleman of the highest order; and to dance with a young mercer at Hampstead Assembly gave the utmost delight to the young lady. When George first went to wait upon his mother's friends, he found our old acquaintance, Mr. Draper, of the Temple, sedulous in his attentions to her; and the lawyer, who was married, told Mr. Warrington to look out, as the young lady had a plum to her fortune. Mr. Drabshaw, a young Quaker gentleman, and nephew of Mr. Trail, Madam Esmond's Bristol agent, was also in constant attendance upon the young lady, and in dreadful alarm and suspicion when Mr. Warrington first made his appearance. Wishing to do honour to his mother's neighbours, Mr. Warrington invited them to an entertainment at his own apartments: and who should so naturally meet them as his friends from Soho? Not one of them but was forced to own little Miss Lydia's beauty. She had the foot of a fairy: the arms, neck, flashing eyes of a little brown huntress of Diana. She had brought a little plaintive accent from home with her—of which I, *moi qui vous parle*, have heard a hundred gross Cockney imitations, and watched as many absurd disguises, and which I say (in moderation) is charming in the mouth of a charming woman. Who sets up to say No, forsooth? You dear Miss Whittington, with whose *h*'s fate has dealt so unkindly?—you lovely Miss Nicol Jarvie, with your Northern burr?—you beautiful Miss Molony, with your Dame Street warble? All accents are pretty from pretty lips, and who shall set the standard up? Shall it be a rose, or a thistle, or a shamrock, or a star and stripe? As for Miss Lydia's accent, I have no doubt it was not odious even from the first day when she set foot on these polite shores, otherwise Mr. Warrington, as a man of taste, had certainly disapproved of her manner of talking, and her schoolmistress at Kensington had not done her duty by her pupil.

After the six months were over, during which, according to

her grandfather's calculation, she was to learn all the accomplishments procurable at the Kensington Academy, Miss Lydia returned nothing loth to her grandfather, and took her place in the world. A narrow world at first it was to her; but she was a resolute little person, and resolved to enlarge her sphere in society: and whither she chose to lead the way, the obedient grandfather followed her. He had been thwarted himself in early life, he said, and little good came of the severity he underwent. He had thwarted his own son, who had turned out but ill. As for little Lyddy, he was determined she should have as pleasant a life as was possible. Did not Mr. George think he was right? 'Twas said in Virginia—he did not know with what reason—that the young gentlemen of Castlewood had been happier if Madam Esmond had allowed them a little of their own way. George could not gainsay this public rumour, or think of inducing the benevolent old gentleman to alter his plans respecting his granddaughter. As for the Lambert family how could they do otherwise than welcome the kind old man the parent so tender and liberal, Madam Esmond's good friend?

When Miss came from school, grandpapa removed from Monument Yard to an elegant house in Bloomsbury; whither they were followed at first by their City friends. There were merchants from Virginia Walk: there were worthy tradesmen with whom the worthy old merchant had dealings; there were their ladies and daughters and sons, who were all highly gracious to Miss Lyddy. It would be a long task to describe how these disappeared one by one—how there were no more junketings at Belsize, or trips to Highgate, or Saturday jaunts to deputy Higgs's villa, Highbury, or country-dances at honest Mr. Lutestring's house at Hackney. Even the Sunday practice was changed; and, O abomination of abominations! Mr. Van den Bosch left Bethesda Chapel in Bunhill Row, and actually took a pew in Queen Square Church!

Queen Square Church, and Mr. George Warrington lived hard by in Southampton Row! 'Twas easy to see at whom Miss Lyddy was setting her cap, and Mr. Draper, who had been full of her and her grandfather's praises before, now took occasion to warn Mr. George, and gave him very different reports regarding Mr. Van den Bosch to those which had first been current. Mr. Van d. B., for all he bragged so of his Dutch parentage, came from Albany, and was nobody's son at all. He had made his money by land speculation, or by privateering (which was uncommonly like piracy), and by the Guinea trade.

His son had married—if marriage it could be called, which was very doubtful—an assigned servant, and had been cut off by his father, and had taken to bad courses, and had died, luckily for himself, in his own bed.

"Mr. Draper has told you bad tales about me," said the placid old gentleman to George. "Very likely we are all sinners, and some evil may be truly said of all of us, with a great deal more that is untrue. Did he tell you that my son was unhappy with me? I told you so too. Did he bring you wicked stories about my family? He liked it so well that he wanted to marry my Lyddy to his brother. Heaven bless her! I have had a many offers for her. And you are the young gentleman I should have chose for her, and I like you none the worse because you prefer somebody else; though what you can see in your Miss, as compared to my Lyddy, begging your honour's pardon, I am at a loss to understand."

"There is no accounting for tastes, my good sir," said Mr. George, with his most superb air.

"No, sir; 'tis a wonder of nature, and daily happens. When I kept store at Albany, there was one of your tip-top gentry there that might have married my dear daughter that was alive then, and with a pretty piece of money, whereby—for her father and I had quarrelled—Miss Lyddy would have been a pauper, you see; and in place of my beautiful Bella, my gentleman chooses a little homely creature, no prettier than your Miss, and without a dollar to her fortune. The more fool he, saving your presence, Mr. George."

"Pray don't save my presence, my good sir," says George, laughing. "I suppose the gentleman's word was given to the other lady, and he had seen her first, and hence was indifferent to your charming daughter."

"I suppose when a young fellow gives his word to perform a cursed piece of folly, he always sticks to it, my dear sir, begging your pardon. But Lord, Lord, what am I speaking of? I am a-speaking of twenty year ago. I was well-to-do-then, but I may say Heaven has blessed my store, and I am three times as well off now. Ask my agents how much they will give for Joseph Van den Bosch's bill at six months on New York—or at sight may be—for forty thousand pound? I warrant they will discount the paper."

"Happy he who has the bill, sir!" says George, with a bow, not a little amused with the candour of the old gentleman.

"Lord, Lord, how mercenary you young men are!" cries the

elder simply. "Always thinking about money nowadays! Happy he who has the girl, I should say—the money ain't the question, my dear sir, when it goes along with such a lovely young thing as that—though I humbly say it, who oughtn't, and who am her fond silly old grandfather. We were talking about you, Lyddy darling—come, give me a kiss, my blessing! We were talking about you, and Mr. George said he wouldn't take you with all the money your poor old grandfather can give you."

"Nay, sir," says George.

"Well, you are right to say nay, for I didn't say all, that's the truth. My Blessing will have a deal more than that trifle I spoke of, when it shall please Heaven to remove me out of this world to a better—when poor old Gappy is gone, Lyddy will be a rich little Lyddy, that she will. But she don't wish me to go yet, does she?"

"Oh, you darling dear grandpapa!" says Lyddy.

"This young gentleman won't have you." (Lyddy looks an arch, "Thank you, sir," from her brown eyes.) "But at any rate he is honest, and that is more than we can say of some folks in this wicked London. Oh, Lord, Lord, how mercenary they are! Do you know that yonder, in Monument Yard, they were all at my poor little Blessing for her money? There was Tom Lutestring; there was Mr. Draper, your precious lawyer; there was actually Mr. Tubbs, of Bethesda Chapel; and they must all come buzzing like flies round the honey-pot. That is why we came out of the quarter where my brother tradesmen live."

"To avoid the flies, to be sure!" says Miss Lydia, tossing up her little head.

"Where my brother tradesmen live," continues the old gentleman. "Else who am I to think of consorting with your grandees and fine folk? I don't care for the fashions, Mr. George; I don't care for plays and poetry, begging your honour's pardon; I never went to a play in my life, but to please this little minx."

"Oh, sir, 'twas lovely! and I cried so, didn't I, grandpapa?" says the child.

"At what, my dear?"

"At—at Mr. Warrington's play, grandpapa."

"Did you, my dear? I dare say; I dare say. It was mail day: and my letters had come in: and my ship the 'Lovely Lyddy' had just come into Falmouth: and Captain Joyce reported how he had mercifully escaped a French privateer; and my head was so full of thanks for that escape, which saved me a deal of money, Mr. George—for the rate at which ships is underwrote this war-time is so scandalous that I often prefer to venture than to insure—that I confess I didn't listen much to the play, sir, and only went to please this little Lyddy."

"And you *did* please me, dearest Gappy!" cries the young lady.

"Bless you! then it's all I want. What does a man want more here below than to please his children, Mr. George? especially me, who knew what it was to be unhappy when I was young, and to repent of having treated this darling's father too hard."

"Oh, grandpapa!" cries the child, with more caresses.

"Yes, I *was* too hard with him, dear; and that's why I spoil my little Lydkin so!"

More kisses ensue between Lyddy and Gappy. The little creature flings the pretty polished arms round the old man's neck, presses the dark red lips on his withered cheek, surrounds the venerable head with a halo of powder beaten out of his wig by her caresses; and eyes Mr. George the while, as much as to say, There, sir! should you not like me to do as much for you!

We confess;—but do we confess all? George certainly told the story of his interview with Lyddy and Gappy, and the old man's news regarding his granddaughter's wealth; but I don't think he told everything; else Theo would scarce have been so much interested, or so entirely amused and good-humoured with Lyddy when next the two young ladies met.

They met now pretty frequently, especially after the old American gentleman took up his residence in Bloomsbury. Mr. Van den Bosch was in the City for the most part of the day, attending to his affairs, and appearing at his place upon 'Change. During his absence Lyddy had the command of the house, and received her guests there like a lady, or rode abroad in a fine coach, which she ordered her grandpapa to keep for her, and into which he could very seldom be induced to set his foot. Before long Miss Lyddy was as easy in the coach as if she had ridden in one all her life. She ordered the domestics here and there; she drove to the mercer's and the jeweller's, and she called upon her friends with the utmost stateliness, or rode abroad with them to take the air. Theo and Hetty were both greatly diverted with her: but would the elder have been quite as well pleased had she known all Miss Lyddy's doings? Not that Theo was of a jealous disposition—far otherwise; but there are cases when a lady has a right to a little jealousy, as I maintain, whatever my fair readers may say to the contrary.

It was because she knew he was engaged, very likely, that Miss Lyddy permitted herself to speak so frankly in Mr. George's praise. When they were alone—and this blessed chance occurred pretty often at Mr. Van den Bosch's house, for we have said he was constantly absent on one errand or the other—it was wonderful how artlessly the little creature would show her enthusiasm, asking him all sorts of simple questions about himself, his genius, his way of life at home and in London, his projects of marriage, and so forth.

" I am glad you are going to be married,—oh, so glad! " she would say, heaving the most piteous sigh the while; " for I can talk to you frankly, quite frankly, as a brother, and not be afraid of that odious politeness about which they were always scolding me at boarding-school. I may speak to you frankly; and if I like you, I may say so, mayn't I, Mr. George? "

" Pray, say so," says George, with a bow and a smile. " That is a kind of talk which most men delight to hear, especially from such pretty lips as Miss Lydia's."

" What do you know about my lips? " says the girl, with a pout and an innocent look into his face.

" What, indeed? " asks George. " Perhaps I should like to know a great deal more."

" They don't tell nothin' but truth, anyhow! " says the girl; " that's why some people don't like them! If I have anything on my mind, it must come out. I am a country-bred girl, I am —with my heart in my mouth—all honesty and simplicity; not like your English girls, who have learned I don't know what at their boarding-schools, and from the men afterwards."

" Our girls are monstrous little hypocrites, indeed! " cries George.

" You are thinking of Miss Lamberts? and I might have thought of them; but I declare I did not then. They have been at boarding-school; they have been in the world a great deal—so much the greater pity for them, for be certain they learned no good there. And now I have said so, of course you will go and tell Miss Theo, won't you, sir? "

" That she has learned no good in the world? She has scarce spoken to men at all, except her father, her brother, and me. Which of us would teach her any wrong, think you? "

"Oh, not you! Though I can understand its being very dangerous to be with you!" says the girl, with a sigh.

"Indeed there is no danger, and I don't bite!" says George, laughing.

"I didn't say bite," says the girl softly. "There's other things dangerous besides biting, I should think. Aren't you very witty? Yes, and sarcastic, and clever, and always laughing at people? Haven't you a coaxing tongue? If you was to look at me in that kind of way, I don't know what would come to me. Was your brother like you as I was to have married? Was he as clever and witty as you? I have heard he was like you: but he hadn't your coaxing tongue. Heigho! 'Tis well you are engaged, Master George, that is all. Do you think if you had seen me first, you would have liked Miss Theo best?"

"They say marriages are made in heaven, my dear; and let us trust that mine has been arranged there," says George.

"I suppose there was no such thing never known, as a man having two sweethearts?" asks the artless little maiden. "Guess it's a pity. Oh me! What nonsense I'm a-talking; there now! I'm like the little girl who cried for the moon; and I can't have it. 'Tis too high for me—too high and splendid and shining; can't reach up to it nohow. Well, what a foolish, wayward, little spoilt thing I am now! But one thing you promise—on your word and your honour, now, Mr. George?"

"And what is that?"

"That you won't tell Miss Theo, else she'll hate me."

"Why should she hate you?"

"Because I hate her and wish she was dead!" breaks out the young lady. And the eyes that were looking so gentle and lachrymose but now, flame with sudden wrath, and her cheeks flush up. "For shame!" she adds, after a pause. "I'm a little fool to speak! But whatever is in my heart must come out. I am a girl of the woods, I am. I was bred where the sun is hotter than in this foggy climate. And I am not like your cold English girls; who, before they speak, or think, or feel, must wait for mamma to give leave. There, there! I may be a little fool for saying what I have. I know you'll go and tell Miss Lambert. Well, do!"

But, as we have said, George didn't tell Miss Lambert. Even from the beloved person there must be some things kept secret: even to himself, perhaps, he did not quite acknowledge what was the meaning of the little girl's confession; or, if he acknowledged it, did not act on it; except in so far as this, perhaps, that my gentleman, in Miss Lydia's presence, was particularly courteous and tender; and in her absence thought of her very kindly, and always with a certain pleasure. It were hard, indeed, if a man might not repay by a little kindness and gratitude the artless affection of such a warm young heart.

What was that story meanwhile which came round to our friends, of young Mr. Lutestring and young Mr. Drabshaw the Quaker, having a boxing-match at a tavern in the City, and all about this young lady? They fell out over their cups, and fought probably. Why did Mr. Draper, who had praised her so at first, tell such stories now against her grandfather? " I suspect," says Madame de Bernstein, " that he wants the girl for some client or relation of his own; and that he tells these tales in order to frighten all suitors from her. When she and her grandfather came to me, she behaved perfectly well; and I confess, sir, I thought it was a great pity that you should prefer yonder red-cheeked countrified little chit, without a halfpenny, to this pretty, wild, artless girl, with such a fortune as I hear she has."

" Oh, she has been with you, has she, aunt? " asks George of his relative.

" Of course she has been with me," the other replies curtly. " Unless your brother has been so silly as to fall in love with that other little Lambert girl——"

" Indeed, ma'am, I think I can say he has not," George remarks.

" Why, then, when he comes back with Mr. Wolfe should he not take a fancy to this little person, as his mamma wishes— only, to do us justice, we Esmonds care very little for what our mammas wish—and marry her, and set up beside you in Virginia? She is to have a great fortune, which you won't touch. Pray, why should it go out of the family? "

George now learned that Mr. Van den Bosch and his grand-daughter had been often at Madame de Bernstein's house. Taking his favourite walk with his favourite companion to Kensington Gardens, he saw Mr. Van den Bosch's chariot turning into Kensington Square. The Americans were going to visit Lady Castlewood then? He found, on some little inquiry, that they had been more than once with her Ladyship. It was, per-haps, strange that they should have said nothing of their visits to George; but, being little curious of other people's affairs, and having no intrigues or mysteries of his own, George was quite slow to imagine them in other people. What mattered to him how often Kensington entertained Bloomsbury, or Bloomsbury made its bow at Kensington?

A number of things were happening at both places, of which our Virginian had not the slightest idea. Indeed, do not things happen under our eyes, and we not see them? Are not comedies and tragedies daily performed before us of which we understand neither the fun nor the pathos? Very likely George goes home thinking to himself, " I have made an impression on the heart of this young creature. She has almost confessed as much. Poor artless little maiden! I wonder what there is in me that she should like me? " Can he be angry with her for this unlucky preference? Was ever a man angry at such a reason? He would not have been so well pleased, perhaps, had he known all; and that he was only one of the performers in the comedy, not the principal character by any means; Rosencrantz and Guildenstern in the tragedy, the part of Hamlet by a gentleman unknown. How often are our little vanities shocked in this way, and subjected to wholesome humiliation! Have you not fancied that Lucinda's eye beamed on you with a special tenderness, and presently become aware that she ogles your neighbour with the very same killing glances? Have you not exchanged exquisite whispers with Lalage at the dinner-table (sweet murmurs heard through the hum of the guests, and clatter of the banquet!), and then overheard her whispering the very same delicious phrases to old Surdus in the drawing-room? The sun shines for everybody; the flowers smell sweet for all noses; and the nightingale and Lalage warble for all ears—not your long ones only, good brother!

CHAPTER LXX

IN WHICH CUPID PLAYS A CONSIDERABLE PART

WE must now, however, and before we proceed with the history of Miss Lydia and her doings, perform the duty of explaining that sentence in Mr. Warrington's letter to his brother which refers to Lady Maria Esmond, and which, to some simple readers, may be still mysterious. For how, indeed, could well-regulated persons divine such a secret? How could innocent and respectable young people suppose that a woman of noble birth, of ancient family, of mature experience,—a woman whom we have seen exceedingly in love only a score of months ago,—should so far forget herself as (oh, my very finger-tips blush as I write the sentence!),—as not only to fall in love with a person of low origin, and very many years her junior, but actually to marry him in the face of the world? That is, not exactly in the face, but behind the back of the world, so to speak; for Parson Sampson privily tied the indissoluble knot for the pair at his chapel in Mayfair.

Now stop before you condemn her utterly. Because Lady Maria had had, and overcome, a foolish partiality for her young cousin, was that any reason why she should never fall in love with anybody else? Are men to have the sole privilege of change, and are women to be rebuked for availing themselves, now and again, of their little chance of consolation? No invectives can be more rude, gross, and unphilosophical than, for instance, Hamlet's to his mother about her second marriage. The truth very likely is, that that tender parasitic creature wanted a something to cling to, and, Hamlet senior out of the way, twined herself round Claudius. Nay, we have known females so bent on attaching themselves, that they can twine round two gentlemen at once. Why, forsooth, shall there not be marriage-tables after funeral baked-meats? If you said grace for your feast yesterday, is that any reason why you shall not be hungry to-day? Your natural fine appetite and relish for this evening's feast, shows that to-morrow evening at eight o'clock you will most probably be in want of your dinner. I, for my part, when Flirtilla or Jiltissa were partial to me (the kind reader will please to fancy that I am alluding here to persons of the most ravishing beauty and lofty rank), always used to bear in mind that a time would come when they would be fond of somebody else. We are served *à la Russe*, and gobbled up a dish at a time, like the folks in Polyphemus's cave. 'Tis *hodie mihi, cras tibi*: there are some Anthropophagi who devour dozens of us,—the old, the young, the tender, the tough, the plump, the lean, the ugly, the beautiful: there's no escape, and one after another, as our fate is, we disappear down their omnivorous maws. Look at Lady Ogresham! We all remember, last year, how she served poor Tom Kydd: seized upon him, devoured him, picked his bones, and flung them away. Now it is Ned Suckling she has got into her den. He lies under her great eyes, quivering and fascinated. Look at the poor little trepid creature, panting and helpless under the great eyes! She trails towards him nearer and nearer: he draws to her, closer and closer. Presently, there will be one or two feeble squeaks for pity, and—hobblegobble—he will disappear! Ah me! it is pity, too. I knew, for instance, that Maria Esmond had lost her heart ever so many times before Harry Warrington found it; but I liked to fancy that he was going to keep it; that bewailing mischance and times out of joint, she would yet have preserved her love, and fondled it in decorous celibacy. If, in some paroxysm of senile folly, I should fall in love to-morrow, I shall still try and think I have acquired the fee-simple of my charmer's heart:—not that I am only a tenant, on a short lease, of an old battered furnished apartment, where the dingy old wine-glasses have been clouded by scores of pairs of lips, and the tumbled old sofas are muddy with the last lodger's boots. Dear dear nymph! Being beloved and beautiful! Suppose I had a little passing passion for Glycera (and her complexion really was as pure as splendent Parian marble); suppose you had a fancy for Telephus, and his low collars and absurd neck;—those follies are all over now, aren't they? We love each other for good now, don't we? Yes, for ever; and Glycera may go to Bath, and Telephus take his *cervicem roseam* to Jack Ketch, *n'est-ce pas ?*

No. *We* never think of changing, my dear. However winds blow, or time flies, or spoons stir, *our* pottage, which is now so piping hot, will never get cold. Passing fancies we may have allowed ourselves in former days; and really your infatuation for Telephus (don't frown so, my darling creature: and make the wrinkles in your forehead worse)—I say, really it was the talk of the whole town; and as for Glycera, she behaved confoundedly ill to me. Well, well, now that we understand each other it is for ever that our hearts are united, and we can look at Sir Cresswell Cresswell, and snap our fingers at his wig. But this Maria of the last century was a woman of an ill-regulated mind. You, my love, who know the world, know that in the course of this lady's career a great deal must have passed that would not bear the light, or edify in the telling. You know (not, my dear creature, that I mean you have any experience; but you have heard people say—you have heard your mother say) that an old flirt, when she has done playing the fool with one passion, will play the fool with another; that flirting is like drinking; and the brandy being drunk up, you—no, not you—Glycera— the brandy being drunk up, Glycera, who has taken to drinking, will fall upon the gin. So, if Maria Esmond has found a successor for Harry Warrington, and set up a new sultan in the precious empire of her heart, what, after all, could you expect from her? That territory was, like the Low Countries, accustomed to being conquered, and for ever open to invasion.

And Maria's present enslaver was no other than Mr. Geoghegan, or Hagan, the young actor who had performed in George's tragedy. His tones were so thrilling, his eyes so bright, his mien so noble, he looked so beautiful in his gilt leather armour and large buckle periwig, giving utterance to the poet's glowing verses, that the lady's heart was yielded up to him, even as Ariadne's to Bacchus when her affair with Theseus was over. The young Irishman was not a little touched and elated by the high-born damsel's partiality for him. He might have preferred a Lady Maria Hagan more tender in years, but one more tender in disposition it were difficult to discover. She clung to him closely, indeed. She retired to his humble lodgings in Westminster with him, when it became necessary to disclose their marriage, and when her furious relatives disowned her.

General Lambert brought the news home from his office in Whitehall one day, and made merry over it with his family. In those homely times a joke was none the worse for being a little broad; and a fine lady would laugh at a jolly page of Fielding, and weep over a letter of Clarissa, which would make your present Ladyship's eyes start out of your head with horror. He uttered all sorts of waggeries, did the merry General, upon the subject of this marriage; upon George's share in bringing it about; upon Harry's jealousy when he should hear of it. He vowed it was cruel that Cousin Hagan had not selected George as groomsman; that the first child should be called Carpezan or Sybilla, after the tragedy, and so forth. They would not quite be able to keep a coach, but they might get a chariot and pasteboard dragons from Mr. Rich's theatre. The baby might be christened in Macbeth's cauldron: and Harry and harlequin ought certainly to be godfathers.

"Why shouldn't she marry him if she likes him?" asked little Hetty. "Why should he not love her because she is a little old? Mamma is a little old, and you love her none the worse. When you married my mamma, sir, I have heard you say you were very poor; and yet you were very happy, and nobody laughed at you!" Thus this impudent little person spoke by reason of her tender age, not being aware of Lady Maria Esmond's previous follies.

So her family has deserted her? George described what wrath they were in; how Lady Castlewood had gone into mourning; how Mr. Will swore he would have the rascal's ears; how furious Madame de Bernstein was, the most angry of all. " It is an insult to the family," says haughty little Miss Het; " and I fancy how ladies of that rank must be indignant at their relative's marriage with a person of Mr. Hagan's condition; but to desert her is a very different matter."

" Indeed, my dear child," cries mamma, " you are talking of what you don't understand. After my Lady Maria's conduct, no respectable person can go to see her."

" What conduct, mamma? "

" Never mind," cries mamma. " Little girls can't be expected to know, and ought not to be too curious to inquire, what Lady Maria's conduct has been! Suffice it, miss, that I am shocked her Ladyship should ever have been here; and I say again, no honest person should associate with her! "

" Then, Aunt Lambert, I must be whipped and sent to bed," says George, with mock gravity. " I own to you (though I did not confess sooner, seeing that the affair was not mine) that I have been to see my cousin the player, and her Ladyship his wife. I found them in very dirty lodgings in Westminster, where the wretch has the shabbiness to keep not only his wife, but his old mother, and a little brother, whom he puts to school. I found Mr. Hagan, and came away with a liking, and almost a respect for him, although I own he has made a very improvident marriage. But how improvident some folks are about marriage, aren't they, Theo? "

" Improvident, if they marry such spendthrifts as you," says the General. " Master George found his relations, and I'll be bound to say he left his purse behind him."

" No, not the purse, sir," says George, smiling very tenderly. " Theo made that. But I am bound to own it came empty away. Mr. Rich is in great dudgeon. He says he hardly dares have Hagan on his stage, and is afraid of a riot, such as Mr. Garrick had about the foreign dancers. This is to be a fine gentleman's riot. The macaronis are furious, and vow they will pelt Mr. Hagan, and have him cudgelled afterwards. My cousin Will, at Arthur's, has taken his oath he will have the actor's ears. Meanwhile, as the poor man does not play, they have cut off his salary; and without his salary, this luckless pair of lovers have no means to buy bread and cheese."

" And you took it to them, sir? It was like you, George! " says Theo, worshipping him with her eyes.

" It was your purse took it, dear Theo! " replies George.

"Mamma, I hope you will go and see them to-morrow!" prays Theo.

"If she doesn't I shall get a divorce, my dear!" cries papa. "Come and kiss me, you little wench—that is, avec la bonne permission de monsieur mon beau-fils."

"Monsieur mon beau fiddlestick, papa!" says Miss Lambert, and I have no doubt complies with the paternal orders. And this was the first time George Esmond Warrington, Esquire was ever called a fiddlestick.

Any man, even in our time, who makes an imprudent marriage, knows how he has to run the gauntlet of the family, and undergo the abuse, the scorn, the wrath, the pity of his relations. If your respectable family cry out because you marry the curate's daughter, one in ten, let us say, of his charming children; or because you engage yourself to the young barrister whose only present pecuniary resources come from the court which he reports, and who will have to pay his Oxford bills out of your slender little fortune;—if your friends cry out for making such engagements as these, fancy the feelings of Lady Maria Hagan's friends, and even those of Mr. Hagan's, on the announcement of this marriage.

There is old Mrs. Hagan, in the first instance. Her son has kept her dutifully and in tolerable comfort, ever since he left Trinity College at his father's death, and appeared as Romeo at Crow Street Theatre. His salary has sufficed of late years to keep the brother at school, to help the sister who has gone out as companion, and to provide fire, clothing, tea, dinner, and comfort for the old clergyman's widow. And now, forsooth, a fine lady, with all sorts of extravagant habits, must come and take possession of the humble home, and share the scanty loaf and mutton! Were Hagan not a high-spirited fellow, and the old mother very much afraid of him, I doubt whether my Lady's life at the Westminster lodgings would be very comfortable. It *was* very selfish perhaps to take a place at that small table, and in poor Hagan's narrow bed. But Love in some passionate and romantic dispositions never regards consequences, or measures accommodation. Who has not experienced that frame of mind; what thrifty wife has not seen and lamented her husband in that condition; when, with rather a heightened colour and a deuce-may-care smile on his face, he comes home and announces that he has asked twenty people to dinner next Saturday? He doesn't know whom exactly; and he does know the dining-room will only hold sixteen. Never mind! Two of the prettiest girls can sit upon young gentlemen's knees: others won't come: there's sure to be plenty! In the intoxication of love people venture upon this dangerous sort of housekeeping; they don't calculate the resources of their dining-table, or those inevitable butchers' and fishmongers' bills which will be brought to the ghastly housekeeper at the beginning of the month.

Yes: it was rather selfish of my Lady Maria to seat herself at Hagan's table and take the cream off the milk, and the wings of the chickens, and the best half of everything where there was only enough before; and no wonder the poor old mamma-in-law was disposed to grumble. But what was her outcry compared to the clamour at Kensington among Lady Maria's noble family! Think of the talk and scandal all over the town! Think of the titters and whispers of the ladies in attendance at the Princess's Court, where Lady Fanny had a place; of the jokes of Mr. Will's brother officers at the usher's table; of the waggeries in the daily prints and magazines; of the comments of the outraged prudes; of the laughter of the clubs and the sneers of the ungodly! At the receipt of the news Madam Bernstein had fits and ran off to the solitude of her dear rocks at Tunbridge Wells, where she did not see above forty people of a night at cards. My Lord refused to see his sister: and the Countess, in mourning, as we have said, waited upon one of her patronesses, a gracious Princess, who was pleased to condole with her upon the disgrace and calamity which had befallen her house. For one, two, three whole days the town was excited and amused by the scandal; then there came other news—a victory in Germany: doubtful accounts from America; a general officer coming home to take his trial; an exquisite new soprano singer from Italy; and the public forgot Lady Maria in her garret, eating the hard-earned meal of the actor's family.

This is an extract from Mr. George Warrington's letter to his brother, in which he describes other personal matters, as well as a visit he had paid to the newly-married pair:—

" My dearest little Theo," he writes, " was eager to accompany her mamma upon this errand of charity; but I thought Aunt Lambert's visit would be best under the circumstances, and without the attendance of her little spinster *aide-de-camp*. Cousin Hagan was out when we called; we found her Ladyship in a loose undress, and with her hair in not the neatest papers, playing at cribbage with a neighbour from the second-floor, while good Mrs. Hagan sat on the other side of the fire with a glass of punch, and the ' Whole Duty of Man.'

" Maria your Maria once, cried a little when she saw us; and

Aunt Lambert, you may be sure, was ready with her sympathy. While she bestowed it on Lady Maria, I paid the best compliments I could invent to the old lady. When the conversation between Aunt L. and the bride began to flag, I turned to the latter, and between us we did our best to make a dreary interview pleasant. Our talk was about you, about Wolfe, about war; you must be engaged face to face with the Frenchmen by this time, and God send my dearest brother safe and victorious out of the battle! Be sure we follow your steps anxiously—we fancy you at Cape Breton. We have plans of Quebec, and charts of the St. Lawrence. Shall I ever forget your face of joy that day when you saw me return safe and sound from the little combat with the little Frenchman? So will my Harry, I know, return from his battle. I feel quite assured of it; elated somehow with the prospect of your certain success and safety. And I have made all here share my cheerfulness. We talk of the campaign as over, and Captain Warrington's promotion as secure. Pray Heaven all our hopes may be fulfilled one day ere long.

"How strange it is that you who are the mettlesome fellow (you know you are) should escape quarrels hitherto, and I, who am a peaceful man, wishing no harm to anybody, should have battles thrust upon me! What do you think actually of my having had another affair upon my wicked hands, and with whom, think you? With no less a personage than your old enemy, our kinsman Mr. Will.

"What or who set him to quarrel with me, I cannot think. Spencer (who acted as second for me, for matters actually have gone this length; don't be frightened; it is all over, and nobody is a scratch the worse) thinks some one set Will on me: but who, I say? His conduct has been most singular; his behaviour quite unbearable. We have met pretty frequently lately at the house of good Mr. Van den Bosch, whose pretty granddaughter was consigned to both of us by our good mother. Oh, dear mother! did you know that the little thing was to be such a *causa belli*, and to cause swords to be drawn, and precious lives to be menaced? But so it has been. To show his own spirit, I suppose, or having some reasonable doubt about mine, whenever Will and I have met at Mynheer's house—and he is for ever going there—he has shown such downright rudeness to me, that I have required more than ordinary patience to keep my temper. He has contradicted me once, twice, thrice, in the presence of the family, and out of sheer spite and rage, as it appeared to me. Is he paying his addresses to Miss Lydia, and her father's ships, negroes, and forty thousand pounds? I should guess so. The old gentleman is for ever talking about his money, and adores his granddaughter, and as she is a beautiful little creature, numbers of folk here are ready to adore her too. Was Will rascal enough to fancy that I would give up my Theo for a million of guineas, and negroes, and Venus to boot? Could the thought of such baseness enter into the man's mind? I don't know that he has accused me of stealing Van den Bosch's spoons and tankards when we dine there, or of robbing on the highway. But for one reason or the other he has chosen to be jealous of me, and as I have parried his impertinences with little sarcastic speeches (though perfectly civil before company), perhaps I have once or twice made him angry. Our little Miss Lydia has unwittingly added fuel to the fire on more than one occasion, especially yesterday, when there was talk about your worship.

" ' Ah!' says the heedless little thing, as we sat over our dessert, ' 'tis lucky for you, Mr. Esmond, that Captain Harry is not here.'

" ' Why, miss?' asks he, with one of his usual conversational ornaments. He must have offended some fairy in his youth, who has caused him to drop curses for ever out of his mouth, as she did the girl to spit out toads and serpents. (I know some one from whose gentle lips there only fall pure pearls and diamonds.) ' Why?' says Will, with a cannonade of oaths.

" ' O fie!' says she, putting up the prettiest little fingers to the prettiest little rosy ears in the world. ' O fie, sir! to use such naughty words. 'Tis lucky the Captain is not here, because he might quarrel with you; and Mr. George is so peaceable and quiet, that he won't. Have you heard from the Captain, Mr. George?'

" ' From Cape Breton,' says I. ' He is very well, thank you; that is——' I couldn't finish the sentence, for I was in such a rage, that I scarce could contain myself.

" ' From the Captain, as you call him, Miss Lyddy,' says Will. ' He'll distinguish himself as he did at St. Cas. Ho, ho!'

" ' So I apprehend he did, sir,' says Harry's brother.

" ' Did he?' says our dear cousin; ' always thought he ran away; took to his legs; got a ducking, and ran away as if a bailiff was after him.'

" ' La!' says miss, ' did the Captain ever have a bailiff after him?'

" ' Didn't he! Ho, ho!' laughs Mr. Will.

" I suppose I must have looked very savage, for Spencer, who was dining with us, trod on my foot, under the table. ' Don't laugh so loud, cousin,' I said, very gently; ' you may wake good old Mr. Van den Bosch.' The good old gentleman was asleep in his arm-chair, to which he commonly retires for a nap after dinner.

" ' Oh, indeed, cousin,' says Will, and he turns and winks at a friend of his, Captain Deuceace, whose own and whose wife's reputation I dare say you heard of when you frequented the clubs, and whom Will has introduced into this simple family as a man of the highest fashion. ' Don't be afraid, miss,' says Mr. Will, ' nor my cousin needn't be.'

" ' Oh, what a comfort!' cries Miss Lyddy. ' Keep quite quiet, gentlemen, and don't quarrel, and come up to me when I send to say the tea is ready.' And with this she makes a sweet little curtsey and disappears.

" ' Hang it, Jack, pass the bottle, and don't wake the old gentleman!' continues Mr. Will. ' Won't you help yourself, cousin?' he continues; being particularly facetious in the tone of that word cousin.

" ' I am going to help myself,' I said, ' but I am not going to drink the glass; and I'll tell you what I am going to do with it, if you will be quite quiet, cousin?' (Desperate kicks from Spencer all this time.)

"'And what the deuce do I care what you are going to do with it?' asks Will, looking rather white.

"'I am going to fling it into your face, cousin,' says I, very rapidly performing that feat.

"'By Jove, and no mistake!' cries Mr. Deuceace; and as he and William roared out an oath together, good old Van den Bosch woke up, and, taking the pocket-handkerchief off his face, asked what was the matter.

"I remarked it was only a glass of wine gone the wrong way; and the old man said, 'Well, well, there is more where that came from! Let the butler bring you what you please, young gentlemen!' and he sank back in his great chair, and began to sleep again.

"'From the back of Montagu House Gardens there is a beautiful view of Hampstead at six o'clock in the morning; and the statue of the King on St. George's Church is reckoned elegant, cousin!' says I, resuming the conversation.

"'D—— the statue!' begins Will: but I said, 'Don't, cousin! or you will wake up the old gentleman. Had we not best go upstairs to Miss Lyddy's tea-table?'

"We arranged a little meeting for the next morning; and a coroner might have been sitting upon one or other, or both, of our bodies this afternoon; but—would you believe it?—just as our engagement was about to take place, we were interrupted by three of Sir John Fielding's men, and carried to Bow Street, and ignominiously bound over to keep the peace.

"Who gave the information? Not I, or Spencer, I can vow. Though I own I was pleased when the constables came running to us, bludgeon in hand: for I had no wish to take Will's blood, or sacrifice my own to such a rascal. Now, sir, have you such a battle as this to describe to me—a battle of powder and no shot?—a battle of swords as bloody as any on the stage? I have filled my paper, without finishing the story of Maria and her Hagan. You must have it by the next ship. You see, the quarrel with Will took place yesterday, very soon after I had written the first sentence or two of my letter. I had been dawdling till dinner-time (I looked at the paper last night, when I was grimly making certain little accounts up, and wondered shall I ever finish this letter?), and now the quarrel has been so much more interesting to me than poor Molly's love-adventures, that behold my paper is full to the brim! Wherever my dearest Harry reads it, I know that there will be a heart full of love for his loving brother,   G. E. W."

CHAPTER LXXI

WHITE FAVOURS

THE little quarrel between George and his cousin caused the former to discontinue his visits to Bloomsbury in a great measure; for Mr. Will was more than ever assiduous in his attentions; and, now that both were bound over to peace, so outrageous in his behaviour, that George found the greatest difficulty in keeping his hands from his cousin. The artless little Lydia had certainly a queer way of receiving her friends. But six weeks before madly jealous of George's preference for another, she now took occasion repeatedly to compliment Theo in her conversation. Miss Theo was such a quiet, gentle creature, Lyddy was sure George was just the husband for her. How fortunate that horrible quarrel had been prevented! The constables had come up just in time; and it was quite ridiculous to hear Mr. Esmond cursing and swearing, and the rage he was in at being disappointed of his duel! "But the arrival of the constables saved your valuable life, dear Mr. George, and I am sure Miss Theo ought to bless them for ever," says Lyddy, with a soft smile. "You won't stop and meet Mr. Esmond at dinner to-day? You don't like being in his company! He can't do you any harm; and I am sure you will do him none." Kind speeches like those addressed by a little girl to a gentleman, and spoken by a strange inadvertency in company, and when other gentlemen and ladies were present, were not likely to render Mr. Warrington very eager for the society of the young American lady.

George's meeting with Mr. Will was not known for some days in Dean Street, for he did not wish to disturb those kind folks with his quarrel; but when the ladies were made aware of it, you may be sure there was a great flurry and to do. "You were actually going to take a fellow-creature's life, and you came to see us, and said not a word! Oh, George, it was shocking!" said Theo.

"My dear, he had insulted me and my brother," pleaded George. "Could I let him call us both cowards, and sit by and say, Thank you?"

The General sat by and looked very grave.

"You know you think, papa, it is a wicked and un-Christian

practice; and have often said you wished gentlemen would have the courage to refuse!"

"To refuse? Yes," says Mr. Lambert, still very glum.

"It must require a prodigious strength of mind to refuse," says Jack Lambert, looking as gloomy as his father; "and I think if any man were to call me a coward, I should be apt to forget my orders."

"You see brother Jack is with me!" cries George.

"I must not be against you, Mr. Warrington," says Jack Lambert.

"Mr. Warrington!" cries George, turning very red.

"Would you, a clergyman, have George break the Commandments, and commit murder, John?" asks Theo, aghast.

"I am a soldier's son, sister," says the young divine drily. "Besides, Mr. Warrington has committed no murder at all. We must soon be hearing from Canada, father. The great question of the supremacy of the two races must be tried there ere long!" He turned his back on George as he spoke, and the latter eyed him with wonder.

Hetty, looking rather pale at this original remark of brother Jack, is called out of the room by some artful pretext of her sister. George started up and followed the retreating girls to the door.

"Great powers, gentlemen!" says he, coming back, "I believe, on my honour, you are giving me the credit of shirking this affair with Mr. Esmond!" The clergyman and his father looked at one another.

"A man's nearest and dearest are always the first to insult him," says George, flashing out.

"You mean to say, 'Not guilty?' God bless thee, my boy!" cries the General. "I told thee so, Jack." And he rubbed his hand across his eyes, and blushed, and wrung George's hand with all his might.

"Not guilty of what, in Heaven's name?" asks Mr. Warrington.

"Nay," said the General. "Mr. Jack, here, brought the story. Let him tell it. I believe 'tis a —— lie, with all my heart." And uttering this wicked expression, the General fairly walked out of the room.

The Rev. J. Lambert looked uncommonly foolish.

"And what is this—this d—— lie, sir, that somebody has been telling of me?" asked George, grinning at the young clergyman.

"To question the courage of any man is always an offence to him," says Mr. Lambert, "and I rejoice that yours has been belied."

"Who told the falsehood, sir, which you repeated?" bawls out Mr. Warrington. "I insist on the man's name!"

"You forget you are bound over to keep the peace," says Jack.

"Curse the peace, sir! We can go and fight in Holland. Tell me the man's name, I say!"

"Fair and softly, Mr. Warrington!" cries the young parson; "my hearing is perfectly good. It was not a man who told me the story which, I confess, I imparted to my father."

"What?" asks George, the truth suddenly occurring. "Was it that artful wicked little vixen in Bloomsbury Square?"

"Vixen is not the word to apply to any young lady, George Warrington!" exclaims Lambert, "much less to the charming Miss Lydia. She artful — the most innocent of Heaven's creatures! She wicked—that angel! With unfeigned delight that the quarrel should be over—with devout gratitude to think that blood consanguineous should not be shed—she spoke in terms of the highest praise of you for declining this quarrel, and of the deepest sympathy with you for taking the painful but only method of averting it."

"What method?" demands George, stamping his foot.

"Why, of laying an information, to be sure!" says Mr. Jack; on which George burst forth into language much too violent for us to repeat here, and highly uncomplimentary to Miss Lydia.

"Don't utter such words, sir!" cried the parson—who, as it seemed, now took his turn to be angry. "Do not insult, in my hearing, the most charming, the most innocent of her sex! If she has been mistaken in her information regarding you, and doubted your willingness to commit what, after all, is a crime —for a crime homicide is, and of the most awful description— you, sir, have no right to blacken that angel's character with foul words: and, innocent yourself, should respect the most innocent as she is the most lovely of women! O George, are you to be my brother?"

"I hope to have that honour," answered George, smiling. He began to perceive the other's drift.

"What, then, what—though 'tis too much bliss to be hoped for by sinful man—what if she should one day be your sister? Who could see her charms without being subjugated by them?

I own that I am a slave. I own that those Latin Sapphics in the September number of the *Gentleman's Magazine*, beginning ' Lydiæ quondam cecinit venustæ ' (with an English version by my friend Hickson of Corpus), were mine. I have told my mother what hath passed between us, and Mrs. Lambert also thinks that the most lovely of her sex has deigned to look favourably on me. I have composed a letter—she another. She proposes to wait on Miss Lydia's grandpapa this very day, and to bring me the answer, which shall make me the happiest or the most wretched of men! It was in the unrestrained intercourse of family conversation that I chanced to impart to my father the sentiments which my dear girl had uttered. Perhaps I spoke slightingly of your courage, which I don't doubt—by Heaven, I don't doubt: it may be, she has erred, too, regarding you. It may be that the fiend jealousy has been gnawing at my bosom, —and horrible suspicion!—that I thought my sister's lover found too much favour with her I would have all my own. Ah, dear George, who knows his faults? I am as one distracted with passion. Confound it, sir! What right have you to laugh at me? I would have you to know that *risu inepto*——"

" What, have you two boys made it up? " cries the General, entering at this moment, in the midst of a roar of laughter from George.

" I was giving my opinion to Mr. Warrington upon laughter, and upon his laughter in particular," says Jack Lambert, in a fume.

" George is bound over to keep the peace, Jack! Thou canst not fight him for two years: and, between now and then, let us trust you will have made up your quarrel. Here is dinner, boys! We will drink absent friends, and an end to the war, and no fighting out of the profession! "

George pleaded an engagement, as a reason for running away early from his dinner; and Jack must have speedily followed him, for when the former, after transacting some brief business at his own lodgings, came to Mr. Van den Bosch's door in Bloomsbury Square, he found the young parson already in parley with a servant there. " His master and mistress had left town yesterday," the servant said.

" Poor Jack! and you had the decisive letter in your pocket? " George asked of his future brother-in-law.

" Well, yes,"—Jack owned he had the document—" and my mother has ordered a chair, and was coming to wait on Miss

Lyddy," he whispered piteously, as the young men lingered on the steps.

George had a note, too, in his pocket for the young lady, which he had not cared to mention to Jack. In truth, his business at home had been to write a smart note to Miss Lyddy, with a message for the gentleman who had brought her that funny story of his giving information regarding the duel! The family being absent, George, too, did not choose to leave his note. "If cousin Will has been the slander-bearer, I will go and make him recant," thought George. "Will the family soon be back?" he blandly asked.

"They are gone to visit the quality," the servant replied. "Here is the address on this paper;" and George read, in Miss Lydia's hand, "The box from Madam Hocquet's to be sent by the Farnham Flying Coach: addressed to Miss Van den Bosch, at the Right Honourable the Earl of Castlewood's, Castlewood, Hants."

"*Where?*" cried poor Jack, aghast.

"His Lordship and their Ladyships have been here often," the servant said, with much importance. "The families is quite intimate."

This was very strange; for, in the course of their conversation, Lyddy had owned but to one single visit from Lady Castlewood.

"And they must be a-going to stay there some time, for Miss have took a power of boxes and gowns with her!" the man added. And the young men walked away, each crumpling his letter in his pocket.

"What was that remark you made?" asks George of Jack, at some exclamation of the latter. "I think you said——"

"Distraction! I am beside myself, George! I—I scarce know what I am saying," groans the clergyman. "She is gone to Hampshire, and Mr. Esmond is gone with her."

"Othello could not have spoken better! and she has a pretty scoundrel in her company!" says Mr. George. "Ha! here is your mother's chair!" Indeed, at this moment poor Aunt Lambert came swinging down Great Russell Street, preceded by her footman. "'Tis no use going farther, Aunt Lambert!" cries George. "Our little bird has flown."

"What little bird?"

"The bird Jack wished to pair with;—the Lyddy bird, aunt. Why, Jack, I protest you are swearing again! This morning 'twas the Sixth Commandment you wanted to break; and now——"

"Confound it! leave me alone, Mr. Warrington, do you hear?" growls Jack, looking very savage; and away he strides far out of the reach of his mother's bearers.

"What is the matter, George?" asks the lady.

George, who has not been very well pleased with brother Jack's behaviour all day, says: "Brother Jack has not a fine temper, Aunt Lambert. He informs you all that I am a coward, and remonstrates with me for being angry. He finds his mistress gone to the country, and he bawls, and stamps, and swears. O fie! Oh, Aunt Lambert, beware of jealousy! Did the General ever make you jealous?"

"You will make me very angry if you speak to me in this way," says poor Aunt Lambert, from her chair.

"I am respectfully dumb. I make my bow. I withdraw," says George, with a low bow, and turns towards Holborn.

His soul was wroth within him. He was bent on quarrelling with somebody. Had he met Cousin Will that night, it had gone ill with his sureties.

He sought Will at all his haunts, at Arthur's, at his own house. There Lady Castlewood's servants informed him that they believed Mr. Esmond had gone to join the family in Hants. He wrote a letter to his cousin:—

"My dear kind Cousin William," he said, "you know I am bound over, and would not quarrel with any one, much less with a dear, truth-telling, affectionate kinsman, whom my brother insulted by caning. But if you can find any one who says that I prevented a meeting the other day by giving information, will you tell your informant that I think it is not I but somebody else is the coward? And I write to Mr. Van den Bosch by the same post, to inform him and Miss Lyddy that I find some rascal has been telling them lies to my discredit, and to beg them have a care of such persons." And, these neat letters being despatched, Mr. Warrington dressed himself, showed himself at the play, and took supper cheerfully at the "Bedford."

In a few days George found a letter on his breakfast-table franked "Castlewood," and, indeed, written by that nobleman:—

"Dear Cousin," my Lord wrote, "there has been so much annoyance in our family of late, that I am sure 'tis time our quarrels should cease. Two days since my brother William brought me a very angry letter, signed G. Warrington, and at the same time, to my great grief and pain, acquainted me with a quarrel that had taken place between you, in which, to say the least, your conduct was violent. 'Tis an ill use to put good wine to—that to which you applied good Mr. Van den Bosch's. Sure, before an old man, young ones should be more respectful. I do not deny that William's language and behaviour are often irritating. I know he has often tried my temper, and that within the 24 hours.

"Ah! why should we not all live happily together? You know, cousin, I have ever professed a sincere regard for you—that I am a sincere admirer of the admirable young lady to whom you are engaged, and to whom I offer my most cordial compliments and remembrances. I would live in harmony with all my family where 'tis possible—the more because I hope to introduce to it a Countess of Castlewood.

"At my mature age, 'tis not uncommon for a man to choose a young wife. My Lydia (you will divine that I am happy in being able to call mine the elegant Miss Van den Bosch) will naturally survive me. After soothing my declining years, I shall not be jealous if at their close she should select some happy man to succeed me; though I shall envy him the possession of so much perfection and beauty. Though of a noble Dutch family, her rank, the girl declares, is not equal to mine, which she confesses that she is pleased to share. I, on the other hand, shall not be sorry to see descendants to my house, and to have it, through my Lady Castlewood's means, restored to something of the splendour which it knew before two or three improvident predecessors impaired it. My Lydia, who is by my side, sends you and the charming Lambert family her warmest remembrances.

"The marriage will take place very speedily here. May I hope to see you at church? My brother will not be present to quarrel with you. When I and dear Lydia announced the match to him yesterday, he took the intelligence in bad part, uttered language that I know he will one day regret, and is at present on a visit to some neighbours. The Dowager Lady Castlewood retains the house at Kensington; we having our own establishment, where you will be ever welcomed, dear cousin, by your affectionate humble servant,   CASTLEWOOD."

From the *London Magazine* of November 1759:—

"Saturday, October 13th, married at his seat, Castlewood, Hants, the Right Honourable Eugene, Earl of Castlewood, to the beautiful Miss Van den Bosch, of Virginia. £70,000."

CHAPTER LXXII

(FROM THE WARRINGTON MS.) IN WHICH MY LADY IS ON THE TOP OF THE LADDER

LOOKING across the fire, towards *her* accustomed chair, who has been the beloved partner of my hearth during the last half of my life, I often ask (for middle-aged gentlemen have the privilege of repeating their jokes, their questions, their stories), whether two young people ever were more foolish and imprudent than we were, when we married, as we did, in the year of the old King's death? My son, who has taken some prodigious leaps in the heat of his fox-hunting, says he surveys the gaps and rivers which he crossed so safely over, with terror afterwards, and astonishment at his own foolhardiness in making such desperate ventures; and yet there is no more eager sportsman in the two counties than Miles. He loves his amusement so much that he cares for no other. He has broken his collar-bone, and had a hundred tumbles (to his mother's terror); but so has his father (thinking, perhaps, of a copy of verse, or his speech at Quarter Sessions) been thrown over his old mare's head, who has slipped on a stone, as they were both dreaming along a park road at four miles an hour; and Miles's reckless sport has been the delight of his life, as my marriage has been the blessing of mine; and I never think of it but to thank Heaven. Mind, I don't set up my worship as an example: I don't say to all young folks, " Go and marry upon twopence a year; " or people would look very black at me at our vestry-meetings; but my wife is known to be a desperate match-maker; and when Hodge and Susan appear in my justice-room with a talk of allowance, we urge them to spend their half-crown a week at home, add a little contribution of our own, and send for the vicar.

Now, when I ask a question of my dear oracle, I know what the answer will be; and hence, no doubt, the reason why I so often consult her. I have but to wear a particular expression of face, and my Diana takes her reflection from it. Suppose I say, " My dear, don't you think the moon was made of cream-cheese, to-night? " She will say, " Well, papa, it did look very like cream-cheese indeed—there's nobody like you for droll similes." Or, suppose I say, " My love, Mr. Pitt's speech was very fine, but I don't think he is equal to what I remember his

father." " Nobody was equal to my Lord Chatham," says my
wife. And then one of the girls cries, " Why, I have often
heard our papa say Lord Chatham was a charlatan!" On
which mamma says, " How like she is to her Aunt Hetty!"

As for Miles, Tros Tyriusve is all one to him. He only reads
the sporting announcements in the Norwich paper. So long as
there is good scent, he does not care about the state of the
country. I believe the rascal has never read my poems, much
more my tragedies (for I mentioned Pocahontas to him the other
day, and the dunce thought she was a river in Virginia); and
with respect to my Latin verses, how can he understand them,
when I know he can't construe Corderius? Why, this note-
book lies publicly on the little table at my corner of the fireside,
and any one may read in it who will take the trouble of lifting
my spectacles off the cover: but Miles never hath. I insert in
the loose pages caricatures of Miles; jokes against him: but he
never knows nor heeds them. Only once, in place of a neat
drawing of mine, in China-ink, representing Miles asleep after
dinner, and which my friend Bunbury would not disown, I
found a rude picture of myself going over my mare Sultana's
head, and entitled " The Squire on Horseback, or Fish out of
Water." And the fellow began to roar with laughter, and all
the girls to titter, when I came upon the page! My wife said
she never was in such a fright as when I went to my book: but
I can bear a joke against myself, and have heard many, though
(strange to say for one who has lived among some of the chief
wits of the age) I never heard a good one in my life. Never
mind, Miles, though thou art not a wit, I love thee none the
worse (there never was any love lost between two wits in a
family); though thou hast no great beauty, thy mother thinks
thee as handsome as Apollo, or His Royal Highness the Prince
of Wales, who was born in the very same year with thee.
Indeed, she always thinks Coates's picture of the Prince is very
like her eldest boy, and has the print in her dressing-room to
this very day.[1]

In that same year, with what different prospects! my Lord
Esmond, Lord Castlewood's son, likewise appeared to adorn
the world. My Lord C. and his humble servant had already
come to a coolness at that time, and, Heaven knows! my honest

[1] Note in a female hand: " My son is *not a spendthrift*, nor a *breaker of
women's hearts*, as *some* gentlemen are; but that he was *exceeding like*
H.R.H. when they were both babies *is most certain*, the Duchess of An-
caster *having herself remarked* him in St. James's Park, where Gumbo and
my poor Molly used often to take him for an airing.—Th. W."

Miles's godmother, at his entrance into life, brought no gold papboats to his christening! Matters have mended since, *laus Deo*—laus Deo, indeed! for I suspect neither Miles nor his father would ever have been able to do much for themselves, and by their own wits.

Castlewood House has quite a different face now from that venerable one which it wore in the days of my youth, when it was covered with the wrinkles of time, the scars of old wars, the cracks and blemishes which years had marked on its hoary features. I love best to remember it in its old shape, as I saw it when young Mr. George Warrington went down at the owner's invitation, to be present at his Lordship's marriage with Miss Lydia Van den Bosch—" an American lady of noble family of Holland," as the county paper announced her Ladyship to be. Then the Towers stood as Warrington's grandfather the Colonel (the Marquis, as Madam Esmond would like to call her father) had seen them. The woods (thinned not a little to be sure) stood, nay, some of the self-same rooks may have cawed over them, which the Colonel had seen threescore years back. His picture hung in the hall, which might have been his, had he not preferred love and gratitude to wealth and worldly honour; and Mr. George Esmond Warrington (that is, Egomet Ipse who write this page down), as he walked the old place, pacing the long corridors, the smooth dew-spangled terraces, and cool darkling avenues, felt awhile as if he was one of Mr. Walpole's cavaliers with ruff, rapier, buff-coat, and gorget, and as if an Old Pretender, or a Jesuit emissary in disguise, might appear from behind any tall tree-trunk round about the mansion, or antique carved cupboard within it. I had the strangest, saddest, pleasantest old-world fancies as I walked the place: I imagined tragedies, intrigues, serenades, escaladoes, Oliver's Roundheads battering the towers, or bluff Hal's Beefeaters pricking over the plain before the castle. I was then courting a certain young lady (Madam, your ladyship's eyes had no need of spectacles then, and on the brow above them there was never a wrinkle or a silver hair), and I remember I wrote a ream of romantic description, under my Lord Castlewood's franks, to the lady who never tired of reading my letters then. She says, I only send her three lines now, when I am away in London or elsewhere. 'Tis that I may not fatigue your old eyes, my dear!

Mr. Warrington thought himself authorised to order a genteel

new suit of clothes for my Lord's marriage, and with Monsieur
Gumbo in attendance, made his appearance at Castlewood a few
days before the ceremony. I may mention that it had been
found expedient to send my faithful Sady home on board a
Virginian ship. A great inflammation attacking the throat
and lungs, and proving fatal in very many cases, in that year of
Wolfe's expedition, had seized and well-nigh killed my poor lad,
for whom his native air was pronounced to be the best cure.
We parted with an abundance of tears, and Gumbo shed as
many when his master went to Quebec: but he had attractions
in this country and none for the military life, so he remained
attached to my service. We found Castlewood House full of
friends, relations, and visitors. Lady Fanny was there upon
compulsion, a sulky bridesmaid. Some of the virgins of the
neighbourhood also attended the young Countess. A bishop's
widow herself, the Baroness Beatrix brought a holy brother-in-
law of the bench from London to tie the holy knot of matrimony
between Eugene, Earl of Castlewood, and Lydia Van den
Bosch, spinster; and for some time before and after the nuptials
the old house in Hampshire wore an appearance of gaiety to
which it had long been unaccustomed. The county families
came gladly to pay their compliments to the newly-married
couple. The lady's wealth was the subject of everybody's talk,
and no doubt did not decrease in the telling. Those naughty
stories which were rife in town, and spread by her disappointed
suitors there, took some little time to travel into Hampshire;
and when they reached the country found it disposed to treat
Lord Castlewood's wife with civility, and not inclined to be too
curious about her behaviour in town. Suppose she had jilted
this man, and laughed at the other? It was her money they
were anxious about, and she was no more mercenary than they.
The Hampshire folks were determined that it was a great benefit
to the county to have Castlewood House once more open, with
beer in the cellars, horses in the stables, and spits turning before
the kitchen fires. The new lady took her place with great
dignity, and 'twas certain she had uncommon accomplishments
and wit. Was it not written, in the marriage advertisements,
that her Ladyship brought her noble husband seventy thousand
pounds? *On a beaucoup d'esprit* with seventy thousand pounds.
The Hampshire people said this was only a small portion of her
wealth. When the grandfather should fall, ever so many plums
would be found on that old tree.

That quiet old man, and keen reckoner, began quickly to put

the dilapidated Castlewood accounts in order, of which long neglect, poverty, and improvidence had hastened the ruin. The business of the old gentleman's life now, and for some time henceforth, was to advance, improve, mend my Lord's finances; to screw the rents up where practicable, to pare the expenses of the establishment down. He could, somehow, look to every yard of worsted lace on the footmen's coats, and every pound of beef that went to their dinner. A watchful old eye noted every flagon of beer which was fetched from the buttery, and marked that no waste occurred in the larder. The people were fewer, but more regularly paid; the liveries were not so ragged, and yet the tailor had no need to dun for his money; the gardeners and grooms grumbled, though their wages were no longer over-due: but the horses fattened on less corn, and the fruit and vegetables were ever so much more plentiful—so keenly did my Lady's old grandfather keep a watch over the household affairs, from his lonely little chamber in the turret.

These improvements, though here told in a paragraph or two, were the affairs of months and years at Castlewood; where, with thrift, order, and judicious outlay of money (however, upon some pressing occasions, my Lord might say he had none) the estate and household increased in prosperity. That it was a flourishing and economical household no one could deny: not even the dowager lady and her two children, who now seldom entered within Castlewood gates, my Lady considering them in the light of enemies—for who, indeed, would like a stepmother-in-law? The little reigning Countess gave the Dowager battle, and routed her utterly and speedily. Though educated in the colonies, and ignorant of polite life during her early years, the Countess Lydia had a power of language and a strength of will that all had to acknowledge who quarrelled with her. The Dowager and my Lady Fanny were no match for the young American: they fled from before her to their jointure-house in Kensington, and no wonder their absence was not regretted by my Lord, who was in the habit of regretting no one whose back was turned. Could Cousin Warrington, whose hand his Lord-ship pressed so affectionately on coming and parting, with whom Cousin Eugene was so gay and frank and pleasant when they were together, expect or hope that his Lordship would grieve at his departure, at his death, at any misfortune which could happen to him, or any souls alive? Cousin Warrington knew better. Always of a sceptical turn, Mr. W. took a grim delight in watching the peculiarities of his neighbours, and could like this one even though he had no courage and no heart. Courage? Heart? What are these to you and me in the .world? A man may have private virtues as he may have half a million in the funds. What we *du monde* expect is, that he should be lively, agreeable, keep a decent figure, and pay his way. Colonel Esmond, Warrington's grandfather (in whose history and dwelling-place Mr. W. took an extraordinary interest), might once have been owner of this house of Castlewood, and of the titles which belonged to its possessor. The gentleman often looked at the Colonel's grave picture as it still hung in the saloon, a copy or replica of which piece Mr. Warrington fondly remembered in Virginia.

"He must have been a little touched here," my Lord said, tapping his own tall placid forehead.

There are certain actions simple and common with some men, which others cannot understand, and deny as utter lies, or deride as acts of madness.

"I do you the justice to think, cousin," says Mr. Warrington to his Lordship, "that you would not give up any advantage for any friend in the world."

"Eh! I am selfish: but am I more selfish than the rest of the world?" asks my Lord, with a French shrug of his shoulders, and a pinch out of his box. Once, in their walks in the fields, his Lordship happening to wear a fine scarlet coat, a cow ran towards him: and the ordinarily languid nobleman sprang over a stile with the agility of a schoolboy. He did not conceal his tremor, or his natural want of courage "I dare say you respect me no more than I respect myself, George," he would say, in his candid way, and begin a very pleasant sardonical discourse upon the fall of man, and his faults, and shortcomings; and wonder why Heaven had not made us all brave and tall, and handsome and rich? As for Mr. Warrington, who very likely loved to be king of his company (as some people do), he could not help liking this kinsman of his, so witty, graceful, polished, high-placed in the world — so utterly his inferior. Like the animal in Mr. Sterne's famous book, "Do not beat me," his Lordship's look seemed to say, "but, if you will, you may." No man, save a bully and coward himself, deals hardly with a creature so spiritless.

CHAPTER LXXIII

WE know, my dear children, from our favourite fairy story-books, how at all christenings and marriages some one is invariably disappointed, and vows vengeance; and so need not wonder that good Cousin Will should curse and rage energetically at the news of his brother's engagement with the colonial heiress. At first, Will fled the house, in his wrath, swearing he would never return. But nobody, including the swearer, believed much in Master Will's oaths; and this unrepentant prodigal, after a day or two, came back to the paternal house. The fumes of the marriage-feast allured him: he could not afford to resign his knife and fork at Castlewood table. He returned, and drank and ate there in token of revenge. He pledged the young bride in a bumper, and drank perdition to her under his breath. He made responses of smothered maledictions as her grandfather gave her away in the chapel, and my Lord vowed to love, honour, and cherish her. He was not the only grumbler respecting that marriage, as Mr. Warrington knew: he heard then, and afterwards, no end of abuse of my Lady and her grandfather. The old gentleman's city friends, his legal adviser, the Dissenting clergyman at whose chapel they attended on their first arrival in England, and poor Jack Lambert, the orthodox divine, whose eloquence he had fondly hoped had been exerted over her in private, were bitter against the little lady's treachery, and each had a story to tell of his having been enslaved, encouraged, jilted by the young American. The lawyer, who had had such an accurate list of all her properties, estates, moneys, slaves, ships, expectations, was ready to vow and swear that he believed the whole account was false; that there was no such place as New York or Virginia; or, at any rate, that Mr. Van den Bosch had no land there; that there was no such thing as a Guinea trade, and that the negroes were so many black falsehoods invented by the wily old planter. The Dissenting parson moaned over his stray lambling—if such a little, wily, mischievous monster could be called a lamb at all. Poor Jack Lambert ruefully acknowledged to his mamma the possession of a lock of black hair, which he bedewed with tears and apostrophised in quite unclerical language: and as for Mr.

William Esmond, he, with the shrieks and curses in which he always freely indulged, even at Castlewood, under his sister-in-law's own pretty little nose, when under any strong emotion, called Acheron to witness, that out of that region there did not exist such an artful young devil as Miss Lydia. He swore that she was an infernal female Cerberus, and called down all the wrath of this world and the next upon his swindling rascal of a brother, who had cajoled him with fair words, and filched his prize from him.

"Why," says Mr. Warrington (when Will expatiated on these matters with him), "if the girl is such a she-devil as you describe her, you are all the better for losing her. If she intends to deceive her husband, and to give him a dose of poison, as you say, how lucky for you you are not the man! You ought to thank the gods, Will, instead of cursing them for robbing you of such a fury, and can't be better revenged on Castlewood than by allowing him her sole possession."

"All this was very well," Will Esmond said; but—not unjustly, perhaps—remarked that his brother was not the less a scoundrel for having cheated him out of the fortune which he expected to get, and which he had risked his life to win, too.

George Warrington was at a loss to know how his cousin had been made so to risk his precious existence (for which, perhaps, a rope's end had been a fitting termination), on which Will Esmond, with the utmost candour, told his kinsman how the little *Cerbera* had actually caused the meeting between them, which was interrupted somehow by Sir John Fielding's men; how she was always saying that George Warrington was a coward for ever sneering at Mr. Will, and the latter doubly a poltroon for not taking notice of his kinsman's taunts; how George had run away and nearly died of fright in Braddock's expedition; and "Deuce take me," says Will, "I never was more surprised, cousin, than when you stood to your ground so coolly in Tottenham Court Fields yonder, for me and my second offered to wager that you would never come!"

Mr. Warrington laughed, and thanked Mr. Will for this opinion of him.

"Though," says he, "cousin, 'twas lucky for me the constables came up, or you would have whipped your sword through my body in another minute. Didn't you see how clumsy I was as I stood before you? And you actually turned white and shook with anger!"

"Yes, curse me," says Mr. Will (who turned very red this

time), "that's my way of showing my rage; and I was confoundedly angry with you, cousin! But now 'tis my brother I hate, and that little devil of a Countess—a Countess! a pretty Countess, indeed!" And, with another rumbling cannonade of oaths, Will saluted the reigning member of his family.

"Well, cousin," says George, looking him queerly in the face, "you let me off easily, and, I dare say, I owe my life to you, or at any rate a whole waistcoat, and I admire your forbearance and spirit. What a pity that a courage like yours should be wasted as a mere Court usher! You are a loss to His Majesty's army. You positively are!"

"I never know whether you are joking or serious, Mr. Warrington," growls Will.

"I should think very few gentlemen would dare to joke with *you*, cousin, if they had a regard for their own lives or ears!" cries Mr. Warrington, who loved this grave way of dealing with his noble kinsman, and used to watch, with a droll interest, the other choking his curses, grinding his teeth because afraid to bite, and smothering his cowardly anger.

"And you should moderate your expressions, cousin, regarding the dear Countess and my Lord your brother," Mr. Warrington resumed. "Of you they always speak most tenderly. Her Ladyship has told me everything."

"What, *everything*?" cries Will, aghast.

"As much as women ever *do* tell, cousin. She owned that she thought you had been a little *épris* with her. What woman can help liking a man who has admired her?"

"Why, she hates you, and says you were wild about her, Mr. Warrington!" says Mr. Esmond.

"*Spretæ injuria formæ*, cousin!"

"For me,—what's for me?" asks the other.

"I never did care for her, and hence, perhaps, she does not love me. Don't you remember that case of the wife of the Captain of the Guard?"

"Which Guard?" asks Will.

"My Lord Potiphar," says Mr. Warrington.

"Lord Who? My Lord Falmouth is Captain of the Yeomen of the Guard, and my Lord Berkeley of the Pensioners. My Lord Hobert had 'em before. Suppose you haven't been long enough in England to know who's who, cousin!" remarks Mr. William.

But Mr. Warrington explained that he was speaking of a captain of the guard of the King of Egypt, whose wife had persecuted one Joseph for not returning her affection for him. On which Will said that, as for Egypt, he believed it was a confounded long way off; and that if Lord What-d'ye-call's wife told lies about him, it was like her sex, who, he supposed, were the same everywhere.

Now the truth is, that when he paid his marriage visit to Castlewood, Mr. Warrington had heard from the little Countess her version of the story of differences between Will Esmond and herself. And this tale differed, in some respects, though he is far from saying it is more authentic than the ingenuous narrative of Mr. Will. The lady was grieved to think how she had been deceived in her brother-in-law. She feared that his life about the Court and town had injured those high principles which all the Esmonds are known to be born with; that Mr. Will's words were not altogether to be trusted; that a loose life and pecuniary difficulties had made him mercenary, blunted his honour, perhaps even impaired the high chivalrous courage "which we Esmonds, cousin," the little lady said tossing her head, "which we Esmonds must always possess — leastways, you and me, and my Lord, and my cousin Harry have it, I know!" says the Countess. "Oh, Cousin George! and must I confess that I was led to doubt of yours, without which a man of ancient and noble family like ours isn't worthy to be called a man! I shall try, George, as a Christian lady, and the head of one of the first families in this kingdom and the whole world, to forgive my brother William for having spoken ill of a member of our family, though a younger branch and by the female side, and made me for a moment doubt of you. He did so. Perhaps he told me ever so many bad things you had said of me."

"I, my dear lady!" cries Mr. Warrington.

"Which he *said* you said of me, cousin, and I hope you didn't, and heartily pray you didn't: and I can afford to despise 'em. And he paid me his court, that's a fact; and so have others, and that I'm used to; and he might have prospered better than he did perhaps (for I did not know my dear lord, nor come to vally his great and eminent qualities, as I do out of the fulness of this grateful heart now!), but, oh! I found William was deficient in courage, and no man as wants that can ever have the esteem of Lydia, Countess of Castlewood, no more he can! He said 'twas you that wanted for spirit, cousin, and angered me by telling me that you was always abusing of me. But I forgive you, George, that I do! And when I tell you that it was he was afraid—the mean skunk!—and actually sent for them constables to prevent the match between you and he you won't wonder I wouldn't valiy a feller like that—no, not that much!" and her Ladyship snapped her little fingers. "I say, *noblesse oblige*, and a man of our family who hasn't got courage, I don't care not this pinch of snuff for him—there, now, I don't! Look at our ancestors, George, round these walls! Haven't the Esmonds always fought for their country and king? Is there one of us that, when the moment arrives, ain't ready to show that he's an Esmond and a nobleman? If my eldest son was to show the white feather, 'My Lord Esmond!' I would say to him (for that's the second title in our family), 'I disown your Lordship!'" And so saying, the intrepid little woman looked round at her ancestors, whose effigies, depicted by Lely and Kneller, figured round the walls of her drawing-room at Castlewood.

Over that apartment, and the whole house, domain, and village, the new Countess speedily began to rule with an un-limited sway. It was surprising how quickly she learned the ways of command; and, if she did not adopt those methods of precedence usual in England among great ladies, invented regulations for herself, and promulgated them, and made others submit. Having been bred a Dissenter, and not being over-familiar with the Established Church service, Mr. Warrington remarked that she made a blunder or two during the office (not knowing, for example, when she was to turn her face towards the east, a custom not adopted, I believe, in other Reforming churches besides the English); but between Warrington's first bridal visit to Castlewood and his second, my Lady had got to be quite perfect in that part of her duty, and sailed into chapel on her cousin's arm, her two footmen bearing her Ladyship's great prayer-book behind her, as demurely as that delightful old devotee with her lacquey, in Mr. Hogarth's famous picture of "Morning," and as if my Lady Lydia had been accustomed to have a chaplain all her life. She seemed to patronise not only the new chaplain, but the service and the church itself, as if she had never in her own country heard a Ranter in a barn. She made the oldest established families in the country—grave baronets and their wives—worthy squires of twenty descents, who rode over to Castlewood to pay the bride and bridegroom honour—know their distance, as the phrase is, and give her the *pas*. She got an old heraldry book; and a surprising old maiden lady from Winton, learned in politeness and genealogies, from whom she learned the Court etiquette (as the old Winton lady had known it in Queen Anne's time); and ere long she jabbered gules and sables, bends and saltires, not with correctness always, but with a wonderful volubility and perseverance. She made little progresses to the neighbouring towns in her gilt coach and six, or to the village in her chair, and asserted a quasi-regal right of homage from her tenants and other clodpoles. She lectured the parson on his divinity; the bailiff on his farming; instructed the astonished housekeeper how to preserve and pickle; would have taught the great London footman to jump behind the carriage, only it was too high for her little Ladyship to mount: gave the village gossips instructions how to nurse and take care of their children long before she had one herself; and as for physic, Madam Esmond in Virginia was not more resolute about her pills and draughts than Miss Lydia, the earl's new bride. Do you remember the story of the fisherman and the Genie, in the "Arabian Nights"? So one wondered with regard to this lady, how such a prodigious genius could have been corked down into such a little bottle as her body. When Mr. Warrington returned to London after his first nuptial visit, she brought him a little present for her young friends in Dean Streat, as she called them (Theo being older, and Hetty scarce younger than herself), and sent a trinket to one and a book to the other—G. Warrington always vowing that Theo's present was a doll, while Hetty's share was a nursery-book with words of one syllable. As for Mr. Will, her younger brother-in-law, she treated him with a maternal gravity and tenderness, and was in the habit of speaking of and to him with a protecting air, which was infinitely diverting to Warrington, although Will's usual curses and blasphemies were sorely increased by her behaviour.

As for old age, my Lady Lydia had little respect for that accident in the life of some gentlemen and gentlewomen; and, once the settlements were made in her behalf, treated the ancient Van den Bosch and his large periwig with no more ceremony than Dinah, her black attendant, whose great ears she would pinch, and whose wolly pate she would pull without scruple, upon offence given—so at least Dinah told Gumbo, who told his master. And all the household trembled before my Lady the Countess; the housekeeper, of whom even my Lord and the Dowager had been in awe; the pampered London footmen, who used to quarrel if they were disturbed at their cards, and grumbled as they swilled the endless beer, now stepped nimbly about their business when they heard her Ladyship's call; even old Lockwood, who had been gate-porter for half a century or more, tried to rally his poor old wandering wits when she came into his lodge to open his window, inspect his wood-closet, and turn his old dogs out of doors. Lockwood bared his old bald head before his new mistress, turned an appealing look towards his niece, and vaguely trembled before her little Ladyship's authority. Gumbo, dressing his master for dinner, talked about Elisha (of whom he had heard the chaplain read in the morning), " and his bald head and de boys who call 'um names, and de bars eat 'um up, and serve 'um right," says Gumbo. But, as for my Lady, when discoursing with her cousin about the old porter, " Pooh, pooh! Stupid old man!" says she; " past his work, he and his dirty old dogs! They are as old and ugly as those old fish in the pond!" (Here she pointed to two old monsters of carp that had been in a pond in Castlewood gardens for centuries, according to tradition, and had their backs all covered with a hideous grey mould.) " Lockwood must pack off; the workhouse is the place for him; and I shall have a smart, good-looking, tall fellow in the lodge that will do credit to our livery."

" He was my grandfather's man, and served him in the wars of Queen Anne," interposed Mr. Warrington. On which my Lady cried petulantly, " O Lord! Queen Anne's dead, I suppose, and we ain't a-going into mourning for her."

This matter of Lockwood was discussed at the family dinner, when her Ladyship announced her intention of getting rid of the old man.

" I am told," demurely remarks Mr. Van den Bosch, " that, by the laws, poor servants and poor folks of all kinds are admirably provided in their old age here in England. I am sure I wish we had such an asylum for our folks at home, and that we were eased of the expense of keeping our old hands."

" If a man can't work he ought to go!" cries her Ladyship.

" Yes, indeed, and that's a fact!" says grandpapa.

" What! an old servant?" asks my Lord.

" Mr. Van den Bosch possibly was independent of servants when he was young," remarks Mr. Warrington.

" Greased my own boots, opened my own shutters, sanded and watered my own——"

" Sugar, sir?" says my Lord.

" No; floor, son-in-law!" says the old man, with a laugh; " though there is such tricks in grocery-stores, saving your Ladyship's presence."

" La, pa! what should *I* know about stores and groceries? " cries her Ladyship.

" He! Remember stealing the sugar, and what came on it, my dear Ladyship? " says grandpapa.

" At any rate, a handsome well-grown man in our livery will look better than that shrivelled old porter creature! " cries my Lady.

" No livery is so becoming as old age, madam, and no lace as handsome as silver hairs," says Mr. Warrington. " What will the county say if you banish old Lockwood? "

" Oh! if you plead for him, sir, I suppose he must stay. Hadn't I better order a couch for him out of my drawing-room, and send him some of the best wine from the cellar? "

" Indeed, your Ladyship couldn't do better," Mr. Warrington remarked, very gravely.

And my Lord said, yawning, " Cousin George is perfectly right, my dear. To turn away such an old servant as Lockwood would have an ill look."

" You see those mouldy old carps are, after all, a curiosity, and attract visitors," continues Mr. Warrington gravely. " Your Ladyship must allow this old wretch to remain. It won't be for long. And you may then engage the tall porter. It is very hard on us, Mr. Van den Bosch, that we are obliged to keep our old negroes when they are past work. I shall sell that rascal Gumbo in eight or ten years."

" Don't tink you will, master! " says Gumbo, grinning.

" Hold your tongue, sir! He doesn't know English ways, you see, and perhaps thinks an old servant has a claim on his master's kindness," says Mr. Warrington.

The next day, to Warrington's surprise, my Lady absolutely did send a basket of good wine to Lockwood, and a cushion for his arm-chair.

" I thought of what you said, yesterday, at night when I went to bed; and guess you know the world better than I do, cousin; and that it's best to keep the old man, as you say."

And so this affair of the porter's lodge ended, Mr. Warrington wondering within himself at this strange little character out of the West, with her *naïveté* and simplicities, and a heartlessness that would have done credit to the most battered old dowager who ever turned trumps in St. James's.

" You tell me to respect old people! Why? I don't see nothin' to respect in the old people I know," she said to Warrington. " They ain't so funny, and I'm sure they ain't so handsome. Look at grandfather; look at Aunt Bernstein. They say she was a beauty once! That picture painted from her! I don't believe it nohow. No one shall tell me that I shall ever be as bad as that! When they come to that, people oughtn't to live. No, that they oughtn't."

Now, at Christmas, Aunt Bernstein came to pay her nephew and niece a visit, in company with Mr. Warrington. They travelled at their leisure in the Baroness's own landau; the old lady being in particular good health and spirits, the weather delightfully fresh and not too cold; and, as they approached her paternal home, Aunt Beatrix told her companion a hundred stories regarding it and old days. Though often lethargic, and not seldom, it must be confessed, out of temper, the old lady would light up at times, when her conversation became wonderfully lively, her wit and malice were brilliant, and her memory supplied her with a hundred anecdotes of a bygone age and society. Sure 'tis hard with respect to Beauty, that its possessors should not have even a life-enjoyment of it, but be compelled to resign it after, at the most, some forty years' lease. As the old woman prattled of her former lovers and admirers (her auditor having much more information regarding her past career than her Ladyship knew of), I would look in her face, and, out of the ruins, try to build up in my fancy a notion of her beauty in its prime. What a homily I read there! How the courts were grown with grass, the towers broken, the doors ajar, the fine gilt saloons tarnished, and the tapestries cobwebbed and torn! Yonder dilapidated palace was all alive once with splendour and music, and those dim windows were dazzling and blazing with light! What balls and feasts were once here, what splendour and laughter! I could see lovers in waiting, crowds in admiration, rivals furious. I could imagine twilight assignations, and detect intrigues, though the curtains were close and drawn. I was often minded to say to the old woman as she talked, " Madam, I know the story was not as you tell it, but so and so "—(I had read at home the history of her life, as my dear old grandfather had wrote it): and my fancy wandered about in her, amused and solitary, as I had walked about our fathers' house at Castlewood, meditating on departed glories, and imagining ancient times.

When Aunt Bernstein came to Castlewood, her relatives there, more, I think, on account of her own force of character, imperiousness, and sarcastic wit, than from their desire to possess her money, were accustomed to pay her a great deal of respect and deference, which she accepted as her due. She expected the same treatment from the new Countess, whom she was prepared to greet with special good-humour. The match had been of her making. " As you, you silly creature, would not have the heiress," she said, " I was determined she should not go out of the family," and she laughingly told of many little schemes for bringing the marriage about. She had given the girl a coronet and her nephew a hundred thousand pounds. Of course she should be welcome to both of them. She was delighted with the little Countess's courage and spirit in routing the Dowager and Lady Fanny. Almost always pleased with pretty people on her first introduction to them, Madam Bernstein *raffoléd* of her niece Lydia's bright eyes and lovely little figure. The marriage was altogether desirable. The old man was an obstacle, to be sure, and his talk and appearance somewhat too homely. But he will be got rid of. He is old and delicate in health. " He will want to go to America, or perhaps farther," says the Baroness, with a shrug. " As for the child, she had great fire and liveliness, and a Cherokee manner, which is not without its charm," said the pleased old Baroness. " Your brother had it—so have you, Master George! Nous la formerons, cette petite. Eugene wants character and vigour, but he is a finished gentleman, and between us we shall make the little savage perfectly presentable."

In this way we discoursed on the second afternoon as we journeyed towards Castlewood. We lay at the " King's Arms " at Bagshot the first night, where the Baroness was always received with profound respect, and thence drove post to Hexton, where she had written to have my Lord's horses in waiting for her: but these were not forthcoming at the inn, and after a couple of hours we were obliged to proceed with our Bagshot horses to Castlewood.

During this last stage of the journey, I am bound to say the old aunt's testy humour returned, and she scarce spoke a single word for three hours. As for her companion, being prodigiously in love at the time, no doubt he did not press his aunt for conversation, but thought unceasingly about his Dulcinea, until the coach actually reached Castlewood Common, and rolled over the bridge before the house.

The housekeeper was ready to conduct her Ladyship to her apartments. My Lord and Lady were both absent. She did not know what had kept them, the housekeeper said, leading the way.

"Not that door, my Lady!" cries the woman, as Madame de Bernstein put her hand upon the door of the room which she had always occupied. "That's her Ladyship's room now. This way." And our aunt followed, by no means in increased good-humour. I do not envy her maids when their mistress was displeased. But she had cleared her brow before she joined the family, and appeared in the drawing-room before supper-time with a countenance of tolerable serenity.

"How d'ye do, aunt?" was the Countess's salutation. "I declare now, I was taking a nap when your Ladyship arrived! Hope you found your room fixed to your liking!"

Having addressed three brief sentences to the astonished old lady, the Countess now turned to her other guests, and directed her conversation to them. Mr. Warrington was not a little diverted by her behaviour, and by the appearance of surprise and wrath which began to gather over Madam Bernstein's face. "*La Petite*," whom the Baroness proposed to "form," was rather a rebellious subject, apparently, and proposed to take a form of her own. Looking once or twice rather anxiously towards his wife, my Lord tried to atone for her pertness towards his aunt by profuse civility on his own part; indeed, when he so wished, no man could be more courteous or pleasing. He found a score of agreeable things to say to Madam Bernstein. He warmly congratulated Mr. Warrington on the glorious news which had come from America, and on his brother's safety. He drank a toast at supper to Captain Warrington. "Our family is distinguishing itself, cousin," he said; and added, looking with fond significance towards his Countess, "I hope the happiest days are in store for us all."

"Yes, George!" says the little lady. "You'll write and tell Harry that we are all very much pleased with him. This action at Quebec is a most glorious action; and now we have turned the French King out of the country, shouldn't be at all surprised if we set up for ourselves in America."

"My love, you are talking treason!" cries Lord Castlewood.

"I am talking reason, anyhow, my Lord. I've no notion of folks being kept down, and treated as children for ever!"

George! Harry! I protest I was almost as much astonished as amused. "When my brother hears that your Ladyship is satisfied with his conduct, his happiness will be complete," I said gravely.

Next day, when talking beside her sofa, where she chose to lie in state, the little Countess no longer called her cousin

" George," but " Mr. George," as before; on which Mr. George laughingly said she had changed her language since the previous day.

" Guess I did it to tease old Madam Buzwig," says her Ladyship. " She wants to treat me as a child, and do the grandmother over me. I don't want no grandmothers, I don't. I'm the head of this house, and I intend to let her know it. And I've brought her all the way from London in order to tell it her, too! La! how she did look when I called you George! I might have called you George—only you had seen that little Theo first, and liked her best, I suppose."

" Yes, I suppose I like her best," says Mr. George.

" Well, I like you because you tell the truth. Because you was the only one of 'em in London who didn't seem to care for my money, though I was downright mad and angry with you once, and with myself too, and with that little sweetheart of yours, who ain't to be compared to me, I know she ain't."

" Don't let us make the comparison, then! " I said, laughing.

" I suppose people must lie on their beds as they make 'em," says she, with a little sigh. " Dare say Miss Theo is very good, and you'll marry her and go to Virginia, and be as dull as we are here. We were talking of Miss Lambert, my Lord, and I was wishing my cousin joy. How is old Goody to-day? What a supper she did eat last night, and drink!—drink like a dragoon! No wonder she has got a headache, and keeps her room. Guess it takes her ever so long to dress herself."

" You, too, may be feeble when you are old, and require rest and wine to warm you! " says Mr. Warrington.

" Hope I shan't be like *her* when I'm old, anyhow! " says the lady. " Can't see why I am to respect an old woman, because she hobbles on a stick, and has shaky hands, and false teeth! " And the little heathen sank back on her couch, and showed twenty-four pearls of her own.

" La! " she adds, after gazing at both her hearers through the curled lashes of her brilliant dark eyes. " How frightened you both look! My Lord has already given me ever so many sermons about old Goody. You are both afraid of her: and I ain't, that's all. Don't look so scared at one another! I ain't a-going to bite her head off. We shall have a battle, and I intend to win. How did I serve the Dowager, if you please, and my Lady Fanny, with their high and mighty airs, when they tried to put down the Countess of Castlewood in her own house, and laugh at the poor American girl? We had a fight, and which got the best of it, pray? Me and Goody will have another, and when it is over, you will see that we shall both be perfect friends!"

When, at this point of our conversation, the door opened, and Madam Beatrix, elaborately dressed according to her wont, actually made her appearance, I, for my part, am not ashamed to own that I felt as great a panic as ever coward experienced. My Lord, with his profoundest bows and blandest courtesies, greeted his aunt and led her to the fire, by which my Lady (who was already hoping for an heir to Castlewood) lay reclining on her sofa. She did not attempt to rise, but smiled a greeting to her venerable guest. And then, after a brief talk, in which she showed a perfect self-possession, while the two gentlemen blundered and hesitated with the most dastardly tremor, my Lord said:—" If we are to look for those pheasants, cousin, we had better go now."

" And I and aunt will have a cosy afternoon. And you will tell me about Castlewood in the old times, won't you, Baroness?" says the new mistress of the mansion.

Oh les lâches que les hommes ! I was so frightened that I scarce saw anything, but vaguely felt that Lady Castlewood's dark eyes were following me. My Lord gripped my arm in the corridor, we quickened our paces till our retreat became a disgraceful run. We did not breathe freely till we were in the open air in the courtyard, where the keepers and the dogs were waiting.

And what happened? I protest, children, I don't know. But this is certain: if your mother had been a woman of the least spirit, or had known how to scold for five minutes during as many consecutive days of her early married life, there would have been no more humble henpecked wretch in Christendom than your father. When Parson Blake comes to dinner, don't you see how at a glance from his little wife he puts his glass down and says, " No, thank you, Mr. Gumbo," when old Gum brings him wine? Blake wore a red coat before he took to black, and walked up Breed's Hill with a thousand bullets whistling round his ears, before he ever saw *our* Bunker Hill in Suffolk. And the fire-eater of the 43rd now dares not face a glass of old port wine! 'Tis his wife has subdued his courage. The women can master us, and did they know their own strength were invincible.

Well, then, what happened I know not on that disgraceful day of panic when your father fled the field, nor dared to see the heroines engage; but when we returned from our shooting, the battle was over. America had revolted, and conquered the mother country.

CHAPTER LXXIV

NEWS FROM CANADA

Our Castlewood relatives kept us with them till the commencement of the new year, and after a fortnight's absence (which seemed like an age to the absurd and infatuated young man) he returned to the side of his charmer. Madame de Bernstein was not sorry to leave the home of her father. She began to talk more freely as we got away from the place. What passed during that interview in which the battle-royal between her and her niece occurred, she never revealed. But the old Lady talked no more of forming *cette petite*, and, indeed, when she alluded to her, spoke in a nervous laughing way, but without any hostility towards the young Countess. Her nephew Eugene, she said, was doomed to be henpecked for the rest of his days: that she saw clearly. A little order brought into the house would do it all the good possible. The little old vulgar American gentleman seemed to be a shrewd person, and would act advantageously as a steward. The Countess's mother was a convict, she had heard, sent out from England, where no doubt she had beaten hemp in most of the gaols; but this news need not be carried to the town-crier; and, after all, in respect to certain kind of people, what mattered what their birth was? The young woman would be honest for her own sake now: was shrewd enough, and would learn English presently; and the name to which she had a right was great enough to get her into any society. A grocer, a smuggler, a slave-dealer, what mattered Mr. Van den Bosch's pursuit or previous profession? The Countess of Castlewood could afford to be anybody's daughter, and as soon as my nephew produced her, says the old lady, it was our duty to stand by her.

The ties of relationship binding Madame de Bernstein strongly to her nephew, Mr. Warrington hoped that she would be disposed to be equally affectionate to her niece; and spoke of his visit to Mr. Hagan and his wife, for whom he entreated her aunt's favour. But the old lady was obdurate regarding Lady Maria; begged that her name might never be mentioned, and immediately went on for two hours talking about no one else. She related a series of anecdotes regarding her niece, which, as this book lies open *virginibus puerisque*, to all the young people of the

family, I shall not choose to record. But this I will say of the
kind creature, that if she sinned, she was not the only sinner of
the family, and if she repented, that others will do well to
follow her example. Hagan, 'tis known, after he left the stage,
led an exemplary life, and was remarkable for elegance and
eloquence in the pulpit. His lady adopted extreme views, but
was greatly respected in the sect which she joined; and when I
saw her last talked to me of possessing a peculiar spiritual
illumination which I strongly suspected at the time to be occasioned by the too free use of liquor: but I remember when she
and her husband were good to me and mine, at a period when
sympathy was needful, and many a Pharisee turned away.

I have told how easy it was to rise and fall in my fickle aunt's
favour, and how each of us brothers, by turns, was embraced
and neglected. My turn of glory had been after the success of
my play. I was introduced to the town-wits; held my place
in their company tolerably well; was pronounced to be pretty
well-bred by the macaronis and people of fashion, and might
have run a career amongst them had my purse been long enough;
had I chose to follow that life; had I not loved at that time a pair
of kind eyes better than the brightest orbs of the Gunnings or
Chudleighs, or all the painted beauties of the Ranelagh ring.
Because I was fond of your mother, will it be believed, children,
that my tastes were said to be low, and deplored by my genteel
family? So it was, and I know that my godly Lady Warrington
and my worldly Madam Bernstein both laid their elderly heads
together and lamented my way of life.

" Why, with his name, he might marry anybody," says meek
Religion, who had ever one eye on heaven and one on the main
chance. " I meddle with no man's affairs, and admire genius,"
says Uncle, " but it *is* a pity you consort with those poets and
authors, and that sort of people, and that, when you might have
had a lovely creature, with a hundred thousand pounds, you let
her slip and make up to a country girl without a penny-piece."

" But if I had promised her, uncle? " says I.

" Promise, promise! these things are matters of arrangement
and prudence, and demand a careful look-out. When you first
committed yourself with little Miss Lambert, you had not seen
the lovely American lady whom your mother wished you to
marry, as a good mother naturally would. And your duty to
your mother, nephew—your duty to the Fifth Commandment,
would have warranted your breaking with Miss L., and fulfilling
your excellent mother's intentions regarding Miss——what was

the Countess's Dutch name? Never mind. A name is nothing; but a plum, Master George, is something to look at! Why, I have my dear little Miley at a dancing-school with Miss Barwell, Nabob Barwell's daughter, and I don't disguise my wish that the children may contract an attachment which may endure through their lives! I tell the Nabob so. We went from the House of Commons one dancing-day, and saw them. 'Twas beautiful to see the young things walking a minuet together! It brought tears into my eyes, for I have a feeling heart, George, and I love my boy!"

" But if I prefer Miss Lambert, uncle, with twopence to her fortune, to the Countess, with her hundred thousand pounds?"

" Why, then, sir, you have a singular taste, that's all," says the old gentleman, turning on his heel and leaving me. And I could perfectly understand his vexation at my not being able to see the world as he viewed it.

Nor did my Aunt Bernstein much like the engagement which I had made, or the family with which I passed so much of my time. Their simple ways wearied, and perhaps annoyed, the old woman of the world, and she no more relished their company than a certain person (who is not so black as he is painted) likes holy water. The old lady chafed at my for ever dangling at my sweetheart's lap. Having risen mightily in her favour, I began to fall again: and once more Harry was the favourite, and his brother, Heaven knows, not jealous.

He was now our family hero. He wrote us brief letters from the seat of war where he was engaged, Madam Bernstein caring little at first about the letters or the writer, for they were simple, and the facts narrated not over interesting. We had early learned in London the news of the action on the glorious first of August at Minden, where Wolfe's old regiment was one of the British six which helped to achieve the victory on that famous day. At the same hour, the young General lay in his bed, in sight of Quebec, stricken down by fever, and perhaps rage and disappointment, at the check which his troops had just received.

Arriving in the St. Lawrence in June, the fleet which brought Wolfe and his army had landed them on the last day of the month on the Island of Orleans, opposite which rises the great cliff of Quebec. After the great action in which his General fell, the dear brother who accompanied the chief wrote home to me one of his simple letters, describing his modest share in that glorious day, but added nothing to the many descriptions already wrote of the action of the 13th of September, save only

I remembered he wrote, from the testimony of a brother aide-de-camp who was by his side, that the General never *spoke at all* after receiving his death-wound, so that the phrase which has been put into the mouth of the dying hero may be considered as no more authentic than an oration of Livy or Thucydides.

From his position on the island, which lies in the great channel of the river to the north of the town, the General was ever hungrily on the look-out for a chance to meet and attack his enemy. Above the city and below it he landed,—now here and now there; he was bent upon attacking wherever he saw an opening. 'Twas surely a prodigious fault on the part of the Marquis of Montcalm, to accept a battle from Wolfe on equal terms, for the British General had no artillery, and when we had made our famous scalade of the heights, and were on the plains of Abraham, we were a little nearer the city, certainly, but as far off as ever from being within it.

The game that was played between the brave chiefs of those two gallant little armies, and which lasted from July until Mr. Wolfe won the crowning hazard in September, must have been as interesting a match as ever eager players engaged in. On the very first night after the landing (as my brother has narrated it) the sport began. At midnight the French sent a flaming squadron of fire-ships down upon the British ships which were discharging their stores at Orleans. Our seamen thought it was good sport to tow the fire-ships clear of the fleet, and ground them on the shore, where they burned out.

As soon as the French commander heard that our ships had entered the river, he marched to Beauport in advance of the city and there took up a strong position. When our stores and hospitals were established, our General crossed over from his island to the left shore, and drew nearer to his enemy. He had the ships in the river behind him, but the whole country in face of him was in arms. The Indians in the forest seized our advanced parties as they strove to clear it, and murdered them with horrible tortures. The French were as savage as their Indian friends. The Montmorenci river rushed between Wolfe and the enemy. He could neither attack these nor the city behind them.

Bent on seeing whether there was no other point at which his foe might be assailable, the General passed round the town of Quebec and skirted the left shore beyond. Everywhere it was guarded, as well as in his immediate front, and having run the gauntlet of the batteries up and down the river, he returned to his post at Montmorenci. On the right of the French position, across the Montmorenci river, which was fordable at low tide, was a redoubt of the enemy. He would have that. Perhaps, to defend it, the French chief would be forced out from his lines, and a battle be brought on. Wolfe determined to play these odds. He would fetch over the body of his army from the island of Orleans, and attack from the St. Lawrence. He would time his attack, so that, at shallow water, his lieutenants, Murray and Townsend, might cross the Montmorenci, and, at the last day of July, he played this desperate game.

He first, and General Monckton, his second in command (setting out from Point Levi, which he occupied), crossed over the St. Lawrence from their respective stations, being received with a storm of shot and artillery as they rowed to the shore. No sooner were the troops landed than they rushed at the French redoubt without order, were shot down before it in great numbers and were obliged to fall back. At the preconcerted signal the troops on the other side of the Montmorenci advanced across the river in perfect order. The enemy even evacuated the redoubt, and fell back to their lines; but from these the assailants were received with so fierce a fire that an impression on them was hopeless, and the General had to retreat.

That battle of Montmorenci (which my brother Harry and I have fought again many a time over our wine) formed the dismal burthen of the first despatch from Mr. Wolfe which reached England, and plunged us all in gloom. What more might one expect of a commander so rash? What disasters might one not foretell? Was ever scheme so wild as to bring three great bodies of men across broad rivers, in the face of murderous batteries, merely on the chance of inducing an enemy, strongly intrenched and guarded, to leave his position and come out and engage us? 'Twas the talk of the town. No wonder grave people shook their heads, and prophesied fresh disaster. The General, who took to his bed after this failure, shuddering with fever, was to live barely six weeks longer, and die immortal! How is it, and by what, and whom, that Greatness is achieved? Is Merit —is Madness the patron? Is it Frolic or Fortune? Is it Fate that awards successes and defeats? Is it the Just Cause that ever wins? How did the French gain Canada from the savage, and we from the French, and after which of the conquests was the right time to sing Te Deum? We are always for implicating Heaven in our quarrels, and causing the gods to intervene whatever the *nodus* may be. Does Broughton, after pummelling and beating Slack, lift up a black eye to Jove and thank him for the victory? And if ten thousand boxers are to be so heard, why not one? And if Broughton is to be grateful, what is Slack to be?

" By the list of disabled officers (many of whom are of rank) you may perceive, sir, that the army is much weakened. By the nature of this river, the most formidable part of the armament is deprived of the power of acting, yet we have almost the whole force of Canada to oppose. In this situation there is such a choice of difficulties, that I own myself at a loss how to determine. The affairs of Great Britain, I know, require the most vigorous measure; but then the courage of a handful of brave men should be exerted only where there is some hope of a favourable event. The Admiral and I have examined the town with a view to a general assault: and he would readily join in this or any other measure for the public service; but I cannot propose to him an undertaking of so dangerous a nature, and promising so little success. . . . I found myself so ill, and am still so weak, that I begged the general officers to consult together for the public utility. They are of opinion that they should try by conveying up a corps of 4000 or 5000 men (which is nearly the whole strength of the army, after the points of Levi and Orleans are put in a proper state of defence) to draw the enemy from their present position, and bring them to an action. I have acquiesced in their proposal, and we are preparing to put it into execution."

So wrote the General (of whose noble letters it is clear *our* dear scribe was not the author or secretary) from his headquarters at Montmorenci Falls on the 2nd day of September: and on the 14th of October following, the " Rodney " cutter arrived with the sad news in England. The attack had failed, the chief was sick, the army dwindling, the menaced city so strong that assault was almost impossible; " the only chance was to fight the Marquis of Montcalm upon terms of less disadvantage than attacking his intrenchments, and, if possible, to draw him from his present position." Would the French chief, whose great military genius was known in Europe, fall into such a snare? No wonder there were pale looks in the city at the news, and doubt and gloom wheresoever it was known.

Three days after this first melancholy intelligence, came the famous letters announcing that wonderful consummation of fortune with which Mr. Wolfe's wonderful career ended. If no man is to be styled happy till his death, what shall we say of this one? His end was so glorious, that I protest not even his mother nor his mistress ought to have deplored it, or at any rate have wished him alive again. I know it is a hero we speak of; and yet I vow I scarce know whether in the last act of his life I admire the result of genius, invention, and daring, or the boldness of a gambler winning surprising odds. Suppose his ascent discovered a half-hour sooner, and his people, as they would have been assuredly, beaten back? Suppose the Marquis of Montcalm not to quit his intrenched lines to accept that strange challenge? Suppose these points — and none of them depend upon Mr. Wolfe at all—and what becomes of the glory of the young hero, of the great Minister who discovered him, of the intoxicated nation which rose up frantic with self-gratulation at the victory? I say, what fate is it, that shapes our ends, or those of nations? In the many hazardous games which my Lord Chatham played, he won this prodigious one. And as the greedy British hands seized the Canadas, it let fall the United States out of its grasp

To be sure this wisdom *d'après coup* is easy. We wonder at this man's rashness now the deed is done, and marvel at the other's fault. What generals some of us are upon paper; what repartees come to our mind when the talk is finished; and, the game over, how well we see how it should have been played! Writing of an event at a distance of thirty years, 'tis not difficult now to criticise and find fault. But at the time when we first heard of Wolfe's glorious deeds upon the plains of Abraham— of that army marshalled in darkness and carried silently up the midnight river—of those rocks scaled by the intrepid leader and his troops—of that miraculous security of the enemy, of his present acceptance of our challenge to battle, and of his defeat on the open plain by the sheer valour of his conqueror —we were all intoxicated in England by the news. The whole nation rose up and felt itself the stronger for Wolfe's victory. Not merely all men engaged in the battle, but those at home who had condemned its rashness, felt themselves heroes. Our spirit rose as that of our enemy faltered. Friends embraced each other when they met. Coffee-houses and public places were thronged with people eager to talk the news. Courtiers rushed to the King and the great Minister by whose wisdom the campaign had been decreed. When he showed himself, the people followed him with shouts and blessings. People did not deplore the dead warrior, but admired his *euthanasia*. Should James Wolfe's friends weep and wear mourning, because a chariot had come from the skies to fetch him away? Let them watch with wonder, and see him departing, radiant; rising above us superior. To have a friend who had been near or about him was to be distinguished. Every soldier who fought with him was a hero. In our fond little circle I know 'twas a distinction to be Harry's brother. We should not in the least wonder but that he, from his previous knowledge of the place, had found the way up the heights which the British army took, and pointed it out to his General. His promotion would follow as a matter of course. Why, even our Uncle Warrington wrote letters to bless Heaven and congratulate me and himself upon the share Harry had had in the glorious achievement. Our aunt Beatrix opened her house and received company upon the strength of the victory. I became a hero from my likeness to my brother. As for Parson Sampson, he preached such a sermon that his auditors (some of whom had been warned by his reverence of the coming discourse) were with difficulty restrained from huzzaing the orator, and were mobbed as they left the chapel. "Don't talk to me, madam, about grief," says General Lambert to his wife, who, dear soul, was for allowing herself some small indulgence of her favourite sorrow on the day when Wolfe's remains were gloriously buried at Greenwich. "If our boys could come by such deaths as James's, you know you wouldn't prevent them from being shot, but would scale the Abraham heights to see the thing done! Wouldst thou mind dying in the arms of victory, Charley?" he asks of the little hero from the Chartreux. "That I wouldn't," says the little man; "and the Doctor gave us a holiday, too."

Our Harry's promotion was ensured after his share in the famous battle, and our aunt announced her intention of purchasing a company for him.

CHAPTER LXXV

THE COURSE OF TRUE LOVE

HAD your father, young folks, possessed the commonest share of prudence, not only would this chapter of his history never have been written, but you yourselves would never have appeared in the world to plague him in a hundred ways: to shout and laugh in the passages when he wants to be quiet at his books; to wake him when he is dozing after dinner, as a healthy country gentleman should; to mislay his spectacles for him, and steal away his newspaper when he wants to read it; to ruin him with tailors' bills, mantua-makers' bills, tutors' bills, as you all of you do; to break his rest of nights when you have the imprudence to fall ill, and when he would sleep undisturbed, but that your silly mother will never be quiet for half-an-hour; and when Joan can't sleep, what use, pray, is there in Darby putting on his nightcap? Every trifling ailment that any one of you has had, has scared her so that I protest I have never been tranquil; and, were I not the most long-suffering creature in the world, would have liked to be rid of the whole pack of you. And now, forsooth, that you have grown out of childhood, long petticoats, chicken-pox, small-pox, whooping-cough, scarlet fever, and the other delectable accidents of puerile life, what must that unconscionable woman propose but to arrange the south rooms as a nursery for possible grandchildren, and set up the Captain with a wife, and make him marry early because we did! He is too fond, she says, of Brooks's and Goosetree's when he is in London. She has the perversity to hint that, though an entrée to Carlton House may be very pleasant, 'tis very dangerous for a young gentleman: and she would have Miles live away from temptation, and sow his wild oats, and marry, as we did. Marry! my dear creature, we had no business to marry at all! By the laws of common prudence and duty, I ought to have backed out of my little engagement with Miss Theo (who would have married somebody else), and taken a rich wife. Your Uncle John was a parson and couldn't fight; poor Charley was a boy at school; and your grandfather was too old a man to call me to account with sword and pistol. I repeat there never was a more foolish match in the world than ours, and our relations were perfectly right in being angry with us. What are relations made for, indeed, but to be angry and find fault? When Hester marries, do you mind, Master George, to quarrel with her if she does not take a husband of your selecting. When George has got his living, after being senior wrangler and fellow of his college, Miss Hester, do you toss up your little nose at the young lady he shall fancy. As for you, my little Theo, I can't part with *you*.[1] You must not quit your old father; for he likes you to play Haydn to him, and peel his walnuts after dinner.

---

[1] On the blank leaf opposite this paragraph is written, in a large girlish hand:—

" I never intend to go.—THEODOSIA."

" Nor I.—HESTER."

They both married, as I see by the note in the family Bible: Miss Theodosia Warrington to Joseph Clinton, son of the Rev. Joseph Blake, and himself subsequently Master of Rodwell Regis Grammar School; and Miss Hester Mary, in 1804, to Captain F. Handyman, R.N.—ED.

Whilst they had the blessing (forsooth!) of meeting, and billing and cooing every day, the two young people, your parents, went on in a fool's paradise, little heeding the world round about them, and all its tattling and meddling. Rinaldo was as brave a warrior as ever slew Turk, but you know he loved dangling in Armida's garden. Pray, my Lady Armida, what did you mean by flinging your spells over me in youth, so that not glory, not fashion, not gaming-tables, not the society of men of wit in whose way I fell, could keep me long from your apron-strings, or out of reach of your dear simple prattle? Pray, my dear, what used we to say to each other during those endless hours of meeting? I never went to sleep after dinner then. Which of us was so witty? Was it I or you? And how came it our conversations were so delightful? I remember that year I did not even care to go and see my Lord Ferrers tried and hung, when all the world was running after his Lordship. The King of Prussia's capital was taken: had the Austrians and Russians been encamped round the Tower there could scarce have been more stir in London: yet Miss Theo and her young gentleman felt no inordinate emotion of pity or indignation. What to us was the fate of Leipzig or Berlin. The truth is, that dear old house in Dean Street was an enchanted garden of delights. I have been as idle since, but never as happy. Shall we order the post-chaise, my dear, leave the children to keep house; and drive up to London and see if the old lodgings are still to be let? And you shall sit at your old place in the window, and wave a little handkerchief as I walk up the street. Say what we did was imprudent. Would we not do it over again? My good folks, if Venus had walked into the room and challenged the apple, I was so infatuated, I would have given it your mother. And had she had the choice, she would have preferred her humble servant in a threadbare coat to my Lord Clive with all his diamonds.

Once, to be sure, and for a brief time in that year, I had a notion of going on the highway in order to be caught and hung as my Lord Ferrers; or of joining the King of Prussia, and requesting some of His Majesty's enemies to knock my brains out; or of enlisting for the India service, and performing some desperate exploit which should end in my bodily destruction. Ah me! that was indeed a dreadful time! Your mother scarce dares speak of it now, save in a whisper of terror; or think of it—it was such cruel pain. She was unhappy years after on the anniversary of the day, until one of you was born on it. Suppose we had been parted: what had come to us? What had my lot been without her? As I think of that possibility, the whole world is a blank. I do not say were we parted now. It has pleased God to give us thirty years of union. We have reached the autumn season. Our successors are appointed and ready; and that one of us who is first called away, knows the survivor will follow ere long. But we were actually parted in our youth; and I tremble to think what *might* have been, had not a dearest friend brought us together.

Unknown to myself, and very likely meaning only my advantage, my relatives in England had chosen to write to Madam Esmond in Virginia, and represent what they were pleased to call the folly of the engagement I had contracted. Every one of them sang the same song: and I saw the letters, and burned the whole cursed pack of them years afterwards when my mother showed them to me at home in Virginia. Aunt Bernstein was forward with her advice. A young person with no wonderful good looks, of no family, with no money:—was ever such an imprudent connection, and ought it not for dear George's sake to be broken off? She had several eligible matches in view for me. With my name and prospects, 'twas a shame I should throw myself away on this young lady; her sister ought to interpose—and so forth.

My Lady Warrington must write, too, and in her peculiar manner. Her Ladyship's letter was garnished with Scripture texts. She dressed her worldliness out in phylacteries. She pointed out how I was living in an unworthy society of player-folks, and the like people, who she could not say were absolutely without religion (Heaven forbid!), but who were deplorably worldly. She would not say an artful woman had *inveigled me for her daughter*, having in vain tried to captivate my younger brother. She was far from saying any harm of the young woman I had selected; but at the least this was certain, Miss L. had no fortune or expectations, and her parents might naturally be anxious to compromise me. She had taken counsel, etc. etc. She had sought for guidance where it was, etc. Feeling what her *duty* was, she had determined to speak. Sir Miles, a man of excellent judgment in the affairs of this world (though he knew and sought a better), fully agreed with her in opinion, nay, desired her to write, and entreat her sister to interfere, that the ill-advised match should not take place.

And who besides must put a little finger into the pie but the new Countess of Castlewood? She wrote a majestic letter to

Madam Esmond, and stated, that having been placed by
Providence at the head of the Esmond family, it was her duty
to communicate with her kinswoman and warn her to break off
this marriage. I believe the three women laid their heads
together previously; and, packet after packet, sent off their
warnings to the Virginian lady.

One raw April morning, as Corydon goes to pay his usual
duty to Phyllis, he finds, not his charmer with her dear smile as
usual ready to welcome him, but Mrs. Lambert, with very red
eyes, and the General as pale as death. " Read this, George
Warrington! " says he, as his wife's head drops between her
hands; and he puts a letter before me, of which I recognised the
handwriting. I can hear now the sobs of the good Aunt Lambert,
and to this day the noise of fire-irons stirring a fire in a room
overhead gives me a tremor. I heard such a noise that day in
the girls' room where the sisters were together. Poor gentle
child! Poor Theo!

" What can I do after this, George, my poor boy? " asks the
General, pacing the room with desperation in his face.

I did not quite read the whole of Madam Esmond's letter, for
a kind of sickness and faintness came over me; but I fear I could
say some of it now by heart. Its style was good, and its actual
words temperate enough, though they only implied that Mr.
and Mrs. Lambert had inveigled me into the marriage; that
they knew such an union was unworthy of me; that (as Madam E.
understood) they had desired a similar union for her younger
son, which project, not unluckily for him, perhaps, was given up
when it was found that Mr. Henry Warrington was not the
inheritor of the Virginian property. If Mr. Lambert was a man
of spirit and honour, as he was represented to be, Madam
Esmond scarcely supposed that, after her representations, he
would persist in desiring this match. She would not lay commands upon her son, whose temper she knew; but for the sake
of Miss Lambert's own reputation and comfort, she urged that
the dissolution of the engagement should come from *her* family,
and not from the just unwillingness of Rachel Esmond Warrington of Virginia.

" God help us, George! " the General said, " and give us all
strength to bear this grief, and these charges which it has pleased
your mother to bring! They are hard, but they don't matter
now. What is of most importance, is to spare as much sorrow
as we can to my poor girl. I know you love her so well, that you
will help me and her mother to make the blow as tolerable as we

may to that poor gentle heart. Since she was born she has never given pain to a soul alive, and 'tis cruel that she should be made to suffer." And as he spoke he passed his hand across his dry eyes.

" It was my fault, Martin! It was my fault! " weeps the poor mother.

" Your mother spoke us fair, and gave her promise," said the father.

" And do you think I will withdraw mine? " cried I; and protested, with a thousand frantic vows, what they knew full well, " that I was bound to Theo before Heaven, and that nothing should part me from her."

" She herself will demand the parting. She is a good girl, God help me! and a dutiful. She will not have her father and mother called schemers, and treated with scorn. Your mother knew not, very likely, what she was doing, but 'tis done. You may see the child, and she will tell you as much. Is Theo dressed, Molly? I brought the letter home from my office last evening after you were gone. The women have had a bad night. She knew at once by my face that there was bad news from America. She read the letter quite firmly. She said she would like to see you and say Good-bye. Of course, George, you will give me your word of honour not to try and see her afterwards. As soon as my business will let me we will get away from this, but mother and I think we are best all together. 'Tis you, perhaps, had best go. But give me your word, at any rate, that you will not try and see her. We must spare her pain, sir! We must spare her pain! " And the good man sat down in such deep anguish himself that I, who was not yet under the full pressure of my own grief, actually felt his, and pitied it. It could not be that the dear lips I had kissed yesterday were to speak to me only once more. We were all here together loving each other, sitting in the room where we met every day; my drawing on the table by her little work-box: she was in the chamber upstairs; she must come down presently.

Who is this opens the door? I see her sweet face. It was like our little Mary's when we thought she would die of the fever. There was even a smile upon her lips. She comes up and kisses me. " Good-bye, dear George! " she says. Great Heaven! An old man sitting in this room,—with my wife's work-box opposite, and she but five minutes away; my eyes grow so dim and full that I can't see the book before me. I am three-and-twenty years old again. I go through every stage of that agony. I once had it sitting in my own post-chaise, with my wife actually by my side. Who dared to sully her sweet love with suspicion? Who had a right to stab such a soft bosom? Don't you see my ladies getting their knives ready, and the poor child bearing it? My wife comes in. She has been serving out tea or tobacco to some of her pensioners. "What is it makes you look so angry, papa?" she says. "My love!" I say, "it is the thirteenth of April." A pang of pain shoots across her face, followed by a tender smile. She has undergone the martyrdom, and in the midst of the pang comes a halo of forgiveness. I can't forgive; not until my days of dotage come, and I cease remembering anything. "Hal will be home for Easter; he will bring two or three of his friends with him from Cambridge," she says. And straightway she falls to devising schemes for amusing the boys. When is she ever occupied but with plans for making others happy?

A gentleman sitting in spectacles before an old ledger, and writing down pitiful remembrances of his own condition, is a quaint and ridiculous object. My corns hurt me, I know, but I suspect my neighbour's shoes pinch him too. I am not going to howl much over my own grief, or enlarge at any great length on this one. Many another man, I dare say, has had the light of his day suddenly put out, the joy of his life extinguished, and has been left to darkness and vague torture. I have a book I tried to read at this time of grief—"Howel's Letters"—and when I come to the part about Prince Charles in Spain, up starts the whole tragedy alive again. I went to Brighthelmstone, and there, at the inn, had a room facing the east, and saw the sun get up ever so many mornings, after blank nights of wakefulness, and smoked my pipe of Virginia in his face. When I am in that place by chance, and see the sun rising now, I shake my fist at him, thinking, O orient Phœbus, what horrible grief and savage wrath have you not seen me suffer! Though my wife is mine ever so long, I say I am angry just the same. Who dared, I want to know, to make us suffer so? I was forbidden to see her. I kept my promise, and remained away from the house: that is, after that horrible meeting and parting. But at night I would go and look at her window, and watch the lamp burning there; I would go to the Chartreux (where I knew another boy), and call for her brother, and gorge him with cakes and half-crowns. I would meanly have her elder brother to dine, and almost kiss him when he went away. I used to breakfast at a coffee-house in Whitehall, in order to see Lambert go to his office; and we would salute each other sadly, and pass on without speaking. Why did not the women come out? They never did. They were practising on her, and persuading her to try and forget me. Oh, the weary weary days! Oh, the maddening time! At last a doctor's chariot used to draw up before the General's house every day. Was she ill? I fear I was rather glad she was ill. My own suffering was so infernal, that I greedily wanted her to share my pain. And would she not? What grief of mine has it not felt, that gentlest and most compassionate of hearts? What pain would it not suffer to spare mine a pang?

I sought that Doctor out. I had an interview with him. I told my story, and laid bare my heart to him, with an outburst of passionate sincerity which won his sympathy. My confession enabled him to understand this young patient's malady; for which his drugs had no remedy or anodyne. I had promised not to see her, or to go to her: I had kept my promise. I had promised to leave London: I had gone away. Twice, thrice I went back and told my sufferings to him. He would take my fee now and again, and always receive me kindly, and let me speak. Ah, how I clung to him! I suspect he must have been unhappy once in his own life, he knew so well and gently how to succour the miserable.

He did not tell me how dangerously, though he did not disguise from me how gravely and seriously, my dearest girl had been ill. I told him everything—that I would marry her and brave every chance and danger; that, without her, I was a man utterly wrecked and ruined, and cared not what became of me. My mother had once consented, and had now chosen to withdraw her consent, when the tie between us had been, as I held, drawn so closely together, as to be paramount to all filial duty.

" I think, sir, if your mother heard you, and saw Miss Lambert, she would relent," said the Doctor. Who was my mother to hold me in bondage; to claim a right of misery over me; and to take this angel out of my arms?

" He could not," he said, " be a message-carrier between young ladies who were pining and young lovers on whom the sweethearts' gates were shut: but so much he would venture to say, that he had seen me, and was prescribing for me, too." Yes, he *must* have been unhappy once, himself. I saw him, you may be sure, on the very day when he had kept his promise to me. He said she seemed to be comforted by hearing news of me.

" She bears her suffering with an angelical sweetness. I prescribe Jesuit's bark, which she takes; but I am not sure the

hearing of you has not done more good than the medicine."
The women owned afterwards that they had never told the
General of the Doctor's new patient.

I know not what wild expressions of gratitude I poured out
to the good Doctor for the comfort he brought me. His treatment was curing two unhappy sick persons. 'Twas but a drop
of water, to be sure; but then a drop of water to a man raging
in torment. I loved the ground he trod upon, blessed the hand
that took mine, and had felt *her* pulse. I had a ring with a
pretty cameo head of a Hercules upon it. 'Twas too small for
his finger, nor did the good old man wear such ornaments. I
made him hang it to his watch chain, in hopes that she might
see it, and recognise that the token came from me. How I
fastened upon Spencer at this time (my friend of the Temple,
who also had an unfortunate love-match), and walked with him
from my apartments to the Temple, and he back with me to
Bedford Gardens, and our talk was for ever about our women!
I dare say I told everybody of my grief. My good landlady and
Betty the housemaid pitied me. My son Miles, who, for a
wonder, has been reading in my MS., says, " By Jove, sir, I
didn't know you and my mother were took in this kind of way.
The year I joined, I was hit very bad myself. An infernal little
jilt that threw me over for Sir Craven Oaks of our regiment. I
thought I should have gone crazy." And he gives a melancholy
whistle, and walks away.

The General had to leave London presently on one of his
military inspections, as the Doctor casually told me; but having
given my word that I would not seek to present myself at his
house, I kept it, availing myself, however, as you may be sure,
of the good physician's leave to visit him, and have news of his
dear patient. His accounts of her were far from encouraging.
" She does not rally," he said. " We must get her back to
Kent again, or to the sea." I did not know then that the poor
child had begged and prayed so piteously not to be moved, that
her parents, divining, perhaps, the reason of her desire to linger
in London, and feeling that it might be dangerous not to humour
her, had yielded to her entreaty, and consented to remain in
town.

At last one morning I came, pretty much as usual, and took
my place in my doctor's front parlour, whence his patients were
called in their turn to his consulting-room. Here I remained,
looking heedlessly over the books on the table and taking no
notice of any person in the room, which speedily emptied itself

of all, save me and one lady who sat with her veil down. I used to stay till the last, for Osborn, the Doctor's man, knew my business, and that it was not my own illness I came for.

When the room was empty of all save me and the lady, she puts out two little hands, cries in a voice which made me start, " Don't you know me, George? " And the next minute I have my arms round her, and kissed her as heartily as ever I kissed in my life, and gave way to a passionate outgush of emotion the most refreshing, for my parched soul had been in rage and torture for six weeks past, and this was a glimpse of heaven.

Who was it, children? You think it was your mother whom the Doctor had brought to me? No. It was Hetty.

CHAPTER LXXVI

INFORMS US HOW MR. WARRINGTON JUMPED INTO A LANDAU

THE emotion at the first surprise and greeting over, the little maiden began at once.

" So you are come at last to ask after Theo, and you feel very sorry that your neglect has made her so ill? For six weeks she has been unwell, and you have never asked a word about her! Very kind of you, Mr. George, I'm sure! "

" Kind! " gasps out Mr. Warrington.

" I suppose you call it kind to be with her every day and all day for a year, and then to leave her without a word? "

" My dear, you know my promise to your father? "

" Promise! " says Miss Hetty, shrugging her shoulders. " A very fine promise, indeed, to make my darling ill, and then suddenly one fine day to say, ' Good-bye, Theo,' and walk away for ever. I suppose gentlemen make these promises, because they wish to keep 'em. *I* wouldn't trifle with a poor child's heart, and leave her afterwards, if I were a man. What has she ever done to you, but be a fool and too fond of you? Pray, sir, by what right do you take her away from all of us, and then desert her, because an old woman in America don't approve of her? She was happy with us before you came. She loved her sister—there never was such a sister—until she saw you. And now, because your mamma thinks her young gentleman might do better, you must leave her forsooth! "

"Great powers, child!" I cried, exasperated at this wrong-headedness. "Was it I that drew back? Is it not I that am forbidden your house; and did not your father require, on my honour, that I should not see her?"

"Honour! And you are the men who pretend to be our superiors; and it is we who are to respect you and admire you! I declare, George Warrington, you ought to go back to your schoolroom in Virginia again; have your black nurse to tuck you up in bed, and ask leave from your mamma when you might walk out. Oh, George! I little thought that my sister was giving her heart away to a man who hadn't the spirit to stand by her; but, at the first difficulty, left her! When Doctor Heberden said he was attending you, I determined to come and see you, and you do look very ill, that I am glad to see; and I suppose it's your mother you are frightened of. But I shan't tell Theo you are unwell. *She* hasn't left off caring for you. *She* can't walk out of a room, break her solemn engagements, and go into the world the next day as if nothing had happened! That is left for men, our superiors in courage and wisdom; and to desert an angel—yes, an angel ten thousand times too good for you; an angel who used to love me till she saw you, and who was the blessing of life and of all of us—is what you call honour? Don't tell me, sir! I despise you all! You are our betters, are you? We are to worship and wait on you, I suppose? *I* don't care about your wit, and your tragedies, and your verses; and I think they are often very stupid. *I* won't sit up at nights copying your manuscripts, nor watch hour after hour at a window wasting my time and neglecting everybody because I want to see your worship walk down the street with your hat cocked! If you are going away, and welcome, give me back my sister, I say! Give me back my darling of old days, who loved every one of us, till she saw you. And you leave her because your mamma thinks she can find somebody richer for you! Oh, you brave gentleman! Go and marry the person your mother chooses, and let my dear die here deserted!"

"Great heavens, Hetty!" I cry, amazed at the logic of the little woman. "Is it I who wish to leave your sister? Did I not offer to keep my promise, and was it not your father who refused me, and made me promise never to try and see her again? What have I but my word, and my honour?"

"Honour, indeed! You keep your word to him, and you break it to her! Pretty honour! If I were a man I would soon let you know what I thought of your honour! Only I forgot—

you are bound to keep the peace and mustn't—— Oh, George, George! Don't you see the grief I am in? I am distracted, and scarce know what I say. You must not leave my darling. They don't know it at home. They don't think so: but I know her best of all, and she will die if you leave her. Say you won't! Have pity upon me, Mr. Warrington, and give me my dearest back!" Thus the warm-hearted distracted creature ran from anger to entreaty, from scorn to tears. Was my little doctor right in thus speaking of the case of her dear patient? Was there no other remedy than that which Hetty cried for? Have not others felt the same cruel pain of amputation, undergone the same exhaustion and fever afterwards, lain hopeless of anything save death, and yet recovered after all, and limped through life subsequently? Why, but that love is selfish, and does not heed other people's griefs and passions, or that ours was so intense and special that we deemed no other lovers could suffer like ourselves;—here in the passionate young pleader for her sister, we might have shown an instance, that a fond heart could be stricken with the love malady and silently suffer it, live under it, recover from it. What had happened in Hetty's own case? Her sister and I, in our easy triumph and fond confidential prattle, had many a time talked over that matter, and egotists as we were, perhaps drawn a secret zest and security out of her less fortunate attachment. 'Twas like sitting by the fireside, and hearing the winter howling without; 'twas like walking by the *mari magno*, and seeing the ship tossing at sea. We clung to each other only the more closely, and, wrapped in our own happiness, viewed others' misfortunes with complacent pity. Be the truth as it may;—grant that we might have been sundered, and after a while survived the separation, so much my sceptical old age may be disposed to admit. Yet, at that time, I was eager enough to share my ardent little Hetty's terrors and apprehensions, and willingly chose to believe that the life dearest to me in the world would be sacrificed if separated from mine. Was I wrong? I would not say as much now. I may doubt about myself (or not doubt, I know), but of her, never; and Hetty found in me quite a willing sharer in her alarms and terrors. I was for imparting some of these to our Doctor; but the good gentleman shut my mouth. "Hush," says he, with a comical look of fright. " I must hear none of this. If two people who happen to know each other, chance to meet and talk in my patients' room, I cannot help myself; but as for match-making and love-making, I am your humble servant!

What will the General do when he comes back to town? He will have me behind Montagu House as sure as I am a live doctor, and alive I wish to remain, my good sir!" and he skips into his carriage, and leaves me there meditating. "And you and Miss Hetty must have no meetings here again, mind you that," he had said previously.

Oh, no! Of course we would have none! We are gentlemen of honour, and so forth, and our word is our word. Besides, to have seen Hetty, was not that an inestimable boon, and would we not be for ever grateful? I am so refreshed with that *drop of water* I have had, that I think I can hold out for ever so long a time now. I walk away with Hetty to Soho, and never once thought of arranging a new meeting with her. But the little emissary was more thoughtful, and she asks me whether I go to the Museum now to read? And I say, "Oh, yes, sometimes, my dear; but I am too wretched for reading now; I cannot see what is on the paper. I do not care about my books. Even 'Pocahontas' is wearisome to me. I——" I might have continued ever so much farther, when, "Nonsense!" she says, stamping her little foot. "Why, I declare, George, you are more stupid than Harry!"

"How do you mean, my dear child?" I ask.

"When do you go? You go away at three o'clock. You strike across on the road to Tottenham Court. You walk through the village, and return by the Green Lane that leads back towards the new hospital. You know you do! If you walk for a week there, it can't do you any harm. Good morning, sir! You'll please not follow me any further." And she drops me a curtsey, and walks away with a veil over her face.

That Green Lane, which lay to the north of the new hospital, is built all over with houses now. In *my* time, when good old George the Second was yet King, 'twas a shabby rural outlet of London; so dangerous, that the City folks who went to their villas and junketing-houses at Hampstead and the out-lying villages, would return in parties of nights, and escorted by waiters with lanthorns, to defend them from the footpads who prowled about the town and outskirts. Hampstead and Highgate churches, each crowning its hill, filled up the background of the view which you saw as you turned your back to London; and one, two, three days Mr. George Warrington had the pleasure of looking upon this landscape, and walking back in the direction of the new hospital. Along the lane were sundry small houses of entertainment; and I remember at one place, where they sold cakes and beer, at the sign of the "Protestant Hero," a decent woman smiling at me on the third or fourth day, and curtseying in her clean apron, as she says, "It appears the lady don't come, sir! Your honour had best step in, and take a can of my cool beer."

At length, as I am coming back through Tottenham Road, on the 25th of May—O day to be marked with the whitest stone!—a little way beyond Mr. Whitfield's Tabernacle, I see a landau before me, and on the box-seat by the driver is my young friend Charley, who waves his hat to me, and calls out, "George, George!" I ran up to the carriage, my knees knocking together so that I thought I should fall by the wheel; and inside I see Hetty, and by her my dearest Theo, propped with a pillow. How thin the little hand had become since last it was laid in mine! The cheeks were flushed and wasted, the eyes strangely bright, and the thrill of the voice when she spoke a word or two, smote me with a pang, I know not of grief or joy was it, so intimately were they blended.

"I am taking her an airing to Hampstead," says Hetty demurely. "The doctor says the air will do her good."

"I have been ill, but I am better now, George," says Theo. There came a great burst of music from the people in the chapel hard by, as she was speaking. I held her hands in mine. Her eyes were looking into mine once more. It seemed as if we had never been parted.

I can never forget the tune of that psalm. I have heard it all through my life. My wife has touched it on her harpsichord, and her little ones have warbled it. Now, do you understand, young people, why I love it so? Because 'twas the music played at our *amoris redintegratio*. Because it sang hope to me, at the period of my existence the most miserable. Yes, the most miserable: for that dreary confinement of Duquesne had its tendernesses and kindly associations connected with it; and many a time in after days I have thought with fondness of the poor Biche and my tipsy gaoler; and the *réveillée* of the forest birds and military music of my prison.

Master Charley looks down from his box-seat upon his sister and me engaged in beatific contemplation, and Hetty listening too, to the music. "I think I should like to go and hear it. And that famous Mr. Whitfield, perhaps he is going to preach this very day! Come in with me, Charley—and George can drive for half-an-hour with dear Theo towards Hampstead and back."

Charley did not seem to have any very strong desire for witnessing the devotional exercises of good Mr. Whitfield and his congregation, and proposed that George Warrington should take Hetty in; but Het was not to be denied. "I will never help you in another exercise as long as you live, sir," cries Miss Hetty, "if you don't come on,"—while the youth clambered down from his box-seat, and they entered the temple together.

Can any moralist, bearing my previous promises in mind, excuse me for jumping into the carriage and sitting down once more by my dearest Theo? Suppose I did break 'em? Will he blame me much? Reverend sir, you are welcome. I broke my promise; and if you would not do as much, good friend, you are welcome to your virtue. Not that I for a moment suspect my own children will ever be so bold as to think of having hearts of their own, and bestowing them according to their liking. No, my young people, you will let papa choose for you; be hungry when he tells you; be thirsty when he orders; and settle your children's marriages afterwards.

And now of course you are anxious to hear what took place when papa jumped into the landau by the side of poor little mamma, propped up by her pillows. "I am come to your part of the story, my dear," says I, looking over to my wife as she is plying her needles.

"To what, pray?" says my lady. "You should skip all that part, and come to the grand battles, and your heroic defence of——"

"Of Fort Fiddle-de-dee in the year 1778, when I pulled off Mr. Washington's epaulet, gouged General Gates's eye, cut off Charles Lee's head, and pasted it on again!"

"Let us hear all about the fighting," say the boys. Even the Captain condescends to own he will listen to any military details, though only from a militia officer.

"Fair and softly, young people! Everything in its turn. I am not yet arrived at the war. I am only a young gentleman, just stepping into a landau, by the side of a young lady whom I promised to avoid. I am taking her hand, which, after a little ado, she leaves in mine. Do you remember how hot it was, the little thing, how it trembled, and how it throbbed and jumped a hundred and twenty in a minute? And as we trot on towards Hampstead, I address Miss Lambert in the following terms——"

"Ah, ah, ah!" say the girls in a chorus with Mademoiselle,

their French governess, who cries, " Nous écoutons maintenant.
La parole est à vous, Monsieur le Chevalier! "

Here we have them all in a circle: mamma is at her side of
the fire, papa at his; Mademoiselle Eléonore, at whom the
Captain looks rather sweetly (eyes off, Captain!); the two girls,
listening like—like *nymphas discentes* to Apollo, let us say; and
John and Tummas (with obtuse ears), who are bringing in
tea-trays and urns.

" Very good," says the Squire, pulling out the MS., and waving
it before him. " We are going to tell your mother's secrets
and mine."

" I am sure you may, papa," cries the house matron.
" There's nothing to be ashamed of." And a blush rises over
her kind face.

" But before I begin, young folks, permit me two or three
questions."

" Allons, toujours des questions! " says Mademoiselle, with
a shrug of her pretty shoulders. (Florac has recommended her
to us, and I suspect the little Chevalier has himself an eye upon
this pretty Mademoiselle de Blois.)

To the questions, then.

CHAPTER LXXVII

AND HOW EVERYBODY GOT OUT AGAIN

" IF you, Captain Miles Warrington, have the honour of winning
the good graces of a lady—of ever so many ladies—of the
Duchess of Devonshire, let us say, of Mrs. Crew, of Mrs.
Fitzherbert, of the Queen of Prussia, of the goddess Venus, of
Mademoiselle Hillisberg of the Opera—never mind of whom in
fine. If you win a lady's good graces, do you always go to the
ness and tell what happened? "

" Not such a fool, Squire! " says the Captain, surveying his
side-curl in the glass.

" Have you, Miss Theo, told your mother every word you
said to Mr. Joe Blake, junior, in the shrubbery, this morning? "

" Joe Blake, indeed! " cries Theo, junior.

" And you, Mademoiselle? That scented billet which came
to you under Sir Thomas's frank, have you told us all the letter
contains? Look how she blushes! As red as the curtain, on

my word! No, Mademoiselle, we all have our secrets" (says the Squire, here making his best French bow). "No, Theo, there was nothing in the shrubbery—only nuts, my child! No, Miles, my son, we don't tell all, even to the most indulgent of fathers—and if I tell what happened in a landau on the Hampstead Road, on the 25th of May, 1760, may the Chevalier Ruspini pull out every tooth in my head!"

"Pray tell, papa!" cries mamma; "or, as Jobson, who drove us, is in your service now, perhaps you will have him in from the stables! I insist upon your telling!"

"What is, then, this mystery?" asks Mademoiselle in her pretty French accent, of my wife.

"Eh, ma fille!" whispers the lady. "Thou wouldst ask me what I said? I said 'Yes!'—behold all I said." And so 'tis my wife has peached, and not I; and this was the sum of our conversation, as the carriage, all too swiftly as I thought, galloped towards Hampstead, and flew back again. Theo had not agreed to fly in the face of her honoured parents—no such thing. But we would marry no other person; no, not if we lived to be as old as Methuselah; no, not the Prince of Wales himself would she take. Her heart she had given away with her papa's consent—nay, order—it was not hers to resume. So kind a father must relent one of these days; and, if George would keep his promise—were it now, or were it in twenty years, or were it in another world, she knew she should never break hers.

Hetty's face beamed with delight when, my little interview over, she saw Theo's countenance wearing a sweet tranquillity. All the doctor's medicine has not done her so much good, the fond sister said. The girls went home after their act of disobedience. I gave up the place which I had held during a brief period of happiness by my dear invalid's side. Hetty skipped back into her seat, and Charley on to his box. He told me, in after days, that it was a very dull stupid sermon he had heard. The little chap was too orthodox to love dissenting preachers' sermons.

Hetty was not the only one of the family who remarked her sister's altered countenance and improved spirits. I am told that on the girls' return home, their mother embraced both of them, especially the invalid, with more than common ardour of affection. "There was nothing like a country ride," Aunt Lambert said, "for doing her dear Theo good. She had been on the road to Hampstead, had she? She must have another ride to-morrow. Heaven be blessed, my Lord Wrotham's horses were at their orders three or four times a week, and the sweet child might have the advantage of them!" As for the idea that Mr. Warrington might have happened to meet the children on their drive, Aunt Lambert never once entertained it,—at least spoke of it. I leave anybody who is interested in the matter to guess whether Mrs. Lambert could by any possibility have supposed that her daughter and her sweetheart could ever have come together again. Do women help each other in love-perplexities? Do women scheme, intrigue, make little plans, tell little fibs, provide little amorous opportunities, hang up the rope-ladder, coax, wheedle, mystify the guardian or Abigail, and turn their attention away while Strephon and Chloe are billing and cooing in the twilight, or whisking off in the post-chaise to Gretna Green? My dear young folks, some people there are of this nature; and some kind souls who have loved tenderly and truly in their own time, continue ever after to be kindly and tenderly disposed towards their young successors, when they begin to play the same pretty game.

Miss Prim doesn't. If *she* hears of two young persons attached to each other, it is to snarl at them for fools, or to imagine of them all conceivable evil. Because she has a hump-back herself, she is for biting everybody else's. I believe if she saw a pair of turtles cooing in a wood, she would turn her eyes down, or fling a stone to frighten them; but I am speaking, you see, young ladies, of your grandmother, Aunt Lambert, who was one great syllabub of human kindness; and, besides, about the affair at present under discussion, how am I ever to tell whether she knew anything regarding it or not?

So, all she says to Theo on her return home is, " My child, the country air has done you all the good in the world, and I hope you will take another drive to-morrow, and another, and another, and so on."

" Don't you think, papa, the ride has done the child most wonderful good, and must not she be made to go out in the air? " Aunt Lambert asks of the General, when he comes in for supper.

Yes, sure, if a coach and six will do his little Theo good, she shall have it, Lambert says, or he will drag the landau up Hampstead Hill himself, if there are no horses; and so the good man would have spent, freely, his guineas, or his breath, or his blood, to give his child pleasure. He was charmed at his girl's altered countenance; she picked a bit of chicken with appetite;

she drank a little negus, which he made for her; indeed it did seem to be better than the kind doctor's best medicine, which hitherto, God wot, had been of little benefit. Mamma was gracious and happy. Hetty was radiant and rident. It was quite like an evening at home at Oakhurst. Never for months past, never since that fatal cruel day, that no one spoke of, had they spent an evening so delightful.

But, if the other women chose to coax and cajole the good simple father, Theo herself was too honest to continue for long even that sweet and fond delusion. When, for the third or fourth time, he comes back to the delightful theme of his daughter's improved health, and asks, " What has done it? Is it the country air? is it the Jesuit's bark? is it the new medicine? "

" Can't you think, dear, what it is? " she says, laying a hand upon her father's, with a tremor in her voice, perhaps, but eyes that are quite open and bright.

" And what is it, my child? " asks the General.

" It is because I have seen him again, papa! " she says.

The other two women turned pale, and Theo's heart, too, begins to palpitate, and her cheek to whiten, as she continues to look in her father's scared face.

" It was not wrong to see him," she continues, more quickly; " it would have been wrong not to tell you."

" Great God! " groans the father, drawing his hand back, and with such a dreadful grief in his countenance, that Hetty runs to her almost swooning sister, clasps her to her heart, and cries out rapidly, " Theo knew nothing of it, sir! It was my doing—it was all my doing! "

Theo lies on her sister's neck, and kisses it twenty, fifty times.

" Women, women! are you playing with my honour? " cries the father, bursting out with a fierce exclamation.

Aunt Lambert sobs wildly, " Martin! Martin! " " Don't say a word to her! " again calls out Hetty, and falls back herself staggering towards the wall, for Theo has fainted on her shoulder.

I was taking my breakfast next morning, with what appetite I might, when my door opens, and my faithful black announces, " General Lambert." At once I saw, by the General's face, that the yesterday's transaction was known to him. " Your accomplices did not confess," the General said, as soon as my servant had left us, " but sided with you against their father—

a proof how desirable clandestine meetings are. It was from Theo herself I heard that she had seen you."

"Accomplices, sir!" I said (perhaps not unwilling to turn the conversation from the real point at issue). "You know how fondly and dutifully your young people regard their father. If they side against you in this instance, it must be because justice is against you. A man like you is not going to set up *sic volo sic jubeo* as the sole law in his family!"

"Psha, George!" cries the General. "For though we are parted, God forbid I should desire that we should cease to love each other. I had your promise that you would not seek to see her."

"Nor did I go to her, sir," I said, turning red, no doubt; for though this was truth, I own it was untrue.

"You mean she was brought to you?" says Theo's father, in great agitation. "Is it behind Hester's petticoat that you will shelter yourself? What a fine defence for a gentleman!"

"Well, I won't screen myself behind the poor child," I replied. "To speak as I did was to make an attempt at evasion, and I am ill-accustomed to dissemble. I did not infringe the letter of my agreement, but I acted against the spirit of it. From this moment I annul it altogether."

"You break your word given to me!" cries Mr. Lambert.

"I recall a hasty promise made on a sudden at a moment of extreme excitement and perturbation. No man can be for ever bound by words uttered at such a time; and, what is more, no man of honour or humanity, Mr. Lambert, would try to bind him."

"Dishonour to *me!* sir," exclaims the General.

"Yes, if the phrase is to be shuttlecocked between us!" I answered hotly. "There can be no question about love, or mutual regard, or difference of age, when that word is used: and were you my own father—and I love you better than a father, Uncle Lambert,—I would not bear it! What have I done? I have seen the woman whom I consider my wife before God and man, and if she calls me I will see her again. If she comes to me, here is my home for her, and the half of the little I have. 'Tis you, who have no right, having made me the gift, to resume it. Because my mother taunts you unjustly, are you to visit Mrs. Esmond's wrong upon this tender innocent creature? You profess to love your daughter, and you can't bear a little wounded pride for her sake. Better she should perish away in misery, than an old woman in Virginia should say that Mr. Lambert had schemed to marry one of his daughters. Say that to satisfy what you call honour and I call selfishness, we part, we break our hearts well nigh, we rally, we try to forget each other, we marry elsewhere? Can any man be to my dear as I have been? God forbid! Can any woman be to me what she is? You shall marry her to the Prince of Wales to-morrow, and it is a cowardice and treason. How can we, how can you, undo the promises we have made to each other before Heaven? You may part us! and she will die as surely as if she were Jephthah's daughter. Have you made any vow to Heaven to compass her murder? Kill her if you conceive your promise so binds you: but this I swear, that I am glad you have come, so that I may here formally recall a hasty pledge which I gave, and that, call me when she will, I will come to her!"

No doubt this speech was made with the flurry and agitation belonging to Mr. Warrington's youth, and with the firm conviction that death would infallibly carry off one or both of the parties, in case their worldly separation was inevitably decreed. Who does not believe his first passion eternal? Having watched the world since and seen the rise, progress, and—alas, that I must say it!—decay of other amours, I may smile now as I think of my own youthful errors and ardours; but, if it be a superstition, I had rather hold it; I had rather think that neither of us could have lived with any other mate, and that, of all its innumerable creatures, Heaven decreed these special two should be joined together.

"We must come, then, to what I had fain have spared myself," says the General, in reply to my outbreak; "to an unfriendly separation. When I meet you, Mr. Warrington, I must know you no more. I must order—and they will not do other than obey me—my family and children not to recognise you when they see you, since you will not recognise in your intercourse with me the respect due to my age, the courtesy of gentlemen. I had hoped so far from your sense of honour, and the idea I had formed of you, that, in my present great grief and perplexity, I should have found you willing to soothe and help me as far as you might—for, God knows, I have need of everybody's sympathy. But, instead of help, you fling obstacles in my way. Instead of a friend—a gracious Heaven pardon me!—I find in you an enemy! An enemy to the peace of my home and the honour of my children, sir! And as such I shall treat you, and know how to deal with you, when you molest me!"

And, waving his hand to me, and putting on his hat, Mr. Lambert hastily quitted my apartment.

I was confounded, and believed, indeed, there was war between us. The brief happiness of yesterday was clouded over and gone, and I thought that never since the day of the first separation had I felt so exquisitely unhappy as now, when the bitterness of quarrel was added to the pangs of parting, and I stood not only alone but friendless. In the course of one year's constant intimacy I had come to regard Lambert with a reverence and affection which I had never before felt for any mortal man except my dearest Harry. That his face should be turned from me in anger was as if the sun had gone out of my sphere, and all was dark around me. And yet I felt sure that in withdrawing the hasty promise I had made not to see Theo, I was acting rightly—that my fidelity to her, as hers now to me, was paramount to all other ties of duty or obedience, and that, ceremony or none, I was hers, first and before all. Promises were passed between us, from which no parent could absolve either; and all the priests in Christendom could no more than attest and confirm the sacred contract which had tacitly been ratified between us.

I saw Jack Lambert by chance that day, as I went mechanically to my not unusual haunt, the library of the new Museum; and with the impetuousness of youth, and eager to impart my sorrow to some one, I took him out of the room and led him about the gardens, and poured out my grief to him. I did not much care for Jack (who in truth was somewhat of a prig, and not a little pompous and wearisome with his Latin quotations) except in the time of my own sorrow, when I would fasten upon him or any one; and having suffered himself in his affair with the little American, being *haud ignarus mali* (as I knew he would say), I found the college gentleman ready to compassionate another's misery. I told him, what has here been represented at greater length, of my yesterday's meeting with his sister; of my interview with his father in the morning; of my determination at all hazards never to part with Theo. When I found from the various quotations from the Greek and Latin authors which he uttered that he leaned to my side in the dispute, I thought him a man of great sense, clung eagerly to his elbow, and bestowed upon him much more affection than he was accustomed at other times to have from me. I walked with him up to his father's lodgings in Dean Street; saw him enter at the dear door; surveyed the house from without with a sickening desire to know from its exterior appearance how my beloved fared within; and called for a bottle at the coffee-house where I waited Jack's return. I called him brother when I sent him away. I fondled him as the condemned wretch at Newgate hangs about the gaoler or the parson, or any one who is kind to him in his misery. I drank a whole bottle of wine at the coffee-house—by the way, Jack's Coffee-House was its name—called another. I thought Jack would never come back.

He appeared at length with rather a scared face; and, coming to my box, poured out for himself two or three bumpers from my second bottle, and then fell to his story, which, to me at least, was not a little interesting. My poor Theo was keeping her room, it appeared, being much agitated by the occurrences of yesterday; and Jack had come home in time to find dinner on table; after which his good father held forth upon the occurrences of the morning, being anxious and able to speak more freely, he said, because his eldest son was present and Theodosia was not in the room. The General stated what had happened at my lodgings between me and him. He bade Hester be silent, who indeed was as dumb as a mouse, poor thing! he told Aunt Lambert (who was indulging in that madefaction of pocket-handkerchiefs which I have before described), and with something like an imprecation, that the women were all against him, and pimps (he called them) for one another; and frantically turning round to Jack, asked what was his view in the matter?

To his father's surprise and his mother's and sister's delight, Jack made a speech on my side. He ruled with me (citing what ancient authorities I don't know), that the matter had gone out of the hands of the parents on either side; that having given their consent, some months previously, the elders had put themselves out of court. Though he did not hold with a great, a respectable, he might say a host of divines, those sacramental views of the marriage-ceremony—for which there was a great deal to be said—yet he held it, if possible, even more sacredly than they; conceiving that though marriages were made before the civil magistrate, and without the priest, yet they were, before Heaven, binding and indissoluble.

"It is not merely, sir," says Jack, turning to his father, "those whom I, John Lambert, Priest, have joined, let no man put asunder; it is those whom *God* has joined let no man separate." (Here he took off his hat, as he told the story to me.) "My views are clear upon the point, and surely these young people were joined, or permitted to plight themselves to each other by the consent of you, the priest of your own family. My views, I say, are clear, and I will lay them down at length in a series of two or three discourses which, no doubt, will satisfy you. Upon which," says Jack, " my father said, ' I am satisfied already, my dear boy,' and my lively little Het (who has much archness) whispers to me, ' Jack, mother and I will make you a dozen shirts, as sure as eggs is eggs.' "

" Whilst we were talking," Mr. Lambert resumed, " my sister Theodosia made her appearance, I must say very much agitated and pale, kissed our father, and sat down at his side, and took a sippet of toast—(my dear George, this port is excellent, and I drink your health)—and took a sippet of toast and dipped it in his negus.

" ' You should have been here to hear Jack's sermon!' says Hester. ' He has been preaching most beautifully.'

" ' Has he?' asks Theodosia, who is too languid and weak, poor thing, much to care for the exercises of eloquence, or the display of authorities, such as I must own," says Jack, " it was given to me this afternoon to bring forward.

" ' He has talked for three-quarters of an hour by Shrewsbury clock,' says my father, though I certainly had not talked so long or half so long *by my own watch*. ' And his discourse has been you, my dear,' says papa, playing with Theodosia's hand.

" ' Me, papa?'

" ' You and—and Mr. Warrington—and—and George, my love,' says papa. Upon which " (says Mr. Jack) " my sister came closer to the General, and laid her head upon him, and wept upon his shoulder.

" ' This is different, sir,' says I, ' to a passage I remember in Pausanias.'

" ' In Pausanias? Indeed!' said the General. ' And pray, who was he?'

" I smiled at my father's simplicity in exposing his ignorance before his children. ' When Ulysses was taking away Penelope from her father, the King hastened after his daughter and bridegroom, and besought his darling to return. Whereupon it is related, Ulysses offered her her choice,—whether she would return, or go on with him? Upon which the daughter of Icarius covered her face with her veil. For want of a veil my sister has taken refuge in your waistcoat, sir," I said, and we all laughed; though my mother vowed that if such a proposal had been made to *her*, or Penelope had been a girl of spirit, she would have gone home with her father that instant.

"'But I am not a girl of any spirit, dear mother!' says Theodosia, still *in gremio patris*. I do not remember that this habit of caressing was frequent in my own youth," continues Jack. "But after some more discourse, Brother Warrington! I bethought me of you, and left my parents insisting upon Theodosia returning to bed. The late transactions have, it appears, weakened and agitated her much. I myself have experienced, in my own case, how full of *solliciti timoris* is a certain passion; how it racks the spirits; and I make no doubt, if carried far enough, or indulged to the extent to which women (who have little philosophy) will permit it to go—I make no doubt, I say, is ultimately injurious to the health. My service to you, brother!"

From grief to hope, how rapid the change was! What a flood of happiness poured into my soul, and glowed in my whole being! Landlord, more port! Would honest Jack have drunk a binful I would have treated him; and, to say truth, Jack's sympathy was large in this case, and it had been generous all day. I decline to score the bottles of port: and place to the fabulous computations of interested waiters, the amount scored against me in the reckoning. Jack was my dearest, best of brothers. My friendship for him I swore should be eternal. If I could do him any service, were it a bishopric, by George! he should have it. He says I was interrupted by the watchman rhapsodising verses beneath the loved one's window. I know not. I know I awoke joyfully and rapturously, in spite of a racking headache, the next morning.

Nor did I know the extent of my happiness quite, or the entire conversion of my dear noble enemy of the previous morning. It must have been galling to the pride of an elder man to have to yield to representations and objections couched in language so little dutiful as that I had used towards Mr. Lambert. But the true Christian gentleman, retiring from his talk with me, mortified and wounded by my asperity of remonstrance, as well as by the pain which he saw his beloved daughter suffer, went thoughtfully and sadly to his business, as he subsequently told me, and in the afternoon (as his custom not unfrequently was) into a church which was open for prayers. And it was here, on his knees, submitting his case in the quarter whither he frequently, though privately, came for guidance and comfort, that it seemed to him that his child was right in her persistent fidelity to me, and himself wrong in demanding her utter submission. Hence Jack's cause was won almost before he began to plead it; and the brave gentle heart, which could bear no rancour, which bled at inflicting pain on those it loved, which even shrank from asserting authority or demanding submission, was only too glad to return to its natural pulses of love and affection.

CHAPTER LXXVIII

PYRAMUS AND THISBE

In examining the old papers at home, years afterwards, I found, docketed and labelled with my mother's well-known neat handwriting, "From London, April, 1760. My son's dreadful letter."

When it came to be mine I burnt the document, not choosing that that story of domestic grief and disunion should remain amongst our family annals for future Warringtons to gaze on, mayhap, and disobedient sons to hold up as examples of foregone domestic rebellions. For similar reasons, I have destroyed the paper which my mother despatched to me at this time of tyranny, revolt, annoyance, and irritation.

Maddened by the pangs of separation from my mistress, and not unrightly considering that Mrs. Esmond was the prime cause of the greatest grief and misery which had ever befallen me in the world, I wrote home to Virginia a letter, which might have been more temperate, it is true, but in which I endeavoured to maintain the extremest respect and reticence. I said I did not know by what motives she had been influenced, but that I held her answerable for the misery of my future life, which she had chosen wilfully to mar and render wretched. She had occasioned a separation between me and a virtuous and innocent young creature, whose own hopes, health, and happiness were cast down for ever by Mrs. Esmond's interference. The deed was done, as I feared, and I would offer no comment upon the conduct of the perpetrator, who was answerable to God alone; but I did not disguise from my mother that the injury which she had done me was so dreadful and mortal that her life or mine could never repair it; that the tie of my allegiance was broken towards her, and that I never could be, as heretofore, her dutiful and respectful son.

Madam Esmond replied to me in a letter of very great dignity (her style and correspondence were extraordinarily elegant and fine). She uttered not a single reproach or hard word, but coldly gave me to understand that it was before that awful tribunal of God she had referred the case between us, and asked for counsel: that, in respect of her own conduct, as a mother, she was ready, in all humility, to face it. Might I, as a son, be equally able to answer for myself, and to show, when the Great Judge demanded the question of me, whether I had done my own duty, and honoured my father and mother! *O popoi!* My grandfather has quoted in his Memoir a line of Homer, showing how in our troubles and griefs the gods are always called in question. When our pride, our avarice, our interest, our desire to domineer, are worked upon, are we not for ever pestering Heaven to decide in their favour? In our great American quarrel, did we not on both sides appeal to the skies as to the justice of our causes, sing *Te Deum* for victory, and boldly express our confidence that the right should prevail? Was America right because she was victorious? Then I suppose Poland was wrong because she was defeated!—How am I wandering into this digression about Poland, America, and what not, and all the while thinking of a little woman now no more, who appealed to Heaven and confronted it with a thousand texts out of its own book, because her son wanted to make a marriage not of her liking! We appeal, we imprecate, we go down on our knees, we demand blessings, we shriek out for sentence according to law; the great course of the great world moves on; we pant and strive, and struggle; we hate; we rage; we weep passionate tears; we reconcile; we race and win; we race and lose; we pass away, and other little strugglers succeed; our days are spent; our night comes, and another morning rises, which shines on us no more.

My letter to Madam Esmond, announcing my revolt and disobedience (perhaps I myself was a little proud of the composition of that document), I showed in duplicate to Mr. Lambert, because I wished him to understand what my relations to my mother were, and how I was determined, whatever of threats or quarrels the future might bring, never for my own part to consider my separation from Theo as other than a forced one. Whenever I could see her again I would. My word given to her was *in secula seculorum,* or binding at least as long as my life should endure. I implied that the girl was similarly bound to me, and her poor father knew indeed as much. He might separate us; as he might give her a dose of poison, and the gentle obedient creature would take it and die; but the death or separation would be his doing: let him answer them. Now he was tender about his children to weakness, and could not have the heart to submit any one of them—this one especially—to torture. We had tried to part: we could not. He had endeavoured to separate us: it was more than was in his power. The bars were up, but the young couple—the maid within and the knight without—were loving each other all the same. The wall was built, but Pyramus and Thisbe were whispering on either side. In the midst of all his grief and perplexity, Uncle Lambert had plenty of humour, and could not but see that his *rôle* was rather a sorry one. Light was beginning to show through that lime and rough plaster of the wall: the lovers were getting their hands through, then their heads through—indeed, it was wall's best business to retire.

I forget what happened stage by stage and day by day; nor, for the instruction of future ages, does it much matter. When my descendants have love-scrapes of their own, they will find their own means of getting out of their troubles. I believe I did not go back to Dean Street, but that practice of driving in the open air was considered most healthful for Miss Lambert. I got a fine horse, and rode by the side of her carriage. The old woman at Tottenham Court came to know both of us quite well, and nod and wink in the most friendly manner when we passed by. I fancy the old goody was not unaccustomed to interest herself in young couples, and has dispensed the hospitality of her roadside cottage to more than one pair.

The doctor and the country air effected a prodigious cure upon Miss Lambert. Hetty always attended as duenna, and sometimes of his holiday, Master Charley rode my horse, when I got into the carriage. What a deal of love-making Miss Hetty heard!—with what exemplary patience she listened to it! I do not say she went to hear the Methodist sermons any more, but 'tis certain that when we had a closed carriage she would very kindly and considerately look out of the window. Then, what heaps of letters there were!—what running to and fro! Gumbo's bandy legs were for ever on the trot from my quarters to Dean Street; and, on my account or her own, Mrs. Molly, the girls' maid, was for ever bringing back answers to Bloomsbury. By the time when the autumn leaves began to turn pale, Miss Theo's roses were in full bloom again, and my good Doctor Heberden's cure was pronounced to be complete. What else happened during this blessed period? Mr. Warrington completed his great tragedy of "Pocahontas," which was not only accepted by Mr. Garrick this time (his friend Doctor Johnson having spoken not unfavourably of the work), but my friend and cousin, Hagan, was engaged by the manager to perform the part of the hero, Captain Smith. Hagan's engagement was not made before it was wanted. I had helped him and his family with means disproportioned, perhaps, to my power, especially considering my feud with Madam Esmond, whose answer to my angry missive of April came to me towards autumn, and who wrote back from Virginia with war for war, controlment for controlment. These menaces, however, frightened me little: my poor mother's thunder could not reach me; and my conscience, or casuistry, supplied me with other interpretations for her texts of Scripture, so that her oracles had not the least weight with me in frightening me from my purpose. How my new loves speeded I neither informed her, nor any other members of my maternal or paternal family, who, on both sides, had been bitter against my marriage. Of what use wrangling with them? It was better *carpere diem* and its sweet loves and pleasures, and to leave the railers to grumble, or the seniors to advise, at their ease.

Besides Madam Esmond I had, it must be owned, in the frantic rage of my temporary separation, addressed notes of wondrous sarcasm to my uncle Warrington, to my aunt Madame de Bernstein, and to my Lord or Lady of Castlewood (I forget to which individually), thanking them for the trouble which they had taken in preventing the dearest happiness of my life, and promising them a corresponding gratitude from their obliged relative. Business brought the jovial Baronet and his family to London somewhat earlier than usual, and Madame de Bernstein was never sorry to get back to Clarges Street and her cards. I saw them. They found me perfectly well. They concluded the match was broken off, and I did not choose to undeceive them. The Baroness took heart at seeing how cheerful I was, and made many sly jokes about my philosophy, and my prudent behaviour as a man of the world. She was, as ever, bent upon finding a rich match for me: and I fear I paid many compliments at her house to a rich young soap-boiler's daughter from Mile End, whom the worthy Baroness wished to place in my arms.

"You court her with infinite wit and esprit, my dear," says my pleased kinswoman, "but she does not understand half you say, and the other half, I think, frightens her. This *ton de persiflage* is very well in our society, but you must be sparing of it, my dear nephew, amongst these *roturiers*."

Miss Badge married a young gentleman of royal dignity, though shattered fortunes, from a neighbouring island; and I trust Mrs. Mackshane has ere this pardoned my levity. There was another person besides Miss at my aunt's house, who did not understand my *persiflage* much better than Miss herself; and that was a lady who had seen James the Second's reign, and who was alive and as worldly as ever in King George's. I loved to be with her: but that my little folks have access to this volume, I could put down a hundred stories of the great old folks whom she had known in the great old days—of George the First and his ladies, of St. John and Marlborough, of his reigning Majesty and the late Prince of Wales, and the causes of the quarrel between them—but my modest muse pipes for boys and virgins. Son Miles does not care about Court stories, or if he doth, has a fresh budget from Carlton House, quite as bad as the worst of our old Baroness. No, my dear wife, thou hast no need to shake thy powdered locks at me! Papa is not going to scandalise his nursery with old-world gossip, nor bring a blush over our chaste bread and butter.

But this piece of scandal I cannot help. My aunt used to tell it with infinite gusto; for, to do her justice, she hated your would-be-good people, and sniggered over the faults of the self-styled righteous with uncommon satisfaction. In her later days she had no hypocrisy, at least; and in so far was better than some white-washed—— Well, to the story. My Lady Warrington, one of the tallest and the most virtuous of her sex, who had goodness for ever on her lips and " Heaven in her eye," like the woman in Mr. Addison's tedious tragedy (which has kept the stage, from which some others, which shall be nameless, have disappeared), had the world in her other eye, and an exceedingly shrewd desire of pushing herself in it. What does she do when my marriage with your ladyship yonder was supposed to be broken off, but attempt to play off on me those arts which she had tried on my poor Harry with such signal ill success, and which failed with me likewise! It was not the Beauty—Miss Flora was for my master—(and what a master! I protest I take off my hat at the idea of such an illustrious connection!)—it was Dora, the Muse, was set upon me to languish at me and to pity me, and to read even my godless tragedy, and applaud me and console me. Meanwhile, how was the Beauty occupied? Will it be believed that my severe aunt gave a great entertainment to my Lady Yarmouth, presented her boy to her, and placed poor little Miles under her Ladyship's august protection? That, so far, is certain; but can it be that she sent her daughter to stay at my Lady's house, which our gracious lord and master daily visited, and with the views which old Aunt Bernstein attributed to her? "But for that fit of apoplexy, my dear," Bernstein said, "that aunt of yours intended there should have been a *Countess in her own right* in the Warrington family!"[1] My neighbour and kinswoman, my Lady Claypool, is dead and buried. Grow white, ye daisies upon Flora's tomb! I can see my pretty Miles, in a gay little uniform of the Norfolk Militia, led up by his parent to the lady whom the king delighted to honour, and the good-natured old Jezebel laying her hand upon the boy's curly pate. I am accused of being but a lukewarm Royalist; but sure I can contrast those times with ours, and acknowledge the difference between the late Sovereign and the present, who, born a Briton, has given to every family in the empire an example of decorum and virtuous life.[2]

Thus my life sped in the pleasantest of all occupation; and, being so happy myself, I could afford to be reconciled to those who, after all, had done me no injury, but rather added to the zest of my happiness by the brief obstacle which they had placed in my way. No specific plans were formed, but Theo and I knew that a day would come when we need say farewell no more. Should the day befall a year hence—ten years hence— we were ready to wait. Day after day we discussed our little plans with Hetty for our confidante. On our drives we drove out pretty cottages that we thought might suit young people of small means; we devised all sorts of delightful schemes and childish economies. We were Strephon and Chloe to be sure. A cot and a brown loaf should content us! Gumbo and Molly should wait upon us (as indeed they have done from that day until this). At twenty who is afraid of being poor? Our trials would only confirm our attachment. The "sweet sorrow" of every day's parting but made the morrow's meeting more delightful; and when we separated we ran home and wrote each other those precious letters, which we and other young gentle-

---

[1] Compare Walpole's letters in Mr. Cunningham's excellent new edition. See the story of the supper at N. House, to show what great noblemen would do for a king's mistress, and the pleasant account of the waiting for the Prince of Wales before Holland House.—ED.

[2] The Warrington MS. is dated 1793.—ED.

men and ladies write under such circumstances; but though my wife has them all in a great tin sugar-box in the closet in her bedroom, and, I own, I myself have looked at them once, and even thought some of them pretty,—I hereby desire my heirs and executors to burn them all unread, at our demise; specially desiring my son the Captain (to whom I know the perusal of MSS. is not pleasant) to perform this duty. Those secrets whispered to the penny-post, or delivered between Molly and Gumbo, were intended for us alone, and no ears of our descendants shall overhear them.

We heard in successive brief letters how our dear Harry continued with the army, as General Amherst's aide-de-camp, after the death of his own glorious General. By the middle of October there came news of the capitulation of Montreal and the whole of Canada, and a brief postscript in which Hal said he would ask for leave now, and must go and see the old lady at home, who wrote *as sulky as a bare*, Captain Warrington remarked. I could guess why, though the claws could not reach me. I had written pretty fully to my brother how affairs were standing with me in England.

Then on the 25th October comes the news that His Majesty has fallen down dead at Kensington, and that George the Third reigned over us. I feared we grieved but little. What do those care for the Atridæ whose hearts are strung only to *erota mounon ?* A modest, handsome, brave new Prince, we gladly accept the common report that he is endowed with every virtue; and we cry huzzay with the loyal crowd that hails his accession: it could make little difference to us, as we thought, simple young sweethearts, whispering our little love-stories in our corner.

But who can say how great events affect him? Did not our little Charley, at the Chartreux, wish impiously for a new king immediately, because on His Gracious Majesty's accession Doctor Crusius gave his boys a holiday? He and I, and Hetty, and Theo (Miss Theo was strong enough to walk many a delightful mile now), heard the heralds proclaim his new Majesty before Savile House in Leicester Fields, and a pickpocket got the watch and chain of a gentleman hard by us, and was caught and carried to Bridewell, all on account of His Majesty's accession. Had the King not died, the gentleman would not have been in the crowd: the chain would not have been seized; the thief would not have been caught and soundly whipped; in this way many of us, more or less remotely, were implicated in the great change which ensued, and even we humble folks were affected by it presently.

As thus. My Lord Wrotham was a great friend of the august family of Savile House, who knew and esteemed his many virtues. Now, of all living men, my Lord Wrotham knew and loved best his neighbour and old fellow-soldier, Martin Lambert, declaring that the world contained few better gentlemen. And my Lord Bute, being all potent, at first, with His Majesty, and a nobleman, as I believe, very eager at the commencement of his brief and luckless tenure of power to patronise merit wherever he could find it, was strongly prejudiced in Mr. Lambert's favour by the latter's old and constant friend.

My (and Harry's) old friend Parson Sampson, who had been in and out of gaol I don't know how many times of late years, and retained an ever-enduring hatred for the Esmonds of Castlewood, and as lasting a regard for me and my brother, was occupying poor Hal's vacant bed at my lodgings at this time (being, in truth, hunted out of his own by the bailiffs). I liked to have Sampson near me, for a more amusing Jack-friar never walked in cassock; and, besides, he entered into all my rhapsodies about Miss Theo: was never tired (so he vowed) of hearing me talk of her; admired " Pocahontas " and " Carpezan " with, I do believe, an honest enthusiasm; and could repeat whole passages of those tragedies with an emphasis and effect that Barry or Cousin Hagan himself could not surpass. Sampson was the go-between between Lady Maria and such of her relations as had not disowned her; and, always in debt himself, was never more happy than in drinking a pot, or mingling his tears with his friends in similar poverty. His acquaintance with pawnbrokers' shop was prodigious. He could procure more money, he boasted, on an article than any gentleman of his cloth. He never paid his own debts, to be sure, but he was ready to forgive his debtors. Poor as he was, he always found means to love and help his needy little sister, and a more prodigal, kindly, amiable rogue never probably grinned behind bars. They say that I love to have parasites about me. I own to have had a great liking for Sampson, and to have esteemed him much better than probably much better men.

When he heard how my Lord Bute was admitted into the Cabinet, Sampson vowed and declared that his Lordship—a great lover of the drama, who had been to see " Carpezan," who had admired it, and who would act the part of the King very

finely in it—he vowed, by George! that my Lord must give me
a place worthy of my birth and merits. He insisted upon it
that I should attend his Lordship's levée. I wouldn't? The
Esmonds were all as proud as Lucifer; and, to be sure, my birth
was as good as that of any man in Europe. Where was my
Lord himself when the Esmonds were lords of great counties,
warriors, and Crusaders? Where were they? Beggarly Scotchmen, without a rag to their backs—by George! tearing raw
fish in their islands. But now the times were changed. The
Scotchmen were in luck. Mum's the word! "I don't envy
him," says Sampson, "but he shall provide for you and my
dearest, noblest, heroic Captain! He SHALL, by George!"
would my worthy parson roar out. And when, in the month
after his accession, His Majesty ordered the play of "Richard
III." at Drury Lane, my chaplain cursed, vowed, swore, but he
would have him to Covent Garden to see "Carpezan" too.
And now, one morning, he bursts into my apartment, where I
happened to lie rather late, waving the newspaper in his hand,
and singing "Huzzay!" with all his might.

"What is it, Sampson?" says I. "Has my brother got
his promotion?"

"No, in truth: but some one else has. Huzzay! Huzzay!
His Majesty has appointed Major-General Martin Lambert to
be Governor and Commander-in-Chief of the Island of Jamaica."

I started up. Here was news indeed! Mr. Lambert would
go to his government: and who would go with him? I had
been supping with some genteel young fellows at the "Cocoa-
tree." The rascal Gumbo had a note for me from my dear
mistress on the night previous, conveying the same news to
me, and had delayed to deliver it. Theo begged me to see her
at the old place at midday the next day without fail.[1]

There was no little trepidation in our little council when we
reached our place of meeting. Papa had announced his acceptance of the appointment, and his speedy departure. He would
have a frigate given him, and *take his family with him*. Merciful
powers! and were we to be parted? My Theo's old deathly
paleness returned to her. Aunt Lambert thought she would
have swooned; one of Mrs. Goodison's girls had a bottle of salts,
and ran up with it from the work-room. "Going away?
Going away in a frigate, Aunt Lambert? Going to tear her

---

[1] In the Warrington MS. there is not a word to say what the "old place"
was. Perhaps some obliging reader of *Notes and Queries* will be able to
inform me, and who Mrs. Goodison was.—ED.

away from me? Great God! Aunt Lambert, I shall die!"
She was better when mamma came up from the work-room
with the young lady's bottle of salts. You see the women used
to meet me: knowing dear Theo's delicate state, how could
they refrain from compassionating her? But the General was
so busy with his levées and his waiting on Ministers, and his
outfit, and the settlement of his affairs at home, that they never
happened to tell him about our little walks and meetings: and
even when orders for the outfit of the ladies were given, Mrs.
Goodison, who had known and worked for Miss Molly Benson
as a school-girl (she remembered Miss Esmond of Virginia perfectly, the worthy lady told me, and a dress she made for the
young lady to be presented at Her Majesty's Ball)—" even
when the outfit was ordered for the three ladies," says Mrs.
Goodison demurely, "why, I thought I could do no harm in
completing the order."

Now I need not say in what perturbation of mind Mr. Warrington went home in the evening to his lodgings, after the discussion with the ladies of the above news. No, or at least a
very few, more walks; no more rides to dear dear old Hampstead
or beloved Islington; no more fetching and carrying of letters
for Gumbo and Molly! The former blubbered so, that Mr.
Warrington was quite touched by his fidelity, and gave him a
crown-piece to go to supper with the poor girl, who turned out
to be his sweetheart. What, you too unhappy, Gumbo, and
torn from the maid you love? I was ready to mingle with him
tear for tear.

What a solemn conference I had with Sampson that evening!
He knew my affairs, my expectations, my mother's anger.
Psha! that was far off, and he knew some excellent liberal people
(of the order of Melchisedec) who would discount the other. The
General would not give his consent? Sampson shrugged his
broad shoulders and swore a great roaring oath. My mother
would not relent? What then? A man was a man, and to
make his own way in the world, he supposed. He is only a
churl who won't play for such a stake as that, and lose or win,
by George! shouts the chaplain, over a bottle of Burgundy at the
"Bedford Head," where we dined. I need not put down our
conversation. We were two of us, and I think there was only
one mind between us. Our talk was of a Saturday night. . . .

I did not tell Theo, nor any relative of hers, what was being
done. But when the dear child faltered and talked, trembling,
of the coming departure, I bade her bear up and vowed all

would be well, so confidently, that she, who ever has taken her alarms and joys from my face (I wish, my dear, it were sometimes not so gloomy), could not but feel confidence; and placed (with many fond words that need not here be repeated) her entire trust in me—murmuring those sweet words of Ruth that must have comforted myriads of tender hearts in my dearest maiden's plight; that whither I would go she would go, and that my people should be hers. At last, one day, the General's preparations being made, the trunks encumbering the passages of the dear old Dean Street lodging, which I shall love as long as I shall remember at all—one day, almost the last of his stay, when the good man (his Excellency we called him now) came home to his dinner—a comfortless meal enough it was in the present condition of the family—he looked round the table at the place where I had used to sit in happy old days, and sighed out—" I wish, Molly, George was here."

" Do you, Martin? " says Aunt Lambert, flinging into his arms.

" Yes, I do; but I don't wish you to choke me, Molly," he says. " I love him dearly. I may go away and never see him again, and take his foolish little sweetheart along with me. I suppose you will write to each other, children? I can't prevent that, you know; and until he changes his mind, I suppose Miss Theo won't obey papa's orders, and get him out of her foolish little head. Wilt thou, Theo? "

" No, dearest, dearest, best papa! "

" What! more embraces and kisses! What does all this mean? "

" It means that—that George is in the drawing-room," says mamma.

" Is he? My dearest boy! " cries the General. " Come to me—come in! " And when I entered he held me to his heart and kissed me.

I confess at this I was so overcome that I fell down on my knees before the dear good man, and sobbed on his own.

" God bless you, my dearest boy! " he mutters hurriedly. " Always loved you as a son—haven't I, Molly? Broke my heart nearly when I quarrelled with you about this little— What!—odds marrow-bones!—*all* down on your knees! Mrs. Lambert, pray what is the meaning of all this? "

" Dearest, dearest papa! I will go with you all the same! " whimpers one of the kneeling party. " And I will wait—oh! as long as ever my dearest father wants me! "

"In Heaven's name!" roars the General, "tell me what has happened?"

What had happened was, that George Esmond Warrington and Theodosia Lambert had been married in Southwark that morning, their banns having been duly called in the church of a certain friend of the Reverend Mr. Sampson.

CHAPTER LXXIX

CONTAINING BOTH COMEDY AND TRAGEDY

WE, who had been active in the guilty scene of the morning, felt trebly guilty when we saw the effect which our conduct had produced upon him, whom, of all others, we loved and respected. The shock to the good man was strange, and pitiful to us to witness who had administered it. The child of his heart had deceived and disobeyed him—I declare I think, my dear, now, we would not or could not do it over again;—his whole family had entered into a league against him. Dear kind friend and father! We know thou hast pardoned our wrong—in the heaven where thou dwellest amongst purified spirits who learned on earth how to love and pardon! To love and forgive were easy duties with that man. Beneficence was natural to him, and a sweet smiling humility; and to wound either was to be savage and brutal, as to torture a child, or strike blows at a nursing woman. The deed done, all we guilty ones grovelled in the earth, before the man we had injured. I pass over the scenes of forgiveness, of reconciliation, of common worship together, of final separation when the good man departed to his government, and the ship sailed away before us, leaving me and Theo on the shore. We stood there hand in hand horribly abashed, silent, and guilty. My wife did not come to me till her father went: in the interval between the ceremony of our marriage and his departure, she had remained at home, occupying her old place by her father, and bed by her sister's side: he as kind as ever, but the women almost speechless among themselves; Aunt Lambert, for once, unkind and fretful in her temper; and little Hetty feverish and strange, and saying, "I wish we were gone. I wish we were gone." Though admitted to the house, and forgiven, I slunk away during those last days, and only saw my wife for a minute or two in the street, or with her family. She was not mine till they were gone. We went to Winchester and Hampton for what may be called our wedding. It was but a dismal business. For a while we felt utterly lonely: and of our dear father as if we had buried him, or drove him to the grave by our undutifulness.

I made Sampson announce our marriage in the papers. (My wife used to hang down her head before the poor fellow afterwards.) I took Mrs. Warrington back to my old lodgings in Bloomsbury, where there was plenty of room for us, and our modest married life began. I wrote home a letter to my mother in Virginia, informing her of no particulars, but only that Mr. Lambert being about to depart for his government, I considered myself bound in honour to fulfil my promise towards his dearest daughter; and stated that I intended to carry out my intention of completing my studies for the Bar, and qualifying myself for employment at home, or in our own or any other colony. My good Mrs. Mountain answered this letter, by desire of Madam Esmond, she said, who thought that for the sake of peace my communications had best be conducted that way. I found my relatives in a fury which was perfectly amusing to witness. The butler's face, as he said " Not at home," at my uncle's house in Hill Street, was a bland tragedy that might have been studied by Garrick when he sees Banquo. My poor little wife was on my arm, and we were tripping away laughing at the fellow's *accueil*, when we came upon my Lady in a street stoppage in her chair. I took off my hat and made her the lowest possible bow. I affectionately asked after my dear cousins. " I—I wonder you dare look me in the face! " Lady Warrington gasped out. " Nay, don't deprive me of *that* precious privilege! " says I. " Move on, Peter," she screams to her chairman. " Your Ladyship would not impale your husband's own flesh and blood? " says I. She rattles up the glass of her chair in a fury. I kiss my hand, take off my hat and perform another of my very finest bows.

Walking shortly afterwards in Hyde Park with my dearest companion, I met my little cousin exercising on horseback with a groom behind him. As soon as he sees us, he gallops up to us, the groom pounding afterwards and bawling out, " Stop, Master Miles, stop! " " I am not to speak to my cousin," says Miles, " but telling you to send my love to Harry is not speaking to you, is it? Is that my new cousin? I'm not told not to speak to her. I'm Miles, cousin, Sir Miles Warrington Baronet's son, and you are very pretty!" "Now, *duee* now, Master Miles," says the groom, touching his hat to us; and the boy trots away laughing and looking at us over his shoulder. "You see how my relations have determined to treat me," I say to my partner. "As if I married you for your relations!" says Theo, her eyes beaming joy and love into mine. Ah! how happy we were! how brisk and pleasant the winter! How snug the kettle by the fire (where the abashed Sampson some-times came and made the punch); how delightful the night at the theatre, for which our friends brought us tickets of admis-sion, and where we daily expected our new play of "Poca-hontas" would rival the successes of all former tragedies.

The fickle old aunt of Clarges Street, who received me on my first coming to London with my wife, with a burst of scorn, mollified presently, and as soon as she came to know Theo (whom she had pronounced to be an insignificant little country-faced chit), fell utterly in love with her, and would have her to tea and supper every day when there was no other company. "As for company, my dears," she would say, "I don't ask you. You are no longer du monde. Your marriage has put that entirely out of the question." So she would have had us come to amuse her, and go in and out by the back-stairs. My wife was fine lady enough to feel only amused at this reception; and I must do the Baroness's domestics the justice to say that, had we been duke and duchess, we could not have been received with more respect. Madame de Bernstein was very much tickled and amused with my story of Lady Warrington and the chair. I acted it for her, and gave her anecdotes of the pious Baronet's lady and her daughters, which pleased the mis-chievous lively old woman.

The Dowager Countess of Castlewood, now established in her house at Kensington, gave us that kind of welcome which genteel ladies extend to their poorer relatives. We went once or twice to her ladyship's drums at Kensington; but losing more money at cards, and spending more money in coach-hire than I liked to afford, we speedily gave up those entertainments, and, I dare say, were no more missed or regretted than other people in the fashionable world, who are carried by death, debt, or other accident out of the polite sphere. My Theo did not in the least regret this exclusion. She had made her appearance at one of these drums, attired in some little ornaments which her mother left behind her, and by which the good lady set some store; but I thought her own white neck was a great deal prettier than these poor twinkling stones; and there were dowagers, whose wrinkled old bones blazed with rubies and diamonds, which, I am sure, they would gladly have exchanged for her modest *parure* of beauty and freshness. Not a soul spoke to her—except, to be sure, Beau Lothair, a friend of Mr. Will's, who prowled about Bloomsbury afterwards, and even sent my wife a billet. I met him in Covent Garden shortly after, and promised to break his ugly face if ever I saw it in the neighbourhood of my lodgings, and Madam Theo was molested no further.

The only one of our relatives who came to see us (Madame de Bernstein never came; she sent her coach for us sometimes, or made inquiries regarding us by her woman or her major-domo) was our poor Maria, who, with her husband, Mr. Hagan, often took a share of our homely dinner. Then we had friend Spencer from the Temple, who admired our Arcadian felicity, and gently asked our sympathy for his less fortunate loves; and twice or thrice the famous Doctor Johnson came in for a dish of Theo's tea. A dish? a pailful! "And a pail the best thing to feed him, sar!" says Mr. Gumbo indignantly: for the Doctor's appearance was not pleasant, nor his linen particularly white. He snorted, he grew red, and sputtered in feeding; he flung his meat about, and bawled out in contradicting people: and annoyed my Theo, whom he professed to admire greatly, by saying, every time he saw her, "Madam, you do not love me; I see by your manner you do not love me; though I admire you, and come here for your sake. Here is my friend Mr. Reynolds that shall paint you: he has no ceruse in his paint-box that is as brilliant as your complexion." And so Mr. Reynolds, a most perfect and agreeable gentleman, would have painted my wife: but I knew what his price was, and did not choose to incur that expense. I wish I had now, for the sake of the children, that they might see what yonder face was like some five-and-thirty years ago. To me, madam, 'tis the same now as ever; and your ladyship is always young!

What annoyed Mrs. Warrington with Doctor Johnson more than his contradictions, his sputterings, and his dirty nails, was, I think, an unfavourable opinion which he formed of my new tragedy. Hagan once proposed that he should read some scenes from it after tea.

"Nay, sir, conversation is better," says the Doctor. "I can read for myself, or hear you at the theatre. I had rather hear Mrs. Warrington's artless prattle than your declamation of Mr. Warrington's decasyllables. Tell us about your household affairs, madam, and whether his Excellency your father is well, and whether you made the pudden and the butter sauce. The butter sauce was delicious!" (He loved it so well that he had kept a large quantity in the bosom of a very dingy shirt.) "You made it as though you loved me. You helped me as though you loved me, though you don't."

"Faith, sir, you are taking some of the present away with you in your waistcoat," says Hagan, with much spirit.

"Sir, you are rude!" bawls the Doctor. "You are unacquainted with the first principles of politeness, which is courtesy before ladies. Having received a university education I am surprised that you have not learnt the rudiments of politeness. I respect Mrs. Warrington. I should never think of making personal remarks about her guests before her!"

"Then, sir," says Hagan fiercely, "why did you speak of my theatre?"

"Sir, you are saucy!" roars the Doctor.

"De te fabula," says the actor. "I think it is your waistcoat that is saucy. Madam, shall I make some punch in the way we make it in Ireland?"

The Doctor, puffing, and purple in the face, was wiping the dingy shirt with a still more dubious pocket-handkerchief, which he then applied to his forehead. After this exercise, he blew a hyperborean whistle as if to blow his wrath away. "It *is* de me, sir—though, as a young man, perhaps you need not have told me so."

"I drop my point, sir! If you have been wrong, I am sure I am bound to ask your pardon for setting you so!" says Mr. Hagan, with a fine bow.

"Doesn't he look like a god?" says Maria, clutching my wife's hand: and indeed Mr. Hagan did look like a handsome young gentleman. His colour had risen; he had put his hand to his breast with a noble air: Chamont or Castalio could not present himself better.

"Let me make you some lemonade, sir; my papa has sent us a box of fresh limes. May we send you some to the Temple?"

"Madam, if they stay in your house, they will lose their quality and turn sweet," says the Doctor. "Mr. Hagan, you are a young saucebox, that's what you are! Ho! ho! It is I have been wrong."

"O my Lord, my Polidore!" bleats Lady Maria, when she was alone in my wife's drawing-room:—

> "'Oh, I could hear thee talk forever thus,
> Eternally admiring,—fix and gaze
> On those dear eyes, for every glance they send
> Darts through my soul, and fills my heart with rapture!'

Thou knowest not, my Theo, what a pearl and paragon of a man my Castalio is; my Chamont, my—O dear me, child, what a pity it is that in your husband's tragedy he should have to take the horrid name of Captain Smith!"

Upon this tragedy not only my literary hopes, but much of my financial prospects were founded. My brother's debts discharged, my mother's drafts from home duly honoured, my own expenses paid, which, though moderate, were not inconsiderable,—pretty nearly the whole of my patrimony had been spent, and this auspicious moment I must choose for my marriage! I could raise money on my inheritance: that was not impossible, though certainly costly. My mother could not leave her eldest son without a maintenance, whatever our quarrels might be. I had health, strength, good wits, some friends, and reputation—above all, my famous tragedy, which the manager had promised to perform, and upon the proceeds of this I counted for my present support. What becomes of the arithmetic of youth? How do we then calculate that a hundred pounds is a maintenance, and a thousand a fortune? How did I dare play against Fortune with such odds? I succeeded, I remember, in convincing my dear General, and he left home convinced that his son-in-law had for the present necessity at least a score of hundred pounds at his command. He and his dear Molly had begun life with less, and the ravens had somehow always fed them. As for the women, the question of poverty was one of pleasure to those sentimental souls, and Aunt Lambert, for her part, declared it would be wicked and irreligious to doubt of a provision being made for her children. Was the righteous ever forsaken? Did the just man ever have to beg his bread? She knew better than that! "No, no, my dears! I am not going to be afraid on *that* account, I warrant you! Look at me and my General!"

Theo believed all I said and wished to believe myself. So we actually began life upon a capital of Five Acts, and about three hundred pounds of ready money in hand!

Well, the time of the appearance of the famous tragedy drew near, and my friends canvassed the town to get a body of supporters for the opening night. I am ill at asking favours from the great; but when my Lord Wrotham came to London, I went, with Theo in my hand, to wait on his Lordship, who received us kindly, out of regard for his old friend, her father—though he good-naturedly shook a finger at me (at which my little wife hung down her head) for having stole a march on the good General. However, he would do his best for her father's daughter; hoped for a success; said he had heard great things of the piece; and engaged a number of places for himself and his friends. But this patron secured, I had no other. "*Mon cher*, at my age," says the Baroness, "I should bore myself to death at a tragedy: but I will do my best; and I will certainly send my people to the boxes. Yes! Case in his best black looks like a nobleman; and Brett in one of my gowns has a *faux air de moi* which is quite distinguished. Put down my name for two in the front boxes. Good-bye, my dear. *Bonne chance !*" The Dowager Countess presented compliments (on the back of the nine of clubs), had a card-party that night, and was quite sorry she and Fanny could not go to my tragedy. As for my uncle and Lady Warrington, they were out of the question. After the affair of the sedan chair I might as well have asked Queen Elizabeth to go to Drury Lane. These were all my friends —that host of aristocratic connections about whom poor Sampson had bragged; and on the strength of whom the manager, as he said, had given Mr. Hagan his engagement! "Where was my Lord Bute? Had I not promised his Lordship should come?" he asks snappishly, taking snuff (how different from the brisk, and engaging, and obsequious little manager of six months ago!)—" I promised Lord Bute should come?"

"Yes," says Mr. Garrick, "and Her Royal Highness the Princess of Wales, and His Majesty too."

Poor Sampson owned that he, buoyed up by vain hopes, had promised the appearance of these august personages.

The next day, at rehearsal, matters were worse still, and the manager in a fury.

" Great Heavens, sir ! " says he, " into what a pretty *guetapens* have you led me? Look at that letter, sir !—read that letter ! " And he hands me one:—

" MY DEAR SIR " (said the letter),—" I have seen his Lordship, and conveyed to him Mr. Warrington's request that he would honour the tragedy of ' Pocahontas ' by his presence. His lordship is a patron of the drama, and a magnificent friend of all the liberal arts: but he desires me to say that he cannot think of attending himself, much less of asking his Gracious Master to witness the performance of a play, a principal part in which is given to an actor who has made a clandestine marriage with a daughter of one of His Majesty's nobility.—Your well-wisher,

"SAUNDERS M'DUFF.

"MR. D. GARRICK,
    "At the Theatre Royal in Drury Lane."

My poor Theo had a nice dinner waiting for me after the rehearsal. I pleaded fatigue as the reason for looking so pale; I did not dare to convey to her this dreadful news.

CHAPTER LXXX

POCAHONTAS

THE English public, not being so well acquainted with the history of Pocahontas as we of Virginia, who still love the memory of that simple and kindly creature, Mr. Warrington, at the suggestion of his friends, made a little ballad about this Indian princess, which was printed in the magazines a few days before the appearance of the tragedy. This proceeding, Sampson and I considered to be very artful and ingenious. "It is like ground-bait, sir," says the enthusiastic parson, "and you will see the fish rise in multitudes, on the great day!" He and Spencer declared that the poem was discussed and admired at several coffee-houses in their hearing, and that it had been attributed to Mr. Mason, Mr. Cowper of the Temple, and even to the famous Mr. Gray. I believe poor Sam had himself set abroad these reports; and, if Shakspeare had been named as the author of the tragedy, would have declared "Pocahontas" to be one of the poet's best performances. I made acquaintance with brave Captain Smith, as a boy, in my grandfather's library at home, where I remember how I would sit at the good old man's knees, with my favourite volume on my own, spelling out the exploits of our Virginian hero. I loved to read of Smith's travels, sufferings, captivities, escapes, not only in America, but Europe. I become a child again almost as I take from the shelf before me in England the familiar volume, and all sorts of recollections of my early home come crowding over my mind. The old grandfather would make pictures for me of Smith doing battle with the Turks on the Danube, or led out by our Indian savages to death. Ah, what a terrific fight was that in which he was engaged with the three Turkish champions, and how I used to delight over the story of his combat with Bonny Molgro, the last and most dreadful of the three! What a name Bonny Molgro was, and with what a prodigious turban, scimitar, and whiskers we represented him! Having slain and taken off the heads of his first two enemies, Smith and Bonny Molgro met, falling to (says my favourite old book) " with their battle-axes, whose piercing bills made sometimes the one, sometimes the other to have scarce sense to keep their saddles: especially the Christian received such a wound that he lost his battle-axe, whereat the supposed conquering Turke had a great shout from the rampires. Yet, by the readinesse of his horse, and his great judgment and dexteritie, he not only avoided the Turke's blows, but, having drawn his falchion, so pierced the Turke under the cutlets, through back and body, that though he alighted from his horse, he stood not long, ere *hee* lost his head *as the rest had done.* In reward for which deed, Duke Segismundus gave him 3 Turke's head in a shield for armes and 300 Duckats yeerely for a pension." Disdaining time and place (with that daring which is the privilege of poets) in my tragedy, Smith is made to perform similar exploits on the banks of our Potomac and James's River. Our " ground-bait " verses ran thus:—

POCAHONTAS

Wearied arm and broken sword
  Wage in vain the desperate fight;
Round him press a countless horde;
  He is but a single knight.
Hark! a cry of triumph shrill
  Through the wilderness resounds,
  As, with twenty bleeding wounds,
Sinks the warrior, fighting still.

Now they heap the fatal pyre,
  And the torch of death they light:
Ah! 'tis hard to die of fire!
  Who will shield the captive knight?
Round the stake with fiendish cry
  Wheel and dance the savage crowd,
  Cold the victim's mien and proud,
And his breast is bared to die.

Who will shield the fearless heart?
  Who avert the murderous blade?
From the throng, with sudden start,
  See, there springs an Indian maid.
Quick she stands before the knight,
  " Loose the chain, unbind the ring,
  I am daughter of the King,
And I claim the Indian right! "

Dauntlessly aside she flings
  Lifted axe and thirsty knife:
Fondly to his heart she clings,
  And her bosom guards his life!
In the woods of Powhattan,
  Still 'tis told, by Indian fires,
How a daughter of their sires
Saved the captive Englishman.

I need not describe at length the plot of my tragedy, as my children can take it down from the shelves any day and peruse it for themselves. Nor shall I, let me add, be in a hurry to offer to read it again to my young folks, since Captain Miles and the parson both chose to fall asleep last Christmas, when, at mamma's request, I read aloud a couple of acts. But any person having a moderate acquaintance with plays and novels can soon, out of the above sketch, fill out a picture to his liking. An Indian king; a lovely princess, and her attendant, in love with the British captain's servant; a traitor in the English fort; a brave Indian warrior, himself entertaining an unhappy passion for Pocahontas; a medicine-man and priest of the Indians (very well played by Palmer), capable of every treason, stratagem, and crime, and bent upon the torture and death of the English prisoner; these, with the accidents of the wilderness, the war dances and cries (which Gumbo had learned to mimic very accurately from the red people at home), and the arrival of the English fleet, with allusions to the late glorious victories in Canada, and the determination of Britons ever to rule and conquer in America, some of us not unnaturally thought might contribute to the success of our tragedy.

But I have mentioned the ill omens which preceded the day; the difficulties which a peevish, and jealous, and timid management threw in the way of the piece, and the violent prejudice which was felt against it in *certain high quarters*. What wonder then, I ask, that "Pocahontas" should have turned out not to be a victory? I laugh to scorn the malignity of the critics who found fault with the performance. Pretty critics, forsooth, who said that "Carpezan" was a masterpiece, whilst *a far superior and more elaborate work* received only their sneers! I insist on it that Hagan acted his part so admirably that *a certain actor and manager of the theatre* might well be jealous of him; and that, but for the cabal made outside, the piece would have succeeded. The order had been given that the play could not succeed; so at least Sampson declared to me. "The house swarmed with Macs, by George, and they should have the galleries washed with brimstone," the honest fellow swore, and always vowed that Mr. Garrick himself would not have had the piece succeed for the world; and was never in such a rage as during that grand scene in the second act, where Smith (poor Hagan) being bound to the stake, Pocahontas comes and saves him, and when the whole house was thrilling with applause and sympathy.

Anybody who has curiosity sufficient may refer to the published tragedy (in the octavo form, or in the subsequent splendid quarto edition of my Collected Works, and Poems Original and Translated), and say whether the scene is without merit, whether the verses are not elegant, the language rich and noble? One of the causes of the failure was my actual *fidelity to history*. I had copied myself at the Museum, and tinted neatly, a figure of Sir Walter Raleigh in a frill and beard; and (my dear Theo giving some of her mother's best lace for the ruff) we dressed Hagan accurately after this drawing, and no man could look better. Miss Pritchard as Pocahontas, I dressed too as a Red Indian, having seen enough of *that* costume in my own experience at home. Will it be believed that the house tittered when she first appeared? They got used to her, however, but just at the moment when she rushes into the prisoner's arms, and a number of people were actually in tears, a fellow in the pit bawls out, " Bedad! here's the Belle Savage kissing the Saracen's Head; " on which an impertinent roar of laughter sprang up in the pit, breaking out with fitful explosions during the remainder of the performance. As the wag in Mr. Sheridan's amusing " Critic " admirably says about the morning guns, the playwrights were not content with one of them, but must fire two or three; so with this wretched pot-house joke of the Belle Savage (the ignorant people not knowing that Pocahontas herself was the very Belle Sauvage from whom the tavern took its name!). My friend of the pit repeated it *ad nauseam* during the performance, and as each new character appeared, saluted him by the name of some tavern—for instance, the English governor (with a long beard) he called the " Goat and Boots; " his lieutenant (Barker), whose face certainly was broad, the " Bull and Mouth," and so on! And the curtain descended amidst a shrill storm of whistles and hisses, which especially assailed poor Hagan, every time he opened his lips. Sampson saw Master Will in the green boxes, with some pretty acquaintances of his, and had no doubt that the treacherous scoundrel was one of the ringleaders in the conspiracy. " I would have flung him over into the pit," the faithful fellow said (and

Sampson was man enough to execute his threat), " but I saw a couple of Mr. Nadab's followers prowling about the lobby, and was obliged to sheer off." And so the eggs we had counted on selling at market were broken, and our poor hopes lay shattered before us!

I looked in at the house from the stage before the curtain was lifted, and saw it pretty well filled, especially remarking Mr. Johnson in the front boxes, in a laced waistcoat, having his friend Mr. Reynolds by his side; the latter could not hear, and the former could not see, and so they came good-naturedly à *deux* to form an opinion of my poor tragedy. I could see Lady Maria (I knew the hood she wore) in the lower gallery, where she once more had the opportunity of sitting and looking at her beloved actor performing a principal character in a piece. As for Theo, she fairly owned that, unless I ordered her, she had rather not be present, nor had I any such command to give, for, if things went wrong, I knew that to see her suffer would be intolerable pain to myself, and so acquiesced in her desire to keep away.

Being of a pretty equanimous disposition, and, as I flatter myself, able to bear good or evil fortune without disturbance; I myself, after taking a light dinner at the " Bedford," went to the theatre a short while before the commencement of the play, and proposed to remain there, until the defeat or victory was decided. I own now, I could not help seeing which way the fate of the day was likely to turn. There was something gloomy and disastrous in the general aspect of all things around. Miss Pritchard had the headache: the barber who brought home Hagan's wig had powdered it like a wretch; amongst the gentlemen and ladies in the green-room, I saw none but doubtful faces: and the manager (a very flippant, not to say impertinent gentleman, in my opinion, and who himself on that night looked as dismal as a mute at a funeral) had the insolence to say to me, " For Heaven's sake, Mr. Warrington, go and get a glass of punch at the ' Bedford,' and don't frighten us all here by your dismal countenance!" " Sir," says I, " I have a right, for five shillings, to comment upon your face, but I never gave you any authority to make remarks upon mine." " Sir," says he in a pet, " I most heartily wish I had never seen your face at all!" " Yours, sir!" said I, " has often amused me greatly; and when painted for Abel Drugger is exceedingly comic "— and indeed I have always done Mr. G. the justice to think that in low comedy he was unrivalled.

I made him a bow, and walked off to the coffee-house, and for five years after never spoke a word to the gentleman. When he apologised to me, at a nobleman's house where we chanced to meet, I said I had utterly forgotten the circumstance to which he alluded, and that, on the first night of a play, no doubt, author and manager were flurried alike. And added, " After all, there is no shame in not being made for the theatre. Mr. Garrick—you were." A compliment with which he appeared to be as well pleased as I intended he should.

Fidus Achates ran over to me at the end of the first act to say that all things were going pretty well; though he confessed to the titter in the house upon Miss Pritchard's first appearance dressed exactly like an Indian princess.

" I cannot help it, Sampson," said I (filling him a bumper of good punch), " if Indians are dressed so."

" Why," says he, " would you have had Caractacus painted blue like an ancient Briton, or Bonduca with nothing but a cow-skin? "—And indeed it may be that the fidelity to history was the cause of the ridicule cast on my tragedy, in which case I, for one, am not ashamed of its defeat.

After the second act, my aide-de-camp came from the field with dismal news indeed. I don't know how it is that, nervous before action,[1] in disaster I become pretty cool and cheerful. " Are things going ill? " says I. I call for my reckoning, put on my hat, and march to the theatre as calmly as if I was going to dine at the Temple; fidus Achates walking by my side, pressing my elbow, kicking the link-boys out of the way, and crying, " By George, Mr. Warrington, you are a man of spirit— a Trojan, sir! " So, there were men of spirit in Troy; but, alas! fate was too strong for them.

At any rate, no man can say that I did not bear my misfortune with calmness: I could no more help the clamour and noise of the audience than a captain can help the howling and hissing of the storm in which his ship goes down. But I was determined that the rushing waves and broken masts should *impavidum ferient*, and flatter myself that I bore my calamity without flinching. " Not Regulus, my dear madam, could step into his barrel more coolly," Sampson said to my wife. 'Tis unjust to say of men of the parasitic nature that they are unfaithful in misfortune. Whether I was prosperous or poor, the

---

[1] The writer seems to contradict himself here, having just boasted of possessing a pretty equanimous disposition. He was probably mistaken in his own estimate of himself, as other folks have been besides.—Ed.

wild parson was equally true and friendly, and shared our crust as eagerly as ever he had partaken of our better fortune.

I took my place on the stage, whence I could see the actors of my poor piece, and a portion of the audience who condemned me. I suppose the performers gave me a wide berth out of pity for me. I must say that I think I was as little moved as any spectator; and that no one would have judged from my mien that I was the unlucky hero of the night.

But my dearest Theo, when I went home, looked so pale and white, that I saw from the dear creature's countenance that the knowledge of my disaster had preceded my return. Spencer, Sampson, Cousin Hagan, and Lady Maria were to come after the play, and congratulate the author, God wot! (Poor Miss Pritchard was engaged to us likewise, but sent word that I must understand that she was a great deal too unwell to sup that night.) My friend the gardener of Bedford House had given my wife his best flowers to decorate her little table. There they were; the poor little painted standards—and the battle lost! I had borne the defeat well enough, but as I looked at the sweet pale face of the wife across the table, and those artless trophies of welcome which she had set up for her hero, I confess my courage gave way, and my heart felt a pang almost as keen as any that ever has smitten it.

Our meal, it may be imagined, was dismal enough, nor was it rendered much gayer by the talk we strove to carry on. Old Mrs. Hagan was, luckily, very ill at this time; and her disease, and the incidents connected with it, a great blessing to us. Then we had His Majesty's approaching marriage, about which there was a talk. (How well I remember the most futile incidents of the day: down to a tune which a carpenter was whistling by my side at the playhouse, just before the dreary curtain fell!) Then we talked about the death of good Mr. Richardson, the author of "Pamela" and "Clarissa," whose works we all admired exceedingly. And as we talked about "Clarissa," my wife took on herself to wipe her eyes once or twice, and say, faintly, "You know, my love, mamma and I could never help crying over that dear book. Oh, my dearest dearest mother" (she adds), "how I wish she could be with me now!" This was an occasion for more open tears, for of course a young lady may naturally weep for her absent mother. And then we mixed a gloomy bowl with Jamaica limes, and drank to the health of his Excellency the Governor: and then, for a second toast, I filled a bumper, and, with a smiling face, drank to " our better fortune!"

This was too much. The two women flung themselves into each other's arms, and irrigated each other's neck-handkerchiefs with tears. " O Maria! Is not—is not my George good and kind?" sobs Theo. " Look at my Hagan—how great, how god-like he was in his part!" gasps Maria. " It was a beastly cabal which threw him over—and I could plunge this knife into Mr. Garrick's black heart—the odious little wretch!" and she grasps a weapon at her side. But throwing it presently down the enthusiastic creature rushes up to her lord and master, flings her arms round him, and embraces him in the presence of the little company.

I am not sure whether some one else did not do likewise. We were all in a state of extreme excitement and enthusiasm. In the midst of grief, Love the consoler appears amongst us, and soothes us with such fond blandishments and tender caresses, that one scarce wishes the calamity away. Two or three days afterwards, on our birthday, a letter was brought me in my study, which contained the following lines:—

FROM POCAHONTAS

Returning from the cruel fight
How pale and faint appears my knight!
He sees me anxious at his side;
" Why seek, my love, your wounds to hide?
Or deem your English girl afraid
To emulate the Indian maid?"

    Be mine my husband's grief to cheer,
In peril to be ever near;
Whate'er of ill or woe betide,
To bear it clinging at his side;
The poisoned stroke of fate to ward,
His bosom with my own to guard;
Ah! could it spare a pang to his,
It could not know a purer bliss!
'Twould gladden as it felt the smart,
And thank the hand that flung the dart!

I do not say the verses are very good, but that I like them as well as if they were—and that the face of the writer (whose sweet young voice I fancy I can hear as I hum the lines), when I went into her drawing-room after getting the letter, and when I saw her blushing and blessing me—seemed to me more beautiful than any I can fancy out of heaven.

CHAPTER LXXXI

RES ANGUSTA DOMI

I HAVE already described my present feelings as an elderly
gentleman, regarding that rash jump into matrimony, which I
persuaded my dear partner to take with me when we were both
scarce out of our teens. As a man and a father—with a due
sense of the necessity of mutton-chops, and the importance of
paying the baker—with a pack of rash children round about us
who might be running off to Scotland to-morrow, and pleading
papa's and mamma's example for their impertinence,—I know
that I ought to be very cautious in narrating this early part of
the married life of George Warrington, Esquire, and Theodosia
his wife—to call out *mea culpa*, and put on a demure air, and
sitting in my comfortable easy-chair here, profess to be in a
white sheet and on the stool of repentance, offering myself up
as a warning to imprudent and hot-headed youth.

But, truth to say, that married life, regarding which my dear
relatives prophesied so gloomily, has disappointed all those
prudent and respectable people. It has had its trials: but I
can remember them without bitterness—its passionate griefs,
of which time, by God's kind ordinance, has been the benign
consoler—its days of poverty, which we bore, who endured it,
to the wonder of our sympathising relatives looking on—its
precious rewards and blessings, so great that I scarce dare to
whisper them to this page; to speak of them, save with awful
respect and to One Ear, to which are offered up the prayers and
thanks of all men. To marry without a competence is wrong
and dangerous, no doubt, and a crime against our social codes;
but do not scores of thousands of our fellow-beings commit the
crime every year with no other trust but in Heaven, health, and
their labour? Are young people entering into the married life
not to take hope into account, nor dare to begin their housekeeping until the cottage is completely furnished, the cellar and
larder stocked, the cupboard full of plate, and the strong-box of
money? The increase and multiplication of the world would
stop, were the laws which regulate the genteel part of it to be
made universal. Our gentlefolks tremble at the brink in their
silk stockings and pumps, and wait for whole years, until they
find a bridge or a gilt barge to carry them across; our poor do

not fear to wet their bare feet, plant them in the brook, and trust to fate and strength to bear them over. Who would like to consign his daughter to poverty? Who would counsel his son to undergo the countless risks of poor married life, to remove the beloved girl from comfort and competence, and subject her to debt, misery, privation, friendlessness, sickness, and the hundred gloomy consequences of the *res angusta domi*? I look at my own wife and ask her pardon for having imposed a task so fraught with pain and danger upon one so gentle. I think of the trials she endured, and am thankful for them and for that unfailing love and constancy with which God blessed her and strengthened her to bear them all. On this question of marriage I am not a fair judge: my own was so imprudent and has been so happy, that I must not dare to give young people counsel. I have endured poverty, but scarcely ever found it otherwise than tolerable: had I not undergone it, I never could have known the kindness of friends, the delight of gratitude, the surprising joys and consolations which sometimes accompany the scanty meal and narrow fire, and cheer the long day's labour. This at least is certain, in respect of the lot of the decent poor, that a great deal of superfluous pity is often thrown away upon it. Good-natured fine folks, who sometimes stepped out of the sunshine of their riches into our narrow obscurity, were blinded, as it were, whilst we could see quite cheerfully and clearly: they stumbled over obstacles which were none to us: they were surprised at the resignation with which we drank small beer, and that we could heartily say grace over such very cold mutton.

The good General, my father-in-law, had married his Molly, when he was a subaltern of a foot regiment, and had a purse scarce better filled than my own. They had had their ups and downs of fortune. I think (though my wife will never confess to this point) they had married, as people could do in their young time, without previously asking papa's and mamma's leave.[1] At all events, they were so well pleased with their own good luck in matrimony, that they did not grudge their children's, and were by no means frightened at the idea of any little hardships which we in the course of our married life might be called upon to undergo. And I suppose when I made my own pecuniary statements to Mr. Lambert, I was anxious to deceive both of us. Believing me to be master of a couple of

---

[1] The editor has looked through Burn's *History of the Fleet Marriages* without finding the names of Martin Lambert and Mary Benson.

thousand pounds he went to Jamaica quite easy in his mind as to his darling daughter's comfort and maintenance, at least for some years to come. After paying the expenses of his family's outfit the worthy man went away not much richer than his son-in-law: and a few trinkets, and some lace of Aunt Lambert's, with twenty new guineas in a purse which her mother and sisters made for her, were my Theo's marriage portion. But in valuing my stock, I chose to count as a good debt a sum which my honoured mother never could be got to acknowledge up to the day when the resolute old lady was called to pay the last debt of all. The sums I had disbursed for her, she urged, were spent for the improvement and maintenance of the estate which was to be mine at her decease. What money she could spare was to be for my poor brother, who had nothing, who would never have spent his own means had he not imagined himself to be *sole heir* of the Virginian property, *as he would have been*—the good lady took care to emphasise this point in many of her letters—but for a half-hour's accident of birth. He was now distinguishing himself in the service of his king and country. To purchase his promotion was his mother's, *she should suppose* his brother's duty! When I had finished my bar-studies and my *dramatic amusements*, Madam Esmond informed me that I was welcome to return home and take that place in our colony to which my birth entitled me. This statement she communicated to me more than once through Mountain, and before the news of my marriage had reached her.

There is no need to recall her expressions of maternal indignation when she was informed of the step I had taken. On the pacification of Canada, my dear Harry asked for leave of absence, and dutifully paid a visit to Virginia. He wrote, describing his reception at home, and the splendid entertainments which my mother made in honour of her son. Castlewood, which she had not inhabited since our departure for Europe, was thrown open again to our friends of the colony; and the friend of Wolfe, and the soldier of Quebec, was received by all our acquaintance with every becoming honour. Some dismal quarrels, to be sure, ensued, because my brother persisted in maintaining his friendship with Colonel Washington, of Mount Vernon, whose praises Harry was never tired of singing. Indeed I allow the gentleman every virtue; and in the struggles which terminated so fatally for England a few years since, I can admire as well as his warmest friends, General Washington's glorious constancy and success.

If these battles between Harry and our mother were frequent, as, in his letters, he described them to be, I wondered, for my part, why he should continue at home? One reason naturally suggested itself to my mind, which I scarcely liked to communicate to Mrs. Warrington; for we had both talked over our dear little Hetty's romantic attachment for my brother, and wondered that he had never discovered it. I need not say, I suppose, that my gentleman had found some young lady at home more to his taste than our dear Hester, and hence accounted for his prolonged stay in Virginia.

Presently there came, in a letter from him, not a full confession, but an admission of this interesting fact. A person was described, not named—a being all beauty and perfection, like other young ladies under similar circumstances. My wife asked to see the letter: I could not help showing it, and handed it to her, with a very sad face. To my surprise she read it, without exhibiting any corresponding sorrow of her own.

"I have thought of this before, my love," I said. "I feel with you for your disappointment regarding poor Hetty."

"Ah! poor Hetty," says Theo, looking down at the carpet.

"It would never have done," says I.

"No—they would not have been happy," sighs Theo.

"How strange he never should have found out her secret!" I continued.

She looked me full in the face with an odd expression.

"Pray, what does that look mean?" I asked.

"Nothing, my dear—nothing! only I am not surprised!" says Theo, blushing.

"What," I ask, "can there be another?"

"I am sure I never said so, George," says the lady hurriedly. "But if Hetty has overcome her childish folly, ought we not all to be glad? Do you gentlemen suppose that you only are to fall in love and grow tired, indeed?"

"What!" I say, with a strange commotion of my mind. "Do you mean to tell me, Theo, that you ever cared for any one but me?"

"Oh, George," she whimpers, "when I was at school, there was —there was one of the boys of Doctor Backhouse's school, who sat in the loft next to us; and I thought he had lovely eyes, and I was so shocked when I recognised him behind the counter at Mr. Grigg the mercer's, when I went to buy a cloak for baby, and I wanted to tell you, my dear, and I didn't know how!"

I went to see this creature with the lovely eyes, having made my wife describe the fellow's dress to me, and I saw a little bandy-legged wretch in a blue camlet coat, with his red hair tied with a dirty ribbon, about whom I forbore generously even to reproach my wife; nor will she ever know that I have looked at the fellow, until she reads the confession in this page. If our wives saw us as we are, I thought, would they love us as they do? Are we as much mistaken in them, as they in us? I look into one candid face at least, and think it never has deceived me.

Lest I should encourage my young people to an imitation of my own imprudence, I will not tell them with how small a capital Mrs. Theo and I commenced life. The unfortunate tragedy brought us nothing; though the reviewers, since its publication of late, have spoken not unfavourably as to its merits, and Mr. Kemble himself has done me the honour to commend it. Our kind friend Lord Wrotham was for having the piece published by subscription, and sent me a bank-note, with a request that I would let him have a hundred copies for his friends; but I was always averse to that method of levying money, and preferring my poverty *sine dote*, locked up my manuscript, with my poor girl's verses inserted at the first page. I know not why the piece should have given such offence at court, except for the fact that an actor who had run off with an earl's daughter performed a principal part in the play; but I was told that sentiments which I had put into the mouths of some of the Indian characters (who were made to declaim against ambition, the British desire of rule, and so forth) were pronounced dangerous and unconstitutional; so that the little hope of Royal favour, which I might have had, was quite taken away from me.

What was to be done? A few months after the failure of the tragedy, as I counted up the remains of my fortune (the calculation was not long or difficult), I came to the conclusion that I must beat a retreat out of my pretty apartments in Bloomsbury, and so gave warning to our good landlady, informing her that my wife's health required that we should have lodgings in the country. But we went no farther than Lambeth, our faithful Gumbo and Molly following us: and here, though as poor as might be, we were waited on by a maid and a lacquey in livery, like any folks of condition. You may be sure kind relatives cried out against our extravagance; indeed, are they not the people who find our faults out for us, and proclaim them to the rest of the world?

Returning home from London one day, whither I had been

on a visit to some booksellers, I recognised the family arms and livery on a grand gilt chariot which stood before a public-house near to our lodgings. A few loitering inhabitants were gathered round the splendid vehicle, and looking with awe at the footmen, resplendent in the sun, and quaffing blazing pots of beer. I found my Lady Castlewood sitting opposite to my wife in our little apartment (whence we had a very bright pleasant prospect of the river, covered with barges and wherries, and the ancient towers and trees of the Archbishop's place and garden, and Mrs. Theo, who has a very droll way of describing persons and scenes, narrated to me all the particulars of her Ladyship's conversation, when she took her leave.

" I have been here this ever-so-long," says the Countess, " gossiping with Cousin Theo, while you have been away at the coffee-house, I dare say, making merry with your friends, and drinking your punch and coffee. Guess she must find it rather lonely here, with nothing to do but work them little caps, and hem them frocks. Never mind, dear; reckon you'll soon have a companion who will amuse you when Cousin George is away at his coffee-house! What a nice lodging you have got here, I do declare! Our new house which we have took is twenty times as big, and covered with gold from top to bottom: but I like this quite as well. Bless you! being rich is no better than being poor. When we lived to Albany, and I did most all the work myself, scoured the rooms, biled the kettle, helped the wash, and all, I was just as happy as I am now. We only had one old negro to keep the store. Why don't you sell Gumbo, Cousin George? He ain't no use here idling and dawdling about, and making love to the servant-girl. Fogh! guess they ain't particular, these English people! " So she talked, rattling on with perfect good-humour, until her hour for departure came; when she produced a fine repeating watch, and said it was time for her to pay a call upon Her Majesty at Buckingham House. " And mind you come to us, George," says her Lady-ship, waving a little parting hand out of the gilt coach. " Theo and I have settled all about it."

" Here, at least," said I, when the laced footmen had clam-bered up behind the carriage, and our magnificent little patroness had left us;—" here is one who is not afraid of our poverty, nor ashamed to remember her own."

" Ashamed! " said Theo, resuming her lilliputian needlework. " To do her justice, she would make herself at home in any kitchen or palace in the world. She has given me and Molly twenty lessons in housekeeping. She says, when she was at home to Albany, she roasted, baked, swept the house, and milked the cow." (Madam Theo pronounced the word cow archly in our American way, and imitated her Ladyship's accent very divertingly.)

"And she has no pride," I added. "It was good-natured of her to ask us to dine with her and my Lord. When will Uncle Warrington ever think of offering us a crust again, or a glass of his famous beer?"

"Yes, it was not ill-natured to invite us," says Theo slily. "But, my dear, you don't know all the conditions!" And then my wife, still imitating the Countess's manner, laughingly informed me what these conditions were. "She took out her pocket-book, and told me," says Theo, "what days she was engaged abroad and at home. On Monday she received a Duke and a Duchess, with several other members of my Lord's house, and their ladies. On Tuesday came more earls, two bishops, and an ambassador. 'Of course you won't come on them days?' says the Countess. 'Now you are so poor, you know that fine company ain't no good for you. Lord bless you! father never dines on our company days! he don't like it; he takes a bit of cold meat anyways.' On which," says Theo, laughing, "I told her that Mr. Warrington did not care for any but the best of company, and proposed that she should ask us on some day when the Archbishop of Canterbury dined with her, and his Grace must give us a lift home in his coach to Lambeth. And she is an economical little person, too," continues Theo. "'I thought of bringing with me some of my baby's caps and things, which his Lordship has outgrown 'em, but they may be wanted again, you know, my dear.' And so we lose that addition to our wardrobe," says Theo, smiling, "and Molly and I must do our best without her Ladyship's charity. 'When people are poor, they are poor,' the Countess said, with her usual outspokenness, 'and must get on the best they can. What we shall do for that poor Maria, goodness only knows! we can't ask her to see us as we can you, though you are so poor: but an earl's daughter to marry a play-actor! La, my dear, it's dreadful: His Majesty and the Princess have both spoken of it! Every other noble family in this kingdom as has ever heard of it, pities us; though I have a plan for helping those poor unhappy people, and have sent down Simons, my groom of the chambers, to tell them on it.' This plan was, that Hagan, who had kept almost all his terms at Dublin College, should return thither and take his degree, and enter into holy orders, ' when we will provide him with a chaplaincy at home, you know,' Lady Castlewood added." And I may mention here, that this benevolent plan was executed a score of months later; when I was enabled myself to be of service to Mr. Hagan, who was one of the kindest and best of our friends during our own time of want and distress. Castlewood then executed his promise loyally enough, got orders and a colonial appointment for Hagan, who distinguished himself both as a soldier and preacher, as we shall presently hear; but not a guinea did his Lordship spare to aid either his sister or his kinsman in their trouble. I never asked him, thank Heaven, to assist me in my own; though, to do him justice, no man could express himself more amiably, and with a joy which I believe was quite genuine, when my days of poverty were ended.

As for my Uncle Warrington, and his virtuous wife and daughters, let me do them justice likewise, and declare that, throughout my period of trial, their sorrow at my poverty was consistent and unvarying. I still had a few acquaintances who saw them, and of course (as friends will) brought me a report of their opinions and conversation; and I never could hear that my relatives had uttered one single good word about me or my wife. They spoke even of my tragedy as a crime—I was accustomed to hear that sufficiently maligned—of the author as a miserable reprobate, for ever reeling about Grub Street in rags and squalor. They held me out no hand of help. My poor wife might cry in her pain, but they had no twopence to bestow upon her. They went to church a half-dozen times in the week. They subscribed to many public charities. Their tribe was known eighteen hundred years ago, and will flourish as long as men endure. They will still thank Heaven that they are not as other folks are; and leave the wounded and miserable to other succour.

I don't care to recall the dreadful doubts and anxieties which began to beset me: the plan after plan which I tried, and in which I failed, for procuring work and adding to our dwindling stock of money. I bethought me of my friend Mr. Johnson, and when I think of the eager kindness with which he received me, am ashamed of some pert speeches which I own to have made regarding his manners and behaviour. I told my story and difficulties to him, the circumstance of my marriage, and the prospects before me. He would not for a moment admit ' they were gloomy, or, *si male nunc*, that they would continue to be so. I had before me the chances, certainly very slender, of a place in England; the inheritance which must be mine in the course of nature, or at any rate would fall to the heir I was expecting. I had a small stock of money for present actual necessity—a possibility, " though, to be free with you, sir " (says he) " after the performance of your tragedy, I doubt whether nature has endowed you with those peculiar qualities which are necessary for achieving a remarkable literary success " —and finally a submission to the maternal rule, and a return to Virginia, where plenty and a home were always ready for me. " Why, sir ! " he cried, " such a sum as you mention would have been a fortune to me when I began the world, and my friend Mr. Goldsmith would set up a coach and six on it. With youth, hope, to-day, and a couple of hundred pounds in cash—no young fellow need despair. Think, sir, you have a year at least before you, and who knows what may chance between now and then. Why, sir, your relatives here may provide for you, or you may succeed to your Virginian property, or you may come into a fortune ! " I did not in the course of that year, but he did. My Lord Bute gave Mr. Johnson a pension, which set all Grub Street in a fury against the recipient, who, to be sure, had published his own not very flattering opinion upon pensions and pensioners.

Nevertheless, he did not altogether discourage my literary projects, promised to procure me work from the booksellers, and faithfully performed that kind promise. " But," says he, " sir, you must not appear amongst them *in formâ pauperis*. Have you never a friend's coach in which we can ride to see them ? You must put on your best-laced hat and waistcoat; and we must appear, sir, as if you were doing *them* a favour." This stratagem answered, and procured me respect enough at the first visit or two: but when the booksellers knew that I wanted to be paid for my work, their backs refused to bend any more, and they treated me with a familiarity which I could ill stomach. I overheard one of them, who had been a footman, say, " Oh, it's Pocahontas, is it? let him wait." And he told his boy to say as much to me. " Wait, sir ! " says I, fuming with rage and putting my head into his parlour. " I'm not accustomed to waiting, but I have heard you are." And I strode out of the shop into Pall Mall in a mighty fluster.

And yet Mr. D. was in the right. I came to him, if not to ask a favour, at any rate to propose a bargain, and surely it was my business to wait his time and convenience. In more fortunate days I asked the gentleman's pardon, and the kind author of the " Muse in Livery " was instantly appeased.

I was more prudent, or Mr. Johnson more fortunate, in an application elsewhere, and Mr. Johnson procured me a little work from the booksellers in translating from foreign languages, of which I happen to know two or three. By a hard day's labour I could earn a few shillings; so few that a week's work would hardly bring me a guinea: and that was flung to me with insolent patronage by the low hucksters who employed me. I can put my finger upon two or three magazine articles written at this period,[1] and paid for with a few wretched shillings, which papers as I read them awaken in me the keenest pangs of bitter remembrance. I recall the doubts and fears which agitated me, see the dear wife nursing her infant and looking up into my face with hypocritical smiles that vainly try to mask her alarm: the struggles of pride are fought over again: the wounds under which I smarted, reopen. There are some acts of injustice committed against me which I don't know how to forgive; and which, whenever I think of them, awaken in me the same feelings of revolt and indignation. The gloom and darkness gather over me—till they are relieved by a reminiscence of that love and tenderness which through all gloom and darkness have been my light and consolation.

CHAPTER LXXXII

MILES'S MOIDORE

LITTLE Miles made his appearance in this world within a few days of the gracious Prince who commands his regiment. Illuminations and cannonading saluted the Royal George's birth, multitudes were admitted to see him as he lay behind a gilt railing at the Palace with noble nurses watching over him.

---

[1] Mr. George Warrington, of the Upper Temple, says he remembers a book containing his grandfather's book-plate, in which were pasted various extracts from reviews and newspapers in an old type, and lettered outside *Les Chaînes de l'Esclavage.* These were no doubt the contributions above mentioned; but the volume has not been found, either in the town-house or in the library at Warrington Manor. The editor, by the way, is not answerable for a certain inconsistency, which may be remarked in the narrative. The writer says, p. 289, that he speaks " without bitterness " of past times, and presently falls into a fury with them. The same manner of forgiving our enemies is not uncommon in the present century.

Few nurses guarded the cradle of our little prince: no courtiers, no faithful retainers saluted it, except our trusty Gumbo and kind Molly, who to be sure loved and admired the little heir of my poverty as loyally as our hearts could desire. Why was our boy not named George like the other paragon just mentioned, and like his father? I gave him the name of a little scapegrace of my family, a name which many generations of Warringtons had borne likewise; but my poor little Miles's love and kindness touched me at a time when kindness and love were rare from those of my own blood, and Theo and I agreed that our child should be called after that single little friend of my paternal race.

We wrote to acquaint our royal parents with the auspicious event, and bravely inserted the child's birth in the *Daily Advertiser*, and the place, Church Street, Lambeth, where he was born. " My dear," says Aunt Bernstein, writing to me in reply to my announcement, " how could you point out to all the world that you live in such a *trou* as that in which you have buried yourself? I kiss the little mamma, and send a remembrance for the child." This remembrance was a fine silk coverlid, with a lace edging fit for a prince. It was not very useful: the price of the lace would have served us much better, but Theo and Molly were delighted with the present, and my eldest son's cradle had a cover as fine as any nobleman's.

Good Doctor Heberden came over several times to visit my wife, and see that all things went well. He knew and recommended to us a surgeon in the vicinage, who took charge of her: luckily, my dear patient needed little care, beyond that which our landlady and her own trusty attendant could readily afford her. Again our humble precinct was adorned with the gilded apparition of Lady Castlewood's chariot wheels; she brought a pot of jelly, which she thought Theo might like, and which, no doubt, had been served at one of her Ladyship's banquets on a previous day. And she told us of all the ceremonies at Court, and of the splendour and festivities attending the birth of the august heir to the Crown. Our good Mr. Johnson happened to pay me a visit on one of those days when my Lady Countess's carriage flamed up to our little gate. He was not a little struck by her magnificence, and made her some bows, which were more respectful than graceful. She called me cousin very affably, and helped to transfer the present of jelly from her silver dish into our crockery pan with much benignity. The Doctor tasted the sweetmeat, and pronounced it to be excellent. " The great, sir," says he, "are fortunate in every way. They can engage the most skilful practitioners of the culinary art, as they can assemble the most amiable wits round their table. If, as you think, sir, and from the appearance of the dish your suggestion at least is plausible, this sweetmeat may have appeared already at his Lordship's table, it has been there in good company. It has quivered under the eyes of celebrated beauties, it has been tasted by ruby lips, it has divided the attention of the distinguished company, with fruits, tarts, and creams, which I make no doubt were like itself, delicious." And so saying, the good Doctor absorbed a considerable portion of Lady Castlewood's benefaction; though as regards the epithet delicious I am bound to say, that my poor wife, after tasting the jelly, put it away from her as not to her liking; and Molly, flinging up her head, declared it was mouldy.

My boy enjoyed at least the privilege of having an earl's daughter for his godmother; for this office was performed by his cousin, our poor Lady Maria, whose kindness and attention to the mother and the infant were beyond all praise; and who, having lost her own solitary chance for maternal happiness, yearned over our child in a manner not a little touching to behold. Captain Miles is a mighty fine gentleman, and his uniforms of the Prince's Hussars as splendid as any that ever bedizened a soldier of fashion; but he hath too good a heart, and is too true a gentleman, let us trust, not to be thankful when he remembers that his own infant limbs were dressed in some of the little garments which had been prepared for the poor player's child. Sampson christened him in that very chapel in Southwark, where our marriage ceremony had been performed. Never were the words of the Prayer-book more beautifully and impressively read than by the celebrant of the service; except at its end, when his voice failed him, and he and the rest of the little congregation were fain to wipe their eyes. "Mr. Garrick himself, sir," says Hagan, "could not have read those words so nobly. I am sure little innocent never entered the world accompanied by wishes and benedictions more tender and sincere."

And now I have not told how it chanced that the Captain came by his name of Miles. A couple of days before his christening, when as yet I believe it was intended that our firstborn should bear his father's name, a little patter of horse's hoofs comes galloping up to our gate; and who should pull at the bell but young Miles, our cousin? I fear he had disobeyed his parents when he galloped away on that undutiful journey.

"You know," says he, "Cousin Harry gave me my little horse: and I can't help liking you, because you are so like Harry, and because they are always saying things of you at home, and it's a shame: and I have brought my whistle and coral that my godmamma Lady Suckling gave me, for your little boy; and if you're so poor, Cousin George, here's my gold moidore, and it's worth ever so much, and it's no use to me, because I mayn't spend it, you know."

We took the boy up to Theo in her room (he mounted the stair in his little tramping boots, of which he was very proud); and Theo kissed him, and thanked him; and his moidore has been in her purse from that day.

My mother, writing through her ambassador as usual, informed me of her royal surprise and displeasure on learning that my son had been christened Miles—a name not known, at least in the Esmond family. I did not care to tell the reason at the time; but when, in after years, I told Madam Esmond how my boy came by his name, I saw a tear roll down her wrinkled cheek, and I heard afterwards that she had asked Gumbo many questions about the boy who gave his name to *our* Miles: our Miles Gloriosus of Pall Mall, Valenciennes, Almack's Brighton.

CHAPTER LXXXIII

TROUBLES AND CONSOLATIONS

In our early days at home, when Harry and I used to be so undutiful to our tutor, who would have thought that Mr. Esmond Warrington of Virginia would turn bear-leader himself? My mother (when we came together again) never could be got to speak directly of this period of my life; but would allude to it as "that terrible time, my love, which I can't bear to think of," "those dreadful years when there was difference between us," and so forth, and though my pupil, a worthy and grateful man, sent me out to Jamestown several barrels of that liquor by which his great fortune was made, Madam Esmond spoke of him as "your friend in England," "your wealthy Lambeth friend," etc., but never by his name; nor did she ever taste a drop of his beer. We brew our own too at Warrington Manor, but our good Mr. Foker never fails to ship to Ipswich every year a couple of butts of his entire. His son is a young sprig of fashion, and has married an earl's daughter; the father is a very worthy and kind gentleman, and it is to the luck of making his acquaintance that I owe the receipt of some of the most welcome guineas that ever I received in my life.

It was not so much the sum, as the occupation and hope given me by the office of Governor, which I took on myself, which were then so precious to me. Mr. F.'s Brewery (the site has since been changed) then stood near to Pedlar's Acre in Lambeth: and the surgeon who attended my wife in her confinement, likewise took care of the wealthy brewer's family. He was a Bavarian, originally named Voelker. Mr. Lance, the surgeon, I suppose, made him acquainted with my name and history. The worthy doctor would smoke many a pipe of Virginia in my garden, and had conceived an attachment for me and my family. He brought his patron to my house: and when Mr. F. found that I had a smattering of his language, and could sing " Prinz Eugen, the noble Ritter " (a song that my grandfather had brought home from the Marlborough wars), the German conceived a great friendship for me: his lady put her chair and her chariot at Mrs. Warrington's service: his little daughter took a prodigious fancy to our baby (and to do him justice, the Captain, who is as ugly a fellow now as ever wore a queue,[1] was beautiful as an infant): and his son and heir, Master Foker, being much maltreated at Westminster School because of his father's profession of brewer, the parents asked if I would take charge of him; and paid me a not insufficient sum for superintending his education.

Mr. F. was a shrewd man of business, and as he and his family really interested themselves in me and mine, I laid all my pecuniary affairs pretty unreservedly before him; and my statement, he was pleased to say, augmented the respect and regard which he felt for me. He laughed at our stories of the aid which my noble relatives had given me—my aunt's coverlid, my Lady Castlewood's mouldy jelly, Lady Warrington's contemptuous treatment of us. But he wept many tears over the story of little Miles's moidore; and as for Sampson and Hagan, " I vow," says he, " dey shall have as much beer als ever dey can drink." He sent his wife to call upon Lady Maria, and treated her with the utmost respect and obsequiousness, whenever she came to visit him. It was with Mr. Foker that Lady Maria stayed when Hagan went to Dublin to complete his

[1] The very image of the Squire at thirty, everybody says so.—M. W. (*Note in the MS.*)

college terms; and the good brewer's purse also ministered to our friend's wants and supplied his outfit.

When Mr. Foker came fully to know my own affairs and position, he was pleased to speak of me with terms of enthusiasm, and as if my conduct showed some extraordinary virtue. I have said how my mother saved money for Harry, and how the two were in my debt. But when Harry spent money, he spent it fancying it to be his; Madam Esmond never could be made to understand she was dealing hardly with me—the money was paid and gone, and there was an end of it. Now, at the end of '62, I remember Harry sent over a considerable remittance for the purchase of his promotion, begging me at the same time to remember that he was in my debt, and to draw on his agents if I had any need. He did not know how great the need was, or how my little capital had been swallowed.

Well, to take my brother's money would delay his promotion, and I naturally did not draw on him, though I own I was tempted; nor, knowing my dear General Lambert's small means, did I care to impoverish him by asking for supplies. These simple acts of forbearance my worthy brewer must choose to consider as instances of exalted virtue. And what does my gentleman do but write privately to my brother in America, lauding me and my wife as the most admirable of human beings, and call upon Madame de Bernstein, who never told me of his visit, indeed, but who, I perceived about this time, treated us with singular respect and gentleness, that surprised me in one whom I could not but consider as selfish and worldly. In after days I remember asking him how he had gained admission to the Baroness? He laughed: " De Baroness! " says he. " I knew de Baron when he was a *walet* at Munich, and I was a brewer-apprentice." I think our family had best not be too curious about our uncle the Baron.

Thus, the part of my life which ought to have been most melancholy was in truth made pleasant by many friends, happy circumstances, and strokes of lucky fortune. The bear I led was a docile little cub, and danced to my piping very readily. Better to lead him about, than to hang round booksellers' doors, or wait the pleasure or caprice of managers! My wife and I, during our exile, as we may call it, spent very many pleasant evenings with these kind friends and benefactors. Nor were we without intellectual enjoyments: Mrs. Foker and Mrs. Warrington sang finely together; and sometimes, when I was in the mood, I read my own play of " Pocahontas " to this friendly audience, in a manner better than Hagan's own, Mr. Foker was pleased to say.

After that little escapade of Miles Warrington, junior, I saw nothing of him, and heard of my paternal relatives but rarely. Sir Miles was assiduous at Court (as I believe he would have been at Nero's), and I laughed one day when Mr. Foker told me that he had heard on 'Change " that they were going to make my uncle a Beer."—" A Beer?" says I in wonder.—" Can't you understand de vort, ven I say it?" says the testy old gentleman. " Vell, vell, a Lort!" Sir Miles indeed was the obedient humble servant of the Minister, whoever he might be. I am surprised he did not speak English with a Scotch accent during the first favourite's brief reign. I saw him and his wife coming from Court, when Mrs. Claypool was presented to Her Majesty on her marriage. I had my little boy on my shoulder. My uncle and aunt stared resolutely at me from their gilt coach window. The footmen looked blank over their nosegays. Had I worn the Fairy's cap and been invisible, my father's brother could not have passed me with less notice.

We did not avail ourselves much, or often, of that queer invitation of Lady Castlewood, to go and drink tea and sup with her Ladyship, when there was no other company. Old Van den Bosch, however shrewd his intellect and great his skill in making a fortune, was not amusing in conversation, except to his daughter, who talked household and City matters, bulling and bearing, raising and selling farming-stock, and so forth, quite as keenly and shrewdly as her father. Nor was my Lord Castlewood often at home or much missed by his wife when absent, or very much at ease in the old father's company. The Countess told all this to my wife in her simple way. " Guess," says she, " my Lord and father don't pull well together nohow. Guess my Lord is always wanting money, and father keeps the key of the box: and quite right too. If he could have the fingering of all our money, my Lord would soon make away with it, and then what's to become of our noble family? We pay everything, my dear, except play debts, and them we won't have nohow. We pay cooks, horses, wine-merchants, tailors, and everybody—and lucky for them, too—reckon my Lord wouldn't pay 'em! And we always take care that he has a guinea in his pocket, and goes out like a real nobleman. What that man do owe to us: what he did before we come—gracious goodness only knows! Me and father does our best to make him respectable: but it's no easy job, my dear. La! he'd melt the plate, only father keeps the key of the strong-room; and when we go to Castlewood, my father travels with me, and papa is armed too, as well as the people."

"Gracious heavens!" cries my wife, "your Ladyship does not mean to say, you suspect your own husband of a desire to——"

"To what? Oh no, nothing of course! And I would trust our brother Will with untold money, wouldn't I? As much as I'd trust the cat with the cream-pan! I tell you, my dear, it's not all pleasure being a woman of rank and fashion: and if I have bought a countess's coronet, I have paid a good price for it—that I have!"

And so had my Lord Castlewood paid a large price for having his estate freed from incumbrances, his houses and stables furnished, and his debts discharged. He was the slave of the little wife and her father. No wonder the old man's society was not pleasant to the poor victim, and that he gladly slunk away from his own fine house, to feast at the club when he had money, or at least to any society save that which he found at home. To lead a bear, as I did, was no very pleasant business to be sure; to wait in a bookseller's ante-room until it should please his honour to finish his dinner and give me audience, was sometimes a hard task for a man of my name and with my pride; but would I have exchanged my poverty against Castlewood's ignominy, or preferred his miserable dependence to my own? At least I earned my wage such as it was; and no man can say that I ever flattered my patrons or was servile to them; or indeed, in my dealings with them, was otherwise than sulky, overbearing, and, in a word, intolerable.

Now there was a certain person with whom Fate had thrown me into a life-partnership, who bore *her* poverty with such a smiling sweetness and easy grace, that niggard Fortune relented before her, and, like some savage Ogre in the fairy tales, melted at the constant goodness and cheerfulness of that uncomplaining, artless, innocent creature. However poor she was, all who knew her saw that here was a fine lady; and the little tradesmen and humble folks round about us treated her with as much respect as the richest of our neighbours. "I think, my dear," says good-natured Mrs. Foker, when they rode out in the latter's chariot, "you look like the mistress of the carriage, and I only as your maid." Our landladies adored her; the tradesfolk executed her little orders as eagerly as if a duchess gave them, or they were to make a fortune by waiting on her. I have

thought often of the lady in "Comus," and how, through all
the rout and rabble, she moves, entirely serene and pure.

Several times, as often as we chose indeed, the good-natured
parents of my young bear lent us their chariot to drive abroad
or to call on the few friends we had. If I must tell the truth,
we drove once to the "Protestant Hero" and had a syllabub
in the garden there; and the hostess would insist upon calling
my wife her Ladyship during the whole afternoon. We also
visited Mr. Johnson, and took tea with him (the ingenious Mr.
Goldsmith was of the company); the Doctor waited upon my
wife to her coach. But our most frequent visits were to Aunt
Bernstein, and I promise you I was not at all jealous because
my aunt presently professed to have a wonderful liking for
Theo.

This liking grew so that she would have her most days in
the week, or to stay altogether with her, and thought that
Theo's child and husband were only plagues to be sure, and
hated us in the most amusing way for keeping her favourite
from her. Not that my wife was unworthy of anybody's favour;
but her many forced absences, and the constant difficulty of
intercourse with her, raised my aunt's liking for a while to a
sort of passion. She poured in notes like love-letters; and her
people were ever about our kitchen. If my wife did not go to
her, she wrote heartrending appeals, and scolded me severely
when I saw her; and, the child being ill once (it hath pleased
Fate to spare our Captain to be a prodigious trouble to us, and
a wholesome trial for our tempers), Madam Bernstein came
three days running to Lambeth; vowed there was nothing the
matter with the baby;—nothing at all,—and that we only
pretended his illness, in order to vex her.

The reigning Countess of Castlewood was just as easy and
affable with her old aunt, as with other folks great and small.
"What *air* you all about, scraping and bowing to that old
woman, I can't tell noways!" her Ladyship would say. "She
a fine lady! Nonsense! She ain't no more fine than any other
lady: and I guess I'm as good as any of 'em with their high
heels and their grand airs! She a beauty once! Take away
her wig, and her rouge, and her teeth; and what becomes of
your beauty, I'd like to know! Guess you'd put it all in a
band-box, and there would be nothing left but a shrivelled old
woman!" And indeed the little homilist only spoke too truly.
All beauty must at last come to this complexion; and decay,
either under ground or on the tree. Here was old age, I fear,

without reverence. Here were grey hairs, that were hidden, or painted. The world was still here, and she tottering on it, and clinging to it with her crutch. For fourscore years she had moved on it, and eaten of the tree, forbidden and permitted. She had had beauty, pleasure, flattery: but what secret rages, disappointments, defeats, humiliations! what thorns under the roses! what stinging bees in the fruit! " You are not a beauty, my dear," she would say to my wife: " and may thank your stars that you are not." (If she contradicted herself in her talk, I suppose the rest of us occasionally do the like.) " Don't tell me that your husband is pleased with your face, and you want no one else's admiration! We all do. Every woman would rather be beautiful, than be anything else in the world—ever so rich, or ever so good, or have all the gifts of the fairies! Look at that picture, though I know 'tis but a bad one, and that stupid vapouring Kneller could not paint my eyes, nor my hair, nor my complexion. What a shape I had then—and look at me now, and this wrinkled old neck! Why have we such a short time of our beauty? I remember Mademoiselle de l'Enclos at a much greater age than mine, quite fresh and well-conserved. We can't hide our ages. They are wrote in Mr. Collins's books for us. I was born in the last year of King James's reign. I am not old yet. I am but seventy-six. But what a wreck, my dear: and isn't it cruel that our time should be so short? "

Here my wife has to state the incontrovertible proposition, that the time of all of us is short here below.

" Ha! " cries the Baroness. " Did not Adam live near a thousand years, and was not Eve beautiful all the time? I used to perplex Mr. Tusher with that—poor creature! What have we done since, that our lives are so much lessened, I say? "

" Has your life been so happy that you would prolong it ever so much more? " asks the Baroness's auditor. " Have you, who love wit, never read Dean Swift's famous description of the deathless people in ' Gulliver ' ? My papa and my husband say 'tis one of the finest and most awful sermons ever wrote. It were better not to live at all, than to live without love; and I'm sure," says my wife, putting her handkerchief to her eyes, " should anything happen to my dearest George, I would wish to go to heaven that moment."

" Who loves me in heaven? I am quite alone, child—that is why I had rather stay here," says the Baroness, in a frightened and rather piteous tone. " You are kind to me, God bless your sweet face! Though I scold, and have a frightful temper, my servants will do anything to make me comfortable, and get up at any hour of the night, and never say a cross word in answer. I like my cards still. Indeed, life would be a blank without 'em. Almost everything is gone except that. I can't eat my dinner now, since I lost those last two teeth. Everything goes away from us in old age. But I still have my cards—thank Heaven, I still have my cards! " And here she would begin to doze: waking up, however, if my wife stirred or rose, and imagining that Theo was about to leave her. " Don't go away, I can't bear to be alone. I don't want you to talk. But I like to see your face, my dear! It is much pleasanter than that horrid old Brett's, that I have had scowling about my bedroom these ever so long years."

" Well, Baroness! still at your cribbage? " (We may fancy a noble Countess interrupting a game at cards between Theo and Aunt Bernstein.) " Me and my Lord Esmond have come to see you! Go and shake hands with grand-aunt, Esmond, and tell her Ladyship that your Lordship's a good boy! "

" My Lordship's a good boy," says the child. (Madam Theo used to act these scenes for me in a very lively way.)

" And if he is, I guess he don't take after his father," shrieks out Lady Castlewood. She chose to fancy that Aunt Bernstein was deaf, and always bawled at the old lady.

" Your Ladyship chose my nephew for better or for worse," says Aunt Bernstein, who was now always very much flurried in the presence of the young Countess.

" But he is a precious deal worse than ever I thought he was. I am speaking of your pa, Ezzy. If it wasn't for your mother, my son, Lord knows what would become of you! We are a-going to see his little Royal Highness. Sorry to see your Ladyship not looking quite so well to-day. We can't always remain young; and la! how we *do* change as we grow old! Go up and kiss that lady, Ezzy. She has got a little boy, too. Why, bless us! have you got the child downstairs? " Indeed, Master Miles was down below, for special reasons accompanying his mother on her visits to Aunt Bernstein sometimes; and our aunt desired the mother's company so much, that she was actually fain to put up with the child. " So you have got the child here? Oh, you sly-boots! " says the Countess. " Guess you come after the old lady's money. La bless you! Don't look so frightened. She can't hear a single word I say. Come,

Ezzy. Good-bye, aunt!" And my Lady Countess rustles out of the room.

Did Aunt Bernstein hear her or not? Where was the wit for which the old lady had been long famous? and was that fire put out, as well as the brilliancy of her eyes? With other people she was still ready enough, and unsparing of her sarcasms. When the Dowager of Castlewood and Lady Fanny visited her (these exalted ladies treated my wife with perfect indifference and charming good-breeding)—the Baroness, in their society, was stately, easy, and even commanding. She would mischievously caress Mrs. Warrington before them; in her absence, vaunt my wife's good-breeding; say that her nephew had made a foolish match perhaps, but that I certainly had taken a charming wife. "In a word, I praise you so to them, my dear," says she, "that I think they would like to tear your eyes out." But before the little American 'tis certain that she was uneasy and trembled. She was so afraid, that she actually did not dare to deny her the door; and, the Countess's back turned, did not even abuse her. However much they might dislike her, my ladies did not tear out Theo's eyes. Once they drove to our cottage at Lambeth, where my wife happened to be sitting at the open window, holding her child on her knee, and in full view of her visitors. A gigantic footman strutted through our little garden, and delivered their Ladyships' visiting tickets at our door. Their hatred hurt us no more than their visit pleased us. When next we had the loan of our friend the brewer's carriage, Mrs. Warrington drove to Kensington, and Gumbo handed over to the giant our cards in return for those which his noble mistresses had bestowed on us.

The Baroness had a coach, but seldom thought of giving it to us; and would let Theo and her maid and baby start from Clarges Street in the rain, with a faint excuse that she was afraid to ask her coachman to take his horses out. But, twice on her return home, my wife was frightened by rude fellows on the other side of Westminster Bridge; and I fairly told my aunt that I should forbid Mrs. Warrington to go to her, unless she could be brought home in safety; so grumbling Jehu had to drive his horses through the darkness. He grumbled at my shillings: he did not know how few I had. Our poverty wore a pretty decent face. My relatives never thought of relieving it, nor I of complaining before them. I don't know how Sampson got a windfall of guineas; but, I remember, he brought me six once; and they were more welcome than any money I ever had in my life. He had been looking into Mr. Miles's crib, as the child lay asleep; and, when the parson went away, I found the money in the baby's little rosy hand. Yes, love is best of all. I have many such benefactions registered in my heart—precious welcome fountains springing up in desert places, kind friendly lights cheering our despondency and gloom.

This worthy divine was willing enough to give as much of his company as she chose to Madame de Bernstein, whether for cards or theology. Having known her Ladyship for many years now, Sampson could see, and averred to us, that she was breaking fast; and as he spoke of her evidently increasing infirmities, and of the probability of their fatal termination, Mr. S. would discourse to us in a very feeling manner of the necessity for preparing for a future world; of the vanities of this, and of the hope that in another there might be happiness for all repentant sinners.

" I have been a sinner for one," says the chaplain, bowing his head, " God knoweth, and I pray him to pardon me. I fear, sir, your aunt, the Lady Baroness, is not in such a state of mind as will fit her very well for the change which is imminent. I am but a poor weak wretch, and no prisoner in Newgate could confess that more humbly and heartily. Once or twice of late, I have sought to speak on this matter with her Ladyship, but she has received me very roughly. ' Parson,' says she, ' if you come for cards 'tis mighty well, but I will thank you to spare me your sermons.' What can I do, sir? I have called more than once of late, and Mr. Case hath told me his lady was unable to see me." In fact Madam Bernstein told my wife, whom she never refused, as I said, that the poor chaplain's *ton* was unendurable, and as for his theology, " Haven't I been a Bishop's wife? " says she, " and do I want this creature to teach me? "

The old lady was as impatient of doctors as of divines; pretending that my wife was ailing, and that it was more convenient for our good Doctor Heberden to visit her in Clarges Street than to travel all the way to our Lambeth lodgings, we got Dr. H. to see Theo at our aunt's house, and prayed him if possible to offer his advice to the Baroness: we made Mrs. Brett, her woman, describe her ailments, and the Doctor confirmed our opinion that they were most serious, and might speedily end. She would rally briskly enough of some evenings, and entertain a little company; but of late she scarcely went abroad at all. A somnolence, which we had remarked in her, was attributable in part to opiates which she was in the habit of taking; and she used these narcotics to smother habitual pain. One night, as we two sat with her (Mr. Miles was weaned by this time, and his mother could leave him to the charge of our faithful Molly), she fell asleep over her cards. We hushed the servants who came to lay out the supper-table (she would always have this luxurious, nor could any injunction of ours or the Doctor's teach her abstinence), and we sat a while as we had often done before, waiting in silence till she should arouse from her doze.

When she awoke, she looked fixedly at me for a while, fumbled with the cards, and dropped them again in her lap, and said, " Henry, have I been long asleep? " I thought at first that it was for my brother she mistook me; but she went on quickly, and with eyes fixed as upon some very far distant object, and said, " My dear, 'tis of no use, I am not good enough for you. I love cards and play, and Court; and oh, Harry, you don't know all! " Here her voice changed, and she flung her head up. " His father married Anne Hyde, and sure the Esmond blood is as good as any that's not Royal. Mamma, you must please to treat me with more respect. Vos sermons me fatiguent; entendez vous?—faites place à mon Altesse Royale: mesdames, me connaissez-vous? je suis la——" Here she broke out into frightful hysterical shrieks and laughter, and as we ran up to her alarmed, " Oui, Henri," she says, " il a juré de m'épouser, et les princes tiennent parole—n'est-ce pas? Oh oui! ils tiennent parole; si non, tu le tueras, cousin; tu le—ah! que je suis folle! " And the pitiful shrieks and laughter recommenced. Ere her frightened people had come up to her summons, the poor thing had passed out of this mood into another; but always labouring under the same delusion—that I was the Henry of past times, who had loved her and had been forsaken by her, whose bones were lying far away by the banks of the Potomac. My wife and the women put the poor lady to bed as I ran myself for medical aid. She rambled, still talking wildly, through the night, with her nurses and the surgeon sitting by her. Then she fell into a sleep, brought on by more opiate. When she awoke, her mind did not actually wander; but her speech was changed, and one arm and side were paralysed.

'Tis needless to relate the progress and termination of her malady, or watch that expiring flame of life as it gasps and flickers. Her senses would remain with her for awhile (and then she was never satisfied unless Theo was by her bedside), or again her mind would wander, and the poor decrepit creature, lying upon her bed, would imagine herself young again, and speak incoherently of the scenes and incidents of her early days. Then she would address me as Henry again, and call upon me to revenge some insult or slight, of which (whatever my suspicions might be) the only record lay in her insane memory. " They have always been so," she would murmur: " they never loved man or woman but they forsook them. Je me vengerai, oh oui, je me vengerai! I know them all: I know them all: and I will go to my Lord Stair with the list. Don't tell me! His religion can't be the right one. I will go back to my mother's, though she does not love me. She never did. Why don't you, mother? Is it because I am too wicked? Ah! pitié! pitié! O mon père! I will make my confession "—and here the unhappy paralysed lady made as if she would move in her bed.

Let us draw the curtain round it. I think with awe still of those rapid words, uttered in the shadow of the canopy, as my pallid wife sits by, her Prayer-book on her knee; as the attendants move to and fro noiselessly; as the clock ticks without, and strikes the fleeting hours; as the sun falls upon the Kneller picture of Beatrix in her beauty, with the blushing cheeks, the smiling lips, the wavering auburn tresses, and the eyes which seem to look towards the dim figure moaning in the bed. I could not for a while understand why our aunt's attendants were so anxious that we should quit it. But towards evening a servant stole in, and whispered her woman; and then Brett, looking rather disturbed, begged us to go downstairs, as the—as the Doctor was come to visit the Baroness. I did not tell my wife, at the time, who " the Doctor " was; but as the gentleman slid by us, and passed upstairs, I saw at once that he was a Catholic ecclesiastic. When Theo next saw our poor lady, she was speechless; she never recognised any one about her, and so passed unconsciously out of life. During her illness her relatives had called assiduously enough, though she would see none of them save us. But when she was gone, and we descended to the lower rooms after all was over, we found Castlewood with his white face, and my Lady from Kensington, and Mr. Will, already assembled in the parlour. They looked greedily at us as we appeared. They were hungry for the prey.

When our aunt's will was opened, we found it was dated five years back, and everything she had was left to her dear nephew,

Henry Esmond Warrington of Castlewood in Virginia, " in affectionate love and remembrance of the name which he bore." The property was not great. Her revenue had been derived from pensions from the Crown as it appeared (for what services I cannot say), but the pensions of course died with her, and there were only a few hundred pounds, besides jewels, trinkets, and the furniture of the house in Clarges Street, of which all London came to the sale. Mr. Walpole bid for her portrait, but I made free with Harry's money so far as to buy the picture in: and it now hangs over the mantelpiece of the chamber in which I write. What with jewels, laces, trinkets, and old china which she had gathered—Harry became possessed of more than four thousand pounds by his aunt's legacy. I made so free as to lay my hand upon a hundred, which came, just as my stock was reduced to twenty pounds; and I procured bills for the remainder, which I forwarded to Captain Henry Esmond in Virginia. Nor should I have scrupled to take more (for my brother was indebted to me in a much greater sum), but he wrote me there was another wonderful opportunity for buying an estate and negroes in our neighbourhood at home; and Theo and I were only too glad to forego our little claim, so as to establish our brother's fortune. As to mine, poor Harry at this time did not know the state of it. My mother had never informed him that she had ceased remitting to me. She helped him with a considerable sum, the result of her savings, for the purchase of his new estate; and Theo and I were most heartily thankful at his prosperity.

And how strange ours was! By what curious good fortune, as our purse was emptied, was it filled again! I had actually come to the end of our stock, when poor Sampson brought me his six pieces—and with these I was enabled to carry on, until my half-year's salary, as young Mr. Foker's Governor, was due: then Harry's hundred, on which I laid *main basse*, helped us over three months (we were behindhand with our rent, or the money would have lasted six good weeks longer): and when this was pretty near expended, what should arrive but a bill of exchange for a couple of hundred pounds from Jamaica, with ten thousand blessings from the dear friends there, and fond scolding from the General that we had not sooner told him of our necessity—of which he had only heard through our friend Mr. Foker, who spoke in such terms of Theo and myself as to make our parents more than ever proud of their children. Was my quarrel with my mother irreparable? Let me go to Jamaica.

There was plenty there for all, and employment which his Excellency as Governor would immediately procure for me. "Come to us!" writes Hetty. "Come to us!" writes Aunt Lambert. "Have my children been suffering poverty, and we rolling in our Excellency's coach, with guards to turn out whenever we pass? Has Charley been home to you for ever so many holidays, from the Chartreux, and had ever so many of my poor George's half-crowns in his pocket, I dare say?" (this was indeed the truth, for where was he to go for holidays but to his sister? and was there any use in telling the child how scarce half-crowns were with us?) "And you always treating him with such goodness, as his letters tell me, which are brimful of love for George and little Miles! Oh, how we long to see Miles!" wrote Hetty and her mother; "and *as for his godfather*" (writes Het), "who has been good to my dearest and her child, I promise him a kiss whenever I see him!"

Our young benefactor was never to hear of our family's love and gratitude to him. That glimpse of his bright face over the railings before our house at Lambeth, as he rode away on his little horse, was the last we ever were to have of him. At Christmas a basket comes to us, containing a great turkey, and three brace of partridges, with a card, and "*shot by M. W.*" wrote on one of them. And on receipt of this present, we wrote to thank the child, and gave him our sister's message.

To this letter there came a reply from Lady Warrington, who said she was bound to inform me, that in visiting me her child had been guilty of *disobedience,* and that she learned his visit to me now for the first time. Knowing *my* views regarding *duty to my parents* (which I had exemplified *in my marriage*), she could not wish her son to adopt them. And fervently hoping that I might be brought to see the errors *of my present course,* she took leave *of this most unpleasant subject,* subscribing herself, etc., etc. And we got this pretty missive as sauce for poor Miles's turkey, which was our family feast for New Year's day. My Lady Warrington's letter choked our meal, though Sampson and Charley rejoiced over it.

Ah me! Ere the month was over, our little friend was gone from amongst us. Going out shooting, and dragging his gun through a hedge after him, the trigger caught in a bush, and the poor little man was brought home to his father's house, only to live a few days and expire in pain and torture. Under the yew-trees yonder, I can see the vault which covers him, and where my bones one day no doubt will be laid. And over our

pew at church my children have often wistfully spelt the
touching epitaph in which Miles's heartbroken father has
inscribed his grief and love for his only son.

CHAPTER LXXXIV

IN WHICH HARRY SUBMITS TO THE COMMON LOT

HARD times were now over with me, and I had to battle with
poverty no more. My little kinsman's death made a vast
difference in my worldly prospects. I became next heir to a
good estate. My uncle and his wife were not likely to have
more children. "The woman is capable of committing any
crime to disappoint you," Sampson vowed; but, in truth, my
Lady Warrington was guilty of no such treachery. Cruelly
smitten by the stroke which fell upon them, Lady Warrington
was taught by her religious advisers to consider it as a chastisement of Heaven, and submit to the Divine Will. "Whilst your
son lived, your heart was turned away from the better world"
(her clergyman told her), "and your Ladyship thought too
much of this. For your son's advantage you desired rank and
title. You asked and might have obtained an earthly coronet.
Of what avail is it now, to one who has but a few years to pass
upon earth—of what importance compared to the heavenly
crown, for which you are an assured candidate?" The accident
caused no little sensation. In the chapels of that enthusiastic
sect, towards which, after her son's death, she now more than
ever inclined, many sermons were preached bearing reference
to the event. Far be it from me to question the course which
the bereaved mother pursued, or to regard with other than
respect and sympathy any unhappy soul seeking that refuge
whither sin and grief and disappointment fly for consolation.
Lady Warrington even tried a reconciliation with myself. A
year after her loss, being in London, she signified that she would
see me, and I waited on her; and she gave me, in her usual
didactic way, a homily upon my position and her own. She
marvelled at the decree of Heaven, which had permitted, and
how dreadfully punished! her poor child's disobedience to her
—a disobedience by which I was to profit. (It appeared my
poor little man had disobeyed orders, and gone out with his
gun, unknown to his mother.) She hoped that, should I ever

succeed to the property, though the Warringtons were, thank Heaven, a long-lived family, except in my own father's case, whose life had been curtailed by the excesses of a very ill-regulated youth,—but should I ever succeed to the family estate and honours, she hoped, she prayed, that my present course of life might be altered; that I should part from my unworthy associates; that I should discontinue all connection with the horrid theatre and its licentious frequenters; that I should turn to that quarter where only peace was to be had; and to those sacred duties which she feared—she very much feared—that I had neglected. She filled her exhortation with Scripture language, which I do not care to imitate. When I took my leave she gave me a packet of sermons for Mrs. Warrington, and a little book of hymns by Miss Dora, who has been eminent in that society of which she and her mother became avowed professors subsequently, and who, after the Dowager's death, at Bath, three years since, married young Mr. Juffles, a celebrated preacher. The poor lady forgave me then, but she could not bear the sight of our boy. We lost our second child, and then my aunt and her daughter came eagerly enough to the poor suffering mother, and even invited us hither. But my uncle was now almost every day in our house. He would sit for hours looking at our boy. He brought him endless toys and sweetmeats. He begged that the child might call him Godpapa. When we felt our own grief, (which at times still, and after the lapse of five-and-twenty years, strikes me as keenly as on the day when we first lost our little one)—when I felt my own grief I knew how to commiserate his. But my wife could pity him before she knew what it was to lose a child of her own. The mother's anxious heart had already divined the pang which was felt by the sorrow-stricken father; mine, more selfish, has only learned pity from experience, and I was reconciled to my uncle by my little baby's coffin.

The poor man sent his coach to follow the humble funeral, and afterwards took out little Miles, who prattled to him unceasingly, and forgot any grief he might have felt in the delights of his new black clothes, and the pleasures of the airing. How the innocent talk of the child stabbed the mother's heart! Would we ever wish that it should heal of that wound? I know her face so well that, to this day, I can tell when, sometimes, she is thinking of the loss of that little one. It is not a grief for a parting so long ago; it is a communion with a soul we love in heaven.

We came back to our bright lodgings in Bloomsbury soon afterwards, and my young bear, whom I could no longer lead, and who had taken a prodigious friendship for Charley, went to the Chartreux School, where his friend took care that he had no more beating than was good for him, and where (in consequence of the excellence of his private tutor, no doubt) he took and kept a good place. And he liked the school so much, that he says, if ever he has a son, he shall be sent to that seminary.

Now, I could no longer lead my bear, for this reason, that I had other business to follow. Being fully reconciled to us, I do believe, for Mr. Miles's sake, my uncle (who was such an obsequious supporter of Government, that I wonder the Minister ever gave him anything, being perfectly sure of his vote) used his influence in behalf of his nephew and heir; and I had the honour to be gazetted as one of His Majesty's Commissioners for licensing hackney-coaches, a post I filled, I trust, with credit, until a quarrel with the Minister (to be mentioned in its proper place) deprived me of *that* one. I took my degree also at the Temple, and appeared in Westminster Hall in my gown and wig. And, this year, my good friend, Mr. Foker, having business at Paris, I had the pleasure of accompanying him thither, where I was received *à bras ouverts* by my dear American preserver, Monsieur de Florac, who introduced me to his noble family, and to even more of the polite society of the capital than I had leisure to frequent; for I had too much spirit to desert my kind patron Foker, whose acquaintance lay chiefly amongst the bourgeoisie, especially with Monsieur Santerre, a great brewer of Paris, a scoundrel who hath since distinguished himself in blood and not beer. Mr. F. had need of my services as interpreter, and I was too glad that he should command them, and to be able to pay back some of the kindness which he had rendered to me. Our ladies, meanwhile, were residing at Mr. Foker's new villa at Wimbledon, and were pleased to say that they were amused with the " Parisian letters " which I sent to them through my distinguished friend Mr. Hume, then of the Embassy, and which subsequently have been published in a neat volume.

Whilst I was tranquilly discharging my small official duties in London, those troubles were commencing which were to end in the great separation between our colonies and the mother country. When Mr. Grenville proposed his Stamp duties, I said to my wife that the Bill would create a mighty discontent at home, for we were ever anxious to get as much as we could from England, and pay back as little; but assuredly I never anticipated the prodigious anger which the scheme created. It was with us as with families or individuals. A pretext is given for a quarrel; the real cause lies in long bickerings and previous animosities. Many foolish exactions and petty tyrannies, the habitual insolence of Englishmen towards all foreigners, all colonists, all folk who dare to think their rivers as good as our Abana and Pharpar; the natural spirit of men outraged by our imperious domineering spirit, set Britain and her colonies to quarrel; and the astonishing blunders of the system adopted in England brought the quarrel to an issue, which I, for one, am not going to deplore. Had I been in Virginia instead of London, 'tis very possible I should have taken the provincial side, if out of mere opposition to that resolute mistress of Castlewood, who might have driven me into revolt, as England did the Colonies. Was the Stamp Act the cause of the revolution?—a tax no greater than that cheerfully paid in England. Ten years earlier, when the French were within our territory, and we were imploring succour from home, would the colonies have rebelled at the payment of this tax? Do not most people consider the tax-gatherer their natural enemy? Against the British in America there were arrayed thousands and thousands of the high-spirited and brave, but there were thousands more who found their profit in the quarrel, or had their private reasons for engaging in it. I protest I don't know now whether mine were selfish or patriotic, or which side was the right, or whether both were not? I am sure we in England had nothing to do but to fight the battle out; and, having lost the game, I do vow and believe that, after the first natural soreness, the loser felt no rancour.

What made brother Hal write home from Virginia, which he seemed exceedingly loth to quit, such flaming patriotic letters? My kind best brother was always led by somebody; by me when we were together (he had such an idea of my wit and wisdom, that if I said the day was fine, he would ponder over the observation as though it was one of the sayings of the Seven Sages), by some other wiseacre when I was away. Who inspired these flaming letters, this boisterous patriotism, which he sent to us in London? " He is rebelling against Madam Esmond," said I. " He is led by some colonial person—by that lady, perhaps," hinted my wife. Who " that lady " was Hal never had told us; and, indeed, besought me never to allude

to the delicate subject in my letters to him; " for Madam wishes
to see 'em all, and I wish to say nothing *about you know what*
until the proper moment," he wrote. No affection could be
greater than that which his letters showed. When he heard
(from the informant whom I have mentioned) that in the midst
of my own extreme straits I had retained no more than a hundred
pounds out of his aunt's legacy, he was for mortgaging the
estate which he had just bought; and had more than one
quarrel with his mother in my behalf, and spoke his mind with a
great deal more frankness than I should ever have ventured to
show. Until her angry recriminations (when she charged him
with ingratitude, after having toiled and saved so much and so
long for him) the poor fellow did not know that our mother had
cut off my supplies, to advance his interests; and by the time
this news came to him his bargains were made, and I was
fortunately quite out of want.

Every scrap of paper which we ever wrote, our thrifty parent
at Castlewood taped and docketed and put away. We boys
were more careless about our letters to one another: I especially,
who perhaps chose rather to look down upon my younger
brother's literary performances; but my wife is not so supercilious, and hath kept no small number of Harry's letters, as
well as those of the angelic being whom we were presently to
call sister.

" To think whom he has chosen, and whom he might have
had! Oh, 'tis cruel!" cries my wife, when we got that notable
letter in which Harry first made us acquainted with the name of
his charmer.

" She was a very pretty little maid when I left home, she may
be a perfect beauty now," I remarked, as I read over the longest
letter Harry ever wrote on private affairs.

" But is she to compare to my Hetty?" says Mrs. Warrington.

" We agreed that Hetty and Harry were not to be happy
together, my love," say I.

Theo gives her husband a kiss. " My dear, I wish they had
tried," she says, with a sigh. " I was afraid lest—lest Hetty
should have led him, you see; and I think she hath the better
head. But, from reading this, it appears that the new lady has
taken command of poor Harry," and she hands me the letter:—

" My dearest George hath been prepared by previous letters to
understand how a certain lady has made a conquest of my heart,
which I have given away in exchange for something infinitely more

valuable, *namely, her own.* She is at my side as I write this letter, and if there is no bad spelling such as you often used to laugh at, 'tis because I have my pretty dictionary at hand, which makes no fault in the longest word, nor *in anything* else I know of: being of opinion that she is *perfection.*

" As Madam Esmond saw all your letters, I writ you not to give any hint of a certain delicate matter—but now *'tis no secret,* and is known to all the country. Mr. George is not the only one of our family who has made a secret marriage, and been scolded by his mother. As a dutiful younger brother I *have followed his example ;* and now I may tell you how this mighty event came about.

" I had not been at home long before I saw *my fate was accomplisht.* I will not tell you how beautiful Miss Fanny Mountain had grown since I had been away in Europe. She saith, ' You *never will think so,*' and I am glad, as she is the only thing in life I would grudge to my dearest brother.

" That neither Madam Esmond nor my *other* mother (as Mountain is now) should have seen our mutual attachment, is a wonder —only to be accounted for by supposing that love makes other folks blind. Mine for my Fanny was increased by seeing what the treatment was she had from Madam Esmond, who indeed was very rough and haughty with her, which my love bore with a sweetness perfectly angelic (this I will say, though she will order me not to write any such nonsense). She was scarce better treated than a servant of the house—indeed our negroes can talk much more free before Madam Esmond than ever my Fanny could.

" And yet my Fanny says she doth not regret Madam's unkindness, as without it I possibly never should have been what I am to her. Oh, dear brother! when I remember how great your goodness hath been, how, in my own want, you paid my debts, and rescued me out of prison; how you have been living in poverty which never need have occurred but for my fault; how you might have paid yourself back my just debt to you and would not, preferring my advantage to your own comfort, indeed I am lost at the thought of such goodness; and ought I not to be thankful to Heaven that hath given me such a wife and such a brother!

" When I writ to you requesting you to send me my aunt's legacy money, for which indeed I had the most profitable and urgent occasion, I had no idea that you were yourself suffering poverty. That you, the head of our family, should condescend to be governor to a brewer's son!—that you should have to write for booksellers (except in so far as your own genius might prompt you), never once entered my mind, until Mr. Foker's letter came to us, and this would never have been shown—for Madam kept it secret—had it not been for the difference which sprang up between us.

" Poor Tom Diggle's estate and negroes being for sale, owing to Tom's losses and extravagance at play, and his father's debts before him—Madam Esmond saw here was a great opportunity of making a provision for me, and that with six thousand pounds for the farm and stock, I should be put in possession of as pretty a property as falls to most younger sons in this country. It lies handy enough to Richmond, between Kent and Hanover Court House—the mansion nothing for elegance compared to ours at Castlewood, but the land excellent and the people extraordinary healthy.

" Here was a second opportunity, Madam Esmond said, such as never might again befall. By the sale of my commissions and her own savings I might pay more than half of the price of the property, and get the rest of the money on mortgage; though here, where money is scarce to procure, it would have been difficult and dear. At this juncture, with our new relative, Mr. Van den Bosch, bidding against us (his agent is wild that we should have bought the property over him), my aunt's legacy most opportunely fell in. And now I am owner of a good house and negroes in my native country, shall be called, no doubt, to our House of Burgesses, and hope to see my dearest brother and family under my own roof-tree. To sit at my own fireside, to ride my own horses to my own hounds, is better than going a-soldiering, now war is over, and there are no French to fight. Indeed, Madam Esmond made a condition that I should leave the army, and live at home, when she brought me her £1750 of savings. She had lost one son, she said, who chose to write play-books, and live in England—let the other stay with her at home.

" But after the purchase of the estate was made, and my papers for selling out were sent home, my mother would have had me marry a person of *her* choosing, but by no means of mine. You remember Miss Betsy Pitts at Williamsburg? She is in nowise improved by having had her face dreadfully scarred with small-pock, and though Madam Esmond saith the young lady hath every virtue, I own her virtues did not suit me. Her eyes do not look straight; she hath one leg shorter than another; and oh, brother! didst thou never remark Fanny's ankles when we were boys? *Neater I never saw at the Opera.*

" Now, when 'twas agreed that I should leave the army, a certain dear girl (canst thou guess her name?) one day, when we were private, burst into tears of such happiness, that I could not but feel immensely touched by her sympathy.

" ' Ah! ' says she, ' do you think, sir, that the idea of the son of my revered benefactress going to battle doth not inspire me with terror? Ah, Mr. Henry! do you imagine I have no heart? When Mr. George was with Braddock, do you fancy we did not pray for him? And when you were with Mr. Wolfe—oh! '

" Here the dear creature hid her eyes in her handkerchief, and had hard work to prevent her mamma, who came in, from seeing that she was crying. But my dear Mountain declares that, though she might have fancied, might have prayed in secret for such a thing (she owns to that now), she never imagined it for one moment. Nor, indeed, did my good mother, who supposed that Sam Lintot, the apothecary's lad at Richmond, was Fanny's flame—an absurd fellow that I near kicked into James River.

" But when the commission was sold, and the estate bought, what does Fanny do but fall into a deep melancholy? I found her crying, one day, in her mother's room, where the two ladies had been at work trimming hats for my negroes.

" ' What! crying, miss? ' says I. ' Has my mother been scolding you? '

" ' No,' says the dear creature. ' Madam Esmond has been kind to-day.'

" And her tears drop down on a cockade which she is sewing on to a hat for Sady, who is to be head groom.

" ' Then why, miss, are those dear eyes so red? ' say I.

" ' Because I have the toothache,' she says, ' or because—because I am a fool.' Here she fairly bursts out. ' Oh, Mr. Harry! oh, Mr. Warrington! You are going to leave us, and 'tis as well. You will take your place in your country, as becomes you. You will leave us poor women in our solitude and dependence. You will come to visit us from time to time. And when you are happy, and honoured, and among your gay companions, you will remember your——'

" Here she could say no more, and hid her face with one hand as I, I confess, seized the other.

" ' Dearest, sweetest Miss Mountain! ' says I. ' Oh, could I think that the parting from me has brought tears to those lovely eyes! Indeed, I fear, I should be almost happy! Let them look upon your——'

" ' Oh, sir! ' cries my charmer. ' Oh, Mr. Warrington! consider who I am, sir, and who you are! Remember the difference between us! Release my hand, sir! What would Madam Esmond say if—if——'

" If what, I don't know, for here our mother was in the room.

" ' What would Madam Esmond say? ' she cries out. ' She would say that you are an ungrateful, artful, false little——'

" ' Madam! ' says I.

" ' Yes, an ungrateful, artful, false little wretch! ' cries out my mother. ' For shame, miss! What would Mr. Lintot say if he saw you making eyes at the Captain? And for you, Harry, I will have you bring none of your garrison manners hither. This is a Christian family, sir, and you will please to know that my house is not intended for captains and their misses! '

" ' Misses, mother! ' says I. ' Gracious powers, do you ever venture for to call Miss Mountain by such a name? Miss Mountain, the purest of her sex! '

" ' The purest of her sex! Can I trust my own ears? ' asks Madam, turning very pale.

" ' I mean that if a man would question her honour, I would fling him out of window,' says I.

" ' You mean that you—your mother's son—are actually paying honourable attentions to this young person? '

" ' He would never dare offer any other! ' cries my Fanny; ' nor any woman but you, madam, to think so! '

" ' Oh! I didn't know, miss! ' says mother, dropping her a fine curtsey, ' I didn't know the honour you were doing our family! You propose to marry with us, do you? Do I understand Captain Warrington aright, that he intends to offer me Miss Mountain as a daughter-in-law? '

" ' 'Tis to be seen, madam, that I have no protector, or you would not insult me so! ' cries my poor victim.

" ' I should think the apothecary protection sufficient!' says our mother.

" ' I don't, mother!' I bawled out, for I was very angry; ' and if Lintot offers her any liberty, I'll brain him with his own pestle!'

" ' Oh! if Lintot has withdrawn, sir, I suppose I must be silent. But I did not know of the circumstance. He came hither, as I supposed, to pay court to Miss: and we all thought the match equal, and I encouraged it.'

" ' He came because I had the toothache!' cries my darling. (And indeed she had *a dreadful bad* tooth. And he took it out for her, and there is no end to the suspicions and calumnies of women.)

" ' What more natural than that he should marry my house-keeper's daughter — 'twas a very suitable match!' continues Madam, taking snuff. ' But I confess,' she adds, going on, ' I was not aware that you intended to jilt the apothecary for my son!'

" ' Peace, for Heaven's sake; peace, Mr. Warrington!' cries my angel.

" ' Pray, sir, before you fully make up your mind, had you not better look round the rest of my family?' says Madam. ' Dinah is a fine tall girl, and not very black; Cleopatra is promised to Ajax the blacksmith, to be sure; but then we could break the marriage, you know. If with an apothecary, why not with a blacksmith? Martha's husband has run away, and——'

" Here, dear brother, I own I broke out swearing. I can't help it; but at times, when a man is angry, it *do* relieve him immensely. I'm blest but I should have gone wild, if it hadn't been for them oaths.

" ' Curses, blasphemy, ingratitude, disobedience,' says mother, leaning now on her tortoiseshell stick, and then waving it—something like a queen in a play. ' These are my rewards!' says she. ' O Heaven, what have I done, that I should merit this awful punishment? and does it please you to visit the sins of my fathers upon me? Where do my children inherit their pride? When I was young, had I any? When my papa bade me marry, did I refuse? Did I ever think of disobeying? No, sir. My fault hath been, and I own it, that my love was centred upon you, perhaps to the neglect of your elder brother.' (Indeed, brother, there was some truth in what Madam said.) ' I turned from Esau, and I clung to Jacob. And now I have my reward, I have my reward! I fixed my vain thoughts on this world and its distinctions. To see my son advanced in worldly rank was my ambition. I toiled, and spared, that I might bring him worldly wealth. I took unjustly from my eldest son's portion, that my younger might profit. And oh! that I should live to see him seducing the daughter of my own housekeeper under 'my own roof, and replying to my just anger with oaths and blasphemies!'

" ' I try to seduce no one, madam,' I cried out. ' If I utter oaths and blasphemies, I beg your pardon; but you are enough to provoke a saint to speak 'em. I won't have this young lady's character assailed—no, not by my own mother nor any mortal alive. No, dear Miss Mountain! If Madam Esmond chooses to say that my designs on you are dishonourable,—let this undeceive her!' And, as I spoke, I went down on my knees, seizing my adorable Fanny's hand. ' And if you will accept this heart and hand, miss,' says I, ' they are yours for ever.'

" ' *You*, at least, I knew, sir,' says Fanny with a noble curtsey, ' never said a word that was disrespectful to me, or entertained any doubt of my honour. And I trust it is only Madam Esmond, in the world, who can have such an opinion of me. After what your Ladyship hath said of me, of course I can stay no longer in your house.'

" ' Of course, madam, I never intended you should; and the sooner you leave it the better,' cries our mother.

" ' If you are driven from my mother's house, mine, miss, is at your service,' says I, making her a low bow. ' It is nearly ready now. If you will take it and stay in it for ever, it is yours! And as Madam Esmond insulted your honour, at least let me do all in my power to make a reparation!' I don't know what more I exactly said, for you may fancy I was not a little flustered and excited by the scene. But here Mountain came in, and my dearest Fanny, flinging herself into her mother's arms, wept upon her shoulder; whilst Madam Esmond, sitting down in her chair, looked at us as pale as a stone. Whilst I was telling my story to Mountain (who, poor thing, had not the least idea, not she, that Miss Fanny and I had the slightest inclination for one another), I could hear our mother once or twice still saying, ' I am punished for my crime!'

" Now, what our mother meant by her crime I did not know at first, or indeed take much heed of what she said; for you know her way, and how, when she is angry, she always talks sermons. But Mountain told me afterwards, when we had some talk together, as we did at the tavern, whither the ladies presently removed with their bag and baggage—for not only would they not stay at Madam's house after the language she used, but my mother determined to go away likewise. She called her servants together, and announced her intention of going home instantly to Castlewood; and I own to you 'twas with a horrible pain I saw the family coach roll by, with six horses, and ever so many of the servants on mules and on horseback, as I and Fanny looked through the blinds of the tavern.

" After the words Madam used to my spotless Fanny, 'twas impossible that the poor child or her mother should remain in our house: and indeed M. said that she would go back to her relations in England: and, a ship bound homewards lying in James River, she went and bargained with the captain about a passage, so bent was she upon quitting the country, and so little did *she* think of making a match between me and my angel. But the cabin was mercifully engaged by a North Carolina gentleman and his family, and before the next ship sailed (which bears this letter to my dear George) they have agreed to stop with me. Almost all the ladies in this neighbourhood have waited on them. When the marriage takes place, I hope Madam Esmond will be reconciled. My Fanny's father was a British officer; and, sure, ours was no more. Some day, please Heaven, we shall visit Europe, and the places where *my wild oats* were sown, and where I committed so many extravagances from which my dear brother rescued me.

" The ladies send you their affection and duty, and to my sister.

We hear His Excellency General Lambert is much beloved in Jamaica: and I shall write to our dear friends there *announcing my happiness*. My dearest brother will participate in it, and I am ever his grateful and affectionate   H. E. W.

"*P.S.*—Till Mountain told me, I had no more notion than the *ded* that Madam E. had actially stopt your allowances; besides making you pay for ever so much—near upon £1000 Mountain says—for goods, etc., provided for the Virginian *proparty*. Then there was all the charges of me *out of prison*, which *I. O. U. with all my hart*. Draw upon me, please, dearest brother—*to any amount*—adressing me to care of Messrs. Horn and Sandon, Williamsburg, *privit ;* who remitt by present occasion a bill for £225, payable by their London agents on demand. *Please don't acknolledge this in answering :* as there's no good in *botharing women with accounts :* and with the extra £5 by a capp or what she likes for my dear sister, and a toy for my nephew from *Uncle Hal.*"

The conclusion to which we came on the perusal of this document was, that the ladies had superintended the style and spelling of my poor Hal's letter, but that the postscript was added without their knowledge. And I am afraid we argued that the Virginian Squire was under female domination—as Hercules, Samson, and *fortes multi* had been before him.

CHAPTER LXXXV

INVENI PORTUM

WHEN my mother heard of my acceptance of a place at home, I think she was scarcely well pleased. She may have withdrawn her supplies in order to starve me into a surrender, and force me to return with my family to Virginia, and to dependence under her. We never, up to her dying day, had any explanation on the pecuniary dispute between us. She cut off my allowances: I uttered not a word; but managed to live without her aid. I never heard that she repented of her injustice, or acknowledged it, except from Harry's private communication to me. In after days, when we met, by a great gentleness in her behaviour, and an uncommon respect and affection shown to my wife, Madam Esmond may have intended I should understand her tacit admission that she had been wrong; but she made no apology, nor did I ask one. Harry being provided for (whose welfare I could not grudge), all my mother's savings and economical schemes went to my advantage, who was her heir. Time was when a few guineas would have been more useful to me than hundreds which might come to me when I had no need; but when Madam Esmond and I met, the period of necessity was long passed away; I had no need to scheme ignoble savings, or to grudge the doctor his fee: I had plenty, and she could but bring me more. No doubt she suffered in her own mind to think that my children had been hungry, and she had offered them no food; and that strangers had relieved the necessity from which her proud heart had caused her to turn aside. Proud? Was she prouder than I? A soft word of explanation between us might have brought about a reconciliation years before it came: but I would never speak, nor did she. When I commit a wrong, and know it subsequently, I love to ask pardon; but 'tis as a satisfaction to my own pride, and to myself I am apologising for having been wanting to myself. And hence, I think (out of regard to that personage of *ego*), I scarce ever could degrade myself to do a meanness. How do men feel whose whole lives (and many men's lives are) are lies, schemes, and subterfuges? What sort of company do they keep when they are alone? Daily in life I watch men whose every smile is an artifice, and every wink an hypocrisy. Doth such a fellow wear a mask in his own privacy, and to his own conscience? If I choose to pass over an injury, I fear 'tis not from a Christian and forgiving spirit: 'tis because I can afford to remit the debt, and disdain to ask a settlement of it. One or two sweet souls I have known in my life (and perhaps tried) to whom forgiveness is no trouble,—a plant that grows naturally, as it were, in the soil. I know how to remit, I say, not forgive. I wonder are we proud men proud of being proud?

So I showed not the least sign of submission towards my parent in Virginia yonder, and we continued for years to live in estrangement, with occasionally a brief word or two (such as the announcement of the birth of a child, or what not) passing between my wife and her. After our first troubles in America about the Stamp Act, troubles fell on me in London likewise. Though I have been on the Tory side in our quarrel (as indeed upon the losing side in most controversies), having no doubt that the Imperial Government had a full right to levy taxes in the colonies, yet at the time of the dispute I must publish a pert letter to a member of the House of Burgesses in Virginia, in which the question of the habitual insolence of the mother country to the colonies was so freely handled, and sentiments were uttered so disagreeable to persons in power, that I was deprived of my place as hackney-coach licenser, to the terror and horror of my uncle, who never could be brought to love people in disgrace. He had grown to have an extreme affection for my wife as well as my little boy; but towards myself, personally, entertained a kind of pitying contempt which always infinitely amused me. He had a natural scorn and dislike for poverty, and a corresponding love for success and good fortune. Any opinion departing at all from the regular track shocked and frightened him, and all truth-telling made him turn pale. He must have had originally some warmth of heart and genuine love of kindred: for, spite of the dreadful shocks I gave him, he continued to see Theo and the child (and me too, giving me a mournful recognition when we met); and though broken-hearted by my free-spokenness, he did not refuse to speak to me as he had done at the time of our first differences, but looked upon me as a melancholy lost creature, who was past all worldly help or hope. Never mind, I must cast about for some new scheme of life; and the repayment of Harry's debt to me at this juncture enabled me to live at least for some months, or even years to come. O strange fatuity of youth! I often say. How was it that we dared to be so poor and so little cast down?

At this time His Majesty's Royal uncle of Cumberland fell down and perished in a fit; and, strange to say, his death occasioned a remarkable change in my fortune. My poor Sir Miles Warrington never missed any Court ceremony to which he could introduce himself. He was at all the drawing-rooms, christenings, balls, funerals of the Court. If ever a prince or princess was ailing, his coach was at their door: Leicester Fields, Carlton House, Gunnersbury, were all the same to him, and nothing must satisfy him now but going to the stout Duke's funeral. He caught a great cold and an inflammation of the throat from standing bareheaded at this funeral in the rain; and one morning, before almost I had heard of his illness, a lawyer waits upon me at my lodgings in Bloomsbury, and salutes me by the name of Sir George Warrington.

Poverty and fear of the future were over now. We laid the poor gentleman by the side of his little son, in the family churchyard where so many of his race repose. Little Miles and I were the chief mourners. An obsequious tenantry bowed and curtseyed before us, and did their utmost to conciliate my honour and my worship. The Dowager and her daughter with-

drew to Bath presently; and I and my family took possession
of the house, of which I have been master for thirty years. Be
not too eager, O my son! Have but a little patience, and I too
shall sleep under yonder yew-trees, and the people will be tossing
up their caps for Sir Miles.

The records of a prosperous country life are easily and briefly
told. The steward's books show what rents were paid and forgiven, what crops were raised, and in what rotation. What
visitors came to us, and how long they stayed: what pensioners
my wife had, and how they were doctored and relieved, and how
they died: what year I was sheriff, and how often the hounds
met near us: all these are narrated in our house-journals, which
any of my heirs may read who choose to take the trouble. We
could not afford the fine mansion in Hill Street, which my pre-
decessor had occupied; but we took a smaller house, in which,
however, we spent more money. We made not half the show
(with liveries, equipages, and plate) for which my uncle had been
famous; but our beer was stronger, and my wife's charities
were perhaps more costly than those of the Dowager Lady
Warrington. No doubt she thought there was no harm in
spoiling the Philistines; for she made us pay unconscionably
for the goods she left behind her in our country-house, and I
submitted to most of her extortions with unutterable good-
humour. What a value she imagined the potted plants in her
green-houses bore! What a price she set upon that horrible
old spinet she left in her drawing-room! And the framed pieces
of worsted-work, performed by the accomplished Dora and the
lovely Flora, had they been masterpieces of Titian or Vandyck,
to be sure my Lady Dowager could hardly have valued them
at a higher price. But though we paid so generously, though
we were, I may say without boast, far kinder to our poor than
ever she had been, for a while we had the very worst reputation
in the county, where all sorts of stories had been told to my
discredit. I thought I might perhaps succeed to my uncle's
seat in Parliament, as well as to his landed property; but I
found, I knew not how, that I was voted to be a person of very
dangerous opinions. I would not bribe. I would not coerce my
own tenants to vote for me in the election of '68. A gentleman
came down from Whitehall with a pocket-book full of bank-notes;
and I found that I had no chance against my competitor.

Bon Dieu! Now that we were at ease in respect of worldly
means—now that obedient tenants bowed and curtseyed as we
went to church; that we drove to visit our friends, or to the

neighbouring towns, in the great family coach with the four fat
horses; did we not often regret poverty, and the dear little
cottage at Lambeth, where Want was ever prowling at the
door? Did I not long to be bear-leading again, and vow that
translating for booksellers was not such very hard drudgery?
When we went to London, we made sentimental pilgrimages to
all our old haunts. I dare say my wife embraced all her landladies. You may be sure we asked all the friends of those old
times to share the comforts of our new home with us. The
Reverend Mr. Hagan and his lady visited us more than once.
His appearance in the pulpit at B—— (where he preached very
finely, as we thought) caused an awful scandal there. Sampson
came too, another unlucky Levite, and was welcome as long as
he would stay among us. Mr. Johnson talked of coming, but
he put us off once or twice. I suppose our house was dull.
I know that I myself would be silent for days, and fear that
my moodiness must often have tried the sweetest-tempered
woman in the world who lived with me. I did not care for field
sports. The killing one partridge was so like killing another,
that I wondered how men could pass days after days in the
pursuit of that kind of slaughter. Their fox-hunting stories
would begin at four o'clock, when the table-cloth was removed,
and last till supper-time. I sat silent, and listened: day after
day I fell asleep: no wonder I was not popular with my company.

What admission is this I am making? Here was the storm
over, the rocks avoided, the ship in port, and the sailor not
over-contented! Was Susan I had been sighing for during the
voyage, not the beauty I expected to find her? In the first
place, Susan and all the family can look in her William's log-
book, and so, madam, I am not going to put my secrets down
there. No, Susan, I never had secrets from thee. I never cared
for another woman. I have seen more beautiful, but none that
suited me as well as your Ladyship. I have met Mrs. Carter
and Miss Mulso, and Mrs. Thrale and Madam Kaufmann, and
the angelic Gunnings, and her Grace of Devonshire, and a host
of beauties who were not angelic by any means; and I was not
dazzled by them. Nay, young folks, I may have led your
mother a weary life, and been a very Blue-beard over her, but
then I had no other heads in the closet. Only, the first pleasure
of taking possession of our kingdom over, I own I began to be
quickly tired of the crown. When the Captain wears it, His
Majesty will be a very different Prince. He can ride a-hunting
five days in the week, and find the sport amusing. I believe

he would hear the same sermon at church fifty times, and not yawn more than I do at the first delivery. But sweet Joan, beloved Baucis! being thy faithful husband and true lover always, thy Darby is rather ashamed of having been testy so often; and, being arrived at the consummation of happiness, Philemon asks pardon for falling asleep so frequently after dinner. There came a period of my life when, having reached the summit of felicity, I was quite tired of the prospect I had there: I yawned in Eden, and said, " Is this all? What, no lions to bite? no rain to fall? no thorns to prick you in the rose-bush when you sit down?—only Eve, for ever sweet and tender, and figs for breakfast, dinner, supper, from week's end to week's end!" Shall I make my confessions? Hearken! Well, then, if I must make a clean breast of it.

.   .   .   .

[Here three pages are torn out of Sir George Warrington's MS. book, for which the Editor is sincerely sorry.]

I know the theory and practice of the Roman Church; but, being bred of another persuasion (and sceptical and heterodox regarding that), I can't help doubting the other, too, and wondering whether Catholics, in their confessions, confess all? Do we Protestants ever do so; and has education rendered those other fellow-men so different from us? At least, amongst us, we are not accustomed to suppose Catholic priests or laymen more frank and open than ourselves. Which brings me back to my question,—does any man confess all? Does yonder dear creature know all my life who has been the partner of it for thirty years; who, whenever I have told her a sorrow, has been ready with the best of her gentle power to soothe it; who has watched when I did not speak, and when I was silent has been silent herself, or with the charming hypocrisy of woman has worn smiles and an easy appearance so as to make me imagine she felt no care, or would not even ask to disturb her lord's secret when he seemed to indicate a desire to keep it private? Oh the dear hypocrite! Have I not watched her hiding the boys' peccadilloes from papa's anger? Have I not known her cheat out of her housekeeping to pay off their little extravagances; and talk to me with an artless face, as if she did not know that our revered Captain had had dealings with the gentlemen of Duke's Place, and our learned collegian, at the end of his terms, had very pressing reasons for sporting his oak (as the phrase is) against some of the University tradesmen? Why, from the very earliest days, thou wise woman, thou wert for ever concealing something from me,—this one stealing jam from the cupboard; that one getting into disgrace at school; that naughty rebel (put on the caps, young folks, according to the fit) flinging an inkstand at mamma in a rage, whilst I was told the gown and the carpet were spoiled by accident. We all hide from one another. We have all secrets. We are all alone. We sin by ourselves, and, let us trust, repent too. Yonder dear woman would give her foot to spare mine a twinge of the gout; but, when I have the fit, the pain is in my slipper. At the end of the novel or the play, the hero and heroine marry or die, and so there is an end of them as far as the poet is concerned, who huzzays for his young couple till the postchaise turns the corner; or fetches the hearse and plumes, and shovels them underground. But when Mr. Random and Mr. Thomas Jones are married, is all over? Are there no quarrels at home? Are there no Lady Bellastons abroad? are there no constables to be outrun? no temptations to conquer us, or be conquered by us? The Sirens sang after Ulysses long after his marriage, and the suitors whispered in Penelope's ear, and he and she had many a weary day of doubt and care, and so have we all. As regards money I was put out of trouble by the inheritance I made: but does not *Atra Cura* sit behind baronets as well as *equites* ? My friends in London used to congratulate me on my happiness. Who would not like to be master of a good house and a good estate? But can Gumbo shut the hall-door upon blue devils, or lay them always in a red sea of claret? Does a man sleep the better who has four-and-twenty hours to doze in? Do his intellects brighten after a sermon from the dull old vicar; a ten minutes' cackle and flattery from the village apothecary; or the conversation of Sir John and Sir Thomas with their ladies, who came ten moonlight muddy miles to eat a haunch, and play a rubber? 'Tis all very well to have tradesmen bowing to your carriage-door, room made for you at quarter-sessions, and my lady wife taken down the second or the third to dinner: but these pleasures fade—nay, have their inconveniences. In our part of the country, for seven years after we came to Warrington Manor, our two what they called best neighbours were my Lord Tutbury and Sir John Mudbrook. We are of an older date than the Mudbrooks, consequently, when we dined together, my Lady Tutbury always fell to my lot, who was deaf and fell asleep after dinner; or if I had Lady Mudbrook, she chattered with a folly so incessant and intense, that even my wife could hardly keep her complacency (consummate hypocrite as her Ladyship is), knowing the rage with which I was fuming at the other's clatter. I come to London. I show my tongue to Doctor Heberden. I pour out my catalogue of complaints. "Psha, my dear Sir George!" says the unfeeling physician. "Headaches, languor, bad sleep, bad temper——" ("Not bad temper: Sir George has the sweetest temper in the world, only he is sometimes a little melancholy," says my wife.) "Bad sleep, bad temper," continues the implacable Doctor. "My dear lady, his inheritance has been his ruin, and a little poverty and a great deal of occupation would do him all the good in life."

No, my brother Harry ought to have been the squire, with remainder to my son Miles, of course. Harry's letters were full of gaiety and good spirits. His estate prospered; his negroes multiplied; his crops were large; he was a member of our House of Burgesses; he adored his wife: could he but have a child his happiness would be complete. Had Hal been master of Warrington Manor-house in my place, he would have been beloved through the whole country; he would have been steward at all the races, the gayest of all the jolly huntsmen, the *bien venu* at all the mansions round about, where people scarce cared to perform the ceremony of welcome at sight of my glum face. As for my wife, all the world liked her, and agreed in pitying her. I don't know how the report got abroad, but 'twas generally agreed that I treated her with awful cruelty, and that for jealousy I was a perfect Bluebeard. Ah me! And so it is true that I have had many dark hours; that I pass days in long silence; that the conversation of fools and whipper-snappers makes me rebellious and peevish, and that, when I feel contempt, I sometimes don't know how to conceal it, or I should say did not. I hope as I grow older I grow more charitable. Because I do not love bawling and galloping after a fox, like the Captain yonder, I am not his superior; but in this respect, humbly own that he is mine. He has perceptions which are denied me; enjoyments which I cannot understand. Because I am blind the world is not dark. I try now and listen with respect when Squire Codgers talks of the day's run. I do my best to laugh when Captain Rattleton tells his garrison stories. I step up to the harpsichord with old Miss Humby (our neighbour from Beccles) and try and listen as she warbles her ancient ditties. I play whist laboriously. Am I not trying to do the duties of life? and I have a right to be garrulous and egotistical, because I have been reading Montaigne all the morning.

I was not surprised, knowing by what influences my brother was led, to find his name in the list of Virginia burgesses who declared that the sole right of imposing taxes on the inhabitants of this colony is now, and ever has been, legally and constitutionally vested in the House of Burgesses, and called upon the other colonies to pray for the Royal interposition in favour of the violated rights of America. And it was now, after we had been some three years settled in our English home, that a correspondence between us and Madam Esmond began to take place. It was my wife who (upon some pretext such as women always know how to find) re-established the relations between us. Mr. Miles must need have the small-pox, from which he miraculously recovered without losing any portion of his beauty; and on this recovery the mother writes her prettiest little wheedling letter to the grandmother of the fortunate babe. She coaxes her with all sorts of modest phrases and humble offerings of respect and goodwill. She narrates anecdotes of the precocious genius of the lad (what hath subsequently happened, I wonder, to stop the growth of that gallant young officer's brains?), and she must have sent over to his grandmother a lock of the darling boy's hair, for the old lady, in her reply, acknowledged the receipt of some such present. I wonder, as it came from England, they allowed it to pass our custom-house at Williamsburg. In return for these peace-offerings and smuggled tokens of submission, comes a tolerably gracious letter from my lady of Castlewood. She inveighs against the dangerous spirit pervading the colony: she laments to think that her unhappy son is consorting with people who, she fears, will be no better than rebels and traitors. She does not wonder, considering *who his friends and advisers are*. How can a wife taken from an *almost menial situation* be expected to sympathise with persons of rank and dignity who have the honour of the Crown at heart? If evil times were coming for the monarchy (for the folks in America appeared to be disinclined to pay taxes, and required that everything should be done for them without cost), she remembered how to monarchs in misfortune the Esmonds —her father the Marquis especially—had ever been faithful. She knew not what opinions (though she might judge from my *new-fangled* Lord Chatham) were in fashion in England. She prayed, at least, she might hear that *one* of her sons was not on the side of *rebellion*. When we came, in after days, to look over old family papers in Virginia, we found " Letters from my daughter Lady Warrington," neatly tied up with a ribbon.

My Lady Theo insisted I should not open them; and the truth, I believe, is, that they were so full of praises of her husband that she thought my vanity would suffer from reading them.

When Madam began to write, she gave us brief notices of Harry and his wife. "The two women," she wrote, "still govern everything with my poor boy at Fannystown (as he chooses to call his house). They must save money there, for I hear but a *shabby account* of their manner of entertaining. The *Mount Vernon gentleman* continues to be his great friend, and he votes in the House of Burgesses very much as *his guide* advises him. Why he should be so sparing of his money I cannot understand: I heard, of five negroes who went with his equipages to my Lord Bottetourt's, only two had shoes to their feet. I had reasons to save, having sons for whom I wished to provide, but he hath no children, wherein he certainly is spared from much grief, though, no doubt, Heaven in its wisdom means our good by the trials which, through our children, it causes us to endure. His mother-in-law," she added in one of her letters, "has been ailing. Ever since his marriage, my poor Henry has been the creature of these two artful women, and they rule him entirely. Nothing, my dear daughter, is more contrary to common sense and to Holy Scripture than this. Are we not told, *Wives, be obedient to your husbands?* Had Mr. Warrington lived, I should have endeavoured to follow up that sacred precept holding that nothing so becomes a woman as *humility and obedience.*"

Presently we had a letter sealed with black, and announcing the death of our dear good Mountain, for whom I had a hearty regret and affection, remembering her sincere love for us as children. Harry deplored the event in his honest way, and with tears which actually blotted his paper. And Madam Esmond, alluding to the circumstance, said: "My late housekeeper, Mrs. Mountain, as soon as she found her illness was fatal, sent to me requesting a last interview on her death-bed, intending, doubtless, to pray my forgiveness for her treachery towards me. I sent her word that I could forgive her *as a Christian*, and heartily hope (though I confess I doubt it) that she had a due sense of her crime towards me. But our meeting, I considered, was of no use, and could only occasion unpleasantness between us. If she repented, *though at the eleventh hour*, it was not too late, and I sincerely trusted that she was now doing so. And, would you believe her lamentable and hardened condition? she sent me word through Dinah, my woman, whom I despatched to her with medicines for *her soul's and her body's health*, that she had nothing to repent of as far as regarded her conduct to me, and she wanted to be left alone! Poor Dinah distributed the medicine to my negroes, and our people took it *eagerly*—while Mrs. Mountain, left to herself, succumbed to the fever. Oh the perversity of human kind! This poor creature was *too proud* to take my remedies, and is now beyond the reach of cure and physicians. You tell me your little Miles is subject to fits of cholic. *My* remedy, and I will beg you to let me know if effectual, is," etc. etc.—and here followed the prescription which thou didst not take, O my son, my heir, and my pride! because thy fond mother had *her* mother's favourite powder, on which in his infantine troubles our first-born was dutifully nurtured. Did words not exactly consonant with truth pass between the ladies in their correspondence? I fear my Lady Theo was not altogether candid: else how to account for a phrase in one of Madam Esmond's letters, who said, " I am glad to hear the powders have done the dear child good! They are, if not on a first, on a second or third application, *almost infallible*, and have been the blessed means of relieving many persons round me, both infants and adults, white and coloured. I send my grandson an Indian bow and arrows. Shall these old eyes never behold him at Castlewood, I wonder, and is Sir George so busy with his books and his politics that he can't afford a few months to his mother in Virginia? I am much alone now. My son's chamber is just as he left it: the same books are in the presses: his little hanger and fowling-piece over the bed, and my father's picture over the mantelpiece. I never allow anything to be altered in his room or his brother's. I fancy the children playing near me sometimes, and that I can see my dear father's head as he dozes in his chair. Mine is growing almost as white as my father's. Am I never to behold my children ere I go hence? The Lord's will be done! "

CHAPTER LXXXVI

AT HOME

Such an appeal as this of our mother would have softened hearts much less obdurate than ours; and we talked of a speedy visit to Virginia, and of hiring all the " Young Rachel's " cabin accommodation. But our child must fall ill, for whom the voyage would be dangerous, and from whom the mother of course could not part; and the "Young Rachel" made her voyage without us that year. Another year there was another difficulty, in my worship's first attack of the gout (which occupied me a good deal, and afterwards certainly cleared my wits and enlivened my spirits); and now came another much sadder cause for delay in the sad news we received from Jamaica. Some two years after our establishment at the Manor, our dear General returned from his government, a little richer in the world's goods than when he went away, but having undergone a loss for which no wealth could console him, and after which, indeed, he did not care to remain in the West Indies. My Theo's poor mother—the most tender and affectionate friend (save one) I have ever had—died abroad of the fever. Her last regret was that she should not be allowed to live to see our children and ourselves in prosperity.

"She sees us, though we do not see her; and she thanks you, George, for having been good to her children," her husband said.

He, we thought, would not be long ere he joined her. His love for her had been the happiness and business of his whole life. To be away from her seemed living no more. It was pitiable to watch the good man as he sat with us. My wife, in her air and in many tones and gestures, constantly recalled her mother to the bereaved widower's heart. What cheer we could give him in his calamity we offered; but, especially, little Hetty was now, under Heaven, his chief support and consolation. She had refused more than one advantageous match in the island, the General told us; and on her return to England, my Lord Wrotham's heir laid himself at her feet. But she loved best to stay with her father, Hetty said. As long as he was not tired of her she cared for no husband.

"Nay," said we, when this last great match was proposed, "let the General stay six months with us at the Manor here, and you can have him at Oakhurst for the other six."

But Hetty declared her father never could bear Oakhurst again now that her mother was gone; and she would marry no man for his coronet and money—not she! The General, when we talked this matter over, said gravely that the child had no desire for marrying, owing possibly to some disappointment in early life, of which she never spoke; and we, respecting her feelings, were for our parts equally silent. My brother Lambert had by this time a college living near to Winchester, and a wife of course to adorn his parsonage. We professed but a moderate degree of liking for this lady, though we made her welcome when she came to us. *Her* idea regarding our poor Hetty's determined celibacy was different to that which I had. This Mrs. Jack was a chatterbox of a woman, in the habit of speaking her mind very freely, and of priding herself excessively on her skill in giving pain to her friends.

" My dear Sir George," she was pleased to say, " *I* have often and often told our dear Theo that *I* wouldn't have a pretty sister in my house to make tea for Jack when I was up-stairs, and always to be at hand when I was wanted in the kitchen or nursery, and always to be dressed neat and in her best when I was very likely making pies or puddings or looking to the children. I have every confidence in Jack, of course. I should like to see him look at another woman, indeed! And so I have in Jemima: but they don't come together in *my* house when I'*m* upstairs—that I promise you! And so I told my sister Warrington."

" Am I to understand," says the General, " that you have done my Lady Warrington the favour to warn her against her sister, my daughter Miss Hester? "

" Yes, pa, of course I have. A duty is a duty, and a woman is a woman, and a man's a man, as I know very well. Don't tell me. He *is* a man. Every man is a man, with all his sanctified airs! "

" You yourself have a married sister, with whom you were staying when my son Jack first had the happiness of making your acquaintance? " remarks the General.

" Yes, of course I have a married sister, every one knows that, and I have been as good as a mother to her children, that I have! "

" And am I to gather from your conversation that your attractions proved a powerful temptation for your sister's husband? "

" La, General! I don't know how you can go for to say I ever said any such a thing! " cries Mrs. Jack, red and voluble.

" Don't you perceive, my dear madam, that it is you who have insinuated as much, not only regarding yourself, but regarding my own two daughters? "

" Never, never, never, as I'm a Christian woman! And it's most cruel of you to say so, sir. And I *do* say a sister is best out of the house, that I do! And as Theo's time is coming I warn her, that's all."

" Have you discovered, my good madam, whether my poor Hetty has stolen any of the spoons? When I came to breakfast this morning, my daughter was alone, and there must have been a score of pieces of silver on the table."

" La, sir! who ever said a word about spoons? Did *I* ever accuse the poor dear? If I did, may I drop down dead at this moment on this hearth-rug! And I ain't used to be spoke to in this way. And me and Jack have both remarked it; and I've done my duty, that I have." And here Mrs. Jack flounces out of the room, in tears.

" And has the woman had the impudence to tell you this, my child? " asks the General, when Theo (who is a little delicate) comes to the tea-table.

" She has told me every day since she has been here. She comes into my dressing-room to tell me. She comes to my nursery, and says, ' Ah, *I* wouldn't have a sister prowling about my nursery, that I wouldn't.' Ah, how pleasant it is to have amiable and well-bred relatives, say I."

" Thy poor mother has been spared this woman," groans the General.

" Our mother would have made her better, papa," says Theo, kissing him.

" Yes, dear." And I see that both of them are at their prayers.

But this must be owned, that to love one's relatives is not always an easy task; to live with one's neighbours is sometimes not amusing. From Jack Lambert's demeanour next day, I could see that his wife had given him her version of the conversation. Jack was sulky, but not dignified. He was angry, but his anger did not prevent his appetite. He preached a sermon for us which was entirely stupid. And little Miles, once more in sables, sat at his grandfather's side, his little hand placed in that of the kind old man.

Would he stay and keep house for us during our Virginian trip? The housekeeper should be put under the full domination of Hetty. The butler's keys should be handed over to him; for Gumbo, not I thought with an over good grace, was to come with us to Virginia: having, it must be premised, united himself with Mrs. Molly in the bonds of matrimony, and peopled a cottage in my park with sundry tawny Gumbos. Under the care of our good General and his daughter we left our house then; we travelled to London, and thence to Bristol, and our obsequious agent there had the opportunity of declaring that he should offer up prayers for our prosperity, and of vowing that children so beautiful as ours (we had an infant by this time to accompany Miles) were never seen on any ship before. We made a voyage without accident. How strange the feeling was as we landed from our boat at Richmond! A coach and a host of negroes were there in waiting to receive us; and hard by a gentleman on horseback, with negroes in our livery, too, who sprang from his horse and rushed up to embrace us. Not a little charmed were both of us to see our dearest Hal. He rode with us to our mother's door. Yonder she stood on the steps to welcome us: and Theo knelt down to ask her blessing.

Harry rode in the coach with us as far as our mother's house! but would not, as he said, spoil sport by entering with us. " She sees me," he owned, " and we are pretty good friends; but Fanny and she are best apart; and there is no love lost between 'em, I can promise you. Come over to me at the tavern, George, when thou art free. And to-morrow I shall have the honour to present her sister to Theo. 'Twas only from happening to be in town yesterday that I heard the ship was signalled, and waited to see you. I have sent a negro boy home to my wife, and she'll be here to pay her respects to my Lady Warrington." And Harry, after this brief greeting, jumped out of the carriage, and left us to meet our mother alone.

Since I parted from her I had seen a great deal of fine company, and Theo and I had paid our respects to the King and Queen at St. James's; but we had seen no more stately person than this who welcomed us, and raising my wife from her knee, embraced her and led her into the house. 'Twas a plain wood-built place, with a gallery round, as our Virginian houses are; but if it had been a palace, with a little empress inside, our reception could not have been more courteous. There was old Nathan, still the major-domo, a score of kind black faces of blacks grinning welcome. Some whose names I remembered as children were grown out of remembrance, to be sure, to be buxom lads and lasses; and some I had left with black pates were grizzling now with snowy polls: and some who were born since my time were peering at doorways with their great eyes and little naked feet. It was, " I'm little Sip, Master George! " and " I'm Dinah, Sir George! " and " I'm Master Miles's boy! " says a little chap in a new livery and boots of nature's blacking. Ere the day was over the whole household had found a pretext for passing before us, and grinning and bowing and making us welcome. I don't know how many repasts were served to us. In the evening my

Lady Warrington had to receive all the gentry of the little town, which she did with perfect grace and good-humour, and I had to shake hands with a few old acquaintances—old enemies I was going to say; but I had come into a fortune and was no longer a naughty prodigal. Why, a drove of fatted calves was killed in my honour! My poor Hal was of the entertainment, but gloomy and crestfallen. His mother spoke to him, but it was as a queen to a rebellious prince, her son, who was not yet forgiven. We two slipped away from the company, and went up to the rooms assigned to me: but there, as we began a free conversation, our mother, taper in hand, appeared with her pale face. Did I want anything? Was everything quite as I wished it? She had peeped in at the dearest children, who were sleeping like cherubs. How she did caress them, and delight over them! How she was charmed with Miles's dominating airs, and the little Theo's smiles and dimples! "Supper is just coming on the table, Sir George. If you like our cookery better than the tavern, Henry, I beg you to stay." What a different welcome there was in the words and tone addressed to each of us! Hal hung down his head, and followed to the lower room. A clergyman begged a blessing on the meal. He touched with not a little art and eloquence upon our arrival at home, upon our safe passage across the stormy waters, upon the love and forgiveness which awaited us in the mansions of the Heavenly Parent when the storms of life were over.

Here was a new clergyman, quite unlike some whom I remembered about us in earlier days, and I praised him, but Madam Esmond shook her head. She was afraid his principles were very dangerous: she was afraid others had adopted those dangerous principles. Had I not seen the paper signed by the burgesses and merchants at Williamsburg the year before—the Lees, Randolphs, Bassets, Washingtons, and the like, and oh, my dear, that I should have to say it, our name, that is, your brother's (by what influence I do not like to say), and this unhappy Mr. Belman's who begged a blessing last night?

If there had been quarrels in our little colonial society when I left home, what were these to the feuds I found raging on my return? We had sent the Stamp Act to America, and been forced to repeal it. Then we must try a new set of duties on glass, paper, and what not, and repeal that Act too, with the exception of a duty on tea. From Boston to Charleston the tea was confiscated. Even my mother, loyal as she was, gave up her favourite drink; and my poor wife would have had to forego

hers, but we had brought a quantity for our private drinking
on board ship, which had paid four times as much duty at home.
Not that I for my part would have hesitated about paying duty.
The home Government must have some means of revenue, or its
pretensions to authority were idle. They say the colonies were
tried and tyrannised over: I say the home Government was
tried and tyrannised over. ('Tis but an affair of argument and
history, now: we tried the question, and were beat; and the
matter is settled as completely as the conquest of Britain by the
Normans.) And all along, from conviction, I trust, I own to
have taken the British side of the quarrel. In that brief and
unfortunate experience of war which I had had in my early life,
the universal cry of the army and well-affected persons was, that
Mr. Braddock's expedition had failed, and defeat and disaster
had fallen upon us in consequence of the remissness, the selfishness, and the rapacity of many of the very people for whose
defence against the French arms had been taken up. The
colonists were for having all done for them, and for doing
nothing. They made extortionate bargains with the champions
who came to defend them; they failed in contracts; they
furnished niggardly supplies; they multiplied delays until the
hour for beneficial action was past, and until the catastrophe
came which never need have occurred but for their ill-will.
What shouts of joy were there, and what ovations for the great
British Minister who had devised and effected the conquest of
Canada! Monsieur de Vaudreuil said justly that that conquest
was the signal for the defection of the North American colonies
from their allegiance to Great Britain; and my Lord Chatham,
having done his best to achieve the first part of the scheme, contributed more than any man in England towards the completion
of it. The colonies were insurgent, and he applauded their
rebellion. What scores of thousands of waverers must he have
encouraged into resistance! It was a general who says to an
army in revolt, " God save the King! My men, you have a
right to mutiny!" No wonder they set up his statue in this
town, and his picture in t'other; whilst here and there they
hanged Ministers and Governors in effigy. To our Virginian
town of Williamsburg, some wiseacres must subscribe to bring
over a portrait of my Lord, in the habit of a Roman orator
speaking in the Forum, to be sure, and pointing to the palace
of Whitehall, and the special window out of which Charles I.
was beheaded! Here was a neat allegory, and a pretty compliment to a British statesman! I hear, however, that my

Lord's head was painted from a bust, and so was taken off without his knowledge.

Now my country is England, not America or Virginia: and I take, or rather took, the English side of the dispute. My sympathies had always been with home, where I was now a squire and a citizen: but had my lot been to plant tobacco, and live on the banks of James River or Potomac, no doubt my opinions had been altered. When, for instance, I visited my brother at his new house and plantation, I found him and his wife as staunch Americans as we were British. We had some words upon the matter in dispute,—who had not in those troublesome times?—but our argument was carried on without rancour; even my new sister could not bring us to that, though she did her best when we were together, and in the curtain lectures, which I have no doubt she inflicted on her spouse, like a notable housewife as she was. But we trusted each other so entirely that even Harry's duty towards his wife would not make him quarrel with his brother. He loved me from old time, when my word was law with him; he still protested that he and every Virginian gentleman of his side was loyal to the Crown. War was not declared as yet, and gentlemen of different opinions were courteous enough to one another. Nay, at our public dinners and festivals, the health of the King was still ostentatiously drunk: and the Assembly of every colony, though preparing for Congress, though resisting all attempts at taxation on the part of the home authorities, was loud in its expressions of regard for the King our father, and pathetic in its appeals to that paternal sovereign to put away evil counsellors from him, and listen to the voice of moderation and reason. Up to the last, our Virginian gentry were a grave, orderly, aristocratic folk, with the strongest sense of their own dignity and station. In later days, and nearer home, we have heard of fraternisation and equality. Amongst the great folks of our Old World I have never seen a gentleman standing more on his dignity and maintaining it better than Mr. Washington: no — not the King against whom he took arms. In the eyes of all the gentry of the French Court, who gaily joined in the crusade against us, and so took their revenge for Canada, the great American chief always appeared as *anax andron*, and they allowed that his better could not be seen in Versailles itself.

Though they were quarrelling with the Governor, the gentlemen of the House of Burgesses still maintained amicable relations with him, and exchanged dignified courtesies. When my Lord Bottetourt arrived, and held his court at Williamsburg in no small splendour and state, all the gentry waited upon him, Madam Esmond included. And at his death, Lord Dunmore, who succeeded him, and brought a fine family with him, was treated with the utmost respect by our gentry privately, though publicly the House of Assembly and the Governor were at war.

Their quarrels are a matter of history, and concern me personally only so far as this, that our burgesses being convened for the 1st of March in the year after my arrival in Virginia, it was agreed that we should all pay a visit to our capital, and our duty to the Governor. Since Harry's unfortunate marriage Madam Esmond had not performed this duty, though always previously accustomed to pay it; but now that her eldest son was arrived in the colony, my mother opined that we must certainly wait upon his Excellency the Governor, nor were we sorry, perhaps, to get away from our little Richmond to enjoy the gaieties of the provincial capital. Madam engaged, and at a great price, the best house to be had at Richmond for herself and her family. Now I was rich, her generosity was curious. I had more than once to interpose (her old servants likewise wondering at her new way of life), and beg her not to be so lavish. But she gently said, in former days she had occasion to save, which now existed no more. Harry had enough, sure, with such a wife as he had taken out of the housekeeper's room. If she chose to be a little extravagant now, why should she hesitate? She had not her dearest daughter and grandchildren with her every day (she fell in love with all three of them, and spoiled them as much as they were capable of being spoiled). Besides, in former days I certainly could not accuse her of too much *extravagance*, and this I think was almost the only allusion she made to the pecuniary differences between us. So she had her people dressed in their best, and her best wines, plate, and furniture from Castlewood by sea at no small charge, and her dress in which she had been married in George the Second's reign, and we all flattered ourselves that our coach made the greatest figure of any except his Excellency's, and we engaged Signor Formicalo, his Excellency's major-domo, to superintend the series of feasts that were given in my honour; and more flesh-pots were set a-stewing in our kitchens in one month, our servants said, than had been known in the family since the young gentlemen went away. So great was Theo's influence over my mother, that she actually persuaded her, that year, to receive our sister Fanny, Hal's wife, who would have stayed upon the plantation rather than face Madam Esmond. But trusting to Theo's promise of amnesty, Fanny (to whose house we had paid more than one visit) came up to town, and made her curtsey to Madam Esmond, and was forgiven. And rather than be forgiven in that way, I own, for my part, that I would prefer perdition or utter persecution.

"You know these, my dear?" says Madam Esmond, pointing to her fine silver sconces. "Fanny hath often cleaned them when she was with me at Castlewood. And this dress, too, Fanny knows, I dare say? Her poor mother had the care of it. I always had the greatest confidence in her."

Here there is wrath flashing from Fanny's eyes, which our mother, who has forgiven her, does not perceive—not she!

"Oh, she was a treasure to me!" Madam resumes. "I never should have nursed my boys through their illnesses but for your mother's admirable care of them. Colonel Lee, permit me to present you to my daughter, my Lady Warrington. Her Ladyship is a neighbour of your relatives the Bunburys at home. Here comes his Excellency. Welcome, my Lord!"

And our princess performs before his Lordship one of those curtseys of which she was not a little proud; and I fancy I see some of the company venturing to smile.

"By George, madam," says Mr. Lee, "since Count Borulawski, I have not seen a bow so elegant as your ladyship's."

"And pray, sir, who was Count Borulawski?" asks Madam.

"He was a nobleman high in favour with his Polish Majesty," replies Mr. Lee. "May I ask you, madam, to present me to your distinguished son?"

"This is Sir George Warrington," says my mother, pointing to me.

"Pardon me, madam. I meant Captain Warrington, who was by Mr. Wolfe's side when he died. I had been contented to share his fate, so I had been near him."

And the ardent Lee swaggers up to Harry, and takes his hand with respect, and pays him a compliment or two, which makes me, at least, pardon him for his late impertinence: for my dearest Hal walks gloomily through his mother's rooms, in his old uniform of the famous corps which he has quitted.

We had had many meetings, which the stern mother could not interrupt, and in which that instinctive love which bound us to one another, and which nothing could destroy, had opportunity to speak. Entirely unlike each other in our pursuits, our tastes, our opinions—his life being one of eager exercise, active sport, and all the amusements of the field, while mine is to dawdle over books and spend my time in languid self-contemplation—we have, nevertheless, had such a sympathy as almost passes the love of women. My poor Hal confessed as much to me, for his part, in his artless manner, when we went away without wives or womankind, except a few negroes left in the place, and passed a week at Castlewood together.

The ladies did not love each other. I know enough of my Lady Theo, to see after a very few glances whether or not she takes a liking to another of her amiable sex. All my powers of persuasion or command fail to change the stubborn creature's opinion. Had she ever said a word against Mrs. This or Miss That? Not she! Has she been otherwise than civil? No, assuredly! My Lady Theo is polite to a beggar-woman, treats her kitchen-maids like duchesses, and murmurs a compliment to the dentist for his elegant manner of pulling her tooth out. She would black my boots, or clean the grate, if I ordained it (always looking like a duchess the while); but as soon as I say to her, "My dear creature, be fond of this lady, or t'other!" all obedience ceases; she executes the most refined curtseys; smiles and kisses even to order; but performs that mysterious undefinable freemasonic signal, which passes between women, by which each knows that the other hates her. So, with regard to Fanny, we had met at her house, and at others. I remembered her affectionately from old days, I fully credited poor Hal's violent protests and tearful oaths, that, by George, it was our mother's persecution which made him marry her. He couldn't stand by and see a poor thing tortured as she was, without coming to her rescue; no, by heavens, he couldn't! I say I believed all this; and had for my sister-in-law a genuine compassion, as well as an early regard; and yet I had no love to give her: and, in reply to Hal's passionate outbreaks in praise of her beauty and worth, and eager queries to me whether I did not think her a perfect paragon, I could only answer with faint compliments or vague approval, feeling all the while that I was disappointing my poor ardent fellow, and cursing inwardly that revolt against flattery and falsehood into which I sometimes frantically rush. Why should I not say, "Yes, dear Hal, thy wife is a paragon; her singing is delightful, her hair and shape are beautiful;" as I might have said by a little common stretch of politeness? Why could I not cajole this or that stupid neighbour or relative, as I have heard Theo do a thousand times, finding all sorts of lively prattle to amuse them, whilst I sit before them dumb and gloomy? I say it was a sin not to have more words to say in praise of Fanny. We ought to have praised her, we ought to have liked her. My Lady Warrington certainly ought to have liked her, for she can play the hypocrite, and I cannot. And there was this young creature —pretty, graceful, shaped like a nymph, with beautiful black eyes—and we cared for them no more than for two gooseberries! At Warrington my wife and I, when we pretended to compare notes, elaborately complimented each other on our new sister's beauty. What lovely eyes!—Oh, yes! What a sweet little dimple on her chin!—*Ah oui!* What wonderful little feet!— Perfectly Chinese! where should we in London get slippers small enough for her? And, these compliments exhausted, we knew that we did not like Fanny the value of one penny-piece; we knew that we disliked her; we knew that we ha—— Well, what hypocrites women are! We heard from many quarters how eagerly my brother had taken up the new anti-English opinion, and what a champion he was of so-called American rights and freedom. " It is her doing, my dear," says I to my wife. " If I had said so much, I am sure you would have scolded me," says my Lady Warrington, laughing: and I did straightway begin to scold her, and say it was most cruel of her to suspect our new sister; and what earthly right had we to do so? But I say again, I know Madam Theo so well, that when once she has got a prejudice against a person in her little head, not all the King's horses nor all the King's men will get it out again. I vow nothing would induce her to believe that Harry was not henpecked—nothing.

Well, we went to Castlewood together without the women, and stayed at the dreary, dear old place, where we had been so happy, and I, at least, so gloomy. It was winter, and duck time, and Harry went away to the river, and shot dozens and scores and bushels of canvas-backs, whilst I remained in my grandfather's library amongst the old mouldering books which I loved in my childhood—which I see in a dim vision still resting on a little boy's lap, as he sits by an old white-headed gentleman's knee. I read my books; I slept in my own bed and room—religiously kept, as my mother told me, and left as on the day when I went to Europe. Hal's cheery voice would wake me, as of old. Like all men who love to go a-field, he was an early riser: he would come and wake me, and sit on the foot of the bed and perfume the air with his morning pipe, as the house negroes laid great logs on the fire. It was a happy time!

Old Nathan had told me of cunning crypts where ancestral rum and claret were deposited. We had had cares, struggles, battles, bitter griefs, and disappointments; we were boys again as we sat there together. I am a boy now even, as I think of the time.

That unlucky tea-tax, which alone of the taxes lately imposed upon the colonies the home Government was determined to retain, was met with defiance throughout America. 'Tis true we paid a shilling in the pound at home, and asked only threepence from Boston or Charleston; but, as a question of principle, the impost was refused by the provinces, which indeed ever showed a most spirited determination to pay as little as they could help. In Charleston, the tea-ships were unloaded, and the cargoes stored in cellars. From New York and Philadelphia, the vessels were turned back to London. In Boston (where there was an armed force, whom the inhabitants were perpetually mobbing), certain patriots, painted and disguised as Indians, boarded the ships, and flung the obnoxious cargoes into the water. The wrath of our white Father was kindled against this city of Mohocks in masquerade. The notable Boston Port Bill was brought forward in the British House of Commons: the port was closed, and the Custom House removed to Salem. The Massachusetts Charter was annulled; and—in just apprehension that riots might ensue, in dealing with the perpetrators of which the colonial courts might be led to act partially—Parliament decreed that persons indicted for acts of violence and armed resistance might be sent home, or to another colony, for trial. If such acts set all America in a flame, they certainly drove all well-wishers of our country into a fury. I might have sentenced Master Miles Warrington, at five years old, to a whipping, and he would have cried, taken down his little small-clothes, and submitted: but suppose I offered (and he richly deserving it) to chastise Captain Miles of the Prince's Dragoons? He would whirl my paternal cane out of my hand, box my hair-powder out of my ears. Lord a-mercy! I tremble at the very idea of the controversy! He would *assert his independence*, in a word! and if, I say, I think the home Parliament had a right to levy taxes in the colonies, I own that we took means most captious, most insolent, most irritating, and, above all, most impotent, to assert our claim.

My Lord Dunmore, our Governor of Virginia, upon Lord Bottetourt's death, received me into some intimacy soon after my arrival in the colony, being willing to live on good terms with all our gentry. My mother's severe loyalty was no secret to him; indeed, she waved the King's banner in all companies, and talked so loudly and resolutely, that Randolph and Patrick Henry himself were struck dumb before her. It was Madam Esmond's celebrated reputation for loyalty (his Excellency laughingly told me) which induced him to receive her eldest son to grace.

"I have had the worst character of you from home," his Lordship said. "Little birds whisper to me, Sir George, that you are a man of the most dangerous principles. You are a friend of Mr. Wilkes and Alderman Beckford. I am not sure you have not been at Medmenham Abbey. You have lived with players, poets, and all sorts of wild people. I have been warned against you, sir, and I find you——"

"Not so black as I have been painted," I interrupted his Lordship with a smile.

"Faith," says my Lord, "if I tell Sir George Warrington that he seems to me a very harmless quiet gentleman, and that 'tis a great relief to me to talk to him amidst these loud politicians; these lawyers with their perpetual noise about Greece and Rome; these Virginian squires who are for ever professing their loyalty and respect, whilst they are shaking their fists in my face—I hope nobody overhears us," says my Lord, with an arch smile, "and nobody will carry my opinions home."

His Lordship's ill opinion having been removed by a better knowledge of me, our acquaintance daily grew more intimate; and, especially between the ladies of his family and my own, a close friendship arose—between them and my wife at least. Hal's wife, received kindly at the little provincial Court, as all ladies were, made herself by no means popular there by the hot and eager political tone which she adopted. She assailed all the Government measures with indiscriminating acrimony. Were they lenient? She said the perfidious British Government was only preparing a snare, and biding its time until it could forge heavier chains for unhappy America. Were they angry? Why did not every American citizen rise, assert his rights as a freeman, and serve every British governor, officer, soldier, as they had treated the East India Company's tea? My mother, on the other hand, was pleased to express her opinions with equal frankness, and, indeed, to press her advice upon his Excellency with a volubility which may have fatigued that representative of the Sovereign. Call out the militia; send for fresh troops from New York, from home, from anywhere; lock up the

Capitol! (this advice was followed, it must be owned) and send every one of the ringleaders amongst those wicked burgesses to prison! was Madam Esmond's daily counsel to the Governor by word and letter. And if not only the burgesses, but the burgesses' wives could have been led off to punishment and captivity, I think this Brutus of a woman would scarce have appealed against the sentence.

CHAPTER LXXXVII

THE LAST OF "GOD SAVE THE KING"

WHAT perverse law of Fate is it that ever places me in a minority? Should a law be proposed to hand over this realm to the Pretender of Rome, or the Grand Turk, and submit it to the new sovereign's religion, it might pass, as I should certainly be voting against it. At home in Virginia, I found myself disagreeing with everybody as usual. By the Patriots I was voted (as indeed I professed myself to be) a Tory; by the Tories I was presently declared to be a dangerous Republican. The time was utterly out of joint. O cursed spite! Ere I had been a year in Virginia, how I wished myself back by the banks of Waveney! But the aspect of affairs was so troublous, that I could not leave my mother, a lone lady, to face possible war and disaster, nor would she quit the country at such a juncture, nor should a man of spirit leave it. At his Excellency's table, and over his Excellency's plentiful claret, that point was agreed on by numbers of well-affected, that vow was vowed over countless brimming bumpers. No; it was *statue signum, signifer!* We Cavaliers would all rally round it; and at these times, our Governor talked like the bravest of the brave.

Now, I will say, of all my Virginian acquaintance, Madam Esmond was the most consistent. Our gentlefolks had come in numbers to Williamsburg; and a great number of them proposed to treat her Excellency the Governor's lady to a ball, when the news reached us of the Boston Port Bill. Straightway the House of Burgesses adopts an indignant protest against this measure of the British Parliament, and decrees a solemn day of fast and humiliation throughout the country, and of solemn prayer to Heaven to avert the calamity of Civil War. Meanwhile the invitation to my Lady Dunmore having been already given and accepted, the gentlemen agreed that their ball should take place on the appointed evening, and then sackcloth and ashes should be assumed some days afterwards.

" A ball!" says Madam Esmond. " I go to a ball which is given by a set of rebels who are going publicly to insult His Majesty a week afterwards! I will die sooner!" And she wrote to the gentlemen who were stewards for the occasion to say, that viewing the dangerous state of the country, she, for her part, could not think of attending a ball.

What was her surprise then, the next time she went abroad in her chair, to be cheered by a hundred persons, white and black, and shouts of " Huzzah, madam!" " Heaven bless your Ladyship!" They evidently thought her patriotism had caused her determination not to go to the ball.

Madam, that there should be no mistake, puts her head out of the chair, and cries out " God save the King!" as loud as she can. The people cried " God save the King!" too. Everybody cried " God save the King!" in those days. On the night of that entertainment, my poor Harry, as a Burgess of the House, and one of the givers of the feast, donned his uniform red coat of Wolfe's (which he so soon was to exchange for another colour) and went off with Madam Fanny to the ball. My Lady Warrington and her humble servant, as being strangers in the country, and English people as it were, were permitted by Madam to attend the assembly, from which she of course absented herself. I had the honour to dance a country-dance with the lady of Mount Vernon, whom I found a most lively, pretty, and amiable partner; but am bound to say that my wife's praises of her were received with a very grim acceptance by my mother, when Lady Warrington came to recount the events of the evening. Could not Sir George Warrington have danced with my Lady Dunmore or her daughters, or with anybody but Mrs. Washington; to be sure the Colonel thought so well of himself and his wife, that no doubt he considered her the grandest lady in the room; and she who remembered him a road surveyor at a guinea a day! Well, indeed! there was no measuring the pride of these provincial upstarts, and as for this gentleman, my Lord Dunmore's partiality for him had evidently turned his head. I do not know about Mr. Washington's pride, I know that my good mother never could be got to love him or anything that was his.

She was no better pleased with him for going to the ball, than with his conduct three days afterwards, when the day of fast and humiliation was appointed, and when he attended the service which our new clergyman performed. She invited Mr. Belman to dinner that day, and sundry colonial authorities. The clergyman excused himself: Madam Esmond tossed up her head, and said he might do as he liked. She made a parade of a dinner; she lighted her house up at night, when all the rest of the city was in darkness and gloom; she begged Mr. Hardy, one of his Excellency's aides-de-camp, to sing "God save the King," to which the people in the street outside listened, thinking that it might be a part of some religious service which Madam was celebrating; but then she called for "Britons, strike home!" which the simple young gentleman, just from Europe, began to perform, when a great yell arose in the street, and a large stone, flung from some rebellious hand, plumped into the punch-bowl before me, and scattered it and its contents about our dining-room.

My mother went to the window nothing daunted. I can see her rigid little figure now, as she stands with a tossed-up head, outstretched frilled arms, and the twinkling stars for a background, and sings in chorus, "Britons, strike home! strike home!" The crowd in front of the palings shout and roar, "Silence! for shame! go back!" but she will not go back, not she. "Fling more stones, if you dare!" says the brave little lady; and more might have come, but some gentlemen issuing out of the "Raleigh Tavern" interpose with the crowd. "You mustn't insult a lady," says a voice I think I know. "Huzzah, Colonel! Hurrah, Captain! God bless your honour!" say the people in the street. And thus the enemies are pacified.

My mother, protesting that the whole disturbance was over, would have had Mr. Hardy sing another song; but he gave a sickly grin, and said, "He really did not like to sing to such accompaniments," and the concert for that evening was ended; though I am bound to say that some scoundrels returned at night, frightened my poor wife almost out of wits, and broke every single window in the front of our tenement. "Britons, strike home!" was a little too much; Madam should have contented herself with "God save the King." Militia were drilled, bullets were cast, supplies of ammunition got ready, running plans for disappointing the Royal ordinances devised and carried out; but, to be sure, "God save the King" was the cry everywhere, and in reply to my objections to the gentlemen-patriots, "Why, you are scheming for a separation; you are bringing down upon you the inevitable wrath of the greatest power in the world!"—the answer to me always was, "We mean no separation at all; we yield to no men in loyalty; we glory in the name of Britons," and so forth, and so forth. The powder-barrels were heaped in the cellar, the train was laid, but Mr. Fawkes was persistent in his dutiful petitions to King and Parliament, and meant no harm, not he! 'Tis true when I spoke of the power of our country, I imagined she would exert it; that she would not expect to overcome three millions of fellow-Britons on their own soil with a few battalions, a half-dozen generals from Bond Street, and a few thousand bravos hired out of Germany. As if we wanted to insult the thirteen colonies as well as to subdue them, we must set upon them these hordes of Hessians, and the murderers out of the Indian wigwams. Was our great quarrel not to be fought without *tali auxilio* and *istis defensoribus ?* Ah! 'tis easy, now we are worsted, to look over the map of the great empire wrested from us, and show how we ought not to have lost it. Long Island ought to have exterminated Washington's army; he ought never to have come out of Valley Forge except as a prisoner. The South was ours after the battle of Camden but for the inconceivable meddling of the Commander-in-Chief at New York, who paralysed the exertions of the only capable British General who appeared during the war, and sent him into that miserable *cul-de-sac* at York Town, whence he could only issue defeated and a prisoner. Oh, for a week more! a day more, an hour more of darkness or light! In reading over our American campaigns from their unhappy commencement to their inglorious end, now that we are able to see the enemy's movements and condition as well as our own, I fancy we can see how an advance, a march, might have put enemies into our power who had no means to withstand it, and changed the entire issue of the struggle. But it was ordained by Heaven, and for the good, as we can now have no doubt, of both empires, that the great Western Republic should separate from us: and the gallant soldiers who fought on her side, their indomitable Chief above all, had the glory of facing and overcoming, not only veterans amply provided and inured to war, but wretchedness, cold, hunger, dissensions, treason within their own camp, where all must have gone to rack but for the pure unquenchable flame of patriotism that was for ever burning in the bosom of the heroic leader. What a constancy, what a magnanimity, what a surprising persistence against fortune! Washington before the enemy was no better nor braver than hundreds that fought with him or against him (who has not heard the repeated sneers against "Fabius" in which his factious captains were accustomed to indulge?); but Washington the Chief of a nation in arms, doing battle with distracted parties; calm in the midst of conspiracy; serene against the open foe before him and the darker enemies at his back; Washington inspiring order and spirit into troops hungry and in rags; stung by ingratitude, but betraying no anger, and ever ready to forgive; in defeat invincible, magnanimous in conquest, and never so sublime as on that day when he laid down his victorious sword and sought his noble retirement:—here indeed is a character to admire and revere; a life without a stain, a fame without a flaw. *Quando invenies parem?* In that more extensive work, which I have planned and partly written on the subject of this great war, I hope I have done justice to the character of its greatest leader.[1] And this from the sheer force of respect which his eminent virtues extorted. With the young Mr. Washington of my own early days I had not the honour to enjoy much sympathy: though my brother, whose character is much more frank and affectionate than mine, was always his fast friend in early times, when they were equals, as in latter days when the General, as I do own and think, was all mankind's superior.

I have mentioned that contrariety in my disposition, and, perhaps, in my brother's, which somehow placed us on wrong sides in the quarrel which ensued, and which from this time forth raged for five years, until the mother-country was fain to acknowledge her defeat. Harry should have been the Tory and I the Whig. Theoretically my opinions were very much more liberal than those of my brother, who, especially after his marriage, became what our Indian Nabobs call a Bahadoor—a person ceremonious, stately, and exacting respect. When my Lord Dunmore, for instance, talked about liberating the negroes, so as to induce them to join the King's standard, Hal was for hanging the Governor and the Black Guards (as he called them) whom his Excellency had crimped. "If you gentlemen are fighting for freedom," says I, "sure the negroes may fight too."

[1] And I trust that in the opinions I have recorded regarding him, I have shown that I also can be just and magnanimous towards those who view me personally with no favour. For my brother Hal being at Mount Vernon, and always eager to bring me and his beloved Chief on good terms, showed his Excellency some of the early sheets of my history. General Washington (who read but few books, and had not the slightest pretensions to literary taste) remarked, "If you *will* have my opinion, my dear General, I think Sir George's projected work, from the specimen I have of it, is certain to offend both parties."—G. E. W.

On which Harry roars out, shaking his fist, "Infernal villains, if I meet any of 'em, they shall die by this hand!" And my mother agreed that this idea of a negro insurrection was the most abominable and parricidal notion which had ever sprung up in her unhappy country. She at least was more consistent than brother Hal. She would have black and white obedient to the powers that be: whereas Hal only could admit that freedom was the right of the latter colour.

As a proof of her argument, Madam Esmond, and Harry too, would point to an instance in our own family in the person of Mr. Gumbo. Having got his freedom from me, as a reward for his admirable love and fidelity to me when times were hard, Gumbo, on his return to Virginia, was scarce a welcome guest in his old quarters, amongst my mother's servants. He was free, and they were not: he was, as it were, a centre of insurrection. He gave himself no small airs of protection and consequence amongst them; bragging of his friends in Europe (" at home," as he called it), and his doings there; and for a while bringing the household round about him to listen to him and admire him, like the monkey who had seen the world. Now Sady, Hal's boy, who went to America of his own desire, was not free. Hence jealousies between him and Mr. Gum; and battles, in which they both practised the noble art of boxing and butting, which they had learned at Marybone Gardens and Hockley-in-the-Hole. Nor was Sady the only jealous person; almost all my mother's servants hated Signor Gumbo for the airs which he gave himself; and, I am sorry to say, that our faithful Molly, his wife, was as jealous as his old fellow-servants. The blacks could not pardon her for having demeaned herself so far as to marry one of their kind. She met with no respect, could exercise no authority, came to her mistress with ceaseless complaints of the idleness, knavery, lies, stealing of the black people; and finally with a story of jealousy against a certain Dinah, or Diana, who, I heartily trust, was as innocent as her namesake, the moonlight visitant of Endymion. Now, on the article of morality, Madam Esmond was a very Draconess; and a person accused was a person guilty. She made charges against Mr. Gumbo to which he replied with asperity. Forgetting that he was a free gentleman, my mother now ordered Gumbo to be whipped, on which Molly flew at her Ladyship, all her wrath at her husband's infidelity vanishing at the idea of the indignity put upon him: there was a rebellion in our house at Castlewood. A quarrel took place between me and my mother, as I took my man's side. Hal and Fanny sided with her, on the contrary; and in so far the difference did good, as it brought about some little intimacy between madam and her younger children. This little difference was speedily healed; but it was clear that the Standard of Insurrection must be removed out of our house; and we determined that Mr. Gumbo and his lady should return to Europe.

My wife and I would willingly have gone with them, God wot, for our boy sickened and lost his strength, and caught the fever in our swampy country; but at this time she was expecting to lie in (of our son Henry), and she knew, too, that I had promised to stay in Virginia. It was agreed that we should send the two back; but when I offered Theo to go, she said her place was with her husband;—her father and Hetty at home would take care of our children; and she scarce would allow me to see a tear in her eyes whilst she was making her preparations for the departure of her little ones. Dost thou remember the time, madam, and the silence round the work-tables, as the piles of little shirts are made ready for the voyage? And the stealthy visits to the children's chambers whilst they are asleep and yet with you? and the terrible time of parting, as our barge with the servants and children rows to the ship, and you stand on the shore? Had the Prince of Wales been going on that voyage, he could not have been better provided. Where, sirrah, is the Tompion watch your grandmother gave you? and how did you survive the boxes of cakes which the good lady stowed away in your cabin?

The ship which took out my poor Theo's children returned with the Reverend Mr. Hagan and my Lady Maria on board, who meekly chose to resign her rank, and was known in the colony (which was not to be a colony very long) only as Mrs. Hagan. At the time when I was in favour with my Lord Dunmore, a living falling vacant in Westmoreland county, he gave it to our kinsman, who arrived in Virginia time enough to christen our boy Henry, and to preach some sermons on the then gloomy state of affairs, which Madam Esmond pronounced to be prodigious fine. I think my Lady Maria won Madam's heart by insisting on going out of the room after her. " My father, your brother, was an earl, 'tis true," says she; " but you know your Ladyship is a marquis's daughter, and I never can think of taking precedence of you!" So fond did Madam become of her niece, that she even allowed Hagan to read plays —my own humble compositions amongst others—and was

fairly forced to own that there was merit in the tragedy of
"Pocahontas," which our parson delivered with uncommon
energy and fire.

Hal and his wife came but rarely to Castlewood and Richmond
when the chaplain and his lady were with us. Fanny was very
curt and rude with Maria, used to giggle and laugh strangely
in her company, and repeatedly remind her of her age, to our
mother's astonishment, who would often ask was there any
cause of quarrel between her niece and her daughter-in-law?
I kept my own counsel on these occasions, and was often not a
little touched by the meekness with which the elder lady bore
her persecutions. Fanny loved to torture her in her husband's
presence (who, poor fellow, was also in a happy ignorance about
his wife's early history), and the other bore her agony wincing
as little as might be. I sometimes would remonstrate with
Madam Harry, and ask her was she a Red Indian that she tortured her victims so? " Have not I had torture enough in my
time?" says the young lady, and looked as though she was
determined to pay back the injuries inflicted on her.

" Nay," says I, " you were bred in our wigwam, and I don't
remember anything but kindness!"

" Kindness!" cries she. " No slave was ever treated as I
was. The blows which wound most often are those which
never are aimed. The people who hate us are not those we
have injured."

I thought of little Fanny in our early days, silent, smiling,
willing to run and do all our biddings for us, and I grieved for
my poor brother, who had taken this sly creature into his bosom.

CHAPTER LXXXVIII

YANKEE DOODLE COMES TO TOWN

ONE of the uses to which we put America in the days of our
British dominion was to make it a refuge for our sinners.
Besides convicts and assigned servants whom we transported
to our colonies, we discharged on their shores scapegraces and
younger sons, for whom dissipation, despair, and bailiffs made
the old country uninhabitable. And as Mr. Cook, in his
voyages, made his newly discovered islanders presents of
English animals (and other specimens of European civilisation),

we used to take care to send samples of our *black sheep* over to the colonies, there to browse as best they might, and propagate their precious breed. I myself was perhaps a little guilty in this matter, in busying myself to find a living in America for the worthy Hagan, husband of my kinswoman,—at least was guilty in so far as this, that as we could get him no employment in England, we were glad to ship him to Virginia, and give him a colonial pulpit-cushion to thump. He demeaned himself there as a brave honest gentleman, to be sure; he did his duty thoroughly by his congregation, and his King too; and in so far did credit to my small patronage. Madam Theo used to urge this when I confided to her my scruples of conscience on this subject, and show, as her custom was, and is, that my conduct in this, as in all other matters, was dictated by the highest principles of morality and honour. But would I have given Hagan our living at home, and selected him and his wife to minister to our parish? I fear not. I never had a doubt of our cousin's sincere repentance; but I think I was secretly glad when she went to work it out in the wilderness. And I say this, acknowledging my pride and my error. Twice, when I wanted them most, this kind Maria aided me with her sympathy and friendship. She bore her own distresses courageously, and soothed those of others with admirable affection and devotion. And yet I, and some of mine (not Theo), *would* look down upon her. Oh, for shame, for shame on our pride.

My poor Lady Maria was not the only one of our family who was to be sent out of the way to American wildernesses. Having borrowed, stolen, cheated at home, until he could cheat, borrow, and steal no more, the Honourable William Esmond, Esquire, was accommodated with a place at New York; and his noble brother and Royal master heartily desired that they might see him no more. When the troubles began, we heard of the fellow and his doings in his new habitation. Lies and mischief were his *avant-couriers* wherever he travelled. My Lord Dunmore informed me that Mr. Will declared publicly, that our estate of Castlewood was only ours during his brother's pleasure; that his father, out of consideration for Madam Esmond, his Lordship's half-sister, had given her the place for life, and that he, William, was in negotiation with his brother, the present Lord Castlewood, for the purchase of the reversion of the estate! We had the deed of gift in our strong-room at Castlewood, and it was furthermore registered in due form at Williamsburg; so that we were easy on that score. But the intention was everything;

and Hal and I promised, as soon as ever we met Mr. William, to get from him a confirmation of this pretty story. What Madam Esmond's feelings and expressions were when she heard it, I need scarcely here particularise. "What! my father, the Marquis of Esmond, was a liar, and I am a cheat, am I?" cries my mother. "He will take my son's property at my death, will he?" And she was for writing, not only to Lord Castlewood in England, but to His Majesty himself at St. James's, and was only prevented by my assurances that Mr. Will's lies were notorious amongst all his acquaintance, and that we could not expect, in our own case, that he should be so inconsistent as to tell the truth. We heard of him presently as one of the loudest amongst the Loyalists in New York, as Captain, and presently Major, of a corps of volunteers who were sending their addresses to the well-disposed in all the other colonies, and announcing their perfect readiness to die for the mother-country.

We could not lie in a house without a whole window, and closing the shutters of that unlucky mansion we had hired at Williamsburg, Madam Esmond left our little capital, and my family returned to Richmond, which also was deserted by the members of the (dissolved) Assembly. Captain Hal and his wife returned pretty early to their plantation; and I, not a little annoyed at the course which events were taking, divided my time pretty much between my own family and that of our Governor, who professed himself very eager to have my advice and company. There were the strongest political differences, but as yet no actual personal quarrel. Even after the dissolution of our House of Assembly (the members of which adjourned to a tavern, and there held that famous meeting where, I believe, the idea of a Congress of all the colonies was first proposed), the gentlemen who were strongest in opposition remained good friends with his Excellency, partook of his hospitality, and joined him in excursions of pleasure. The session over, the gentry went home and had meetings in their respective counties; and the Assemblies in most of the other provinces having been also abruptly dissolved, it was agreed everywhere that a General Congress should be held. Philadelphia, as the largest and most important city on our continent, was selected as the place of meeting; and those celebrated conferences began, which were but the angry preface of war. We were still at God save the King; we were still presenting our humble petitions to the throne; but when I went to visit my brother Harry at Fanny's

Mount (his new plantation lay not far from ours, but with Rappahannock between us, and towards Mattaponey river), he rode out on business one morning, and I in the afternoon happened to ride too, and was told by one of the grooms that Master was gone towards " Willis's Ordinary; " in which direction, thinking no harm, I followed. And upon a clear place not far from " Willis's," as I advance out of the wood, I come on Captain Hal on horseback, with three or four and thirty countrymen round about him, armed with every sort of weapon, pike, scythe, fowling-piece, and musket; and the Captain, with two or three likely young fellows as officers under him, was putting the men through their exercise.

As I rode up a queer expression comes over Hal's face. " Present arms! " says he (and the army tries to perform the salute as well as they could). " Captain Cade, this is my brother, Sir George Warrington."

" As a relation of yours, *Colonel*," says the individual addressed as captain, " the gentleman is welcome," and he holds out a hand accordingly.

" And—and a true friend to Virginia," says Hal, with a reddening face.

" Yes, please God! gentlemen," say I, on which the regiment gives a hearty huzzay for the Colonel and his brother. The drill over, the officers, and the men too, were for adjourning to " Willis's " and taking some refreshment, but Colonel Hal said he could not drink with them that afternoon, and we trotted homewards together.

" So, Hal, the cat's out of the bag! " I said.

He gave me a hard look. " I guess there's wilder cats in it. It must come to this, George. I say, you mustn't tell Madam," he adds.

" Good God! " I cried, " do you mean that with fellows such as those I saw yonder, you and your friends are going to make fight against the greatest nation and the best army in the world? "

" I guess we shall get an awful whipping," says Hal, " and that's the fact. But then, George," he added, with his sweet kind smile, " we are young, and a whipping or two may do us good. Won't it do us good, Dolly, you old slut? " and he gives a playful touch with his whip to an old dog of *all trades*, that was running by him.

I did not try to urge upon him (I had done so in vain many times previously) our British side of the question, the side which appears to me to be the best. He was accustomed to put off my reasons by saying, " All mighty well, brother; you speak as an Englishman, and have cast in your lot with your country, as I have with mine." To this argument I own there is no answer, and all that remains for the disputants is to fight the matter out, when the strongest is in the right. Which had the right in the wars of the last century? The King or the Parliament? The side that was uppermost was the right, and on the whole much more humane in their victory than the Cavaliers would have been had they won. Nay, suppose we Tories had won the day in America: how frightful and bloody that triumph would have been! What ropes and scaffolds one imagines, what noble heads laid low! A strange feeling this, I own: I was on the Loyalist side, and yet wanted the Whigs to win. My brother Hal, on the other hand, who distinguished himself greatly with his regiment, never allowed a word of dis- respect against the enemy whom he opposed. " The officers of the British army," he used to say, " are gentlemen: at least, I have not heard that they are very much changed since my time. There may be scoundrels and ruffians amongst the enemy's troops; I dare say we could find some such amongst our own. Our business is to beat His Majesty's forces, not to call them names; any rascal can do that." And, from a name which Mr. Lee gave my brother, and many of his rough horse- men did not understand, Harry was often called " Chevalier Baird " in the Continental army. He was a knight, indeed, without fear and without reproach.

As for the argument, " What could such people as those you were drilling do against the British army? " Hal had a con- fident answer. " They can beat them," says he, " Mr. George, that's what they can do."

" Great Heavens! " I cry, " do you mean with your com- pany of Wolfe's you would hesitate to attack five hundred such? "

" With my company of the 67th I would go anywhere, and agree with you, that at this present moment I know more of soldiering than they;—but place me on that open ground where you found us, armed as you please, and half-a-dozen of my friends, with rifles, in the woods round about me: which would get the better? You know best, Mr. Braddock's aide-de- camp."

There was no arguing with such a determination as this. " Thou knowest my way of thinking, Hal," I said; " and having surprised you at your work, I must tell my Lord what I have seen."

"Tell him, of course. You have seen our county militia exercising. You will see as much in every colony from here to the St. Lawrence or Georgia. As I am an old soldier, they have elected me colonel. What more natural? Come, brother, let us trot on; dinner will be ready, and Mrs. Fan does not like me to keep it waiting." And so we made for his house, which was open, like all the houses of our Virginian gentlemen, and where not only every friend and neighbour, but every stranger and traveller, was sure to find a welcome.

"So, Mrs. Fan," I said, "I have found out what game my brother has been playing."

"I trust the Colonel will have plenty of sport ere long," says she, with a toss of her head.

My wife thought Harry had been hunting, and I did not care to undeceive her, though what I had seen and he had told me made me naturally very anxious.

CHAPTER LXXXIX

A COLONEL WITHOUT A REGIMENT

WHEN my visit to my brother was concluded, and my wife and young child had returned to our maternal house at Richmond, I made it my business to go over to our Governor, then at his country-house, near Williamsburg, and confer with him regarding these open preparations for war, which were being made not only in our own province, but in every one of the colonies, as far as we could learn. Gentlemen with whose names history has since made all the world familiar were appointed from Virginia as Delegates to the General Congress about to be held in Philadelphia. In Massachusetts the people and the Royal troops were facing each other almost in open hostility: in Maryland and Pennsylvania we flattered ourselves that a much more loyal spirit was prevalent: in the Carolinas and Georgia the mother-country could reckon upon staunch adherents, and a great majority of the inhabitants: and it never was to be supposed that our own Virginia would forego its ancient loyalty. We had but few troops in the province, but its gentry were proud of their descent from the cavaliers of the old times: and round about our Governor were swarms of loud and confident Loyalists who were only eager for the moment when they might draw the sword, and scatter the rascally rebels before them. Of course, in these meetings, I was forced to hear many a hard word against my poor Harry. His wife, all agreed (and not without good reason, perhaps), had led him to adopt these extreme anti-British opinions which he had of late declared; and he was infatuated by his attachment to the gentleman of Mount Vernon, it was farther said, whose opinions my brother always followed, and who, day by day, was committing himself farther in the dreadful and desperate course of resistance. " This is your friend," the people about his Excellency said, " this is the man you favoured, who has had your special confidence, and who has repeatedly shared your hospitality!" It could not but be owned much of this was true: though what some of our eager Loyalists called treachery, was indeed rather a proof of the longing desire Mr. Washington and other gentlemen had, not to withdraw from their allegiance to the Crown, but to remain faithful, and exhaust the very last chance of reconciliation, before they risked the other terrible alternative of revolt and separation. Let traitors arm, and villains draw the parricidal sword! We at least would remain faithful; the unconquerable power of England would be exerted, and the misguided and ungrateful provinces punished and brought back to their obedience. With what cheers we drank His Majesty's health after our banquets! We would die in defence of his rights; we would have a Prince of his Royal house to come and govern his ancient dominions! In consideration of my own and my excellent mother's loyalty, my brother's benighted conduct should be forgiven. Was it yet too late to secure him by offering him a good command? Would I not intercede with him, who, it was known, had a great influence over him? In our Williamsburg councils we were alternately in every state of exaltation and triumph, of hope, of fury against the rebels, of anxious expectancy of home succour, of doubt, distrust, and gloom.

I promised to intercede with my brother; and wrote to him, I own, with but little hope of success, repeating, and trying to strengthen the arguments which I had many a time used in our conversations. My mother, too, used her authority; but from this, I own, I expected little advantage. She assailed him, as her habit was, with such texts of Scripture as she thought bore out her own opinion, and threatened punishment to him. She menaced him with the penalties which must fall upon those who were disobedient to the powers that be. She pointed to his elder brother's example; and hinted, I fear, at his subjection to his wife, the very worst argument she could use in such a controversy. She did not show me her own letter to him; possibly she knew I might find fault with the energy of some of the expressions she thought proper to employ; but she showed me his answer, from which I gathered what the style and tenour of her argument had been. And if Madam Esmond brought Scripture to her aid, Mr. Hal, to my surprise, brought scores of texts to bear upon her in reply, and addressed her in a very neat, temperate, and even elegant composition, which I thought his wife herself was scarcely capable of penning. Indeed, I found he had enlisted the services of Mr. Belman, the new Richmond clergyman, who had taken up strong opinions on the Whig side, and who preached and printed sermons against Hagan (who, as I have said, was of our faction), in which I fear Belman had the best of the dispute.

My exhortations to Hal had no more success than our mother's. He did not answer my letters. Being still farther pressed by the friends of the Government, I wrote over most imprudently to say I would visit him at the end of the week at Fanny's Mount; but on arriving, I only found my sister, who received me with perfect cordiality, but informed me that Hal was gone into the country, ever so far towards the Blue Mountains to look at some horses, and was to be away—she did not know how long he was to be away!

I knew then there was no hope. "My dear," I said, "as far as I can judge from the signs of the times, the train that has been laid these years must have a match put to it before long. Harry is riding away. God knows to what end."

"The Lord prosper the righteous cause, Sir George," says she.

"Amen, with all my heart. You and he speak as Americans; I as an Englishman. Tell him from me, that when anything in the course of nature shall happen to our mother, I have enough for me and mine in England, and shall resign all our land here in Virginia to him."

"You don't mean that, George?" she cries, with brightening eyes. "Well, to be sure, it is but right and fair," she presently added. "Why should you, who are the eldest but by an hour, have everything,—a palace and lands in England—the plantation here—the title—and children—and my poor Harry none?

But 'tis generous of you all the same—leastways handsome and proper, and I didn't expect it of you: and you don't take after your mother in this, Sir George, that you don't nohow. Give my love to sister Theo!" And she offers me a cheek to kiss, ere I ride away from her door. With such a woman as Fanny to guide him, how could I hope to make a convert of my brother?

Having met with this poor success in my enterprise, I rode back to our Governor, with whom I agreed that it was time to arm in earnest, and prepare ourselves against the shock that certainly was at hand. He and his whole Court of Officials were not a little agitated and excited; needlessly savage, I thought, in their abuse of the wicked Whigs, and loud in their shouts of Old England for ever; but they were all eager for the day when the contending parties could meet hand to hand, and they could have an opportunity of riding those wicked Whigs down. And I left my Lord, having received the thanks of his Excellency in Council, and engaged to do my best endeavours to raise a body of men in defence of the Crown. Hence the corps, called afterwards the Westmoreland Defenders, had its rise, of which I had the honour to be appointed Colonel, and which I was to command when it appeared in the field. And that fortunate event must straightway take place, as soon as the county knew that a gentleman of my station and name would take the command of the force. The announcement was duly made in the Government *Gazette*, and we filled in our officers readily enough; but the recruits, it must be owned, were slow to come in, and quick to disappear. Nevertheless, friend Hagan eagerly came forward to offer himself as chaplain. Madam Esmond gave us our colours, and progressed about the country engaging volunteers; but the most eager recruiter of all was my good old tutor, little Mr. Dempster, who had been out as a boy on the Jacobite side in Scotland, and who went specially into the Carolinas, among the children of his banished old comrades, who had worn the white cockade of Prince Charles, and who most of all showed themselves in this contest still loyal to the Crown.

Hal's expedition in search of horses led him not only so far as the Blue Mountains in our colony, but thence on a long journey to Annapolis and Baltimore; and from Baltimore to Philadelphia, to be sure; where a second General Congress was now sitting, attended by our Virginian gentlemen of the last year. Meanwhile, all the almanacs tell what had happened. Lexington had happened, and the first shots were fired in the war which was to end in the independence of my native country. We still protested of our loyalty to His Majesty; but we stated our determination to die or be free; and some twenty thousand of our loyal petitioners assembled round about Boston with arms in their hands, and cannon, to which they had helped themselves out of the Government stores. Mr. Arnold had begun that career which was to end so brilliantly, by the daring and burglarious capture of two forts, of which he forced the doors. Three generals from Bond Street, with a large reinforcement, were on their way to help Mr. Gage out of his ugly position at Boston. Presently the armies were actually engaged; and our British generals commenced their career of conquest and pacification in the colonies by the glorious blunder of Breed's Hill. Here they fortified themselves, feeling themselves not strong enough for the moment to win any more glorious victories over the rebels; and the two armies lay watching each other whilst Congress was deliberating at Philadelphia who should command the forces of the confederated colonies.

We all know on whom the most fortunate choice of the nation fell. Of the Virginian regiments which marched to join the new General-in-Chief, one was commanded by Henry Esmond Warrington, Esq., late a Captain in His Majesty's service; and by his side rode his little wife, of whose bravery we often subsequently heard. I was glad, for one, that she had quitted Virginia; for, had she remained after her husband's departure, our mother would infallibly have gone over to give her battle; and I was thankful, at least, that that incident of civil war was spared to our family and history.

The rush of our farmers and country-folk was almost all directed towards the new northern army; and our people were not a little flattered at the selection of a Virginian gentleman for the principal command. With a thrill of wrath and fury the provinces heard of the blood drawn at Lexington; and men yelled denunciations against the cruelty and wantonness of the bloody British invader. The invader was but doing his duty, and was met and resisted by men in arms, who wished to prevent him from helping himself to his own; but people do not stay to weigh their words when they mean to be angry; the colonists had taken their side; and, with what I own to be a natural spirit and ardour, were determined to have a trial of strength with the braggart domineering mother-country.

Breed's Hill became a mountain, as it were, which all men of the American continent might behold, with Liberty, Victory, Glory, on its flaming summit. These dreaded troops could be withstood, then, by farmers and ploughmen. These famous officers could be out-generalled by doctors, lawyers, and civilians! Granted that Britons could conquer all the world;—here were their children who could match and conquer Britons! Indeed, I don't know which of the two deserves the palm, either for bravery or vainglory. We are in the habit of laughing at our French neighbours for boasting, gasconading, and so forth; but for a steady self-esteem and indomitable confidence in our own courage, greatness, magnanimity;—who can compare with Britons, except their children across the Atlantic?

The people round about us took the people's side for the most part in the struggle, and, truth to say, Sir George Warrington found his regiment of Westmoreland Defenders but very thinly manned at the commencement, and woefully diminished in numbers presently, not only after the news of battle from the north, but in consequence of the behaviour of my Lord our Governor, whose conduct enraged no one more than his own immediate partisans, and the loyal adherents of the Crown throughout the colony. That he would plant the King's standard, and summon all loyal gentlemen to rally round it, had been a measure agreed in countless meetings, and applauded over thousands of bumpers. I have a pretty good memory, and could mention the name of many a gentleman, now a smug officer of the United States Government, whom I have heard hiccup out a prayer that he might be allowed to perish under the folds of his country's flag; or roar a challenge to the bloody traitors absent with the rebel army. But let bygones be bygones. This, however, is matter of public history, that his Lordship, our Governor, a peer of Scotland, the Sovereign's representative in his Old Dominion, who so loudly invited all the lieges to join the King's standard, was the first to put it in his pocket and fly to his ships out of reach of danger. He would not leave them, save as a pirate at midnight to burn and destroy. Meanwhile, we loyal gentry remained on shore, committed to our cause, and only subject to greater danger in consequence of the weakness and cruelty of him who ought to have been our leader. It was the beginning of June, our orchards and gardens were all blooming with plenty and summer; a week before I had been over at Williamsburg, exchanging compliments with his Excellency, devising plans for future movements by which we should be able to make good head against rebellion, shaking hands heartily at parting, and *vincere aut mori* the very last words upon all our lips. Our little family was gathered at Richmond, talking over, as we did daily, the prospect of affairs in the north, the quarrels between our own Assembly and his Excellency, by whom they had been afresh convened, when our ghostly Hagan rushes into our parlour, and asks, "Have we heard the news of the Governor?"

"Has he dissolved the Assembly again, and put that scoundrel Patrick Henry in irons?" asks Madam Esmond.

"No such thing! His Lordship with his lady and family have left their palace privately at night. They are on board a man-of-war off York, whence my Lord has sent a despatch to the Assembly, begging them to continue their sitting, and announcing that he himself had only quitted his Government House out of fear of the fury of the people."

What was to become of the sheep, now the shepherd had run away? No entreaties could be more pathetic than those of the gentlemen of the House of Assembly, who guaranteed their Governor security if he would but land, and implored him to appear amongst them, if but to pass bills and transact the necessary business. No: the man-of-war was his seat of Government, and my Lord desired his House of Commons to wait upon him there. This was erecting the King's standard with a vengeance. Our Governor had left us; our Assembly perforce ruled in his stead; a rabble of people followed the fugitive Viceroy on board his ships. A mob of negroes deserted out of the plantations to join this other deserter. He and his black allies landed here and there in darkness, and emulated the most lawless of our opponents in their alacrity at seizing and burning. He not only invited runaway negroes, but he sent an ambassador to Indians with entreaties to join his standard. When he came on shore it was to burn and destroy; when the people resisted, as at Norfolk and Hampton, he retreated and betook himself to his ships again.

Even my mother, after that miserable flight of our chief, was scared at the aspect of affairs, and doubted of the speedy putting down of the rebellion. The arming of the negroes was, in her opinion, the most cowardly blow of all. The loyal gentry were ruined, and robbed, many of them, of their only property. A score of our worst hands deserted from Richmond and Castlewood, and fled to our courageous Governor's fleet; not all of them, though some of them, were slain, and a couple hung by the enemy for plunder and robbery perpetrated whilst with his Lordship's precious army. Because her property was wantonly injured and His Majesty's chief officer an imbecile, would Madam Esmond desert the cause of Royalty and Honour? My good mother was never so prodigiously dignified, and loudly and enthusiastically loyal, as after she heard of our Governor's lamentable defection. The people round about her, though most of them of quite a different way of thinking, listened to her speeches without unkindness. Her oddities were known far and wide through our province; where, I am afraid, many of the wags amongst our young men were accustomed to smoke her, as the phrase then was, and draw out her stories about the Marquis her father, about the splendour of her family, and so forth. But, along with her oddities, her charities and kindness were remembered, and many a rebel, as she called them, had a sneaking regard for the pompous little Tory lady.

As for the Colonel of the Westmoreland Defenders, though that gentleman's command dwindled utterly away after the outrageous conduct of his chief, yet I escaped from some very serious danger which might have befallen me and mine in consequence of some disputes which I was known to have had with my Lord Dunmore. Going on board his ship after he had burnt the stores at Hampton, and issued the proclamation calling the negroes to his standard, I made so free as to remonstrate with him in regard to both measures; I implored him to return to Williamsburg, where hundreds of us, thousands, I hoped, would be ready to defend him to the last extremity; and in my remonstrance used terms so free, or rather, as I suspect, indicated my contempt for his conduct so clearly by my behaviour, that his Lordship flew into a rage, said I was a —— rebel, like all the rest of them, and ordered me under arrest there on board his own ship. In my quality of Militia officer (since the breaking out of the troubles I commonly used a red coat, to show that I wore the King's colour), I begged for a court-martial immediately; and turning round to two officers who had been present during our altercation, desired them to remember all that had passed between his Lordship and me. These gentlemen were no doubt of my way of thinking as to the chief's behaviour, and our interview ended in my going ashore unaccompanied by a guard. The story got wind amongst the Whig gentry, and was improved in the telling. I had spoken out my mind manfully to the Governor; no Whig could have uttered sentiments more liberal. When riots took place in Richmond, and many of the

Loyalists remaining there were in peril of life and betook themselves to the ships, my mother's property and house were never endangered, nor her family insulted. We were still at the stage when a reconciliation was fondly thought possible. " Ah! if all the Tories were like you," a distinguished Whig has said to me, " we and the people at home should soon come together again." This, of course, was before the famous Fourth of July, and that declaration which rendered reconcilement impossible. Afterwards, when parties grew more rancorous, motives much less creditable were assigned for my conduct, and it was said I chose to be a Liberal Tory because I was a cunning fox, and wished to keep my estate whatever way things went. And this, I am bound to say, is the opinion regarding my humble self which has obtained in very high quarters at home, where a profound regard for my own interest has been supposed not uncommonly to have occasioned my conduct during the late unhappy troubles.

There were two or three persons in the world (for I had not told my mother how I was resolved to cede to my brother all my life-interest in our American property) who knew that I had no mercenary motives in regard to the conduct I pursued. It was not worth while to undeceive others; what were life worth, if a man were forced to put himself à la piste of all the calumnies uttered against him? And I do not quite know to this present day, how it happened that my mother, that notorious Loyalist, was left for several years quite undisturbed in her house at Castlewood, a stray troop or company of Continentals being occasionally quartered upon her. I do not know for certain, I say, how this piece of good fortune happened, though I can give a pretty shrewd guess as to the cause of it. Madam Fanny, after a campaign before Boston, came back to Fanny's Mount, leaving her Colonel. My modest Hal, until the conclusion of the war, would accept no higher rank, believing that in command of a regiment he could be more useful than in charge of a division. Madam Fanny, I say, came back, and it was remarkable after her return how her old asperity towards my mother seemed to be removed, and what an affection she showed for her and all the property. She was great friends with the Governor and some of the most influential gentlemen of the new Assembly:—Madam Esmond was harmless, and for her son's sake, who was bravely battling for his country, her errors should be lightly visited:—I know not how it was, but for years she remained unharmed, except in respect of heavy Government

requisitions, which of course she had to pay, and it was not until
the red-coats appeared about our house, that much serious evil
came to it.

CHAPTER XC

IN WHICH WE BOTH FIGHT AND RUN AWAY

WHAT was the use of a Colonel without a regiment? The
Governor and Council who had made such a parade of thanks
in endowing me with mine, were away out of sight, skulking on
board ships, with an occasional piracy and arson on shore. My
Lord Dunmore's black allies frightened away those of his own
blood; and besides these negroes whom he had summoned
around him in arms, we heard that he had sent an envoy among
the Indians of the South, and that they were to come down in
numbers and tomahawk our people into good behaviour. " And
these are to be our allies ! " I say to my mother, exchanging
ominous looks with her, and remembering, with a ghastly dis-
tinctness, that savage whose face glared over mine, and whose
knife was at my throat when Florac struck him down on Braddock's field. We put our house of Castlewood into as good a
state of defence as we could devise; but, in truth, it was more
of the red men and the blacks than of the rebels we were afraid.
I never saw my mother lose courage but once, and then when
she was recounting to us the particulars of our father's death in
a foray of Indians more than forty years ago. Seeing some
figures one night moving in front of our house, nothing could
persuade the good lady but that they were savages, and she sank
on her knees crying out, " The Lord have mercy upon us ! The
Indians—the Indians ! "

My Lord's negro allies vanished on board his ships, or where
they could find pay and plunder; but the painted heroes from
the South never made their appearance, though I own to have
looked at my mother's grey head, my wife's brown hair, and our
little one's golden ringlets, with a horrible pang of doubt lest
these should fall the victims of ruffian war. And it was we who
fought with such weapons, and enlisted these allies ! But that
I *dare* not (so to speak) be setting myself up as interpreter of
Providence, and pointing out the special finger of Heaven (as
many people are wont to do), I would say our employment of

these Indians, and of the German mercenaries, brought their own retribution with them in this war. In the field, where the mercenaries were attacked by the Provincials, they yielded, and it was triumphing over them that so raised the spirit of the Continental army; and the murder of one woman (Miss M'Crea) by a half-dozen Indians, did more harm to the Royal cause than the loss of a battle or the destruction of regiments.

Now, the Indian panic over, Madam Esmond's courage returned: and she began to be seriously and not unjustly uneasy at the danger which I ran myself, and which I brought upon others by remaining in Virginia.

"What harm can they do me," says she, "a poor woman? If I have one son a Colonel without a regiment, I have another with a couple of hundred Continentals behind him in Mr. Washington's camp. If the Royalists come, they will let me off for your sake; if the rebels appear, I shall have Harry's passport. I don't wish, sir, I don't like, that your delicate wife, and this dear little baby should be here, and only increase the risk of all of us! We must have them away to Boston or New York. Don't talk about defending me! Who will think of hurting a poor harmless old woman? If the rebels come, I shall shelter behind Mrs. Fanny's petticoats, and shall be much safer without you in the house than in it." This she said in part, perhaps, because 'twas reasonable; more so because she would have me and my family out of the danger; and danger or not, for her part she was determined to remain in the land where her father was buried, and she was born. She was living *backwards*, so to speak. She had seen the new generation, and blessed them, and bade them farewell. She belonged to the past, and old days and memories.

While we were debating about the Boston scheme, comes the news that the British have evacuated that luckless city altogether, never having ventured to attack Mr. Washington in his camp at Cambridge (though he lay there for many months without powder at our mercy); but waiting until he procured ammunition, and seized and fortified Dorchester heights, which commanded the town, out of which the whole British army and colony was obliged to beat a retreat. That the King's troops won the battle at Bunker's Hill, there is no more doubt than that they beat the French at Blenheim; but through the war their chiefs seem constantly to have been afraid of assaulting intrenched Continentals afterwards; else why, from July to March, hesitate to strike an almost defenceless enemy? Why the hesitation at Long Island, when the Continental army was in our hand? Why that astonishing timorousness of Howe before Valley Forge, where the relics of a force starving, sickening, and in rags, could scarcely man the lines, which they held before a great, victorious, and perfectly appointed army?

As the hopes and fears of the contending parties rose and fell, it was curious to mark the altered tone of the partisans of either. When the news came to us in the country of the evacuation of Boston every little Whig in the neighbourhood made his bow to Madam, and advised her to a speedy submission. She did not carry her loyalty quite so openly as heretofore, and flaunt her flag in the faces of the public, but she never swerved. Every night and morning in private poor Hagan prayed for the Royal Family in our own household, and on Sundays any neighbours were welcome to attend the service, where my mother acted as a very emphatic clerk, and the prayer for the High Court of Parliament under our Most Religious and Gracious King, was very stoutly delivered. The brave Hagan was a parson without a living, as I was a Militia Colonel without a regiment. Hagan had continued to pray stoutly for King George in Williamsburg, long after his Excellency our Governor had run away: but on coming to church one Sunday to perform his duty, he found a corporal's guard at the church door, who told him that the Committee of Safety had put another divine in his place, and he was requested to keep a quiet tongue in his head. He told the men to "lead him before their chiefs" (our honest friend always loved tall words and tragic attitudes); and accordingly was marched through the streets to the Capitol, with a chorus of white and coloured blackguards at the skirts of his gown; and had an interview with Mr. Henry and the new State officers, and confronted the robbers, as he said, in their den. Of course he was for making an heroic speech before these gentlemen (and was one of many men who perhaps would have no objection to be made martyrs, so that they might be roasted *coram populo*, or tortured in a full house), but Mr. Henry was determined to give him no such chance. After keeping Hagan three or four hours waiting in an ante-room in the company of negroes, when the worthy divine entered the new chief magistrate's room with an undaunted mien, and began a prepared speech with—"Sir, by what authority am I, a minister of the—" "Mr. Hagan," says the other, interrupting him, "I am too busy to listen to speeches. And as for King George, he has henceforth no more authority in this country than King Nebuchadnezzar. Mind you that, and hold your tongue, if you please! Stick to King John, sir, and King Macbeth; and if you will send round your benefit-tickets, all the Assembly shall come and hear you. Did you ever see Mr. Hagan, on the boards, when you was in London, General?" And, so saying, Henry turns round upon Mr. Washington's second in command, General Lee, who was now come into Virginia upon State affairs, and our shamefaced good Hagan was bustled out of the room, reddening and almost crying with shame. After this event we thought that Hagan's ministrations were best confined to us in the country, and removed the worthy pastor from his restive lambs in the city.

The selection of Virginians to the very highest civil and military appointments of the new Government bribed and flattered many of our leading people, who but for the outrageous conduct of our Government might have remained faithful to the Crown, and made good head against the rising rebellion. But, although we Loyalists were gagged and muzzled, though the Capitol was in the hands of the Whigs, and our vaunted levies of loyal recruits so many Falstaff's regiments, for the most part, the faithful still kept intelligences with one another in the colony, and with our neighbours; and though we did not rise, and though we ran away, and though, in examination before committees, justices, and so forth, some of our frightened people gave themselves Republican airs, and vowed perdition to kings and nobles; yet we knew each other pretty well, and—according as the chances were more or less favourable to us, the master more or less hard—we concealed our colours, showed our colours, half showed our colours, or downright apostatised for the nonce, and cried " Down with King George! " Our negroes bore about, from house to house, all sorts of messages and tokens. Endless underhand plots and schemes were engaged in by those who could not afford the light. The battle over, the neutrals come and join the winning side, and shout as loudly as the patriots. The runaways are not counted. Will any man tell me that the signers and ardent well-wishers of the Declaration of Independence were not in a minority of the nation, and that the minority did not win? We knew that a part of the defeated army of Massachusetts was about to make an important expedition southward, upon the success of which the very greatest hopes were founded; and I, for one, being anxious to make a movement as soon as there was any chance of activity, had put myself in communication with the ex-Governor Martin, of North Carolina, whom I proposed to join, with three or four of

our Virginian gentlemen, officers of that notable corps of which
we only wanted privates. We made no particular mystery
about our departure from Castlewood; the affairs of Congress
were not going so well yet that the new Government could afford
to lay any particular stress or tyranny upon persons of a doubtful way of thinking. Gentlemen's houses were still open; and in
our Southern fashion we would visit our friends for months at a
time. My wife and I, with our infant and a fitting suite of
servants, took leave of Madam Esmond on a visit to a neighbouring plantation. We went thence to another friend's house, and
then to another, till finally we reached Wilmington, in North
Carolina, which was the point at which we expected to stretch
a hand to the succours which were coming to meet us.

Ere our arrival, our brother Carolinian Royalists had shown
themselves in some force. Their encounters with the Whigs
had been unlucky. The poor Highlanders had been no more
fortunate in their present contest in favour of King George, than
when they had drawn their swords against him in their own
country. We did not reach Wilmington until the end of May,
by which time we found Admiral Parker's squadron there, with
General Clinton and five British regiments on board, whose
object was a descent upon Charleston.

The General, to whom I immediately made myself known,
seeing that my regiment consisted of Lady Warrington, our
infant, whom she was nursing, and three negro servants, received
us at first with a very grim welcome. But Captain Horner of
the "Sphinx" frigate, who had been on the Jamaica station,
and received, like all the rest of the world, many kindnesses
from our dear Governor there, when he heard that my wife was
General Lambert's daughter, eagerly received her on board, and
gave up his best cabin to our service; and so we were refugees,
too, like my Lord Dunmore, having waved our flag, to be sure,
and pocketed it, and slipped out at the back door. From
Wilmington we bore away quickly to Charleston, and in the
course of the voyage and our delay in the river, previous to our
assault on the place, I made some acquaintance with Mr. Clinton
which increased to a further intimacy. It was the King's
birthday when we appeared in the river: we determined it was
a glorious day for the commencement of the expedition.

It did not take place for some days after, and I leave out, pur-
posely, all descriptions of my Andromache parting from her
Hector, going forth on this expedition. In the first place, Hector
is perfectly well (though a little gouty), nor has any rascal of a

Pyrrhus made a prize of his widow: and in times of war and commotion, are not such scenes of woe and terror, and parting, occurring every hour? I can see the gentle face yet over the bulwark, as we descend the ship's side into the boats, and the smile of the infant on her arm. What old stories, to be sure! Captain Miles, having no natural taste for poetry, you have forgot the verses, no doubt, in Mr. Pope's " Homer," in which you are described as parting with your heroic father; but your mother often read them to you as a boy, and keeps the gorget I wore on that day somewhere amongst her dressing-boxes now.

My second venture at fighting was no more lucky than my first. We came back to our ships that evening thoroughly beaten. The madcap Lee, whom Clinton had faced at Boston, now met him at Charleston. Lee, and the gallant garrison there, made a brilliant and most successful resistance. The fort on Sullivan's Island, which we attacked, was a nut we could not crack. The fire of all our frigates was not strong enough to pound its shell; the passage by which we moved up to the assault of the place was not fordable, as those officers found—Sir Henry at the head of them, who was always the first to charge— who attempted to wade it. Death by shot, by drowning, by catching my death of cold, I had braved before I returned to my wife; and our frigate being aground for a time and got off with difficulty, was agreeably cannonaded by the enemy until she got off her bank.

A small incident in the midst of this unlucky struggle was the occasion of a subsequent intimacy which arose between me and Sir Harry Clinton, and bound me to that most gallant officer during the period in which it was my fortune to follow the war. Of his qualifications as a leader there may be many opinions: I fear to say, regarding a man I heartily respect and admire, there ought only to be one. Of his personal bearing and his courage there can be no doubt; he was always eager to show it; and whether at the final charge on Breed's Hill, when at the head of the rallied troops he carried the Continental lines, or here before Sullivan's Fort, or a year later at Fort Washington, when, standard in hand, he swept up the height, and entered the fort at the head of the storming column, Clinton was always foremost in the race of battle, and the King's service knew no more admirable soldier.

We were taking to the water from our boats, with the intention of forcing a column to the fort, through a way which our own guns had rendered practicable, when a shot struck a boat alongside of us, so well aimed, as actually to put three-fourths of the boat's crew *hors de combat*, and knocked down the officer steering, and the flag behind him. I could not help crying out, " Bravo! well aimed! " for no ninepins ever went down more helplessly than these poor fellows before the round shot. Then the General, turning round to me, says rather grimly, " Sir, the behaviour of the enemy seems to please you! " " I am pleased, sir," says I, " that my countrymen, yonder, should fight as becomes our nation." We floundered on towards the fort in the midst of the same amiable attentions from small arms and great, until we found the water was up to our breasts and deepening at every step, when we were fain to take to our boats again and pull out of harm's way. Sir Henry waited upon my Lady Warrington on board the " Sphinx " after this, and was very gracious to her, and mighty facetious regarding the character of the humble writer of the present Memoir, whom his Excellency always described as a rebel at heart. I pray my children may live to see or engage in no great revolutions,—such as that, for instance, raging in the country of our miserable French neighbours. Save a very very few indeed, the actors in those great tragedies do not bear to be scanned too closely; the chiefs are often no better than ranting quacks; the heroes ignoble puppets: the heroines anything but pure. The prize is not always to the brave. In our revolution it certainly did fall, for once and for a wonder, to the most deserving: but who knows his enemies now? His great and surprising triumphs were not in those rare engagements with the enemy where he obtained a trifling mastery; but over Congress; over hunger and disease; over lukewarm friends, or smiling foes in his own camp, whom his great spirit had to meet, and master. When the struggle was over, and our impotent chiefs who had conducted it began to squabble and accuse each other in their own defence before the nation,—what charges and counter-charges were brought; what pretexts of delay were urged; what piteous excuses were put forward that this fleet arrived too late ; that that regiment mistook its orders; that these cannon-balls would not fit those guns: and so to the end of the chapter! Here was a general who beat us with *no* shot at times, and no powder, and no money; and *he* never thought of a convention; *his* courage never capitulated! Through all the doubt and darkness, the danger and long tempest of the war, I think it was only the American leader's indomitable soul that remained entirely steady.

Of course our Charleston expedition was made the most of, and pronounced a prodigious victory by the enemy, who had learnt (from their parents, perhaps) to cry victory if a corporal's guard were surprised, as loud as if we had won a pitched battle. Mr. Lee rushed back to New York, the conqueror of conquerors, trumpeting his glory, and by no man received with more eager delight than by the Commander-in-Chief of the American army. It was my dear Lee and my dear General between them, then; and it hath always touched me in the history of our early Revolution to note that simple confidence and admiration with which the General-in-Chief was wont to regard officers under him, who had happened previously to serve with the King's army. So the Mexicans of old looked and wondered when they first saw an armed Spanish horseman! And this mad flashy braggart (and another Continental General, whose name and whose luck afterwards were sufficiently notorious) you may be sure took advantage of the modesty of the Commander-in-Chief, and advised, and blustered, and sneered, and disobeyed orders; daily presenting fresh obstacles (as if he had not enough otherwise!) in the path over which only Mr. Washington's astonishing endurance could have enabled him to march.

Whilst we were away on our South Carolina expedition, the famous Fourth of July had taken place, and we and the thirteen United States were parted for ever. My own native State of Virginia had also distinguished itself by announcing that all men are equally free; that all power is vested in the people, who have an inalienable right to alter, reform, or abolish their form of government *at pleasure*, and that the idea of an hereditary first magistrate is unnatural and absurd! Our General presented me with this document fresh from Williamsburg, as we were sailing northward by the Virginia capes, and, amidst not a little amusement and laughter, pointed out to me the faith to which, from the Fourth inst. inclusive, I was bound. There was no help for it; I was a Virginian—my godfathers had promised and vowed, in my name, that all men were equally free (including, of course, the race of poor Gumbo), that the idea of a monarchy is absurd, and that I had the right to alter my form of government *at pleasure*. I thought of Madam Esmond at home, and how she would look when these articles of faith were brought her to subscribe: how would Hagan receive them? He demolished them in a sermon, in which all the logic was on his side; but the U.S. Government has not, somehow, been affected by the discourse; and when he came to touch upon the point that all men being free, therefore Gumbo and Sady, and Nathan, had assuredly a right to go to Congress: "Tut, tut! my good Mr. Hagan," says my mother, "let us hear no more of this nonsense; but leave such wickedness and folly to the rebels!"

By the middle of August we were before New York, whither Mr. Howe had brought his army that had betaken itself to Halifax after its inglorious expulsion from Boston. The American Commander-in-Chief was at New York, and a great battle inevitable; and I looked forward to it with an inexpressible feeling of doubt and anxiety, knowing that my dearest brother and his regiment formed part of the troops whom we must attack, and could not but overpower. Almost the whole of the American army came over to fight on a small island, where every officer on both sides knew that they were to be beaten, and whence they had not a chance of escape. Two frigates, out of a hundred we had placed so as to command the enemy's intrenched camp and point of retreat across East River to New York, would have destroyed every bark in which he sought to fly, and compelled him to lay down his arms on shore. He fought: his hasty levies were utterly overthrown; some of his generals, his best troops, his artillery taken; the remnant huddled into their intrenched camp after their rout, the pursuers entering it with them. The victors were called back; the enemy was then pent up in a corner of the island, and could not escape. "They are at our mercy, and are ours to-morrow," says the gentle General. Not a ship was set to watch the American force; not a sentinel of ours could see a movement in their camp. A whole army crossed under our eyes in one single night to the mainland without the loss of a single man; and General Howe was suffered to remain in command after this feat, and to complete his glories of Long Island and Breed's Hill, at Philadelphia! A friend, to be sure, crossed in the night to say the enemy's army was being ferried over, but he fell upon a picket of Germans: they could not understand him: their commander was boozing or asleep. In the morning, when the spy was brought to some one who could comprehend the American language, the whole Continental force had crossed the East River, and our empire over thirteen colonies had slipped away.

The opinions I had about our chief were by no means uncommon in the army; though, perhaps, wisely kept secret by gentlemen under Mr. Howe's immediate command. Am I more unlucky than other folks, I wonder? or why are my imprudent sayings carried about more than my neighbours? My rage that such a use was made of such a victory was no greater than that of scores of gentlemen with the army. Why must my name forsooth be given up to the Commander-in-Chief as that of the most guilty of the grumblers? Personally, General Howe was perfectly brave, amiable, and good-humoured.

"So, Sir George," says he, "you find fault with me, as a military man, because there was a fog after the battle on Long Island, and your friends, the Continentals, gave me the slip! Surely we took and killed enough of them; but there is no satisfying you gentlemen amateurs!" and he turned his back on me, and shrugged his shoulders, and talked to some one else. Amateur I might be, and he the most amiable of men; but if King George had said to him, "Never more be officer of mine," yonder agreeable and pleasant Cassio would most certainly have had his desert.

I soon found how our Chief had come in possession of his information regarding myself. My admirable cousin, Mr. William Esmond—who of course had forsaken New York and his post, when all the Royal authorities fled out of the place, and Washington occupied it,—returned along with our troops and fleets; and, being a gentleman of good birth and name, and well acquainted with the city, made himself agreeable to the new-comers of the Royal army, the young bloods, merry fellows, and macaronis, by introducing them to play-tables, taverns, and yet worse places, with which the worthy gentleman continued to be familiar in the New World as in the Old. *Cœlum non animum.* However Will had changed his air, or whithersoever he transported his carcase, he carried a rascal in his skin.

I had heard a dozen stories of his sayings regarding my family, and was determined neither to avoid him nor seek him; but to call him to account whensoever we met; and, chancing one day to be at a coffee-house in a friend's company, my worthy kinsman swaggered in with a couple of young lads of the army, whom he found it was his pleasure and profit now to lead into every kind of dissipation. I happened to know one of Mr. Will's young companions, an aide-de-camp of General Clinton's, who had been in my close company both at Charleston, before Sullivan's Island, and in the action of Brooklyn, where our General gloriously led the right wing of the English army. They took a box without noticing us at first, though I heard my name three or four times mentioned by my brawling kinsman, who ended some drunken speech he was making by slapping his fist on the table, and swearing, " By ——, I will do for him, and the bloody rebel, his brother! "

" Ah! Mr. Esmond," says I, coming forward with my hat on. (He looked a little pale behind his punch-bowl.) " I have long wanted to see you, to set some little matters right about which there has been a difference between us."

" And what may those be, sir? " says he, with a volley of oaths.

" You have chosen to cast a doubt upon my courage, and say that I shirked a meeting with you when we were young men. Our relationship and our age ought to prevent us from having recourse to such murderous follies " (Mr. Will started up looking fierce and relieved); " but I give you notice, that though I can afford to overlook lies against myself, if I hear from you a word in disparagement of my brother, Colonel Warrington, of the Continental Army, I will hold you accountable."

" Indeed, gentlemen? Mighty fine, indeed! You take notice of Sir George Warrington's words! " cries Mr. Will over his punch-bowl.

" You have been pleased to say," I continued, growing angry as I spoke, and being a fool therefore for my pains, " that the very estates we hold in this country are not ours, but of right revert to your family! "

" So they are ours! By George they're ours! I've heard my brother Castlewood say so a score of times! " swears Mr. Will.

" In that case, sir," says I hotly, " your brother, my Lord Castlewood, tells no more truth than yourself. We have the titles at home in Virginia. They are registered in the courts there; and if ever I hear one word more of this impertinence, I shall call you to account where no constables will be at hand to interfere! "

" I wonder," cries Will, in a choking voice, " that I don't cut him into twenty thousand pieces as he stands there before me with his confounded yellow face. It was my brother Castlewood won his money—no, it was his brother: d—— you, which are you, the rebel or the other? I hate the ugly faces of both of you, and, hic!—if you are for the King, show you are for the King, and drink his health! " and he sank down into his box with a hiccup and a wild laugh, which he repeated a dozen times, with a hundred more oaths and vociferous outcries that I should drink the King's health.

To reason with a creature in this condition, or ask explanations or apologies from him, was absurd. I left Mr. Will to reel to his lodgings under the care of his young friends—who were surprised to find an old toper so suddenly affected and so utterly prostrated by liquor—and limped home to my wife, whom I found happy in possession of a brief letter from Hal, which a countryman had brought in; and who said not a word about the affairs of the Continentals with whom he was engaged, but wrote a couple of pages of rapturous eulogiums upon his brother's behaviour in the field, which my dear Hal was pleased to admire, as he admired everything I said and did.

I rather looked for a message from my amiable kinsman in consequence of the speeches which had passed between us the night before, and did not know but that I might be called by Will to make my words good; and when accordingly Mr. Lacy (our companion of the previous evening) made his appearance at an early hour of the forenoon, I was beckoning my Lady Warrington to leave us, when, with a laugh and cry of " Oh dear, no! " Mr. Lacy begged her Ladyship not to disturb herself.

" I have seen," says he, " a gentleman who begs to send you his apologies if he uttered a word last night which could offend you."

" What apologies? what words? " asks the anxious wife.

I explained that roaring Will Esmond had met me in a coffee-house on the previous evening, and quarrelled with me, as he had done with hundreds before. " It appears the fellow is constantly abusive, and invariably pleads drunkenness, and apologises the next morning, unless he is caned overnight," remarked Captain Lacy. And my Lady, I daresay, makes a little sermon, and asks why we gentlemen will go to idle coffee-houses and run the risk of meeting roaring roystering Will Esmonds?

Our sojourn in New York was enlivened by a project for burning the city which some ardent patriots entertained and partially executed. Several such schemes were laid in the course of the war, and each one of the principal cities was doomed to fire; though, in the interests of peace and goodwill, I hope it will be remembered that these plans never originated with the cruel Government of a tyrant King, but were always proposed by the gentlemen on the Continental side, who vowed that, rather than remain under the ignominious despotism of the ruffian of Brunswick, the fairest towns of America should burn. I presume that the sages who were for burning down Boston were not actual proprietors in that place, and the New York burners might come from other parts of the country—from Philadelphia, or what not. Howbeit, the British spared you, gentlemen, and we pray you give us credit for this act of moderation.

I had not the fortune to be present in the action on the White Plains, being detained by a hurt which I had received at Long Island, and which broke out again and again, and took some time in the healing. The tenderest of nurses watched me through my tedious malady, and was eager for the day when I should doff my militia-coat, and return to the quiet English home where Hetty and our good General were tending our children. Indeed, I don't know that I have yet forgiven myself for the pains and terrors that I must have caused my poor wife, by keeping her separate from her young ones, and away from her home, because, forsooth, I wished to see a little more of the war then going on. Our grand tour in Europe had been all very well. We had beheld St. Peter's at Rome, and the Bishop thereof; the Dauphiness of France (alas, to think that glorious head should ever have been brought so low!) at Paris; and the rightful King of England at Florence. I had dipped my gout in a half-dozen baths and spas, and played cards in a hundred courts, as my " Travels in Europe " (which I propose to publish after the completion of my " History of the American War ") will testify.[1] And, during our peregrinations, my hypochondria diminished (which plagued me woefully at home); and my health and spirits visibly improved. Perhaps it was because she saw the evident benefit I had from excitement and change, that my wife was reconciled to my continuing to enjoy them: and though secretly suffering pangs at being away from her nursery and her eldest boy (for whom she ever has had an absurd infatuation), the dear hypocrite scarce allowed a look of anxiety to appear on her face; encouraged me with smiles; professed herself eager to follow me; asked why it should be a sin in me to covet honour? and, in a word, was ready to stay, to go, to smile, to be sad; to scale mountains, or to go down to the sea in ships; to say that cold was pleasant, heat tolerable, hunger good sport, dirty lodgings delightful; though she is a wretched sailor, very delicate about the little she eats, and an extreme sufferer both of cold and heat. Hence, as I willed to stay on yet awhile on my native continent, she was certain nothing was so good for me; and when I was minded to return home—oh, how she brightened, and kissed her infant, and told

[1] Neither of these two projected works of Sir George Warrington were brought, as it appears, to a completion.

him how he should see the beautiful gardens at home, and Aunt
Hetty, and grandpapa, and his sister, and Miles. "Miles!"
cries the little parrot, mocking its mother—and crowing; as if
there was any mighty privilege in seeing Mr. Miles, forsooth,
who was under Doctor Sumner's care at Harrow-on-the-Hill,
where, to do the gentleman justice, he showed that he could eat
more tarts than any boy in the school, and took most creditable
prizes at football and hare-and-hounds.

CHAPTER XCI

SATIS PUGNÆ

IT has always seemed to me (I speak under the correction of
military gentlemen) that the intrenchments of Breed's Hill
served the Continental army throughout the whole of our
American war. The slaughter inflicted upon us from behind
those lines was so severe, and the behaviour of the enemy so
resolute, that the British chiefs respected the barricades of the
Americans afterwards; and were they firing from behind a row
of blankets, certain of our generals rather hesitated to force
them. In the affair of the White Plains, when, for a second
time, Mr. Washington's army was quite at the mercy of the
victors, we subsequently heard that our conquering troops were
held back before a barricade actually composed of corn-stalks
and straw. Another opportunity was given us, and lasted
during a whole winter, during which the dwindling and dismayed troops of Congress lay starving and unarmed under our
grasp, and the magnanimous Mr. Howe left the famous camp of
Valley Forge untouched, whilst his great, brave, and perfectly
appointed army fiddled and gambled and feasted in Philadelphia. And, by BYNG's countrymen, triumphal arches were
erected, tournaments were held in pleasant mockery of the
middle ages, and wreaths and garlands offered by beautiful
ladies to this clement chief, with fantastical mottoes and posies
announcing that his laurels should be immortal! Why have
my ungrateful countrymen in America never erected statues to
this general? They had not in all their army an officer who
fought their battles better; who enabled them to retrieve their
errors with such adroitness; who took care that their defeats
should be so little hurtful to themselves: and when, in the

course of events, the stronger force naturally got the uppermost, who showed such an untiring tenderness, patience, and complacency in helping the poor disabled opponent on to his legs again. Ah! think of eighteen years before, and the fiery young warrior whom England had sent out to fight her adversary on the American continent. Fancy him for ever pacing round the defences behind which the foe lies sheltered; by night and by day alike sleepless and eager; consuming away in his fierce wrath and longing, and never closing his eye, so intent is it in watching; winding the track with untiring scent that pants and hungers for blood and battle; prowling through midnight forests, or climbing silent over precipices before dawn; and watching till his great heart is almost worn out, until the foe shows himself at last, when he springs on him and grapples with him, and, dying, slays him! Think of Wolfe at Quebec, and hearken to Howe's fiddles as he sits smiling amongst the dancers at Philadelphia.

A favourite scheme with our Ministers at home and some of our generals in America, was to establish a communication between Canada and New York, by which means it was hoped New England might be cut off from the neighbouring colonies, overpowered in detail, and forced into submission. Burgoyne was intrusted with the conduct of the plan, and he set forth from Quebec, confidently promising to bring it to a successful issue. His march began in military state: the trumpets of his proclamations blew before him; he bade the colonists to remember the immense power of England: and summoned the misguided rebels to lay down their arms. He brought with him a formidable English force, an army of German veterans not less powerful, a dreadful band of Indian warriors, and a brilliant train of artillery. It was supposed that the people round his march would rally to the royal cause and standards. The Continental force in front of him was small at first, and Washington's army was weakened by the withdrawal of troops who were hurried forward to meet this Canadian invasion. A British detachment from New York was to force its way up the Hudson, sweeping away the enemy on the route, and make a junction with Burgoyne at Albany. Then was the time when Washington's weakened army should have been struck too; but a greater Power willed otherwise: nor am I, for one, even going to regret the termination of the war. As we look over the game now, how clear seem the blunders which were made by the losing side! From the beginning to the end we were for ever arriving too late. Our supplies and reinforcements from home were too late. Our troops were in difficulty, and our succours reached them too late. Our fleet appeared off York Town just too late, after Cornwallis had surrendered. A way of escape was opened to Burgoyne, but he resolved upon retreat too late. I have heard discomfited officers in after days prove infallibly how a different wind would have saved America to us; how we must have destroyed the French fleet but for a tempest or two; how once, twice, thrice, but for nightfall, Mr. Washington and his army were in our power. Who has not speculated, in the course of his reading of history, upon the " Has been " and the " Might have been " in the world! I take my tattered old map-book from the shelf, and see the board on which the great contest was played; I wonder at the curious chances which lost it: and, putting aside any idle talk about the respective bravery of the two nations, can't but see that we had the best cards, and that we lost the game.

I own the sport had a considerable fascination for me, and stirred up my languid blood. My brother Hal, when settled on his plantation in Virginia, was perfectly satisfied with the sports and occupations he found there. The company of the country neighbours sufficed him; he never tired of looking after his crops and people, taking his fish, shooting his ducks, hunting in his woods, or enjoying his rubber, and his supper. Happy Hal, in his great barn of a house, under his roomy porches, his dogs lying round his feet: his friends, the Virginian Will Wimbles, at free quarters in his mansion; his negroes fat, lazy, and ragged: his shrewd little wife ruling over them and her husband, who always obeyed her implicitly when living, and who was speedily consoled when she died! I say happy, though his lot would have been intolerable to me: wife, and friends, and plantation, and town life at Richmond (Richmond succeeded to the honour of being the capital when our province became a state). How happy he whose foot fits the shoe which fortune gives him! My income was five times as great, my house in England as large, and built of bricks and faced with freestone; my wife—would I have changed her for any other wife in the world? My children—well, I am contented with my Lady Warrington's opinion about *them*. But with all these plums and peaches and rich fruits out of plenty's horn poured into my lap, I fear I have been but an ingrate; and Hodge, my gatekeeper, who shares his bread and scrap of bacon with a family as large as his master's, seems to me to enjoy his meal as

much as I do, though Mrs. Molly prepares her best dishes and
sweetmeats, and Mr. Gumbo uncorks the choicest bottles from
the cellar. Ah me! sweetmeats have lost their savour for me,
however they may rejoice my young ones from the nursery,
and the perfume of claret palls upon old noses! Our parson
has poured out his sermons many and many a time to me, and
perhaps I did not care for them much when he first broached
them. Dost thou remember, honest friend (sure he does, for he
has repeated the story over the bottle as many times as his
sermons almost, and my Lady Warrington pretends as if she
had never heard it)—I say, Joe Blake, thou rememberest ful
well, and with advantages, that October evening when we
scrambled up an embrasure at Fort Clinton, and a clubbed
musket would have dashed these valuable brains out, had not
Joe's sword whipped my rebellious countryman through the
gizzard. Joe wore a red coat in those days (the uniform of the
brave Sixty-third, whose leader, the bold Sill, fell pierced with
many wounds beside him). He exchanged his red for black
and my pulpit. His doctrines are sound and his sermons short.
We read the papers together over our wine. Not two months
ago we read our old friend Howe's glorious deed of the first of
June. We were told how the noble Rawdon, who fought with
us at Fort Clinton, had joined the Duke of York: and to-day
His Royal Highness is in full retreat before Pichegru: and he
and my son Miles have taken Valenciennes for nothing! Ah,
Parson! would you not like to put on your old Sixty-third coat?
(though I doubt Mrs. Blake could never make the buttons and
button-holes meet again over your big body). The boys were
acting a play with my militia sword. Oh, that I were young
again, Mr. Blake! that I had not the gout in my toe; and I
would saddle Rosinante and ride back into the world, and feel
the pulses beat again, and play a little of life's glorious game!

The last " *hit* " which I saw played was gallantly won by our
side; though 'tis true that even in this *parti* the Americans won
the rubber—our people gaining only the ground they stood on,
and the guns, stores, and ships which they captured and destroyed, whilst our efforts at rescue were too late to prevent
the catastrophe impending over Burgoyne's unfortunate army.
After one of those delays which *always* were happening to retard
our plans and weaken the blows which our chiefs intended to
deliver, an expedition was got under way from New York at the
close of the month of September, '77; that, could it but have
advanced a fortnight earlier, might have saved the doomed

force of Burgoyne. *Sed Dis aliter visum.* The delay here was not Sir Henry Clinton's fault, who could not leave his city unprotected; but the winds and weather which delayed the arrival of reinforcements which we had long awaited from England. The fleet which brought them brought us long and fond letters from home, with the very last news of the children under the care of their good Aunt Hetty and their grandfather. The mother's heart yearned towards the absent young ones. She made me no reproaches: but I could read her importunities in her anxious eyes, her terrors for me, and her longing for her children. "Why stay longer?" she seemed to say. "You have no calling to this war, or to draw the sword against your countrymen—why continue to imperil your life and my happiness?" I understood her appeal. We were to enter upon no immediate service of danger; I told her Sir Henry was only going to accompany the expedition for a part of the way. I would return with him, the reconnaissance over, and Christmas, please Heaven, should see our family once more united in England.

A force of three thousand men, including a couple of slender regiments of American Loyalists and New York Militia (with which latter my distinguished relative, Mr. Will Esmond, went as captain), was embarked at New York, and our armament sailed up the noble Hudson river, that presents finer aspects than the Rhine in Europe to my mind: nor was any fire opened upon us from those beetling cliffs and precipitous "palisades," as they are called, by which we sailed; the enemy, strange to say, being for once unaware of the movement we contemplated. Our first landing was on the eastern bank, at a place called Verplancks Point, whence the Congress troops withdrew after a slight resistance, their leader, the tough old Putnam (so famous during the war), supposing that our march was to be directed towards the Eastern Highlands, by which we intended to penetrate to Burgoyne. Putnam fell back to occupy these passes, a small detachment of ours being sent forward as if in pursuit, which he imagined was to be followed by the rest of our force. Meanwhile, before daylight, two thousand men without artillery were carried over to Stoney Point on the western shore, opposite Verplancks, and under a great hill called the Dunderberg by the old Dutch lords of the stream, and which hangs precipitously over it. A little stream at the northern base of this mountain intersects it from the opposite height on which Fort Clinton stood, named not after our General, but after one of the two gentlemen of the same name, who were amongst the oldest and most respected of the provincial gentry of New York, and who were at this moment actually in command against Sir Henry. On the next height to Clinton is Fort Montgomery; and behind them rises a hill called Bear Hill; whilst at the opposite side of the magnificent stream stands "Saint Anthony's Nose," a prodigious peak indeed, which the Dutch had quaintly christened.

The attacks on the two forts were almost simultaneous. Half our men were detached for the assault on Fort Montgomery, under the brave Campbell, who fell before the rampart. Sir Henry, who would never be out of danger where he could find it, personally led the remainder, and hoped, he said, that we should have better luck than before the Sullivan Island. A path led up to the Dunderberg, so narrow as scarcely to admit three men abreast, and in utter silence our whole force scaled it, wondering at every rugged step to meet with no opposition. The enemy had not even kept a watch on it: nor were we descried until we were descending the height, at the base of which we easily dispersed a small force sent hurriedly to oppose us. The firing which here took place rendered all idea of a surprise impossible. The fort was before us. With such arms as the troops had in their hands, they had to assault; and silently and swiftly in the face of the artillery playing upon them, the troops ascended the hill. The men had orders on no account to fire. Taking the colours of the Sixty-third, and bearing them aloft, Sir Henry mounted with the stormers. The place was so steep that the men pushed each other over the wall and through the embrasures; and it was there that Lieutenant Joseph Blake, the father of a certain Joseph Clinton Blake, who looks with the eyes of affection on a certain young lady, presented himself to the living of Warrington by saving the life of the unworthy patron thereof.

About a fourth part of the garrison, as we were told, escaped out of the fort, the rest being killed or wounded, or remaining our prisoners within the works. Fort Montgomery was, in like manner, stormed and taken by our people; and, at night, as we looked down from the heights where the King's standard had been just planted, we were treated to a splendid illumination in the river below. Under Fort Montgomery, and stretching over to that lofty prominence called St. Anthony's Nose, a boom and chain had been laid with a vast cost and labour, behind which several American frigates and galleys were anchored. The fort being taken, these ships attempted to get up the river in the darkness, out of the reach of guns, which they knew must destroy them in the morning. But the wind was unfavourable, and escape was found to be impossible. The crews therefore took to the boats, and so landed, having previously set the ships on fire, with all their sails set; and we beheld these magnificent pyramids of flame burning up to the heavens and reflected in the waters below, until, in the midst of prodigious explosions, they sank and disappeared.

On the next day a *parlementaire* came in from the enemy, to inquire as to the state of his troops left wounded or prisoners in our hands, and the Continental officer brought me a note, which gave me a strange shock, for it showed that in the struggle of the previous evening my brother had been engaged. It was dated October 7, from Major-General George Clinton's divisional headquarters, and it stated briefly that " Colonel H. Warrington, of the Virginia line, hopes that Sir George Warrington escaped unhurt in the assault of last evening, from which the Colonel himself was so fortunate as to retire without the least injury." Never did I say my prayers more heartily and gratefully than on that night, devoutly thanking Heaven that my dearest brother was spared, and making a vow at the same time to withdraw out of the fratricidal contest, into which I only had entered because Honour and Duty seemed imperatively to call me.

I own I felt an inexpressible relief when I had come to the resolution to retire and betake myself to the peaceful shade of my own vines and fig-trees at home. I longed, however, to see my brother ere I returned, and asked, and easily obtained, an errand to the camp of the American General Clinton from our own chief. The headquarters of his division were now some miles up the river, and a boat and a flag of truce quickly brought me to the point where his out-pickets received me on the shore. My brother was very soon with me. He had only lately joined General Clinton's division with letters from headquarters at Philadelphia, and he chanced to hear, after the attack on Fort Clinton, that I had been present during the affair. We passed a brief delightful night together; Mr. Sady, who always followed Hal to the war, cooking a feast in honour of both his masters. There was but one bed of straw in the hut where we had quarters, and Hal and I slept on it, side by side, as we had done when we were boys. We had a hundred things to say regarding past times and present. His kind heart gladdened when I told

him of my resolve to retire to my acres and to take off the red
coat which I wore: he flung his arms round it. " Praised be
God!" said he. " O heavens, George! think what might have
happened had we met in the affair two nights ago!" And he
turned quite pale at the thought. He eased my mind with
respect to our mother. She was a bitter Tory, to be sure, but
the Chief had given special injunctions regarding her safety.
" And Fanny " (Hal's wife) " watches over her, and she is as
good as a company!" cried the enthusiastic husband. " Isn't
she clever? Isn't she handsome? Isn't she good?" cries Hal,
never, fortunately, waiting for a reply to these ardent queries.
" And to think that I was nearly marrying Maria once! O
mercy! what an escape I had!" he added. " Hagan prays for
the King, every morning and night at Castlewood, but they
bolt the doors, and nobody hears. Gracious powers! his wife
is sixty if she is a day; and oh, George! the quantity she
drinks is——" But why tell the failings of our good cousin?
I am pleased to think she lived to drink the health of King
George long after his Old Dominion had passed for ever from
his sceptre.

The morning came when my brief mission to the camp was
ended, and the truest of friends and fondest of brothers accompanied me to my boat, which lay waiting at the river-side. We
exchanged an embrace at parting, and his hand held mine yet
for a moment ere I stepped into the barge which bore me
rapidly down the stream. " Shall I see thee once more, dearest
and best companion of my youth?" I thought. " Amongst
our cold Englishmen, can I ever hope to meet with a friend like
thee? When hadst thou ever a thought that was not kindly
and generous? When a wish, or a possession, but for me you
would sacrifice it? How brave are you, and how modest; how
gentle, and how strong; how simple, unselfish, and humble;
how eager to see others' merit; how diffident of your own!"
He stood on the shore till his figure grew dim before me. There
was that in my eyes which prevented me from seeing him
longer.

Brilliant as Sir Henry's success had been, it was achieved, as
usual, too late: and served but as a small set-off against the
disaster of Burgoyne which ensued immediately, and which our
advance was utterly inadequate to relieve. More than one
secret messenger was despatched to him who never reached
him, and of whom we never learned the fate. Of one wretch
who offered to carry intelligence to him, and whom Sir Henry

despatched with a letter of his own, we heard the miserable doom. Falling in with some of the troops of General George Clinton, who happened to be in red uniform (part of the prize of a British ship's cargo, doubtless, which had been taken by American privateers), the spy thought he was in the English army, and advanced towards the sentries. He found his mistake too late. His letter was discovered upon him, and he had to die for bearing it. In ten days after the success at the Forts occurred the great disaster at Saratoga, of which we carried the dismal particulars in the fleet which bore us home. I am afraid my wife was unable to mourn for it. She had her children, her father, her sister to revisit, and daily and nightly thanks to pay to Heaven that had brought her husband safe out of danger.

CHAPTER XCII

UNDER VINE AND FIG-TREE

NEED I describe, young folks, the delights of the meeting at home, and the mother's happiness with all her brood once more under her fond wings? It was wrote in her face, and acknowledged on her knees. Our house was large enough for all, but Aunt Hetty would not stay in it. She said, fairly, that to resign her *motherhood* over the elder children, who had been hers for nearly three years, cost her too great a pang; and she could not bear for yet awhile to be with them, and to submit to take only the second place. So she and her father went away to a house at Bury St. Edmunds, not far from us, where they lived, and where she spoiled her eldest nephew and niece in private. It was the year after we came home that Mr. B—— the Jamaica planter died, who left her the half of his fortune; and then I heard, for the first time, how the worthy gentleman had been greatly enamoured of her in Jamaica, and, though she had refused him, had thus shown his constancy to her. Heaven knows how much property of Aunt Hetty's Monsieur Miles hath already devoured: the price of his commission and outfit; his gorgeous uniforms; his play debts and little transactions in the Minories;—do you think, sirrah, I do not know what human nature is; what is the cost of Pall Mall taverns, *petits soupers*, play—even in moderation—at the " Cocoa-Tree;"

and that a gentleman cannot purchase all these enjoyments with the five hundred a year which I allow him? Aunt Hetty declares she has made up her mind to be an old maid. " I made a vow never to marry until I could find a man as good as my dear father," she said; " and I never did, Sir George. No, my dearest Theo, not half as good; and Sir George may put *that* in his pipe and smoke it."

And yet when the good General died, calm and full of years, and glad to depart, I think it was my wife who shed the most tears. " I weep because I think I did not love him enough," said the tender creature: whereas Hetty scarce departed from her calm, at least outwardly and before any of us; talks of him constantly still, as though he were alive; recalls his merry sayings, his gentle kind ways with his children (when she brightens up and looks herself quite a girl again), and sits cheerfully looking up to the slab in church which records his name and some of his virtues, and for once tells no lies.

I had fancied, sometimes, that my brother Hal, for whom Hetty had a juvenile passion, always retained a hold of her heart; and when he came to see us, ten years ago, I told him of this childish romance of Het's, with the hope, I own, that he would ask her to replace Mrs. Fanny, who had been gathered to her fathers, and regarding whom my wife (with her usual propensity to consider herself a miserable sinner) always reproached herself, because, forsooth, she did not regret Fanny enough. Hal, when he came to us, was plunged in grief about her loss; and vowed that the world did not contain such another woman. Our dear old General, who was still in life then, took him in and housed him, as he had done in the happy early days. The women played him the very same tunes which he had heard when a boy at Oakhurst. Everybody's heart was very soft with old recollections, and Harry never tired of pouring out his griefs and his recitals of his wife's virtues to Het, and anon of talking fondly about his dear Aunt Lambert, whom he loved with all his heart, and whose praises, you may be sure, were welcome to the faithful old husband, out of whose thoughts his wife's memory was never, I believe, absent for any three waking minutes of the day.

General Hal went to Paris as an American General Officer in his blue and yellow (which Mr. Fox and other gentlemen had brought into fashion here likewise), and was made much of at Versailles, although he was presented by Monsieur le Marquis de Lafayette to the most Christian King and Queen, who did

not love Monsieur le Marquis. And I believe a Marquise took
a fancy to the Virginian General, and would have married him
out of hand, had he not resisted, and fled back to England and
Warrington and Bury again, especially to the latter place, where
the folks would listen to him as he talked about his late wife,
with an endless patience and sympathy. As for us, who had
known the poor paragon, we were civil, but not quite so
enthusiastic regarding her, and rather puzzled sometimes to
answer our children's questions about Uncle Hal's angel wife.

The two Generals and myself, and Captain Miles, and Parson
Blake (who was knocked over at Monmouth, the year after I
left America, and came home to change his coat, and take my
living), used to fight the battles of the Revolution over our
bottle; and the parson used to cry, " By Jupiter, General "
(he compounded for Jupiter, when he laid down his military
habit), " you are the Tory, and Sir George is the Whig! He
is always finding fault with our leaders, and you are for ever
standing up for them; and when I prayed for the King last
Sunday, I heard you following me quite loud."

" And so I do, Blake, with all my heart; I can't forget I
wore his coat," says Hal.

" Ah, if Wolfe had been alive for twenty years more! " says
Lambert.

" Ah, sir," cries Hal, " you should hear the General talk
about *him*! "

" What General? " says I (to vex him).

" *My* General," says Hal, standing up, and filling a bumper.
" His Excellency General George Washington! "

" With all my heart," cry I, but the parson looks as if he
did not like the toast or the claret.

Hal never tired in speaking of his General; and it was on
some such evening of friendly converse, that he told us how he
had actually been in disgrace with this General whom he loved
so fondly. Their difference seems to have been about Monsieur
le Marquis de Lafayette before mentioned, who played such a
fine part in history of late, and who hath so suddenly disappeared out of it. His previous rank in our own service, and
his acknowledged gallantry during the war, ought to have
secured Colonel Warrington's promotion in the Continental
Army, where a whipper-snapper like M. de Lafayette had but
to arrive and straightway to be complimented by Congress with
the rank of Major-General. Hal, with the freedom of an old
soldier, had expressed himself somewhat contemptuously regard-

ing some of the appointments made by Congress, with whom all
sorts of miserable intrigues and cabals were set to work by
unscrupulous officers greedy of promotion. Mr. Warrington,
imitating perhaps in this the example of his now illustrious
friend of Mount Vernon, affected to make the war *en gentilhomme;*
took his pay, to be sure, but spent it upon comforts and clothing
for his men, and as for rank, declared it was a matter of no
earthly concern to him, and that he would as soon serve as
colonel as in any higher grade. No doubt he added contemptuous remarks regarding certain General Officers of Congress
Army, their origin, and the causes of their advancement:
notably he was very angry about the sudden promotion of the
young French lad just named—the Marquis, as they loved to
call him—in the Republican army, and who, by the way, was a
prodigious favourite of the Chief himself. There were not three
officers in the whole Continental force (after poor madcap Lee
was taken prisoner and disgraced) who could speak the Marquis's
language, so that Hal could judge the young Major-General
more closely and familiarly than other gentlemen, including the
Commander-in-Chief himself. Mr. Washington good-naturedly
rated friend Hal for being jealous of the beardless commander
of Auvergne; was himself not a little pleased by the filial regard
and profound veneration which the enthusiastic young nobleman always showed for him; and had, moreover, the very best
politic reasons for treating the Marquis with friendship and
favour.

Meanwhile, as it afterwards turned out, the Commander-in-
Chief was most urgently pressing Colonel Warrington's promotion upon Congress; and, as if his difficulties before the
enemy were not enough, he being at this hard time of winter
intrenched at Valley Forge, commanding five or six thousand
men at the most, almost without fire, blankets, food, or ammunition, in the face of Sir William Howe's army, which was
perfectly appointed, and three times as numerous as his own:
as if, I say, this difficulty was not enough to try him, he had
further to encounter the cowardly distrust of Congress, and
insubordination and conspiracy amongst the officers in his own
camp. During the awful winter of '77, when one blow struck
by the sluggard at the head of the British forces might have
ended the war, and all was doubt, confusion, despair in the
opposite camp (save in one indomitable breast alone), my
brother had an interview with the Chief, which he has subsequently described to me, and of which Hal could never speak

without giving way to deep emotion. Mr. Washington had won no such triumph as that which the dare-devil courage of Arnold and the elegant imbecility of Burgoyne had procured for Gates and the Northern Army. Save in one or two minor encounters, which proved how daring his bravery was, and how unceasing his watchfulness, General Washington had met with defeat after defeat from an enemy in all points his superior. The Congress mistrusted him. Many an officer in his own camp hated him. Those who had been disappointed in ambition, those who had been detected in peculation, those whose selfishness or incapacity his honest eyes had spied out,—were all more or less in league against him. Gates was the chief towards whom the malcontents turned. Mr. Gates' was the only genius fit to conduct the war; and with a vain-gloriousness, which he afterwards generously owned, he did not refuse the homage which was paid him.

To show how dreadful were the troubles and anxieties with which General Washington had to contend, I may mention what at this time was called the "Conway Cabal." A certain Irishman—a Chevalier of St. Louis, and an officer in the French service—arrived in America early in the year '77 in quest of military employment. He was speedily appointed to the rank of brigadier, and could not be contented, forsooth, without an immediate promotion to be major-general.

Mr. C. had friends in Congress, who, as the General-in-Chief was informed, had promised him his speedy promotion. General Washington remonstrated, representing the injustice of promoting to the highest rank the youngest brigadier in the service; and whilst the matter was pending, was put in possession of a letter from Conway to General Gates, whom he complimented, saying, that "Heaven had been determined to save America, or a weak general and bad counsellors would have ruined it." The General enclosed the note to Mr. Conway, without a word of comment; and Conway offered his resignation, which was refused by Congress, who appointed him Inspector-General of the army, with the rank of Major-General.

" And it was at this time," says Harry (with many passionate exclamations indicating his rage with himself and his admiration of his leader), " when, by heavens, the glorious Chief was oppressed by troubles enough to drive ten thousand men mad— that I must interfere with my jealousies about the Frenchman ! I had not said much, only some nonsense to Greene and Cadwalader about getting some frogs against the Frenchman came to dine with us, and having a bagful of Marquises over from Paris, as we were not able to command ourselves;—but I should have known the Chief's troubles, and that he had a better head than mine, and might have had the grace to hold my tongue.

"For a while the General said nothing, but I could remark, by the coldness of his demeanour, that something had occurred to create a schism between him and me. Mrs. Washington, who had come to camp, also saw that something was wrong. Women have artful ways of soothing men and finding their secrets out. I am not sure that I should have ever tried to learn the cause of the General's displeasure, for I am as proud as he is, and besides "(says Hal) "when the Chief is angry, it was not pleasant coming near him, I can promise you." My brother was indeed subjugated by his old friend, and obeyed him and bowed before him as a boy before a schoolmaster.

"At last," Hal resumed, "Mrs. Washington found out the mystery. 'Speak to me after dinner, Colonel Hal,' says she. 'Come out to the parade-ground before the dining-house, and I will tell you all.' I left a half-score of general officers and brigadiers drinking round the General's table, and found Mrs. Washington waiting for me. She then told me it was the speech I had made about the box of Marquises, with which the General was offended. 'I should not have heeded it in another,' he had said, 'but I never thought Harry Warrington would have joined against me.'

"I had to wait on him for the word that night, and found him alone at his table. 'Can your Excellency give me five minutes' time?' I said, with my heart in my mouth. 'Yes, surely, sir,' says he, pointing to the other chair. 'Will you please to be seated?'

"'It used not always to be Sir and Colonel Warrington, between me and your Excellency,' I said.

"He said calmly, 'The times are altered.'

"'Et nos mutamur in illis,' says I. 'Times and people are both changed.'

"'You had some business with me?' he asked.

"'Am I speaking to the Commander-in-Chief or to my old friend?' I asked.

"He looked at me gravely. 'Well,—to both, sir,' he said. 'Pray sit, Harry.'

"'If to General Washington, I tell his Excellency that I, and many officers of this army, are not well pleased to see a boy of twenty made a major-general over us, because he is a Marquis and because he can't speak the English language. If I speak to my old friend, I have to say that he has shown me very little of trust or friendship for the last few weeks; and that I have no desire to sit at your table, and have impertinent remarks made by others there, of the way in which his Excellency turns his back on me.'

" 'Which charge shall I take first, Harry,' he asked, turning his chair away from the table, and crossing his legs as if ready for a talk. 'You are jealous, as I gather, about the Marquis?'

" 'Jealous! sir,' says I. 'An aide-de-camp of Mr. Wolfe is not jealous of a Jack-a-dandy who, five years ago, was being whipped at school!'

" 'You yourself declined higher rank than that which you hold,' says the Chief, turning a little red.

" 'But I never bargained to have a macaroni Marquis to command me!' I cried. 'I will not, for one, carry the young gentleman's orders; and since Congress and your Excellency choose to take your generals out of the nursery, I shall humbly ask leave to resign, and retire to my plantation.'

" 'Do, Harry; that is true friendship!' says the Chief, with a gentleness that surprised me. 'Now that your old friend is in a difficulty, 'tis surely the best time to leave him.'

" 'Sir!' says I.

" 'Do as so many of the rest are doing, Mr. Warrington. *Et tu, Brute*, as the play says. Well, well, Harry! I did not think it of you; but, at least, you are in the fashion.'

" 'You asked which charge you should take first?' I said.

" 'Oh, the promotion of the Marquis? I recommended the appointment to Congress, no doubt; and you and other gentlemen disapprove of it.'

" 'I have spoken for myself, sir,' says I.

" 'If you take me in that tone, Colonel Warrington, I have nothing to answer!' says the Chief, rising up very fiercely; 'and presume that I can recommend officers for promotion without asking your previous sanction.'

" 'Being on that tone, sir,' says I, 'let me respectfully offer my resignation to your Excellency, founding my desire to resign upon the fact, that Congress, at your Excellency's recommendation, offers its highest commands to boys of twenty, who are scarcely even acquainted with our language.' And I rise up, and make his Excellency a bow.

" 'Great Heavens, Harry!' he cries—(about this Marquis's appointment he was beaten, that was the fact, and he could not reply to me)—'can't you believe that in this critical time of our affairs, there are reasons why special favours should be shown to the first Frenchman of distinction who comes amongst us?'

"'No doubt, sir. If your Excellency acknowledges that Monsieur de Lafayette's merits have nothing to do with the question.'

"'I acknowledge or deny nothing, sir!' says the General, with a stamp of his foot, and looking as though he could be terribly angry if he would. 'Am I here to be catechised by you? Stay. Hark, Harry! I speak to you as a man of the world—nay, as an old friend. This appointment humiliates you and others, you say? Be it so! Must we not bear humiliation along with the other burthens and griefs for the sake of our country? It is no more just perhaps that the Marquis should be set over you gentlemen, than that your Prince Ferdinand or your Prince of Wales at home should have a command over veterans. But if in appointing this young nobleman we please a whole nation, and bring ourselves twenty millions of allies, will you and other gentlemen sulk because we do him honour? 'Tis easy to sneer at him (though, believe me, the Marquis has many more merits than you allow him); to my mind it were more generous as well as more polite of Harry Warrington to welcome this stranger for the sake of the prodigious benefit our country may draw from him—not to laugh at his peculiarities, but to aid him, and help his ignorance by your experience as an old soldier: that is what I would do—that is the part I expected of thee— for it is the generous and the manly one, Harry: but you choose to join my enemies, and when I am in trouble you say you will leave me. That is why I have been hurt: that is why I have been cold. I thought I might count on your friendship—and— and you can tell whether I was right or no. I relied on you as on a brother, and you come and tell me you will resign. Be it so! Being embarked in this contest, by God's will I will see it to an end. You are not the first, Mr. Warrington, has left me on the way.'

"He spoke with so much tenderness, and as he spoke his face wore such a look of unhappiness, that an extreme remorse and pity seized me, and I called out I know not what incoherent expressions regarding old times, and vowed that if he would say the word, I never would leave him." "You never loved him, George," says my brother, turning to me, "but I did beyond all mortal men; and, though I am not clever, like you, I think my instinct was in the right.   He has a greatness not approached by other men——"

"I don't say no, brother," said I, " now."

"Greatness, pooh!" says the parson, growling over his wine.

"We walked into Mrs. Washington's tea-room arm-in-arm," Hal resumed; "she looked up quite kind, and saw we were friends. 'Is it all over, Colonel Harry?' she whispered. 'I know he has applied ever so often about your promotion——'

"'I never will take it,' says I." "And that is how I came *to do penance*," says Harry, telling me the story, "with Lafayette the next winter." (Hal could imitate the Frenchman very well.) "'I will go *weez heem*,' says I. 'I know the way to Quebec, and when we are not in action with Sir Guy, I can hear his Excellency the Major-General say his lesson.' There was no fight, you know: we could get no army to act in Canada, and returned to headquarters; and what do you think disturbed the Frenchman most? The idea that people would laugh at him, because his command had come to nothing. And so they did laugh at him, and almost to his face too, and who could help it? If our Chief had any weak point it was this Marquis.

"After our little difference we became as great friends as before —if a man may be said to be friends with a Sovereign Prince, for as such I somehow could not help regarding the General: and one night, when we had sat the company out, we talked of old times, and the jolly days of sport we had together both before and after Braddock's; and that pretty duel you were near having when we were boys. He laughed about it, and said he never saw a man look more wicked and more bent on killing than you did. 'And to do Sir George justice, I think he has hated me ever since,' says the Chief. 'Ah!' he added, 'an open enemy I can face readily enough. 'Tis the secret foe who causes the doubt and anguish! We have sat with more than one at my table to-day to whom I am obliged to show a face of civility, whose hands I must take when they are offered, though I know they are stabbing my reputation, and are eager to pull me down from my place. You spoke but lately of being humiliated because a junior was set over you in command. What humiliation is yours compared to mine, who have to play the farce of welcome to these traitors; who have to bear the neglect of Congress, and see men who have insulted me promoted in my own army. If I consulted my own feelings as a man, would I continue in this command? You know whether my temper is naturally warm or not, and whether as a private gentleman I should be likely to suffer such slights and outrages as are put upon me daily; but in the advancement of the sacred cause in which we are engaged, we have to endure not only hardship and danger, but calumny and wrong, and may God give us strength to do our duty!' And then the General showed me the papers regarding the affair of that fellow Conway, whom Congress promoted in spite of the intrigue, and down whose black throat John Cadwalader sent the best ball he ever fired in his life.

"And it was here," said Hal, concluding his story, "as I looked at the Chief talking at night in the silence of the camp, and remembered how lonely he was, what an awful responsibility he carried; how spies and traitors were eating out of his dish, and an enemy lay in front of him who might at any time overpower him, that I thought, 'Sure, this is the greatest man now in the world: and what a wretch I am to think of my jealousies and annoyances, whilst he is walking serenely under his immense cares!'"

"We talked but now of Wolfe," said I. "Here, indeed, is a greater than Wolfe. To endure is greater than to dare; to tire out hostile fortune; to be daunted by no difficulty; to keep heart when all have lost it; to go through intrigue spotless; and to forego even ambition when the end is gained—who can say this is not greatness, or show the other Englishman who has achieved so much?"

"I wonder, Sir George, you did not take Mr. Washington's side, and wear the blue and buff yourself," grumbles Parson Blake.

"You and I thought scarlet most becoming to our complexion, Joe Blake!" says Sir George. "And my wife thinks there would not have been room for two such great men on one side."

"Well, at any rate, you were better than that odious, swearing, crazy General Lee, who was second in command!" cries Lady Warrington. "And I am certain Mr. Washington never could write poetry and tragedies as you can! What did the General say about George's tragedies, Harry?"

Harry burst into a roar of laughter (in which, of course, Mr. Miles must join his uncle).

"Well!" says he, "it's a fact, that Hagan read one at my house to the General and Mrs. Washington and several more, and they all fell sound asleep!"

"He never liked my husband, that is the truth!" says Theo, tossing up her head, "and 'tis all the more magnanimous of Sir George to speak so well of him."

And then Hal told how, his battles over, his country freed, his great work of liberation completed, the General laid down his victorious sword, and met his comrades of the army in a last adieu. The last British soldier had quitted the shore of the Republics, and the Commander-in-Chief proposed to leave New York for Annapolis, where Congress was sitting, and there resign his commission. About noon on the 4th of December, a barge was in waiting at Whitehall Ferry to convey him across the Hudson. The chiefs of the army assembled at a tavern near the ferry, and there the General joined them. Seldom as he showed his emotion outwardly, on this day he could not disguise it. He filled a glass of wine, and said, " I bid you farewell with a heart full of love and gratitude, and wish your latter days may be as prosperous and happy as those past have been glorious and honourable." Then he drank to them.

" I cannot come to each of you to take my leave," he said, " but shall be obliged if you will each come and shake me by the hand."

General Knox, who was nearest, came forward, and the Chief, with tears in his eyes, embraced him. The others came, one by one, to him, and took their leave without a word. A line of infantry was formed from the tavern to the ferry, and the General, with his officers following him, walked silently to the water. He stood up in the barge, taking off his hat, and waving a farewell. And his comrades remained bareheaded on the shore till their leader's boat was out of view.

As Harry speaks very low, in the grey of evening, with sometimes a break in his voice, we all sit touched and silent. Hetty goes up and kisses her father.

" You tell us of others, General Harry," she says, passing a handkerchief across her eyes, " of Marion and Sumpter, of Greene and Wayne, and Rawdon and Cornwallis, too, but you never mention Colonel Warrington ! "

" My dear, he will tell you his story in private ! " whispers my wife, clinging to her sister, " and you can write it for him."

But it was not to be. My Lady Theo, and her husband too, I own, catching the infection from her, never would let Harry rest, until we had coaxed, wheedled, and ordered him to ask Hetty in marriage. He obeyed, and it was she who now declined. " She had always," she said, " the truest regard for him from the dear old times when they had met as almost children together, but she would never leave her father. When it pleased God to take him, she hoped she would be too old to think of bearing any other name but her own. Harry should have her love always as the best of brothers; and as George and Theo have such a nursery full of children," adds Hester, " we must show our love to *them*, by saving for the young ones." She sent him her answer in writing, leaving home on a visit to friends at a distance, as though she would have him to understand that her decision was final. As such Hal received it. He did not break his heart. Cupid's arrows, ladies, don't bite very deep into the tough skins of gentlemen of our age; though, to be sure, at the time of which I write, my brother was still a young man, being little more than fifty. Aunt Het is now a staid little lady with a voice of which years have touched the sweet chords, and a head which Time has powdered over with silver. There are days when she looks surprisingly young and blooming. Ah me, my dear, it seems but a little while since the hair was golden brown, and the cheeks as fresh as roses! And then came the bitter blast of love unrequited which withered them; and that long loneliness of heart which, they say, follows. Why should Theo and I have been so happy, and thou so lonely? Why should my meal be garnished with love, and spread with plenty, while yon solitary outcast shivers at my gate? I bow my head humbly before the Dispenser of pain and poverty, wealth and health; I feel sometimes as if, for the prizes which have fallen to the lot of me unworthy, I did not *dare* to be grateful. But I hear the voices of my children in their garden, or look up at their mother from my book, or perhaps my sick bed, and my heart fills with instinctive gratitude towards the bountiful Heaven that has so blest me.

Since my accession to my uncle's title and estate my intercourse with my good cousin, Lord Castlewood, had been very rare. I had always supposed him to be a follower of the winning side in politics, and was not a little astonished to hear of his sudden appearance in opposition. A disappointment in respect to a place at Court, of which he pretended to have had some promise, was partly the occasion of his rupture with the Ministry. It is said that the most august person in the realm had flatly refused to receive into the R-y-l Household a nobleman whose character was so notoriously bad, and whose example (so the August Objector was pleased to say) would ruin and corrupt any respectable family. I heard of the Castlewoods during our travels in Europe, and that the mania for play had again seized upon his Lordship. His impaired fortunes having been retrieved by the prudence of his wife and father-in-law, he had again begun to dissipate his income at hombre and lansque-net. There were tales of malpractices in which he had been discovered, and even of chastisement inflicted upon him by the victims of his unscrupulous arts. His wife's beauty and fresh-ness faded early; we met but once at Aix-la-Chapelle, where Lady Castlewood besought my wife to go and see her, and afflicted Lady Warrington's kind heart by stories of the neglect and outrage of which her unfortunate husband was guilty. We were willing to receive these as some excuse and palliation for the unhappy lady's own conduct. A notorious adventurer, gambler, and *spadassin*, calling himself the Chevalier de Barry, and said to be a relative of the mistress of the French King, but afterwards turning out to be an Irishman of low extraction, was in constant attendance upon the Earl and Countess at this time, and conspicuous for the audacity of his lies, the extravagance of his play, and somewhat mercenary gallantry towards the other sex, and a ferocious bravo courage, which, however, failed him on one or two awkward occasions, if common report said true. He subsequently married, and rendered miserable, a lady of title and fortune in England. The poor little American lady's interested union with Lord Castlewood was scarcely more happy.

I remember our little Miles's infantile envy being excited by learning that Lord Castlewood's second son, a child a few months younger than himself, was already an ensign on the Irish estab-lishment, whose pay the fond parents regularly drew. This piece of preferment my Lord must have got for his *cadet* whilst he was on good terms with the Minister, during which period of favour Will Esmond was also shifted off to New York. Whilst I was in America myself, we read in an English journal that Captain Charles Esmond had resigned his commission in His Majesty's service, as not wishing to take up arms against the countrymen of his mother, the Countess of Castlewood. " It is the doing of the old fox, Van den Bosch," Madam Esmond said; " he wishes to keep his Virginian property safe, whatever side should win!" I may mention, with respect to this old worthy, that he continued to reside in England for a while after the Declaration of Independence, not at all denying his sympathy with the American cause, but keeping a pretty quiet tongue, and alleging that such a very old man as himself was past the age of action or mischief, in which opinion the Government con-curred, no doubt, as he was left quite unmolested. But of a sudden a warrant was out after him, when it was surprising with what agility he stirred himself, and skipped off to France, whence he presently embarked upon his return to Virginia.

The old man bore the worst reputation amongst the Loyalists of our colony; and was nicknamed "Jack the Painter" amongst them, much to his indignation, after a certain miscreant who was hung in England for burning naval stores in our ports there. He professed to have lost prodigious sums at home by the persecution of the Government, distinguished himself by the loudest patriotism and the most violent religious outcries in Virginia; where, nevertheless, he was not much more liked by the Whigs than by the party who still remained faithful to the Crown. He wondered that such an old Tory as Madam Esmond of Castlewood was suffered to go at large, and was for ever crying out against her amongst the gentlemen of the new Assembly, the Governor and officers of the State. He and Fanny had high words in Richmond one day, when she told him he was an old swindler and traitor, and that the mother of Colonel Henry Warrington, the bosom friend of his Excellency the Commander-in-Chief, was not to be insulted by such a little smuggling slave-driver as him! I think it was in the year 1780 an accident happened when the old Register Office at Williamsburg was burned down, in which was a copy of the formal assignment of the Virginia property from Francis Lord Castlewood to my grandfather Henry Esmond, Esq. "Oh," says Fanny, "of course this is the work of Jack the Painter!" And Mr. Van den Bosch was for prosecuting her for libel, but that Fanny took to her bed at this juncture, and died.

Van den Bosch made contracts with the new government and sold them bargains, as the phrase is. He supplied horses, meat, forage, all of bad quality; but when Arnold came into Virginia (in the King's service) and burned right and left, Van den Bosch's stores and tobacco-houses somehow were spared. Some secret Whigs now took their revenge on the old rascal. A couple of his ships in James River, his stores, and a quantity of his cattle in their stalls were roasted amidst a hideous bellowing; and he got a note, as he was in Arnold's company, saying that friends had served him as he served others; and containing "Tom the Glazier's compliments to brother Jack the Painter." Nobody pitied the old man, though he went well nigh mad at his loss. In Arnold's suite came the Honourable Captain William Esmond, of the New York Loyalists, as Aide-de-Camp to the General. When Howe occupied Philadelphia, Will was said to have made some money keeping a gambling-house with an officer of the dragoons of Anspach. I know not how he lost it. He could not have had much when he consented to become an aide-de-camp of Arnold.

Now the King's officers having reappeared in the province, Madam Esmond thought fit to open her house at Castlewood and invite them thither—and actually received Mr. Arnold and his suite. " It is not for me," she said, " to refuse my welcome to a man whom my sovereign has admitted to grace." And she threw her house open to him, treating him with great though frigid respect whilst he remained in the district. The General gone, and his precious aide-de-camp with him, some of the rascals who followed in their suite remained behind in the house where they had received so much hospitality, insulted the old lady in her hall, insulted her people, and finally set fire to the old mansion in a frolic of drunken fury. Our house at Richmond was not burned, luckily, though Mr. Arnold had fired the town; and thither the undaunted old lady proceeded, surrounded by her people, and never swerving in her loyalty in spite of her ill-usage. " The Esmonds," she said, " were accustomed to Royal ingratitude."

And now Mr. Van den Bosch, in the name of his grandson and my Lord Castlewood, in England, set up a claim to our property in Virginia. He said it was not my Lord's intention to disturb Madam Esmond in her enjoyment of the estate during her life, but that his father, it had always been understood, had given his kinsman a life-interest in the place, and only continued it to his daughter out of generosity. Now my Lord proposed that his second son should inhabit Virginia, for which the young gentleman had always shown the warmest sympathy. The outcry against Van den Bosch was so great, that he would have been tarred and feathered, had he remained in Virginia. He betook himself to Congress, represented himself as a martyr ruined in the cause of liberty, and prayed for compensation for himself and justice for his grandson.

My mother lived long in dreadful apprehension, having in truth a secret, which she did not like to disclose to any one. *Her titles were burned !* the deed of assignment in her own house, the copy in the Registry at Richmond, had alike been destroyed —by chance? by villainy? who could say? She did not like to confide this trouble in writing to me. She opened herself to Hal, after the surrender of York Town, and he acquainted me with the fact in a letter by a British officer returning home on his parole. Then I remembered the unlucky words I had let

slip before Will Esmond at the coffee-house at New York: and a
part of this iniquitous scheme broke upon me.

As for Mr. Will: there is a tablet in Castlewood Church, in
Hampshire, inscribed, " Dulce et decorum est pro patriâ mori,"
and announcing that " This marble is placed by a mourning
brother, to the memory of the Honourable William Esmond,
Esq., who died in North America, in the service of his King."
But how? When, towards the end of 1781, a revolt took place
in the Philadelphia Line of the Congress Army, and Sir H.
Clinton sent out agents to the mutineers, what became of them?
The men took the spies prisoners, and proceeded to judge them,
and my brother (whom they knew and loved, and had often
followed under fire), who had been sent from camp to make
terms with the troops, recognised one of the spies, just as execution was about to be done upon him—and the wretch, with
horrid outcries, grovelling and kneeling at Colonel Warrington's
feet, besought him for mercy, and promised to confess all to
him. To confess what? Harry turned away sick at heart.
Will's mother and sister never knew the truth. They always
fancied it was in action he was killed.

As for my Lord Earl, whose noble son has been the intendant
of an illustrious Prince, and who has enriched himself at play
with his R—l master: I went to see his Lordship when I heard
of this astounding design against our property, and remonstrated with him on the matter. For myself, as I showed him, I
was not concerned, as I had determined to cede my right to my
brother. He received me with perfect courtesy; smiled when
I spoke of my disinterestedness; said he was sure of my affectionate feelings towards my brother, but what must be his
towards his son? He had always heard from his father: he
would take his Bible oath of that: that, at my mother's death,
the property would return to the head of the family. At the
story of the title which Colonel Esmond had ceded, he shrugged
his shoulders, and treated it as a fable. " On ne fait pas de ces
folies là!" says he, offering me snuff, " and your grandfather
was a man of *esprit!* My little grandmother was *éprise* of him:
and my father, the most good-natured soul alive, lent them the
Virginian property to get them out of the way. C'étoit un
scandale, mon cher, un joli petit scandale!" Oh, if my mother
had but heard him! I might have been disposed to take a high
tone: but he said, with the utmost good-nature, " My dear
Knight, are you going to fight about the character of our grandmother? Allons donc! Come, I will be fair with you! We

will compromise, if you like, about this Virginian property!" and his Lordship named a sum greater than the actual value of the estate.

Amazed at the coolness of this worthy, I walked away to my coffee-house, where, as it happened, an old friend was to dine with me, for whom I have a sincere regard. I had felt a pang at not being able to give this gentleman my living of Warrington-on-Waveney, but I *could* not, as he himself confessed honestly. His life had been too loose, and his example in my village could never have been edifying: besides, he would have died of *ennui* there, after being accustomed to a town life; and he had a prospect finally, he told me, of settling himself most comfortably in London and the Church.[1] My guest, I need not say, was my old friend Sampson, who never failed to dine with me when I came to town, and I told him of my interview with his old patron.

I could not have lighted upon a better confidant. "Gracious powers!" says Sampson, "the man's roguery beats all belief! When I was secretary and factotum at Castlewood, I can take my oath I saw more than once a copy of the deed of assignment by the late lord to your grandfather: ' *In consideration of the love I bear to my kinsman, Henry Esmond, Esq., husband of my dear mother Rachel, Lady Viscountess Dowager of Castlewood, I,*' etc.—so it ran. I know the place where 'tis kept—let us go thither as fast as horses will carry us to-morrow. There is some-body there—never mind whom, Sir George—who has an old regard for me. The papers may be there to this very day, and O Lord, O Lord, but I shall be thankful if I can in any way show my gratitude to you and your glorious brother!" His eyes filled with tears. He was an altered man. At a certain period of the port wine Sampson always alluded with compunction to his past life, and the change which had taken place in his conduct since the awful death of his friend Doctor Dodd.

Quick as we were, we did not arrive at Castlewood too soon. I was looking at the fountain in the court, and listening to that sweet sad music of its plashing, which my grandfather tells of in his Memoirs, and peopling the place with bygone figures, with Beatrix in her beauty; with my Lord Francis in scarlet, calling to his dogs and mounting his grey horse; with the young page of old who won the castle and the heiress—when Sampson comes

---

[1] He was the second Incumbent of Lady Whittlesea's Chapel, Mayfair, and married Elizabeth, relict of Hermann Voelcker, Esq., the eminent brewer.

running down to me with an old volume in rough calf-bound in his hand, containing drafts of letters, copies of agreements, and various writings, some by a secretary of my Lord Francis, some in the slim handwriting of his wife my grandmother, some bearing the signature of the last lord; and here was a copy of the assignment sure enough, as it had been sent to my grandfather in Virginia. "Victoria, Victoria!" cries Sampson, shaking my hand, embracing everybody. "Here is a guinea for thee, Betty. We'll have a bowl of punch at the 'Three Castles' to-night!" As we were talking, the wheels of post-chaises were heard, and a couple of carriages drove into the court containing my Lord and a friend, and their servants in the next vehicle. His Lordship looked only a little paler than usual at seeing me.

"What procures me the honour of Sir George Warrington's visit, and pray, Mr. Sampson, what do you do here?" says my Lord. I think he had forgotten the existence of this book, or had never seen it; and when he offered to take his Bible oath of what he had heard from his father, had simply volunteered a perjury.

I was shaking hands with his companion, a nobleman with whom I had had the honour to serve in America. "I came," I said, "to convince myself of a fact, about which you were mistaken yesterday; and I find the proof in your Lordship's own house. Your Lordship was pleased to take your Lordship's Bible oath, that there was no agreement between your father and his mother, relative to some property which I hold. When Mr. Sampson was your Lordship's secretary, he perfectly remembered having seen a copy of such an assignment, and here it is."

"And do you mean, Sir George Warrington, that unknown to me you have been visiting my papers?" cries my Lord.

"I doubted the correctness of your statement, though backed by your Lordship's Bible oath," I said, with a bow.

"This, sir, is robbery! Give the papers back!" bawled my Lord.

"Robbery is a rough word, my Lord. Shall I tell the whole story to Lord Rawdon?"

"What, is it about the Marquisate? *Connu, connu*, my dear Sir George! We always called you the Marquis in New York. I don't know who brought the story from Virginia."

I never had heard this absurd nickname before, and did not care to notice it. "My Lord Castlewood," I said, "not only doubted, but yesterday laid a claim to my property, taking his Bible oath that——"

Castlewood gave a kind of gasp, and then said, "Great Heaven! Do you mean, Sir George, that there actually is an agreement extant? Yes. Here it is — my father's hand-writing, sure enough! Then the question is clear. Upon my o——, well, upon my honour as a gentleman! I never knew of such an agreement, and must have been mistaken in what my father said. This paper clearly shows the property is yours: and not being mine—why, I wish you joy of it!" and he held out his hand with the blandest smile.

"And how thankful you will be to me, my Lord, for having enabled him to establish the right," says Sampson, with a leer on his face.

"Thankful? No, confound you. Not in the least!" says my Lord. "I am a plain man; I don't disguise from my cousin that I would rather have had the property than he. Sir George, you will stay and dine with us. A large party is coming down here shooting; we ought to have you one of us!"

"My Lord," said I, buttoning the book under my coat, "I will go and get this document copied, and then return it to your Lordship. As my mother in Virginia has had her papers burned, she will be put out of much anxiety by having this assignment safely lodged."

"What, have Madam Esmond's papers been burned? When the deuce was that?" asks my Lord.

"My Lord, I wish you a very good afternoon. Come, Sampson, you and I will go and dine at the 'Three Castles.'" And I turned on my heel, making a bow to Lord Rawdon, and from that day to this I have never set my foot within the halls of my ancestors.

Shall I ever see the old mother again, I wonder? She lives in Richmond, never having rebuilt her house in the country. When Hal was in England, we sent her pictures of both her sons, painted by the admirable Sir Joshua Reynolds. We sat to him, the last year Mr. Johnson was alive, I remember. And the Doctor, peering about the studio, and seeing the image of Hal in his uniform (the appearance of it caused no little excite-ment in those days), asked who was this? and was informed that it was the famous American general—General Warrington, Sir George's brother. "General *Who* ?" cries the Doctor, "General *Where* ? Pooh! I don't know such a service!" and he turned his back and walked out of the premises. My worship is painted in scarlet, and we have replicas of both performances at home. But the picture which Captain Miles and the girls declare to be most like is a family sketch by my ingenious neighbour, Mr. Bunbury, who has drawn me and my Lady with Monsieur Gumbo following us, and written under the piece, " SIR GEORGE, MY LADY, AND THEIR MASTER."

Here my master comes: he has poked out all the house-fires, has looked to all the bolts, has ordered the whole male and female crew to their chambers; and begins to blow my candles out, and says, " Time, Sir George, to go to bed! Twelve o'clock! "

" Bless me! So indeed it is." And I close my book, and go to my rest, with a blessing on those now around me asleep.

THE END